MAKING
IT
WORK

MAKING
IT
WORK

Low-Wage Employment, Family Life, and Child Development

Hirokazu Yoshikawa,
Thomas S. Weisner, and
Edward D. Lowe
Editors

Russell Sage Foundation
New York

The Russell Sage Foundation

The Russell Sage Foundation, one of the oldest of America's general purpose foundations, was established in 1907 by Mrs. Margaret Olivia Sage for "the improvement of social and living conditions in the United States." The Foundation seeks to fulfill this mandate by fostering the development and dissemination of knowledge about the country's political, social, and economic problems. While the Foundation endeavors to assure the accuracy and objectivity of each book it publishes, the conclusions and interpretations in Russell Sage Foundation publications are those of the authors and not of the Foundation, its Trustees, or its staff. Publication by Russell Sage, therefore, does not imply Foundation endorsement.

Library of Congress Cataloging-in-Publication Data

Making it work : low-wage employment, family life, and child development / Hirokazu Yoshikawa, Thomas S. Weisner, Edward D. Lowe, editors.
    p. cm.
Includes bibliographical references and index.
ISBN-10: 0-87154-972-7
ISBN-13: 978-0-87154-972-3
  1. Minimum wage—Wisconsin—Milwaukee—Longitudinal studies. 2. Working poor—Wisconsin—Milwaukee—Longitudinal studies. 3. Family—Wisconsin—Milwaukee—Longitudinal studies. 4. Child development—Wisconsin—Milwaukee—Longitudinal studies. I. Yoshikawa, Hirokazu. II. Weisner, Thomas S., 1943- III. Lowe, Edward D.

HD4919.W6M35 2006
362.509775'95—dc22

2006016173

Text design by Genna Patacsil.

RUSSELL SAGE FOUNDATION
112 East 64th Street, New York, New York 10021
10 9 8 7 6 5 4 3 2 1

Contents

Contributors |

HIROKAZU YOSHIKAWA is professor of education at the Harvard Graduate School of Education.

THOMAS S. WEISNER is professor in the Department of Psychiatry, Semel Institute, Center for Culture and Health, and in the Department of Anthropology at the University of California, Los Angeles.

EDWARD D. LOWE is associate professor of anthropology at Soka University of America.

JOHANNES M. BOS is president and CEO of Berkeley Policy Associates.

FAYE CARTER is a doctoral candidate in the Graduate School of Education and Information Studies at the University of California, Los Angeles.

NOEMÍ ENCHAUTEGUI-DE-JESÚS is visiting assistant professor of psychology at Syracuse University.

ANNA GASSMAN-PINES is a doctoral candidate in community and developmental psychology at New York University.

ERIN B. GODFREY is a doctoral candidate in community and developmental psychology at New York University.

EBONI C. HOWARD is director of the Herr Research Center for Children and Social Policy and holds the Frances Stott Chair in Early Childhood Policy Research at the Erikson Institute in Chicago.

JOANN HSUEH is a research associate in the policy area on family well-being and children's development at MDRC.

VONNIE C. MCLOYD is professor of psychology and senior research scientist at the Center for Developmental Science, University of North Carolina, Chapel Hill.

RASHMITA S. MISTRY is assistant professor of education at the University of California, Los Angeles.

SANDRA NAY is a doctoral candidate in clinical psychology at Duke University.

VALENTINA NIKULINA is a doctoral candidate in clinical psychology at St. John's University.

AMANDA L. ROY is a doctoral candidate in community and developmental psychology at New York University.

Acknowledgments |

IN A PROJECT as collaborative as this one, there are many people to thank. First, we would like to thank every participant in the New Hope Project who talked with our survey teams, child assessment staff, and ethnographers, as well as the teachers who helped us understand how their children were doing in school. We would like to thank the funders of the Next Generation project, especially the David and Lucille Packard, MacArthur, and William T. Grant Foundations. Led initially by Robert Granger and then by Virginia Knox, this unique, multi-year project was a collaboration between Manpower Demonstration Research Corporation (MDRC) and academic investigators that provided an extraordinarily rich collaborative space in which the editors, and most of the contributors, first met. Among those on the Next Generation project we would particularly like to thank are Greg Duncan, Pamela Morris, Lisa Gennetian, Aletha Huston, Kathryn Edin, Andrew London, and Ellen Scott. Hans Bos, who wrote the epilogue for this book, played a central role in the employment group of the Next Generation project, the initial incubator of the work that led to this book. Hans also was the senior impact analyst and data manager for the New Hope Project and its twenty-four- and sixty-month reports.

Among other funders we would like to thank the William T. Grant Foundation, for a faculty scholar's grant that supported much of Yoshikawa's work during the years when this book was developed; and the National Science Foundation, whose grants for the New York University Center for Research on Culture, Development, and Education (NSF grant BCS0218159 to Catherine S. Tamis-LeMonda, Diane Hughes, Niobe Way, and Yoshikawa) and for a project on the effects of income and employment on child development (NSF grant BCS0004076 to Yoshikawa, Pamela Morris, and Lisa Gennetian) also supported the work of Yoshikawa. Weisner thanks the Center for Culture and Health at the UCLA Semel Institute for Neuroscience and Human Behavior for research and administrative support that was essential in providing the continuity that such a collaborative study needed. Warren Thomson provided outstanding administrative support at the Center for Culture and Health.

In the early 1990s, New Hope, Inc. contracted with MDRC to evaluate the New Hope demonstration program. Owing to limited resources, the evaluation initially focused on the implementation of the program and its impact on employment and economic outcomes for adults in the research sample. But from the outset, New Hope, Inc. was interested in expanding the scope of the evaluation to include other outcomes, such as an assessment of the program's effects on children.

The New Hope Child and Family Study (CFS) had its gestation and birth at the MacArthur Foundation's Research Network on Successful Pathways Through Middle Childhood, beginning in 1996. Directed by Jacquelynne Eccles, the network's goals were to design and carry out innovative studies on middle childhood and to consider ways to discover successful pathways during this period of life, particularly among children and families at risk. Robert Granger, Greg Duncan, Aletha Huston, and Weisner were among the core members. By this time, Granger had become the director of the New Hope evaluation, taking over from his MDRC colleague Tom Brock. Members of the network saw the ongoing evaluation as an opportunity to investigate important issues in the middle-childhood age range. Duncan, Granger, Huston, and Weisner had many conversations about what such a study might look like and what it could accomplish. All the network members commented on and contributed to the planning for the New Hope study.[1] The New Hope Child and Family Study survey, child assessments, integrated ethnography, and innovative design would not have been possible without the long-term research investment and new collaborations opened up by MacArthur research networks like this one.

All the survey and ethnographic data on the New Hope participants and families we used came from the New Hope Child and Family Study, which was supported by the MacArthur and William T. Grant Foundations and the National Institute for Child Health and Human Development (grant R01 HD 36038). The ethnographic fieldwork data management and analyses used services of the UCLA Qualitative Fieldwork Core, funded by the National Institute for Child Health and Human Development (grant P30 HD004612); Weisner was principal investigator, and Eli Lieber served as co-director.

The ethnographic data and stories of New Hope participants that are such a central part of every chapter were collected by an outstanding team doing fieldwork in Milwaukee (and elsewhere when families moved) between 1998 and 2004: Conerly Casey (University of California at Los Angeles/Kuwait University), Nelle Chmielwski (University of Wisconsin at Madison), Victor Espinosa (Northwestern University), Christina Gibson (Northwestern/Duke University), Eboni Howard, (Northwestern/Chapin

Hall/Erikson Institute, Chicago), Katherine Magnuson (Northwestern/ University of Wisconsin at Madison), Andrea Robles (University of Wisconsin at Madison), Jennifer Romich (Northwestern/University of Washington at Seattle), and Devarati Syam (University of Wisconsin at Milwaukee). Lucinda Bernheimer of UCLA supervised their efforts and participated in data analysis and management of the ethnographic study. Lowe followed on in all these capacities, besides making his writing and editing contributions to this book. Lowe also was instrumental in helping to run the UCLA qualitative "data camps" where we read, analyzed, and coded field notes. Faye Carter, Helen Davis, Sonya Geis, Claudia Solari, and Karen Quintiliani were excellent research assistants on the UCLA New Hope study. Carter and Geis co-authored papers on child care in the New Hope study. Solari and New York University's Laura Zamborsky were particularly helpful in editing many of these chapters.

Many people provided comments on drafts of chapters, including Marianne Bloch, Ajay Chaudry, Greg Duncan, Lisa Gennetian, Cameron Hay, Rob Hollister, Diane Hughes, Aletha Huston, Ariel Kalil, Virginia Knox, Jacqueline Lerner, Andrew London, Cynthia Miller, Pamela Morris, Katherine Newman, Robert Rector, Irwin Sandler, Marybeth Shinn, Patrick Shrout, and Claudia Strauss. We also received helpful comments from many participants at presentations at the Association for Public Policy Analysis and Management, the Society for Research in Child Development, and the Society for Research in Adolescence and in seminars at Columbia University, Syracuse University, Harvard University, New York University, the Council on Contemporary Families, Tufts University, the University of North Carolina at Chapel Hill, and the National Academy of Sciences Committee on Family and Work Policies. Weisner presented portions of this work at Cornell University, Harvard University, the University of Padua, the Northwestern/Chicago Joint Poverty Center, and UCLA.

We thank Marc Levine of the University of Wisconsin for sharing his insights about low-wage employment in Milwaukee. We would like to give a special thanks to Julie Kerksick, executive director of New Hope, Inc., and David Riemer. They have been unflagging in their dedication to America's working families, and Julie Kerksick was an especially important supporter of this book. Thanks also to the MDRC research team that found the initial set of experimental impacts of the New Hope Project that provided strong evidence for the policy importance of these kinds of supports for working parents.

Finally, we would like to thank our own families, children, and life partners (Stuart Freeman; Susan Weisner, Jeffrey Weisner, Michael Graff-Weisner, Allison Graff-Weisner; and Trish, Sophia, and Emma Lowe) for offering encouragement along the way and putting up with more than their share of distraction as we worked to complete this book.

Chapter One | Introduction:
Raising Children
Where Work
Has Disappeared

Hirokazu Yoshikawa,
Thomas S. Weisner,
and Edward D. Lowe

TAKE A WALK on North Avenue east across the Milwaukee border, from the suburb of Wauwatosa, Wisconsin. It is late summer, a beautiful, cloudless day in the city with a hint of fall in the air. On the Wauwatosa side, you walk down a busy commercial street lined with a Chinese restaurant, a CD store, fast-food joints, eyeglass, clothing, and flower shops, and the occasional restaurant serving breakfast specials. Although nothing on the street indicates luxury, the street is well paved, traffic lines are clearly painted, and banners line the street, proudly drawing attention to the neighborhood ("East Town Tosa").

Sixtieth Street constitutes the boundary between Wauwatosa and Milwaukee. It is a cliff, not quite visible immediately because it is as much social, economic, and political as physical. The moment you cross Sixtieth Street and enter what we will call the "North Side" neighborhood, you notice that the sidewalks and pavement are bumpier and the streets are potholed, with faded traffic lines. Shiny SUVs and minivans have disappeared, and in their place are much older cars, many of them in need of repair. Most noticeably, you encounter boarded-up storefronts; two are right on the eastern corners of North Avenue and Sixtieth Street. You have suddenly entered the landscape of deep inner-city poverty. The service establishments disappear, and

1

the density of urban commercial life is reduced. In late 2004, on a ten-block stretch of North Avenue, not far from Sixtieth Street, there were twenty-one businesses, but twelve boarded-up storefronts and two vacant lots. (West of Sixtieth Street there were no boarded-up storefronts or vacant lots.) The businesses here are oddly restricted to hair salons, bars, child care centers, and small groceries with very little produce. For parents in this corner of Milwaukee, many everyday tasks, such as filling a prescription, getting eyeglasses repaired, buying children's clothing, or taking the family out to a fast-food restaurant, cannot be accomplished without traveling outside the neighborhood.

In addition to the usual signs of U.S. consumer life, local work opportunities seem to have disappeared on this stretch of North Avenue. The neighborhood centered on North Avenue between Sixtieth Street and downtown has been termed the "epicenter" of urban poverty in Milwaukee.[1] Along with most of inner-city Milwaukee, this neighborhood did not participate in the vaunted economic growth of the late 1990s. Nearly all of the job growth in the metropolitan Milwaukee area between 1995 and 2000 occurred in the suburbs. By the early 2000s, Milwaukee had the sixth-highest unemployment rate among the nation's largest fifty cities (University of Wisconsin Center for Economic Development 2003). The rate of working-age adults (sixteen and over) who were not in the labor force in the North Side neighborhood was 36 percent in 2000.[2] These statistics show that it is difficult for working-age adults to find and keep jobs in the inner-city neighborhoods of Milwaukee. Despite these odds, the majority of adults in these neighborhoods do find some work.

What are the consequences for children of growing up in bleak labor markets like Milwaukee's North Side neighborhood, where finding work seems to be so much more difficult than in other places? What are the effects of low-wage job experiences on the development of children? This book examines how working below or near the poverty line affects not just parents' well-being but their children's development—their school performance and engagement, their social behaviors, and their expectations for their future. We use a unique dataset: the New Hope study (Bos et al. 1999; Huston et al. 2001). The New Hope Project was a program to provide supports for Milwaukee adults who worked full-time. We use evidence from the Child and Family Study (CFS)—part of the random-assignment evaluation of New Hope—to examine how changes in work involvement and conditions affect family life and children's prospects. The New Hope data, combining longitudinal survey and ethnographic information, come from families in two neighborhoods in Milwaukee; one is the "North Side" just described, and the other we call the "South Side" neighborhood. These neighborhoods are in the two zip codes that were the sampling base for recruiting participants for the New Hope study. These families were followed over a five-year period from the mid-1990s to the early 2000s.

In this book, we address three sets of questions about the effects of parents' low-wage work on their children's development. The first set addresses parents' experiences of work and the workplace, with an emphasis on how these experiences change over time. How do pathways through the low-wage labor market vary among working-poor parents, and what consequences do those pathways have for their children? Both researchers and the public too often lump the working poor into a single category. After identifying subgroups of the working poor who experience different longitudinal patterns of work, wages, and hours over time, we find great heterogeneity in the work prospects of a large, low-income Milwaukee sample examined over a period of several years. Our evidence reveals six kinds of employment trajectories among the New Hope parents: low-wage work that was mostly part-time; "rapid cycling," or churning from one low-wage job to another; full-time work with wage growth; full-time work with low and stagnant wages; stable employment; and, among a very small group, staying out of the labor market. We describe these employment pathways in depth and use them extensively throughout the book as we argue that there is no one kind of working poor person, job situation, or family circumstance. We then use data on these varied pathways to explore how they influenced outcomes for children. As we will see, some work trajectories, such as full-time wage growth, can have some positive impacts on some aspects of children's development, whereas other trajectories, such as those with very high job instability, can have negative consequences. These questions occupy part I of the book.

In part II, we turn to a second set of questions that address how work and family demands intersect to influence children. New Hope parents were constantly aware of the trade-offs they made between spending more time with their children and making more money for them. What work and family goals did these parents report, and how did they affect their work trajectories and their children? How did New Hope mothers' perceptions of job quality "spill over" to their own well-being and their children's school performance and social behavior? What did money earned from work buy, and how did those earnings influence family and child well-being? What do work pathways have to do with marriage? We will see that job quality does appear to matter for parents' well-being and for their children's academic and behavioral outcomes, as rated by parents and by teachers. We also find that work pathways can make a difference in the probability that single mothers will marry.

Finally, we turn to the question of supports for work. In part III, we ask: How do parents find support, from both informal and formal sources, for their navigation through the low-wage labor market of Milwaukee? We consider three types of support: child care; informal social support from family, friends, and coworkers; and formal work support services. Our analysis of work support services benefits from the experimental design of the New Hope evaluation. Both the adults in the New Hope Project and those randomly assigned to the control group were eligible for the Wisconsin Works (W-2) state welfare program during the period of historic policy upheaval known as welfare reform. The experimental-group mothers were eligible for the additional benefits and incentives of the New Hope antipoverty program, which rewarded full-time work with wage supplements, health care and child care subsidies, a time-limited community service job if other work could not be found, and supportive case management. We find in these chapters that the various work pathways of the New Hope parents are related systematically to the types of child care their children received; that informal social supports carried both benefits and costs; and that the two policy environments of W-2 and New Hope felt strikingly different in the daily lives of the parents in our sample. And we will see that the work supports that New Hope added to W-2 mattered for children's school and behavioral development, above and beyond the income effects of its wage supplement.

We conclude this book by describing the implications of our findings for policies and supports for working poor families and children. Policies and programs for the working poor can be improved in such a way that children's prospects are a priority in their own right rather than a corollary of parents' work effort. We recommend policies that recognize the diversity of work trajectories, improve workplace climates and flexibility, and support the incomes of parents so that they can afford the supports to obtain good jobs as well as provide for their children.

To answer our three sets of questions about work and children's development, we use a combination of quantitative data from comprehensive, repeated surveys filled out by mothers and teachers and in-depth qualitative data. The qualitative information was collected over a three-year period by interviewers talking to families in their living rooms, visiting their child care and school settings, and getting to know their daily routines, dreams, and struggles intimately. We always start with the experiences and perspectives of the workers, parents, and families themselves, using qualitative and ethnographic evidence to tell the stories of how they find and sustain work, struggle to earn more, and deal with the difficult and often marginal world of low-wage work. These qualitative accounts also include what they told us about their goals and values—what they want to achieve in their caregiving and breadwinning and what is most meaningful to them. These rich stories are followed by quantitative analyses of data from parent surveys, administrative records, and assessments of children using tests and teacher reports.

In this book, we describe the circumstances of working-poor parents and children and work contexts using integrated, mixed methods. All of the members of our analytic team conducted both qualitative and quantitative analyses. It is important to combine these two kinds of data sources, we believe, because each provides a window into low-wage employment, family life, and child development that complements the different perspective provided by the other. Our interdisciplinary team of researchers worked together over several years to develop these ideas and to cooperate in using qualitative and quantitative evidence in tandem. This approach ensured a closer relationship between the study of narrative and numbers than is common in most current "mixed-methods" research. Together, these two types of data allow us to examine the fluctuating picture of the intimate interconnection between changes in parents' well-being and children's development and the sometimes smooth, sometimes halting, never easy pathways through low-wage work in Milwaukee at the end of the twentieth century.

In the rest of this chapter, we describe the historical context and policy environment of Milwaukee, particularly the inner-city areas of the city where the New Hope families lived. We then review what is known about the effects of low-wage work on children. Finally, we provide an overview of the sample and the methods we used and an outline of the book.

EMPLOYMENT IN MILWAUKEE'S INNER CITY

Over the last fifty years, there has been a steady erosion of the career blue-collar jobs that once offered the majority of lower-educated workers in the United States the security, benefits, and job advancement opportunities to raise children comfortably and spend time with them after school, during dinner, and in the evening (Wilson 1999). Only a minority of low-wage workers now work standard daytime hours (see Hsueh, this volume; Presser 2003). Unionized jobs, the ones most likely to offer benefits for workers with lower levels of education or skills, represented only 14 percent of jobs in the United States in 1999, a lower proportion than during the recession of the early 1990s.[3] Temporary jobs, in contrast, have become increasingly available.

What are the roots of this decline in good jobs for those with lower levels of education? The story is familiar in cities across the Northeast and the "Rust Belt" of the Midwest—manufacturing jobs, legacies of America's industrial revolution, first began disappearing during the Great Depression, then declined further in numbers in the 1950s and 1960s in an accelerating process that continues up to the present day. This story is no different in Milwaukee, but it has taken shape there in specific ways that have profoundly influenced the daily experiences of the families we describe in this book. We outline this story very briefly here.

The city of Milwaukee grew out of a trading post set on the bluffs above Lake Michigan, on the banks of the Menomenee River. In 1795 the North West Company established a footing in Milwaukee to trade fur. The post grew as its location directly between the larger trading posts of Fort Dearborn (now Chicago) and Green Bay made it strategic. The city's mature industrial period spanned the years of 1870 to 1930, though its population continued to grow until 1960. As the fur trade declined, flour-milling, meatpacking, and leather-tanning grew as the prominent industries. The beer-making expertise of immigrant German settlers also led to the rise of breweries in these decades. Until 1960, Milwaukee's population was overwhelmingly white, with most residents tracing their roots back to Germany or Poland (Gurda 1999).

The city grew rapidly in the early decades of the twentieth century: its size doubled between 1900 and 1930, and then doubled again between 1930 and 1960 (Orum 1995). In a harbinger of more recent tensions between the city and the suburbs, efforts to expand into the areas that surrounded Milwaukee's city limits in the years after World War II were met with resistance by suburban residents, who feared increased taxes. Beginning in the 1950s, an enormous demographic shift occurred in what became known as the center of "inner-city" Milwaukee, or the "Inner Core." An area just west of downtown where the land slopes down from the higher land by the lake, this section includes the Midtown, Walnut Hill, Halyard Park, Washington Park, Sherman Park, and Metcalfe Park neighborhoods and encompasses one of the two neighborhoods sampled for the New Hope study. In 1950 these neighborhoods were overwhelmingly white. Milwaukee was not one of the midwestern cities, like Chicago or Detroit, that drew the great African-American migration from the South prior to the 1940s. But during the 1950s and 1960s, the percentage of African Americans in this neighborhood grew. Racial covenants established by property owners steered black families to areas with lower property values and housing quality. In 1960 a report commissioned by Mayor Zeidler documented what are now familiar U.S. urban problems: low-quality public schools, few recreational resources, and high rents for low-quality housing in the Inner Core. The commission's recommendations—to expand community policing and connect new residents to job and schooling opportunities in the city—were largely ignored (Orum 1995). By the mid-1980s, racial segregation in Milwaukee was deeply entrenched. In 1940, 68 percent of the white population in the metropolitan Milwaukee area had lived in the city. By 1960 this figure had declined to 56 percent, and by 1985 to 36 percent (Levine and Zipp

1993; Levine 2002). By the 1980s the Inner Core of Milwaukee was over-whelmingly black. The city had become one of the most racially segregated in America, with only 2.5 percent of African Americans living in the sub-urbs. And a high proportion of Inner Core households were single mothers on Aid to Families with Dependent Children (AFDC). Single-parent house-holds made up 7 percent of all households in the city in 1960, and 40 per-cent in 1985.

During the same decades that racial segregation soared in Milwaukee, manufacturing jobs were disappearing at an astonishing rate. Factory jobs in Milwaukee had been centered most prominently on the banks of the Menomenee River, which cuts through the city from west to east just south of downtown, but these jobs were also scattered all over the central city. For example, after many large breweries (such as Schlitz, Pabst, Miller, and Blatz) were established in Milwaukee in the early 1900s, the city became the brewing capital of the United States. By the 1990s, however, only Miller was left.[4] The fates of the city's principal manufacturing industries—automotive parts, electrical, and heavy machinery—were similar. In 1960, 123,000 jobs in the city (41 percent of all jobs) were in manufacturing; by 1980 this figure had shrunk to 90,000 jobs, and by 1985 to 72,000 jobs. There were many reasons for the decline in manufacturing in Milwaukee's inner city, including new production technologies, foreign competition, and the increasing preference of employers for suburban locations.

The last three decades also witnessed an increasing divide between the central city and the suburbs in the concentration of jobs. Job growth in the metropolitan area occurred mainly in the suburbs, probably owing in large part to what many employer studies have found: employers strongly prefer white workers over black workers, all other credentials being equal (Wilson 1999). Increasing racial segregation, white flight, and the departure of man-ufacturing jobs from the central city were all factors that facilitated the iso-lation of Inner Core residents from jobs.

By the dawn of the 1990s, over 15 percent of Milwaukee's families were on welfare, with much higher percentages in inner-city neighborhoods (Schultze and Held 2002). Eighteen percent of the city's families were living in poverty. Federal policy to reduce the growing number of families on wel-fare (the Job Opportunity and Basic Skills program, implemented as a result of the Family Support Act of 1988) had recently focused on job training and education. Pressure grew during the early 1990s, however, to institute more radical reforms to reduce the rolls. By 1995 an experimental program, Work Not Welfare, had been started in two Wisconsin counties; it required recip-ients to work and limited their time on welfare to twenty-four months. By the end of 1995 this program was unveiled as Wisconsin Works, or W-2, and it would make Governor Tommy Thompson a leading figure in welfare reform. W-2 became a model for what, after a long and excruciating policy battle, became federal welfare reform—the Personal Responsibility and Work Opportunity Reconciliation Act (PRWORA) of 1996.[5]

The focus in W-2 was on immediate employment positions rather than on intensive job training or basic education. Job "trial periods," such as a workfare program and transitional subsidized jobs, were limited to twenty-four months each, and a cumulative lifetime limit of sixty months was introduced. Additional supports included subsidized child care; transportation assistance; referral to Wisconsin's Medicaid and family health care program, BadgerCare; and changes in the child support system, with payments made directly to custodial parents. All of these changes were implemented through the Job Centers, where caseworkers' duties shifted from eligibility checks to assisting with job searches, workfare, and community service jobs (Wisconsin Department of Workforce Development 2004).

Welfare rolls plunged in Milwaukee after these programs were implemented. In fact, they had dropped by a stunning 66 percent in the city in the two years leading up to full implementation of Wisconsin Works statewide in September 1997. They declined even further after passage of the federal welfare reform law. However, by 1999 the rates of family-level poverty in Milwaukee had dropped only 1.1 percent. Why? Simply put, transitions from welfare to low-wage work do not guarantee a move out of poverty. A longitudinal study in Milwaukee County explored the work experiences of over one thousand applicants for Temporary Assistance for Needy Families (TANF) beginning in 1999, and then again between sixteen and twenty-four months after the first survey (Dworsky, Courtney, and Piliavin 2003). At the outset, 12 percent of survey respondents were employed; during the following year, 77 percent were employed at some point. Between one and two years later, their median earnings were low—just $4,131—and there was little difference ($212) between the group that participated in the meantime in the W-2 program and the group that did not.[6] Including TANF and food stamps payments, the W-2 group had a median income of $8,583 over the first year, compared to $3,380 for those who did not participate in W-2. But the median for the W-2 group was still far below the poverty line for the typical family in the sample (a family of three with two children).[7] For a multitude of reasons we discuss in the next section, the well-being of children whose mothers work below or near the poverty line is still very much a matter of debate in Milwaukee in the post–welfare reform era.

LOW-WAGE WORK DYNAMICS AND CONDITIONS: DO THEY AFFECT CHILDREN?

Several books have recently been written about the working poor in the United States (DeParle 2004; Edin and Lein 1997; Ehrenreich 2001; Heymann

2000; Newman 1999; Shipler 2004). This book differs from these studies in that we explore the implications for family life and children's development of working yet being poor by providing evidence for diverse work trajectories and utilizing the unusual combination of experimental and ethnographic data in New Hope. Our primary focus is on the effects of maternal, not paternal, low-wage work. This is because the data from the Child and Family Study, which includes the child assessments and the ethnographic sample, unfortunately include relatively few fathers as primary informants. We therefore have little information on fathers' employment that is of the depth and breadth of the data on mothers' employment provided by the CFS.[8] The working poor have been too narrowly represented as single women with children. Though our sample does not enable us to study this in depth, we believe that bringing men who work out of poverty is of crucial importance, just as it is for women, as discussed in the chapter in this volume by Gassman-Pines, Yoshikawa, and Nay, as well as at various other points in the book. New Hope was explicitly intended for all adults, not only single women with young children, and New Hope in fact increased employment and earnings for men and adult women without children (Bos et al. 1999).

In this section, we review patterns in maternal employment among the poor and what is known about the effects of low-wage work on children's school performance and social development. As will become apparent, research to date is weak in describing how *changes* in low-wage work and its conditions over time affect children's development, and the effects on children of different conditions of low-wage work, such as wages, hours, benefits, and other dimensions of job quality, are not well understood. Part I addresses these topics.

Maternal employment among the poor surged in the late 1990s. Over the years of the New Hope study (that is, between 1995 and 2001), the rate of work among single mothers with children in the United States increased from 69 percent to 78 percent, a rate of increase that is nearly unheard-of in this statistic (Smolensky and Gootman 2003). Policy analysts agree that some combination of three factors was responsible for this unprecedented increase: the welfare reform of 1996, the strong economy of the late 1990s, and expansions in the earned income tax credit (EITC), which provides an incentive to increase work effort among low-income families.[9]

As urban poverty and reliance on cash welfare grew in the United States in the 1970s and 1980s, researchers examining maternal employment and child well-being began to incorporate some theorizing about families in poverty. Some researchers suggested, for example, that additional earnings in higher-income families may make less of a difference to children because they build on a more stable base of economic resources in the family (Desai, Chase-Lansdale, and Michael 1989). This argument implies that lower-income children benefit more than their higher-income counterparts from their mothers' work. In addition, maternal work may positively affect children because of the benefits of a more regular routine, additional economic resources, or improvements to parenting and psychological well-being from the mother being a working role model to her children.[10] Studies comparing lower-income families to their better-off counterparts also found greater benefits of work for maternal sense of control among lower-income mothers (Hoffman and Youngblade 1999).

But consider other trade-offs of work at the low end of the pay scale. Increased work can bring on stress in the form of difficulties finding and maintaining child care, long commutes, unpredictable and often nonstandard work hours, repetitive and unrewarding work, and, not least, added child care, transportation, and other expenses that cut into the relatively low levels of take-home pay (Crouter and Bumpus 2001; Edin and Lein 1997; Repetti and Wood 1997; Scott et al. 2001). Although all working parents face these issues, they are intensified for low-wage parents. Together, these stressors may swamp any positive effects of work. In line with this trade-off hypothesis, recent reviews have concluded that maternal employment per se has only small effects on the cognitive outcomes or social behaviors of children in poverty. That is, when studies compare children in and near poverty whose mothers work to those whose mothers do not work, the differences are small. But they tend to be positive: children of mothers who work show somewhat higher school performance and lower levels of behavior problems than children of mothers who do not work (Hoffman and Youngblade 1999; Perry-Jenkins, Repetti, and Crouter 2000; Smolensky and Gootman 2003; Zaslow and Emig 1997). Most of this literature is subject to selection bias; that is, it is difficult to conclude that maternal work actually causes these outcomes in children. It may be that unmeasured family factors, such as motivation to work, influences both work effort and children's development.[11]

A variety of work conditions shape the effects of work on children. For example, some studies have found that when duties are simple or repetitive and worker autonomy is low, the effects of maternal employment on the quality of mothers' parenting, and in turn on their children's socio-emotional development and school performance, are more likely to be negative (Parcel and Menaghan 1990, 1994a, 1997).[12] Although these studies have for the most part been carried out on mixed-income, national samples, these particular work conditions are more likely to be experienced by low-wage workers. Other indicators of job quality, such as discrimination in the workplace, have never been examined as influences on children.

Pay and benefits are basics of work life that may affect children in poverty. One study found that maternal work is associated with lower levels of child behavior problems only when wages are above $7.50 an hour (Moore and Driscoll 1997). Another study found that higher mothers' wages, controlling for other background factors, are associated with higher job aspirations among children in poverty (Ripke, Huston, and Mistry 2005). Almost no studies link benefits at work to the development of children in poverty. Jody Heymann (2000) has conducted several studies showing that low-wage jobs are particularly likely to lack flextime, sick leave, vacation leave, and health benefits. Nearly one-third of low-wage workers do not have access even to the unpaid leave provided by the Family and Medical Leave Act, which provides such leave only to employees who have worked 1,250 hours or more in the past twelve months in firms with at least fifty employees (Waldfogel 2001). This lack of benefits may not only increase parents' stress levels but also make it difficult to keep a job when work and family conflicts arise. Using national data, Jody Heymann and her colleagues (Heymann, Earle, and Egleston 1996) estimated a "family illness burden" (the number of sick days of all children in the family that require sick leave) and found that more than one in three families have a family illness burden of two weeks or more each year. If parents have no sick leave, then a mother may leave a sick child home alone or send the child to school or day care, she may have to take unpaid leave, or she may even have to give up her job (Heymann 2000).

One set of conditions particularly relevant to lower-wage workers is shift work. In a series of studies, Harriet Presser has described the increases in rates of work on nonstandard and shifting schedules in the United States.[13] She finds that both of these work conditions are more prominent among low-income families (Presser 1995, 2000, 2003; Presser and Cox 1997). However, we lack information on whether these work schedules and hours have consequences for the development of low-income children. One study on a national sample showed that nonstandard work schedules are associated with lower scores on cognitive assessments of young children (Han 2005).

Several recent studies have found that the timing of maternal employment in children's lives also makes a difference to their development. Specifically, studies on three national datasets found remarkably consistent results about the timing of the return to work following the birth of a child. Specifically, full-time work in the first six months of life appears to lead to lower cognitive ability in early childhood and into middle childhood (Brooks-Gunn, Han, and Waldfogel 2002; Han, Waldfogel, and Brooks-Gunn 2001; Waldfogel, Han, and Brooks-Gunn 2002). Although these studies were carried out on national samples covering a wide range of incomes, the researchers did not find that effects differed by parents' prior incomes.

What is missing from this research literature on the effects of work on children? Astonishingly, almost none of the studies on maternal work and children's development examine the impact of changes in maternal work and its conditions on children. In this book, we examine such work pathways and define six kinds of work trajectories. Economists, working with national panel data, have examined several dynamic work patterns: job stability, job instability, and job mobility. Job instability is defined as work spells interrupted by periods of nonwork. All workers tend to have high job instability early in their careers (think of the typical work of high school or college students or recent graduates). But workers with low levels of education are more likely to experience job instability—transitions from jobs to non-employment—than job-to-job transitions, which are termed job mobility (Johnson and Corcoran 2002; Royalty 1998; Topel and Ward 1992). They are also more likely to experience it longer into their work careers.

Although job mobility is generally accompanied by earnings growth, it is also more likely to occur among more skilled workers. The working poor are more likely to leave jobs for non-job-related reasons because other parts of their lives—child care, partners, informal supports—have less "give" in the context of poverty. The breakdown of one part of a low-resource system may have more serious repercussions on other aspects of the system. In an analysis from the Women's Employment Study, which followed an initially welfare-receiving sample in Michigan, researchers documented women's reasons for job exits. The largest proportion of reasons (57 percent) were not job-related and included difficulties with child care, health problems, transportation problems, and family pressure. Of the rest, 21 percent reported being fired or laid off, while another 21 percent reported quitting because of dissatisfaction with the job (Johnson and Corcoran 2002).

Although economists have been interested in economic predictors and consequences of job dynamics, only a handful of studies have examined how job dynamics are associated with child development. In one study, Vonnie McLoyd and her colleagues found that periods of unemployment and work interruptions were associated with greater psychological distress among African-American adolescents of low-income mothers (McLoyd et al. 1994). In two recent studies of low-income families, job instability was associated with higher levels of withdrawn behaviors in middle childhood and higher levels of high school dropout among teens (Kalil and Ziol-Guest 2005; Yoshikawa and Seidman 2001).

In sum, research shows that employment among lower-income workers can have positive effects on children under certain conditions: higher pay, greater income support, and more complex job responsibilities. Negative effects seem to occur when full-time employment is experienced early in a baby's life or with high levels of instability. However, few studies have examined how changes in employment conditions affect family life and children in the context of poverty. And no studies have examined how changes in employment are experienced in tandem. For example, do those workers who experience the highest job instability also experience the lowest wages? How does the combination of wage growth and job stability affect children? How do lower-income mothers experience differing pathways through low-wage work environments, especially in labor markets as tough as Milwaukee's inner city? Part I of this book considers these questions.

THE WORK-FAMILY BALANCE AMONG LOW-INCOME FAMILIES

So far, we have discussed the characteristics of employment that might affect children but have given little attention to the question of how. What are the processes that might explain how maternal employment affects children's psychological, social, and academic development? Beginning with the very earliest work on parental work and children's development, family processes such as parenting behaviors and parent well-being were identified as factors most likely to explain the link. Research from the 1950s on maternal employment and children's development by Lois Hoffman, for example, established some links between work and parenting practices such as praise and positive affect (Hoffman 1961; see also Siegel et al. 1959; Kanter 1977). Interestingly, some of the central hypotheses at that time about mothers' feelings about their jobs centered on guilt, reflective of societal views of maternal employment as a social problem.[14] Melvin Kohn (1969), in a classic study conducted in the 1960s, found that fathers in jobs with higher complexity of duties and providing more autonomy are more likely to value autonomy and independence in their children. Kohn's research suggested that parents' work can shape their values and beliefs related to parenting.

In the next decades, these themes of parent practices and values as mechanisms explaining the effects of maternal work on children were expanded and other mechanisms were proposed. Toby Parcel and Elizabeth Menaghan's work, for example, showed that parents' work conditions, including wages, occupational complexity, and benefits, indirectly affect children through parents' provision of a warm and supportive home environment (Menaghan and Parcel 1991; Parcel and Menaghan 1994b). A large set of studies on aspects of work stress uncovered the conditions under which stress at work affects the family system, and vice versa (see, for example, Crouter et al. 1999; Hughes, Galinsky, and Morris 1992; Larson and Almeida 1999; Lerner 1994; Repetti and Wood 1997). In addition, as a recent review by Maureen Perry-Jenkins, Rena Repetti, and Ann Crouter (2000) pointed out, a new literature has emerged on how working parents balance the roles of worker, parent, and partner. Interestingly, the goals of low-income working parents concerning their jobs and their family lives have only rarely been studied. Work from the ethnographic study of Urban Change, a four-city study of families before and after welfare reform, showed the complex trade-offs between quality and quantity of time with children and between the roles of caregiver and breadwinner that mothers experienced in Cleveland and Philadelphia (London et al. 2004). Work by Adrie Kusserow (2004) and Annette Lareau (2003), among others, suggests that social class, work, and the neighborhood conditions parents and children face influence parenting goals and practices in the United States. Although individualism is a dominant value, its expression and meaning depend on work and danger. Kusserow, for example, contrasts what she calls the "soft offensive" individualism of the upper middle class in New York, with its emphasis on self-esteem, emotional expressiveness, uniqueness, and individuality, with the lower-class "hard, defensive" individualism, which emphasizes self-defense and protection against violence and poverty. The latter is a truer reflection of the world facing the working poor. In part II of this book, we consider how mothers in the New Hope study balanced their work goals with other personal goals and whether parental goals and values made a difference for their children's development.

The majority of studies examining work and family issues as predictors of children's well-being have focused on middle-class families or national studies across socioeconomic levels. Relatively little in the work-family literature considers the experiences of parents in poverty. The large literature on partner or marital relationships and work, for example, has only recently been extended to low-income families, most notably through the Fragile Families study, a national study of single parents and their infants and young children. Researchers from that study have begun to examine the economic predictors, for example, of single mothers' entry into marriage (Gibson-Davis, Edin, and McLanahan 2005). In addition, surprisingly little attention has been paid to the economic dimensions of work and family life. Kathryn Edin and Laura Lein (1997), in their landmark study, examined household budgeting to explain how mothers on welfare combine formal work, informal contributions from their networks, welfare, and side jobs to make ends meet. Welfare payments alone could never have been sufficient to support their families, yet it was not known at the time how parents managed to keep going financially. The influence of money from earnings and other sources on children, however, through economic well-being and expenditures on children, continues to be understudied. Part II examines questions regarding the relationship between work dynamics, relationships and marriage, and household budgeting to create new perspectives on the work-family interface.

PRIVATE AND PUBLIC SUPPORTS FOR WORK AND THEIR EFFECTS ON CHILDREN

Part III addresses a final set of questions about work and children: How do low-income parents obtain support for their often difficult trajectories through low-wage labor markets? Do the forms of support they utilize—from child care to informal help from social networks and formal work support services—make a difference for children?

The massive increase in work effort among mothers in poverty in the 1990s was predictably accompanied by a surge in the need for child care. State and local child care systems were ill-prepared for this surge in the need for slots. Although federal funding for child care doubled between 1997 and 2000—through the Child Care Development Fund (CCDF) and money from the TANF program (Mezey et al. 2002)—this increase built on a low initial level of support and was not enough to meet the surge in demand. Estimates of the percentage of eligible children who received child care subsidies, based on multiple state studies conducted in the early 2000s, ranged from 12 to 25 percent (Collins et al. 2000). How did the New Hope mothers cope with their need for child care as they embarked on a variety of trajectories through work in the late 1990s? We consider this question in part III.

Informal assistance from family, friends, and coworkers is also important to working parents, yet it has been neglected in studies of parental work and child development. Material or instrumental support, such as help with transportation to and from work and with child care or money to cover bills when unexpected expenses arise, can help buffer the frequent shocks to the fragile system of child care, jobs, and schedules that low-income parents maintain. In addition, emotional support for work varies among partners, friends, and family members to a surprising degree. Few studies have examined the implications of these kinds of support for the career trajectories of the working poor or for their children's development. We examine this topic in part III as well.

Finally, we turn to the role of formal work support services and policies. Do policies that shape maternal employment—most obviously, welfare reform and its variants—affect children's development? This is one area of the research literature where experimental data are available. A series of sixteen experiments were conducted in the early to late 1990s by the Manpower Demonstration Research Corporation (MDRC) and some other policy institutes to test a variety of welfare and work policies for low-income families. Three types of programs were tested: those simply mandating work by introducing reductions in welfare benefits, or sanctions, for failing to work; those "making work pay" by providing earnings supplements to reward increases in work; and those that combined either of these approaches with time limits. In each of the experiments, low-income parents (most often, welfare recipients) were randomly assigned to one of these three types of programs or to a control condition that represented the usual AFDC rules and regulations. In most of these experiments, those assigned to the control condition were not required to work, and there were no time limits on benefit receipt.

Researchers and founders had the foresight, in two- to four-year follow-ups of families in these experiments, to assess indicators of children's school performance and social behaviors (acting-out and withdrawing behaviors). Most of these data were reported by parents, but in some of the studies standardized tests or teachers' reports of children's school performance were collected. These studies showed that the earnings supplement programs were the only programs that had positive effects on children's school performance and social behavior. That is, only the programs that increased both employment and income, and did so without a time limit, benefited primary-grade children (Morris et al. 2001). The other two types of programs—mandatory work programs and those with time limits—had few discernible effects on children, and these were as likely to be negative as positive. The lesson of these experiments thus far is that increasing maternal employment can have positive effects on children's school and social outcomes, but only if the work results in increases in income. Across the programs that made work pay, the increases in income ranged between $1,300 and $1,700 a year—not a lot from a middle-class perspective, but sizable for a low-income family, and enough to bring about small but detectable improvements in the children's outcomes.[15]

For adolescents, these experiments told a different story. Regardless of the policy approach, the programs produced small negative effects on mother-reported adolescent school progress: increases in dropout and suspensions and decreases in ratings of overall school performance (Gennetian et al. 2002). However, these mother reports were not supplemented in any of the studies with teacher reports or standardized tests. And the Three-City study, the largest non-experimental study of the effects of welfare reform on children, found, using more extensive measures, that transitions from welfare to work after passage of federal welfare reform were not associated with negative effects for adolescents (Chase-Lansdale et al. 2003). In fact, adolescents of mothers who made transitions from welfare to work reported lower levels of psychological distress on one measure.

New Hope plays an important role in the literature on employment-policy experiments because it is one of the earnings-supplement programs evaluated in the set of studies conducted by MDRC. It is uniquely valuable among these experiments because it had the additional benefit of an ethnographic study, conducted with a random subsample of parents from the experimental and control groups. We are therefore able to compare parents' experiences of the Wisconsin Works welfare reform program (in the control group) with the additional support services and earnings supplements that New Hope provided (in the experimental group). We make this comparison and ask how work support services in the two groups affected children in the final chapter in part III.

THE NEW HOPE PROJECT: DESIGN, DATA, AND DESCRIPTION OF THE CORE EMPLOYMENT ANALYSIS

The New Hope Project was a program in Milwaukee that offered supports to adults who worked thirty or more hours a week. The idea that "if you work, you should not be poor" fits with the view of many Americans today and was the guiding philosophy behind the New Hope Project. New Hope was in the American social contract tradition of the relationship between citizenship and public investment. New Hope brought supports to working-poor adults who showed an interest in or evidence of working full-time; those supports included child care, health care, income supplementation, and a short-term community service job if needed. The presumption in the program of a "fair, equitable exchange" was part of the kind of policy that Americans today generally support (Strauss 2002). As a goal for U.S. employment policy, and as a goal for assisting families with children, this idea seems appealing. It is difficult enough in the United States today, at most any level of income and across most kinds of jobs, to juggle parenting and work. It is all the more difficult if a parent is hovering around the poverty line, can find only low-wage work, has rapidly cycled among jobs, and enjoys few if any fringe benefits associated with work.[16] The jobs at the bottom of the labor market in the United States often do not pay enough for families with children to be able to survive on a single paycheck (Edin and Lein 1997). This is particularly true for households headed by a single parent.

The state of Wisconsin was a national leader in the 1990s in trying new programs that would assist women with children in moving off of welfare programs and into paid work. Both state agencies and nonprofit community-based organizations (CBOs) were involved in these efforts. One of the more successful programs was the New Hope Project, a CBO initiative based in Milwaukee that operated between late 1994 and 1998 (Bos et al. 1999).

The New Hope Project was conceived by leaders in Wisconsin who were troubled by the existing AFDC welfare system and wanted to start a program that might move more people out of poverty who were able to work. The goal was to make sure that such work would provide many of the same benefits that higher-wage workers receive—wages that would bring participants above the poverty line and offer them health care insurance and child care. The founders of New Hope, among many others, included David Riemer, the author of *Prisoners of Welfare: Liberating America's Poor from Unemployment and Low Wages* (1988), and Julie Kerksick, a member of the Congress for a Working America, a group committed to providing every American who wants one with a decent job (for a more detailed account of the program's development, see Duncan, Huston, and Weisner 2007). Based on advice from an advisory committee, and supported by the Wisconsin Department of Workforce Development and a variety of federal and foundation sources, a random-assignment evaluation was funded to determine the effects of the program on economic and household factors.[17] This evaluation was conducted by MDRC, a policy institute with extensive experience conducting random-assignment, longitudinal evaluations of employment, welfare, and education programs.

Families targeted by New Hope had to meet four eligibility criteria: they had to live in one of the two targeted neighborhoods (zip codes) in Milwaukee; be older than eighteen; have an income at or below 150 percent of the poverty line; and be willing to work thirty or more hours a week. Those who volunteered for the program were randomly assigned either to New Hope or to a control group that was ineligible for the program. The New Hope group offered a suite of benefits to eligible participants: a wage supplement (to ensure that a participant's total family income was substantially above the poverty threshold for that family); subsidies for affordable health insurance; child care vouchers; and a full-time community service job opportunity for those unable to find work on their own. Members of both the control and experimental groups were free to seek help from any federal or state public assistance programs, but only individuals in the experimental program also had access to New Hope benefits. So practically speaking the goal of the program was to lift out of poverty those who were willing to work thirty or more hours a week, on the premise that anyone willing to work full-time should not be poor and would be eligible for all of the New Hope benefits.

Over a period of sixteen months, starting in the fall of 1994, staff for the New Hope Project recruited 1,362 adults from the North Side and South Side neighborhoods in Milwaukee who met the eligibility criteria to participate in the study. This sample received a follow-up assessment at two years, but there was relatively little emphasis in the surveys and administrative data collected on their children's development. (Most of the data collected pertained to employment, income, household changes, service use, and use of public benefits.) Through funding from the MacArthur Foundation's Research Network on Successful Pathways Through Middle Childhood and the National Institute of Child Health and Human Development, a Child and Family Study was added to the evaluation. This smaller sample of 745 consisted of all parents with children between the ages of one and eleven (or more specifically, thirteen months and ten years, eleven months) at baseline. Among them were 54 fathers; we exclude this group of father-headed households from the analyses in this book because they are too few to analyze statistically with any reliability, though they are important for policy purposes. Adult men, whether heading a household or not, were important participants in New Hope. Thus, what we refer to as our full CFS survey sample in this book is a group of 696 mothers. They were followed up at two and at five years with a lengthy survey tapping perceptions of work, well-being, parenting, relationships and marriage, social support, and children's behaviors and activities. In addition, teachers of the children in this sample were asked about their school performance, school engagement, and social behaviors at the two- and five-year follow-ups. Finally, the five-year follow-up also included standardized assessments of children's reading and math achievement.

We present the characteristics, measured at baseline, of the 696 mothers in our survey sample in table 1.1. New Hope mothers were, on average, twenty-nine years old, with children five years old. Fifty-seven percent of the mothers were African American, 26 percent were Latina, and 14 percent were white. The Latina mothers were from a range of backgrounds, including Puerto Rican, Mexican, and Central American, with no single group predominating. Eighty-eight percent of the New Hope mothers were single; the majority of those had never been married. Forty percent were currently working, and 83 percent had worked full-time at some point in their work careers. Fifty-one percent had a high school diploma or GED. Eighty-four percent were receiving some form of government assistance (with just over 70 percent receiving AFDC).

The three-year New Hope Ethnographic Study (NHES) began in the spring of 1998, during the final year of the New Hope experiment, and lasted until the summer of 2001 (Gibson-Davis and Duncan 2005; Gibson and Weisner 2002; Weisner et al. 2000). The NHES took a stratified random sample of forty-four families from the full Child and Family Study, stratified for equal representation of both the experimental and control groups. (Initially forty-six were included; two families dropped out early, one each from the control group and the program group.) In all cases the parent who had been recruited into the larger CFS was recruited into the NHES. Two did not begin until the spring of 1999, leaving a final sample of forty-two NHES parents and their families, who were followed for the entire ethnographic period. Of these, we use as our sample in this book the forty mothers in the NHES, excluding two male-headed households. In return for their participation, each NHES parent was given $50 for every three months of their participation in the study.[18] Thomas Weisner led the NHES fieldwork team through

Table 1.1   Characteristics of New Hope Mothers at Baseline

Variable	Percentage or Mean (Standard Deviation)
Mother's age in years	28.8 (6.4)
Ethnicity	
African American	56.5%
Latina	26.4
White	13.6
Native American	3.4
Single-mother household	88.1
Three or more children	47.5
Youngest child two years old or younger	49.7
Currently working	40.2
Ever worked full-time	83.1
Currently receiving government assistance[a]	84.4
Has high school diploma or GED	51.0
Has access to a car	44.2
Child age in years	5.2 (2.89)
Child female	47.7%

Source: Authors' compilation.
Note: N = 696.
[a]Includes any of the following: AFDC (welfare), general assistance, food stamps, Medicaid.

a series of planning meetings, training, and periodic team meetings over the three-plus years of the fieldwork itself. The fieldwork team included psychologists, anthropologists, and sociologists (graduate students and graduates) from area universities (Northwestern, the University of Wisconsin at Madison, the University of Wisconsin at Milwaukee).[19]

Field-workers visited families roughly every ten weeks, most often in the families' homes, but also in a variety of community settings (Weisner et al. 2002). When visiting families, field-workers used open-ended interviews to engage parents in conversations about their lives, their concerns and hopes, and their everyday routines. The fieldwork team jointly developed a comprehensive set of topics to organize these discussions and home visits and to probe for material relevant to all of them. One topic that received a lot of attention was work life: employers, earnings, hassles at work, work and career goals, juggling work and family. We also covered topics relating to parenting and managing the household: budgeting and debt, child monitoring, school, child care, and parents' goals and fears about their kids. We included a range of other important topics that were sometimes difficult but that we thought would influence work and parenting: partners and husbands, drugs and alcohol, family supports and conflicts (including abuse), and parents' and children's health. We also asked parents their opinions on race, politics, and the welfare system. Field-workers participated in family activities (such as eating meals, shopping, running errands, and going to church) and talked with the children about their home lives, school, and friends. There were no "false negatives" in our interviews and field notes: we made sure that all families were asked about every topic, even those that did not come up naturally during interviews.

After each ethnographic visit, field-workers wrote up the conversations they had with the NHES families in visit summaries and wrote out their observations in more complete descriptive field notes. These field-note entries were based on tape recordings made during each family visit and on written notes taken during and after the day's visit. The data were entered into a database for storing the notes and linked to all the other project data being collected—the EthnoNotes system (Lieber, Weisner, and Presley 2003). In our presentations of case studies of families, quotations from parents about what they think about their lives, and summaries of qualitative patterns in work and family life, it is this EthnoNotes field-note database that we used. We also used these qualitative and ethnographic data files to describe specific topics, such as child care, social supports, or working nonstandard hours, or to detail the different employment trajectories that parents followed. In all analyses, we used the entire corpus of field notes and interview data rather than "cherry-pick" a few apt families or examples.

For an overview of how we conducted our qualitative and quantitative analyses, as well as more details on recruitment, data collection, and measures, see appendix 1.

OVERVIEW OF CHAPTERS

The story we tell here about working-poor parents and children offers new evidence and theory. To begin, we note that there is a fundamental fact about the working poor that, however well-known to researchers and parents, is not typically reflected in the policy and political discourse: the working poor are diverse, and their employment pathways are also diverse. The working poor differ substantially in their employment trajectories. Some experience a combination of wage growth and full-time work, while others are stuck in low-wage jobs at full-time hours. Some have rather stable job histories, but others cycle in and out of multiple jobs without much gain in income or job benefits. Still others struggle perpetually because they never really get or keep jobs. So although the heterogeneity of the working poor and their employment pathways is not news to researchers, the empirical demonstration of this in terms of specific groups of employment trajectories is, as are the implications of these varying employment trajectories for children's prospects and other aspects of work and family life. Our evidence indicates that working-poor parents who were in full-time work with some wage growth were the parents whose children were faring better on a range of child outcomes. High levels of job instability, in contrast, presented a risk to children's academic and social behaviors.

Another important part of the story we tell is that context matters. We consider the family-work interface as well as other contexts that can support work, such as child care, social support, and work support services. As we consider these varied contexts and their relationships to parents' diverse work trajectories and to children's lives and development, what emerges is that no one feature of family life or work circumstances dominates the story—that is, no one variable predicts outcomes or work by itself. Rather, a web of supports is required to support positive job trajectories and children's development. This is a theme across many chapters. The same is true theoretically: we find that a number of theoretical perspectives on how and why income, work, family, and individual characteristics matter for adult and child outcomes deserve some consideration. No one theoretical perspective, taken alone and out of context, predominates. From the family's point of view, their whole cultural ecology contributes to their responses to work and parenting (Weisner 2002). From the point of view of the New Hope Project, the suite of benefits (used in different combinations by families) and the respect shown to families all had some effect on work and child outcomes (Duncan, Huston, and Weisner 2007). Our evidence suggests that the fullest account—and the richest understanding—require economic, developmental, family, sociocultural, and policy perspectives.

The chapters in this book are organized in three parts. Part I describes the world of work, as experienced by New Hope Project participants. These chapters address the dynamics of work over time, their consequences for children's development, and experiences of job quality, work schedules, and discrimination in the workplace.

Chapters 2 and 3 present the results from our core analysis of work trajectories, using both qualitative and quantitative methods. These chapters describe the work trajectories of the New Hope Project members, their antecedents, and the consequences of these trajectories for the parents' well-being and their children's development. In chapter 4, Noemí Enchautegui-de-Jesús, Hirokazu Yoshikawa, and Vonnie McLoyd address job quality by describing what parents in New Hope viewed as the most important dimensions that distinguish good jobs from bad ones. Using the survey data, they also investigate the consequences of job quality for parents' and children's well-being. In chapter 5, JoAnn Hsueh addresses an inescapable fact of low-wage work in the United States: nonstandard hours and shifting schedules. New Hope parents reported wrenching trade-offs related to these work schedules. In quantitative analyses, Hsueh finds associations between nonstandard and shifting schedules and children's school performance and social behaviors. Finally, in chapter 6, Amanda Roy, Hirokazu Yoshikawa, and Sandra Nay examine the understudied topic of discrimination in the low-wage workplace. The New Hope mothers describe race- and sex-based discrimination experiences that were worrisome in their high prevalence and extent of overlap.

In part II, we describe how families balance work and family and how family processes help explain the effects of low-wage work on children's development. Chapter 7 examines how goals for family and work life affect career trajectories and outcomes for children. Thomas Weisner and his colleagues explore participants' personal goals and motivations as they affected and were affected by work. For many of the New Hope parents, low-wage work was a domain of rather high goals and expectations, but too often also a domain of limited growth and opportunity when these goals were thwarted. Breadwinning and caregiving goals were deeply intertwined.

In exploring what work buys for parents and children, chapter 8 integrates economic and psychological perspectives on how work affects economic and psychological processes in the family. Rashmita Mistry and Edward Lowe examine different types of expenditures and the different types of well-being they bring about. They examine parents' well-being, in turn, as it influences their children through effective parenting practices. They find that increases in earned income affect children's school performance and test scores by lowering levels of material hardship and financial worry and thereby increasing effective child management.

In chapter 9, Anna Gassman-Pines and her colleagues find that goals and experiences related to work affect relationships and marriage. In the qualitative data they find, in agreement with recent work on the Fragile Families study, that low-income single mothers state that improvement in their work and economic lives is a prerequisite to feeling ready for marriage. What is new here is their finding that in the New Hope survey data wage growth in the first two years of the study was in fact associated with a greater probability of getting married by year five. In a surprising finding, they discover that the New Hope experiment nearly doubled the rate of marriage among single mothers who had never been married at the beginning of the study. This effect appears to be related to New Hope's impact in increasing income. Entry into marriage in this group, in turn, appears related to children's social behaviors. In qualitative analyses, they explore in richer detail why work and income dynamics may be related to marriage (for example, through changes in relationship quality).

In part III, we conclude by examining child care and other supports for work in the lives of the New Hope mothers. In chapter 10, Lowe and Weisner depict how New Hope mothers juggled child care and work, balancing what they wanted from their children's care providers with their work schedules, available child care, and shifting informal support. The relationship of child care use to work trajectories is also a subject of this chapter.

Finally, Eboni Howard (chapter 11) and Godfrey and Yoshikawa (chapter 12) explore informal and formal work supports. Howard finds that social support was a mixed bag for New Hope parents, bringing with it both benefits and costs. Godfrey and Yoshikawa contrast the work support systems of Wisconsin Works and New Hope. How do New Hope mothers experience the array of work supports in these two very different contexts, one provided by the government in reconstituted welfare offices, the other by a CBO in two neighborhood storefronts? Chapter 12 also investigates whether work support services matter for later employment experiences and children's school performance and social behavior. Godfrey and Yoshikawa find that they in fact do matter, and that utilization of work support services appears causally related to increased income.

It is our hope that the reader will learn in depth the experiences of working parents living in the North Side and South Side neighborhoods of inner-city Milwaukee. We aim to shed some light on the mystery of how children fared as their parents negotiated the daily rhythms of low-wage work at the turn of the twenty-first century. In the concluding chapter, we summarize the major findings of the book and outline recommendations in three areas: income support, work support services, and workplace policies. The goal of our recommendations is to help working parents achieve wage growth and job stability, experience flexibility at work, and obtain the resources to afford important supports for work like transportation and child care. It is our belief that the package of policies we recommend could make a tangible difference in helping working-poor parents not only make ends meet but improve the lives of their children.

Part I | Experiences of Low-Wage Work

Chapter Two | Pathways Through
Low-Wage Work

Hirokazu Yoshikawa, Edward D. Lowe,
Thomas S. Weisner, JoAnn Hsueh,
Noemí Enchautegui-de-Jesús,
Anna Gassman-Pines, Erin B. Godfrey,
Eboni C. Howard, Rashmita S. Mistry,
and Amanda L. Roy

WHAT ARE THE pathways that mothers experience in the low-wage labor markets of Milwaukee? How do particular combinations of job characteristics—hours, wages, entries and exits—unfold over time in these women's lives? Few researchers have attempted to uncover diversity in the pathways—also called longitudinal trajectories—of low-wage work, that is, the subgroups of the working poor who experience different combinations of wages, job length, and hours. Instead, most research has focused on particular job characteristics in isolation and at one point in time. And few studies have utilized both longitudinal survey and ethnographic data to examine how parents' work patterns change over time. With both kinds of data, we identify the very different types of work pathways in the New Hope survey sample and also examine this heterogeneity in more depth in the longitudinal ethnographic data. Chapter 3 will show that different kinds of work trajectories are associated with different developmental outcomes for children.

THE LIVES AND WORK PATHWAYS OF THREE MOTHERS

We begin with the stories of three of the New Hope Ethnographic Study mothers and their work pathways across two and a half years. We chose these three because their stories highlight the tremendous heterogeneity in work trajectories among the working poor.

Evelia

Evelia, a petite single mother, was in her midthirties when our ethnographic study started in the spring of 1998. Although she was born in Milwaukee, both of her parents were born in Puerto Rico. She had lived on the South Side almost all of her life. When our study began, she and her four children were living in an apartment on the second floor of a house.

Evelia was the third child out of six in her family. Her parents divorced when she was four years old, and her mother raised her and her siblings without their father's support. When they were growing up, Evelia says, "We did not have much time to be like a normal child," because her mother took her and her siblings to church five days a week. She realizes now that her mother was using the church as a support as she raised six children on her own. Evelia's siblings have mostly stayed in and around Milwaukee, and she remains close to them, especially her two brothers who live nearby. She is an energetic and organized person who has a keen sense of the injustices of the policies and systems that serve the poor. Independence from welfare and from men is an important value in her life: "I prefer to be poor instead of subjected to a man's fist for the rest of my life."

Evelia did not finish high school because she became pregnant with her first child when she was nineteen. By the start of our study, she had had four children with three different fathers: Mike, who was thirteen years old; her daughter Sol, ten; Pancho, eight; and her youngest daughter, three-year-old Karina. She had a passionate desire to provide them with a better life, but this was difficult to do on a single paycheck; none of their fathers provided child support, despite her efforts to take them to court.

At the time of our first visit, Evelia had been a temp worker in the post office for one and a half years, making $9.00 an hour. This was her first full-time job, and she liked working there, for the most part. Thanks to the job at the post office, she said, she started to think for the first time about her long-term life goals and the things she really wanted. At the same time, she deeply resented the fact that she worked side by side with people who did the same work but, because of their permanent-staff status, were paid more and received benefits. Evelia also felt that the split shift hours she was assigned (3:00 P.M. to 11:30 P.M.) and the occasional overtime she worked kept her away from her children too much. She worried about the impact on them of her absence from the home after school and in the evening. Despite these problems, she stayed at the post office for eighteen months because she was not certain she could find another full-time job that paid as well.

Evelia was tenacious in the pursuit of her dream, which was to move out of Milwaukee to the suburbs to find a better job and more space and safety for her children. But she would wait another year and a half at the post office in vain, putting herself repeatedly on waiting lists for a permanent staff position. She also applied for a job in a post office in a suburb of Milwaukee. She desperately wanted to get herself and her children out of the dangerous South Side. She applied for and received housing assistance in the suburb, but not the job. And she ended up not having enough money to pay for the move, despite her siblings' offers to help her. Finally, when she found out that there was no chance of getting a permanent position at the post office, Evelia quit and took a job at a slaughterhouse, through a referral from her brother. She bet on some advantages of this job—greater job stability (it was a staff position) and better hours. (She worked the first shift from 7:00 A.M. to 5:00 P.M.) Her job at the slaughterhouse was to supervise the line workers for the quality of the meat. She worked in freezing conditions, in the refrigerated portion of the plant, for $8.79 an hour. Her shift lasted ten hours, with one fifteen-minute break and one thirty-minute break. After only a short time in this position, she explained that she felt like an "instrument of exploitation," monitoring Mexican immigrant workers who had to work an even more brutal seven-day workweek. This made her feel "bad and guilty." Evelia quit the slaughterhouse job. This launched her into a series of short-term jobs, one with an electronics manufacturer, and another with the Census Bureau, neither of which lasted for very long or paid much more than she had made at the post office. At the end of the study, she was not employed and was looking for work.

Iris

Iris, a European-American woman, was in her midthirties in 1998. She was overweight, had problems standing for long periods of time, and was missing a number of teeth owing to poor dental care. Iris was one of twelve children, and although she reported being close to her mother growing up, her mother apparently struggled with child-rearing: some of Iris's siblings spent time in foster care. When Iris was younger, she did not like school because she did not have the right clothes and was overweight. She spent two years in a school for troubled girls, but ended up dropping out of high school at age fifteen when that school closed. She said that she did a lot of partying and hanging out with friends in her teen years and after. In her late twenties, she "cleaned up" her life and went back to school to get her GED.

When Iris's field-worker met her for the first time, in 1998, she had been married to Juan, a Mexican immigrant, for five years. She housed and took care of her sister's two sons, seven-year-old Anthony and twelve-year-old

Mark. Iris and her family had just moved to a new apartment on the South Side because their old place was condemned. Their new place was much larger than their previous apartment. Iris especially liked how clean and new it looked, and her nephews were happy that they got their own rooms.

Iris was not working at the outset of our study. She generally stayed home, where she did the housework and took care of Anthony and Mark. Iris recognized that the family could use the money she would earn from working, and at times over the course of the study she said that she wanted to find work outside the home. She gave several reasons why she was not working. First, her husband Juan had "traditional views," preferring that she stay at home, take care of the children, and do the housework while he worked full-time. Iris had worked in the recent past, but that had been a particularly difficult time for Juan. For example, while she was working, Juan had problems taking care of the kids. They would not listen to him. He would call her at work when Anthony or Mark acted up, and she would have to get on the phone to tell the boys what to do. The house was always messy, which also upset Juan. Second, Iris felt that she needed to be home and available for Anthony and Mark when they needed her. This was particularly important because Mark had been getting into trouble both at school and in the neighborhood. Third, Iris believed that her weight, her arthritis and weak legs, and her lack of job skills made it difficult for her to impress employers and get a job. Finally, she had been harassed on several occasions in the few jobs she had held in the past, and these experiences discouraged her. For example, at a temp job in a factory a coworker once threw a piece of aluminum foil shaped like a penis at her. She complained to the manager, and the next day she did not receive a work assignment from the temp service. At other jobs, men made sexual comments to her.

Over the course of our visits with Iris between 1998 and 2001, she did not work outside the home other than during a brief, part-time stint teaching English as a second language (ESL) students and working on her typing skills at the Wisconsin Works Job Center. She did W-2 work in response to pressure from her caseworker, who threatened to cut off her food stamps if she did not come into the work program at the W-2 office. Toward the end of the study, Iris and Juan formally adopted Mark and Anthony, and they applied for and began to receive foster care payments.

Allison

Allison, a divorced African-American woman, was in her late thirties when the ethnography started. She was slender and of medium height. She had two sons, Nick, who was eighteen years old, and Jack, who was eleven. She had been involved with the father of her boys for seventeen years and was married to him for six. The two divorced in 1994 after several rocky years. Her husband left her without providing any support to her or her sons.

Allison and her four siblings grew up in Milwaukee and were raised by their mother. She described her mother as "resourceful" and said that her mother taught her to "mix and fend for yourself." Allison graduated from high school and received further training in medical records and then truck driving. Although her dream was to become a flight attendant, she was not able to pursue it after she found out she was pregnant with Nick.

At the first visit, Allison related that she had been through many financial ups and downs, but that "God provides." She had been working full-time in the service department of a major car dealership since 1993, making $8.50 an hour. Before going to the car dealership, she had worked for a dry cleaner but was fired after the store was robbed. Allison then received unemployment and fought to be included in the job training courses being offered to welfare recipients in office technology, even though she was not on welfare. It was a long battle, and she had to work hard to convince the state authorities that she needed the training in order to get another job. She was grouped with the welfare mothers and received the training, a six-week course. Subsequently, she found the full-time job at the car dealership.

Allison really enjoyed her job. The company provided interesting and informative on-the-job training. She learned a lot about cars and how they work. Allison was also sent to a local technical college for some computer courses. She says she "sucked up the training" like a sponge so that she would know as much as she could about computers. Allison knew that computer experience was marketable and would help her in getting a better job. Although she liked the work at the dealership, she was frustrated that she had not been given a raise. She told her field-worker that she would look for another job in the next few months if she did not get a raise.

Right on schedule, in April 1999, Allison found a new full-time job at an auto parts store through a former coworker at the dealership who had switched jobs and become a manager there. She was not very happy, however, with this new workplace. She thought that the other employees were dishonest and cheap and that the store was "a dump." She also experienced many sexist comments. She knew that there was a lot of sexism in the auto industry, but she had learned to cope with it over the years, often by saying something quick and cutting in response and then moving on. Soon Allison was looking for another job. After a month of searching, she found one at yet another car dealership, through another coworker friend from the first dealership. She really liked that job because she was no longer working directly with customers. By the time of our last interview, in October 2000, Allison was making $12.00 an hour. She felt, however, that given her responsibilities she should have been getting $15.00 an hour.

In reading the stories of Evelia, Iris, and Allison, we are first struck by their common worries and dreams. They share concerns about their children and the wrenching trade-offs of money and time. Earning money requires long, often changing and nonstandard work hours at relatively low wages; moreover, these jobs sometimes do not allow time for managing children who may have challenging behaviors, and many of them do not provide enough resources to support children comfortably. Nowadays, managing this balance between money and time with children is particularly difficult for all American parents, not just for the working poor.

In this chapter, we explore whether Evelia, Iris, and Allison represent typical trajectories through employment experienced by low-wage workers in the New Hope sample. We find five kinds of job trajectories in our sample: two characterized by particularly low-wage work and full-time rather than part-time status; one characterized by particularly high wage growth and full-time work; one characterized by moderately high wages and high job stability; and one characterized by very high job instability. In examining why mothers in our sample experienced the work pathways that they did, we find that human capital factors, mental health, and domestic violence, as well as access to work supports like cars, distinguished these job trajectories. Finally, we explore whether the New Hope Project made it more or less likely that mothers were in particular job trajectories. Assignment to the New Hope group at baseline did in fact increase the probability that mothers would go on to experience one of two of the trajectories: full-time work plus wage growth, and very high job instability.

DIVERSITY IN PATHWAYS THROUGH WORK

There is no standard "working-poor pathway." Among the many differences between Iris's, Evelia's, and Allison's pathways through work, a few stand out. The first is the simple difference in how much each woman was employed outside of the home. Iris clearly worked less than Evelia and Allison, who stayed employed for the majority of the two and a half years of our study. But Iris was in a stable marriage and was able to count on her husband's financial support as the major source of household income. She stayed at home in part because she and her husband believed that was best for the children. Anthony's and Mark's behavior required close monitoring by her, especially since her husband could not seem to manage them.

U.S. public opinion supports women who choose to stay home and care for the children if they do so with the financial support of a reliable spouse or male partner. But if there is no such partner, public opinion is clear, if somewhat ambivalent, in its belief that women must work rather than stay at home for the benefit of their children (Gilens 1999). For single mothers, the American public believes that work is best for them and their children and that welfare is harmful. Of course, most Americans also support providing assistance to the "deserving" among us, and they support programs such as child care assistance and health care for children. Americans' views appear to be influenced by the frame used when they are asked about support for single mothers. For example, an *individualist/moral* frame would suggest that "too many people avoid taking responsibility for their lives (so there should be reductions in support)." A *humanitarian/charity* frame would propose that government "provide help for the poor (but give them time limits)." A *populist/equity* frame would assert that "the average person pays too much in taxes and doesn't get enough in return from the government (so working single mothers should get more)" (Strauss 2002).

In any event, few women in our sample experienced Iris's pathway of limited engagement in work. For example, only two (4.5 percent) of the forty-four women in the ethnographic sample had a stable marriage or a partner who provided the major source of income to the family. A few others relied on welfare and other state supports and made only limited forays into regular employment, while the overwhelming majority were like Evelia and Allison, who worked full-time, most of the time, to support their families. The families in our study, then, were very much like the vast majority of low-income families in the United States who work to support their children and hope that their time away from the home will not harm their children.[1]

The second difference that we see when comparing Iris, Evelia, and Allison is the degree of job stability and instability they experienced. Evelia, after sticking it out at the post office as a temp for one and a half years, finally left in frustration and started a phase of cycling in and out of work that lasted for the rest of the study. For workers at the bottom end of the job market, a decision to leave and take a risk on the next job is momentous. In Evelia's case, the risk did not pay off: the meatpacking job was intolerable, and she left it after four days. At that point, Evelia was desperate because she did not have a lot of money saved up to cover the costs of her household of five (herself and four children). She told her fieldworker with regret that there was no way for her to undo what she had done. Evelia's story shows that, with very little financial cushion available in the form of savings, the hope and risk of job change can lead to real hardships in providing for children.

Allison, in contrast, never went through a period without work. She switched jobs twice, both times using the valuable resource of coworker networks—available to her through her initial job—to make job changes. Economists would describe Evelia's and Allison's work patterns as job instability and job mobility, respectively. Both are forms of job flux, but they are generally associated with different levels of skills. Job *instability*, or frequent transitions from work to nonwork, is more likely to be experienced by those with lower levels of education and fewer job skills (Holzer and LaLonde 1999; Johnson and Corcoran 2002; Royalty 1998; Topel and Ward 1992). Job *mobility*, or voluntary job-to-job transitions, is more common among those with higher education and skills. Although job instability is a natural part of the careers of many workers in the United States—particularly in the early portions of their careers—it is unfortunately more widespread and lasts longer in the work careers of the poor and near-poor.

We also see in Allison's case the advantages of particular job sectors, such as the automotive industry, which generally offers relatively good job benefits. Opportunities in the auto industry span interlocking employment sectors (parts, sales, service) and a range of staff networks for those lucky enough to have experience in the industry. Allison was able to build experience in one sector of an industry that was flexible enough to count that experience in a move within the sector. She also made use of coworker networks in each of her job-to-job transitions. In contrast, at the beginning of our study Evelia was stuck in temp work, which provides very few benefits, lower job stability, and therefore little access to the kinds of coworker networks that enabled Allison's job mobility. A 1997 study conducted in Wisconsin during the time of Evelia's long stint in temp work at the post office found that 30 percent of all jobs engaged in by a sample of women initially on welfare were temp jobs. Most of these were short-term jobs, and over 50 percent of them begun in a quarter did not last until the next quarter (Pawasarat 1997). We can see that despite all of Evelia's best-laid plans, her lack of access to a permanent staff position in the postal system contributed to her difficulty in realizing her goals of a higher-paying job, a move to the suburbs, and a better life for herself and her children.

The third aspect of these women's employment pathways that differentiates them is the degree to which their wages grew over time. The most common employment goal of the parents in our ethnography was a higher wage, which they saw as a step up to middle-class life. For many, however, this goal was not easily realized. Evelia's wages stayed stagnant (hovering around $9.00 an hour) despite all of her efforts to find a higher-paying job. Allison, in contrast, was making about $3.00 more an hour at the end of the study than she did at the beginning. To place Evelia's and Allison's wages in context, studies of welfare recipients conducted in the first year or two after passage of the 1996 reforms found that they were earning between $7.00 and $8.00 an hour (Acs and Loprest 2001). These two women had the advantage of being in one of the most economically robust areas of the country at that time, during a period of almost unprecedented economic growth in the

United States. Yet Evelia was barely making ends meet and had no health benefits or pensions accruing and received no vacation or sick time.

Most studies of low-skilled workers find that wages increase between 1 and 3 percent a year on average (Card, Michalopoulos, and Robins 2001; Friedlander and Burtless 1995). Extrapolated to our study period of two and a half years, this figure would suggest that wages grew between 2.5 and 4.5 percent over that period. Allison, with her increase from $8.50 to $11.50, or 35 percent, in the course of two and a half years was well above the average in the amount of her wage change. Most low-skilled workers who stay at the same job over time do not experience wage growth, an experience that confirms that they are in bottom-of-the-ladder jobs with little opportunity for advancement (Connolly and Gottschalk 2001). Those who transition to new jobs experience somewhat higher wage growth, but of a magnitude that is much lower than it is for more highly educated workers.

Although the existing research on work, job instability, and wage growth is informative, it does not capture the complexity of Iris's, Evelia's, and Allison's work pathways. These three work patterns differed from each other in the particular *combinations* of hours, job lengths, wages, and wage growth they entailed. It was Evelia's combined experience of long work hours, wage stagnation, and job instability that raised her level of work-related stress. Allison may have reported a lower level of job and parenting stress because of the particular combination of job-to-job transitions, accompanied by wage growth, that she experienced. What we see from listening to these women's unfolding stories are dynamic work pathways rather than static characteristics of a particular job at a particular time. Yet the bulk of the research on maternal employment and child development examines particular job characteristics singly and at one point in time. Few studies have examined what propels low-wage working parents into particular combinations of work characteristics, or what the consequences are for their well-being or their children's development.

As three participants in the ethnographic study, do Iris, Evelia, and Allison and their employment pathways represent broader patterns in the full New Hope sample? In the remainder of this chapter, we explore the heterogeneity of the work trajectories in the New Hope survey sample by examining combinations of work dynamic dimensions, including average hours, wages, wage change, job length, and number of jobs over the course of the first twenty-four months of the study. (These survey variables are available only for the period between baseline and twenty-four months.)

We use cluster analysis to capture heterogeneity in work pathways. This statistical technique is suited to uncovering subgroups in a particular population, as defined by a set of dimensional characteristics. It essentially provides a way to categorize a sample based on the particular combinations of these characteristics they embody (for example, distinguishing a group that is high on characteristics A and B and low on C from one that is low on characteristic A, medium on B, and high on C).[2] It is more suited to our analysis than factor analysis, which identifies subgroups of *variables* that covary (correlate) across a sample but does not identify subgroups of people. Using cluster analysis, we identify the diversity of work pathways in our survey sample based on multiple dynamic dimensions of jobs. We then explore how durable these work pathways are over the next three years of the study, using both survey and ethnographic data. Finally, we ask: what prior characteristics of the New Hope families, measured at baseline, predict the kinds of work pathways they experienced over the next two years?

IDENTIFYING WORK PATHWAYS IN THE NEW HOPE SURVEY SAMPLE

For the first two years of the follow-up, we chose variables that tapped the dynamic nature of work. We had information from the survey on up to six jobs that each participant had during the two years. The combination of variables available for each job—start and end dates, wages, and the number of hours of work per week—provided a detailed picture of the economic characteristics of these jobs and therefore of overall job trajectories.[3] We used this information to construct variables representing the average number of months the jobs lasted, the overall number of jobs, the average wage, the amount of change in wages (subtracting the beginning wage from the most recent wage), and the average number of hours worked per week for each survey respondent. Our sample was restricted to those who were followed up at twenty-four months and who reported working at some time during the twenty-four months. (An additional group who reported no work during the two-year survey period was not included in the cluster analysis because their values for each of the work variables was zero; this was a very small group of twenty-two mothers, or 4 percent of the sample.)

Employment variable means for the entire sample who reported any work over the period of the twenty-four-month follow-up were as follows: Mothers worked an average of 2.5 jobs, each with an average length of 11.8 months. The sample reported working an average of 36.8 hours per week, at an average wage of $6.53 an hour. The sample reported an average wage change over the twenty-four months of an increase of $.98.[4] These hourly wage and weekly hours worked are characteristic of those in welfare "leaver" studies (that is, former welfare recipients who went to work following the passage of the 1996 federal welfare reform).[5]

The cluster analysis procedure can identify subgroups that differ in their combinations of dimensions. The five work variables (average job length, number of jobs, average hours worked, average hourly wage, and wage change) were entered into the cluster analysis.[6] Split-half reliability analyses showed essentially the same forms of these clusters across two random halves of the sample. Our analysis identified five subgroups of New Hope parents. Homogeneity coefficients were above the thresholds recommended as standards in cluster analysis; that is, each of the five clusters was sufficiently non-overlapping with the others.[7] Figure 2.1 illustrates the cluster analysis. Each of the five clusters of bars represents a subgroup of our total sample. In each cluster, the bars represent average standardized values of five variables for that subgroup of parents (from left to right for each cluster in the figure: average job length, number of jobs, average hours worked per job, average hourly wage, and wage change over the course of the two-year period). We present standardized values on the Y axis so as to be able to present all the component variables in one figure. The zero line thus represents the average for each variable, across the sample. The small numbers above or below each bar represent that value in its original units (months for job length, hours for hours worked, dollars for wages and wage change). The combination bars that are farthest from the horizontal axis (that is, the ones that are the most *different* from the overall average for the whole sample) are the variables that best distinguish each cluster, or group, from the others.

When examining the low-wage–part-time subgroup, we observe in the graph that all of the lines fall below the samplewide mean. This group comprised 62 members, or 12 percent of the sample. It was characterized by low average hours of work per week (22.7 hours), values lower than the overall sample mean on job length (about 9 months), and average hourly wage ($5.88), number of jobs (2.0), and wage growth (an increase of $.47 over two years) that were each moderately below these variables' means. With 81 members, or 16 percent of the sample, the second group, the rapid cyclers, had by far the highest number of jobs (averaging 4.7) and the shortest average job length (about 5.4 months) and average wage growth (an increase of $.87). They averaged $6.08 in their hourly wage and reported 37.9 average hours of work per week.

The full-time–wage-growth group, with 53 members, or 10 percent of the sample, reported high average work hours (38.9 hours per week across jobs), the highest average wage ($8.07 an hour), and by far the highest wage growth (an increase of $3.80 over the course of two years). The stable employment subgroup, with 139 members, or 27 percent of the sample, had the longest average job length (22 months), higher than average wages ($7.26 an hour), and high hours per week (averaging 38.7 hours).

Finally, the last cluster, the low-wage–full-time group, with 150 members, or 30 percent of the sample, was characterized by lower job duration

Figure 2.1 Cluster Subgroups of Work Pathways

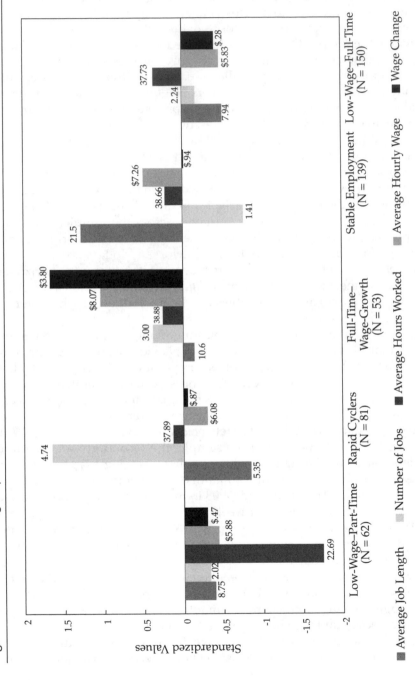

(8 months on average), lower wages (averaging $5.83 an hour), full-time hours (37.8 hours per week), and the lowest wage growth of the five groups (averaging an increase of $.28 over two years).

Our cluster groups, then, showed the characteristics seen in Iris's, Evelia's, and Allison's work pathways—overall work effort, instability, average wage levels, and wage growth—but in varying combinations. We identified one group characterized by very high instability, the rapid cycler group, which had an average of nearly five jobs over two years and relatively low average wages ($6.00 an hour). We found two groups with relatively high average wages, the full-time–wage-growth group and the stable employment group; they differed greatly, however, in their levels of wage *growth,* with average increases of $4.00 and $1.00, respectively.

Finally, two groups were characterized by low wages and significant periods of non-employment. Both the first and last clusters—the low-wage–part-time group and the low-wage–full-time group—had average wages below $6.00 an hour. These two groups also seem to be characterized by significant periods of non-employment, since the average number of jobs multiplied by the average number of jobs worked for each cluster is less than the twenty-four-month period covered by the survey questions (on average, 17.7 months for the low-wage–part-time group and 17.8 months for the low-wage–full-time group). The two groups are primarily distinguished from one another by a large difference in their average number of hours worked per week: 23 hours per week in the low-wage–part-time group and 38 hours a week in the low-wage–full-time group.

Where are Iris, Allison, and Evelia in these clusters? Iris was in the low-wage–part-time group. Like the other members of that group, she did not work to the extent that members of the other groups did, and she worked part-time when she did work. Allison was in the stable employment group; like other members of that group, she made transitions that were more frequently job-to-job transitions (characteristic of job mobility, in economic terms). Finally, Evelia was in the low-wage–full-time group, and like that group generally, she was employed full-time but experienced little increase in her wages over time.

How Durable Are These Employment Pathways?

What happened after the short-term snapshot of the twenty-four-month survey? To answer this question we turn first to the ethnographic sample. Recall that the ethnographic study covered a period of time between the twenty-four- and sixty-month surveys (roughly 1998 to late 2000 for most families in the sample).

We undertook a comprehensive, longitudinal analysis of the field notes for each NHES participant. As we explained in the introduction, we coded each job for start and end date, occupation, title, hourly wage, and types of transitions between jobs and between work and nonwork (promotions or raises at the same job; suspensions or firings; positive reasons for taking on a new job). These results were then summarized into chronological narratives, and the summaries further represented graphically. Figures 2.2 to 2.5 graphically represent each of the employment timelines for each NHES worker, placed within their work pathway groups.[8] The top bar in each figure shows the month of the ethnography in real time. Each row represents one parent; some rows are subdivided in two to represent simultaneous jobs. The different background shades represent different schedules (for example, full-time versus part-time, or odd jobs with no set schedules, such as retrieving junk to sell from a scrap yard). Job-to-job changes are represented by dark vertical lines; dotted lines represent promotions or raises within a particular job. Occupations, titles when available, and wages for each job are indicated within each bar. There were two kinds of job transitions that we did not graph: suspensions or firings, and moves into new jobs because of their positive characteristics. We did analyze these two kinds of transition, however, and they are included in the following discussion.

Our overall finding from the three-year ethnographic study of work dynamic patterns is one of remarkable continuity in trajectories. Many of the women in the ethnographic sample continued in the pattern described by their cluster for several years beyond the twenty-four-month survey. Indeed, of the thirty-four ethnographic families that had enough data to be assigned a cluster membership, we found that twenty-nine (85 percent) persisted in the employment pattern characteristic of the cluster group to which they were assigned using the twenty-four-month data.

For example, four of the five ethnographic families who were part of the low-wage–part-time group continued either working part-time hours or cycling between periods of unemployment and periods of part-time employment (about twenty hours a week; see figure 2.2). The wages for the low-wage–part-time women continued to be lower than for women in the other groups, and their jobs were of shorter duration. In addition, this group was the only group in the ethnographic sample not to experience wage growth. (In this admittedly small group of five, the average wage at the beginning of the ethnography was $6.54, and at the end $6.50.) This group was also the least likely to experience a promotion or a raise at a particular job (average of .4 per person), probably because their work effort was quite low. The low-wage–part-time group's jobs were relatively low-skilled, even compared to the jobs held by women in our overall sample, and there were few clerical jobs in this group; more typical were child care work ($6.00 an hour) and nurse's assistant and crossing guard ($9.00 an hour). Finally, the mothers in this group appeared to be the most likely to experience serious mental illness and some of the most severe levels of domestic violence. A recent large-scale study of mothers on welfare in Michigan (Danziger, Corcoran, et al. 2000; Kalil, Schweingruber, and Seefeldt 2001; Danziger, Kalil, and Anderson 2000) shows that these factors are two of the most powerful barriers to future employment. Unfortunately, Iris's experience with chronic depression and low self-esteem was quite representative of the women in this group. (Iris is the fourth of the five cases in figure 2.2.)

All except one of the six members of the rapid cycler group continued to cycle through short-term jobs (see figure 2.3). The average length of jobs in this group was shorter than in any of the other groups. The rapid cyclers were also characterized by relatively low wages (an average of $6.08 at the beginning of the ethnography and $7.25 at the end, a rise of 19 percent). Interestingly, this group was the most likely to experience a promotion or raise (1.0 per person on average). But they were also the most likely to be suspended or fired, and the least likely to report taking on a new job because of some positive characteristic of it. Jobs in this group were primarily service jobs. However, a greater percentage of jobs in this group, compared to the low-wage–part-time group, were clerical; for example, members of this group held jobs as a bank shipping clerk, administrative assistant, and insurance company clerk.

Turning to figure 2.4, the majority of the women in the stable employment group and the full-time–wage-growth group continued to work stable, full-time jobs. (We combine these two groups in part because of the small number of full-time–wage-growth members who happened to be in the ethnographic sample.) Together, the stable employment group and the full-time–wage-growth group also continued to report higher wages and wage growth than any of the others. The combined group had the highest initial average wage ($8.82) and the largest relative increase (to an average of $11.67, or an increase of 32 percent). Members of this group were also quite likely to experience a promotion or raise (an average of .87 per person), were the least likely to be suspended or fired, and were the most likely to take on a new job because of a positive feature of it. Jobs in both of these groups were more likely than was the case with any of the other groups to be supervisory or managerial positions (such as office manager at a drug treatment center; assistant director, and then director, of a child care agency; payroll manager at a hospital). The two groups also included the few jobs in our sample that were in manufacturing, such as machinist in a factory or Allison's jobs in the auto industry. Allison's job trajectory is depicted in the fourth row from the bottom in figure 2.4.

Figure 2.2 Low-Wage–Part-Time Group

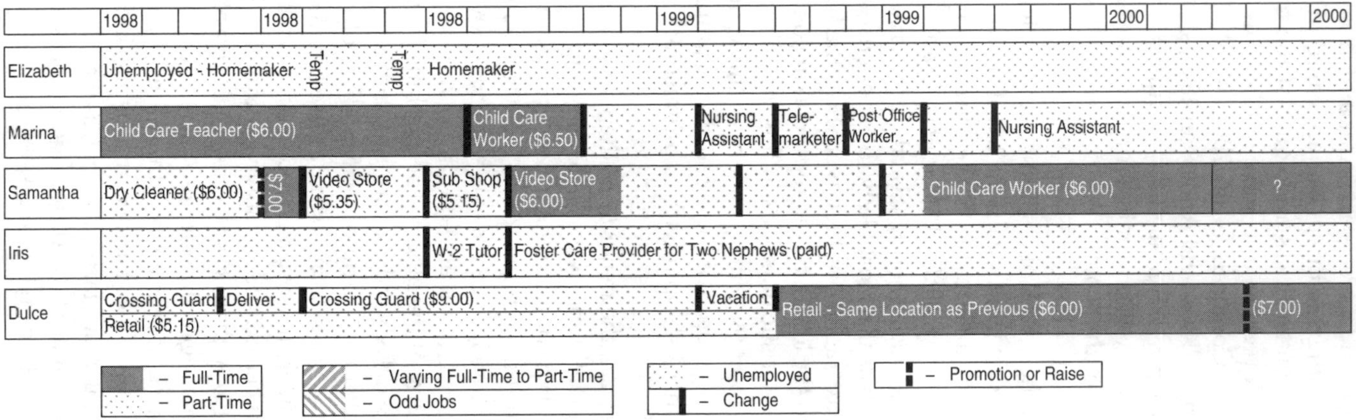

| | 1998 | 1998 | 1998 | 1998 | 1999 | 1999 | 1999 | 2000 | 2000 |

Elizabeth Unemployed - Homemaker Temp Temp Homemaker

Marina Child Care Teacher ($6.00) Child Care Worker ($6.50) Nursing Assistant Tele-marketer Post Office Worker Nursing Assistant

Samantha Dry Cleaner ($6.00) $7.00 Video Store ($5.35) Sub Shop ($5.15) Video Store ($6.00) Child Care Worker ($6.00) ?

Iris W-2 Tutor Foster Care Provider for Two Nephews (paid)

Dulce Crossing Guard ($9.00) Crossing Guard Deliver Vacation Retail - Same Location as Previous ($6.00) ($7.00)
Retail ($5.15)

Legend:
- Full-Time
- Part-Time
- Varying Full-Time to Part-Time
- Odd Jobs
- Unemployed
- Change
- Promotion or Raise

Source: Authors' compilation.

Figure 2.3 Rapid Cycler Group

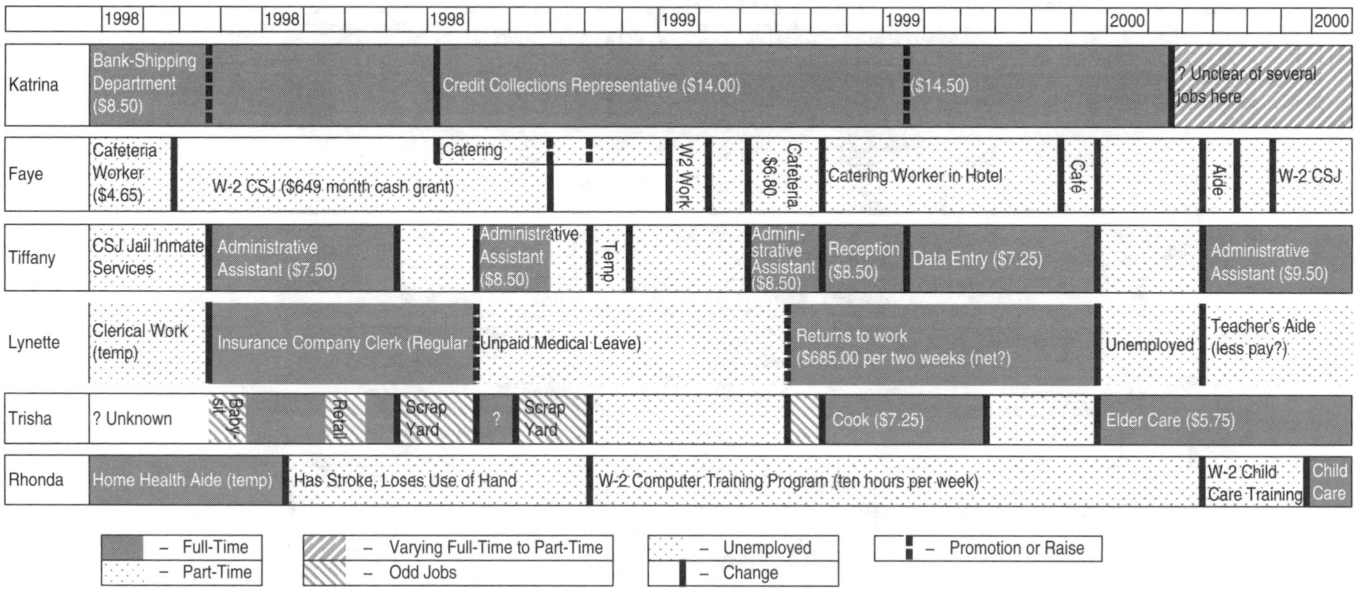

	1998	1998	1998	1998	1999	1999	1999	2000	2000	2000

Katrina: Bank-Shipping Department ($8.50) — Credit Collections Representative ($14.00) — ($14.50) — ? Unclear of several jobs here

Faye: Cafeteria Worker ($4.65) — W-2 CSJ ($649 month cash grant) — Catering — W2 Work — Cafeteria $6.80 — Catering Worker in Hotel — Café — Aide — W-2 CSJ

Tiffany: CSJ Jail Inmate Services — Administrative Assistant ($7.50) — Administrative Assistant ($8.50) — Temp. — Administrative Assistant ($8.50) — Reception ($8.50) — Data Entry ($7.25) — Administrative Assistant ($9.50)

Lynette: Clerical Work (temp) — Insurance Company Clerk (Regular) — Unpaid Medical Leave — Returns to work ($685.00 per two weeks (net?)) — Unemployed — Teacher's Aide (less pay?)

Trisha: ? Unknown — Baby-sit — Retail — Scrap Yard — ? — Scrap Yard — Cook ($7.25) — Elder Care ($5.75)

Rhonda: Home Health Aide (temp) — Has Stroke, Loses Use of Hand — W-2 Computer Training Program (ten hours per week) — W-2 Child Care Training — Child Care

Legend:
- Full-Time
- Part-Time
- Varying Full-Time to Part-Time
- Odd Jobs
- Unemployed
- Change
- Promotion or Raise

Source: Authors' compilation.

Figure 2.4 The Full-Time–Wage-Growth Group (WG) and the Stable Employment (SE) Group

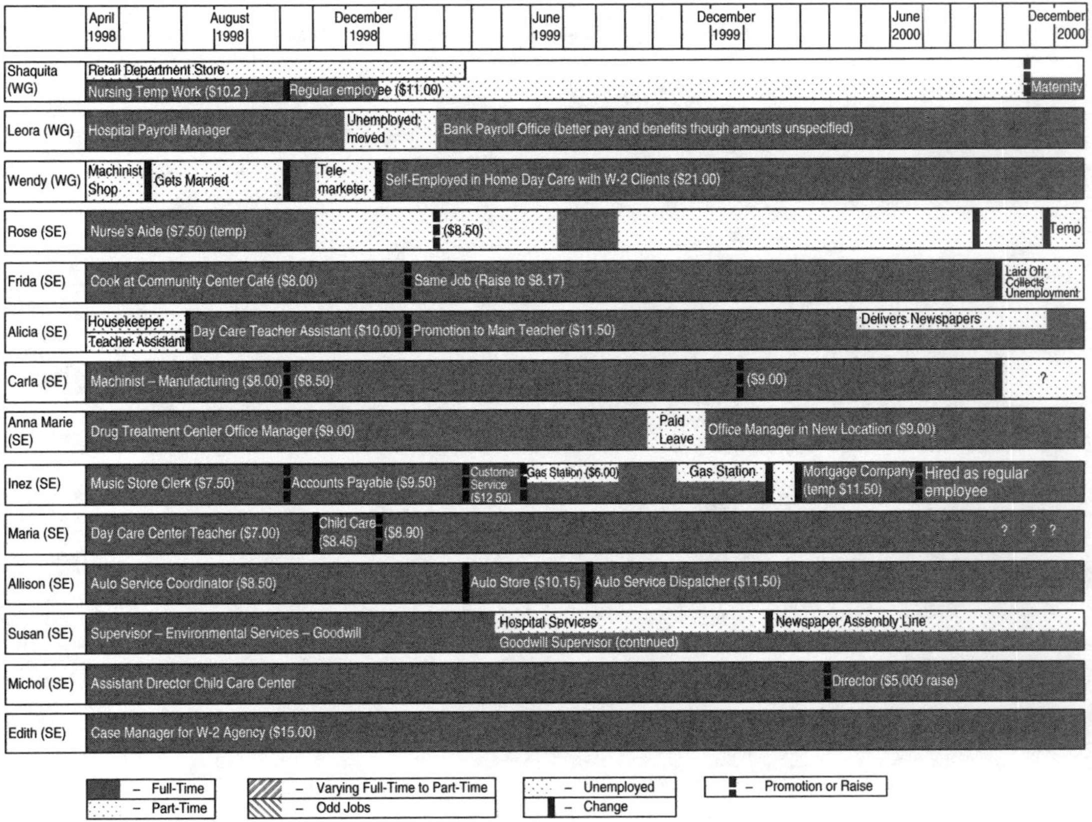

	April 1998	August 1998	December 1998	June 1999	December 1999	June 2000	December 2000

Shaquita (WG): Retail Department Store; Nursing Temp Work ($10.2); Regular employee ($11.00); Maternity

Leora (WG): Hospital Payroll Manager; Unemployed: moved; Bank Payroll Office (better pay and benefits though amounts unspecified)

Wendy (WG): Machinist Shop; Gets Married; Tele-marketer; Self-Employed in Home Day Care with W-2 Clients ($21.00)

Rose (SE): Nurse's Aide ($7.50) (temp); ($8.50); Temp

Frida (SE): Cook at Community Center Café ($8.00); Same Job (Raise to $8.17); Laid Off; Collects Unemployment

Alicia (SE): Housekeeper; Teacher Assistant; Day Care Teacher Assistant ($10.00); Promotion to Main Teacher ($11.50); Delivers Newspapers

Carla (SE): Machinist – Manufacturing ($8.00); ($8.50); ($9.00); ?

Anna Marie (SE): Drug Treatment Center Office Manager ($9.00); Paid Leave; Office Manager in New Location ($9.00)

Inez (SE): Music Store Clerk ($7.50); Accounts Payable ($9.50); Custodial Service ($12.50); Gas Station ($6.00); Gas Station; Mortgage Company Hired as regular (temp $11.50) employee

Maria (SE): Day Care Center Teacher ($7.00); Child Care ($3.45); ($6.90); ? ? ?

Allison (SE): Auto Service Coordinator ($8.50); Auto Store ($10.15); Auto Service Dispatcher ($11.50)

Susan (SE): Supervisor – Environmental Services – Goodwill; Hospital Services; Goodwill Supervisor (continued); Newspaper Assembly Line

Michol (SE): Assistant Director Child Care Center; Director ($5,000 raise)

Edith (SE): Case Manager for W-2 Agency ($15.00)

Legend:
- Full-Time
- Part-Time
- Varying Full-Time to Part-Time
- Odd Jobs
- Unemployed
- Change
- Promotion or Raise

Source: Authors' compilation.

Finally, the low-wage–full-time group (figure 2.5) was characterized by moderate wages and low levels of wage growth (an average of $7.76 at the outset of the ethnography and $8.49 at the end, an increase of only 9 percent). Evelia's difficulties in finding a high-paying job are reflected by her membership in this group; her job trajectory is represented in the second row. This group experienced a moderate probability of promotions or raises relative to the other groups (an average of .75 per person). The jobs in this group were primarily housekeeping, child care, and clerical positions.

Since the job pathways described in figure 2.1 appear quite robust among members of the ethnographic sample, we would expect the reported job characteristics in the sixty-month survey to be strongly predicted by the participants' cluster membership at twenty-four months. For the sixty-month survey, respondents were asked to describe the characteristics of their current or most recent job (if currently not employed).[9] These were for jobs held approximately three years after the last reported job on the twenty-four-month survey. Respondents were asked the number of hours they worked per week, their current or last hourly wage, and how long they had been working in this job. We calculated a wage change score by subtracting the wage reported at sixty months from the last wage they reported at twenty-four months.

Table 2.1 shows the average values of job duration, weekly hours, hourly wage, and wage change between the last job reported at twenty-four months and the reference job (current or most recent) in the sixty-month survey. The cluster groups continue to predict significant mean differences for all of these measures except for wage change. Moreover, the mean differences between pairs of clusters are almost always in the direction predicted at twenty-four months. For example, at sixty months, rapid cyclers continue to have the lowest job duration of any of the groups (18.45 months). Interestingly, however, this group shows the highest average wage growth between twenty-four and sixty months. The stable employment group and the full-time–wage-growth group show the longest job duration (about thirty-six months for both groups, on average). The low-wage–part-time group still reports much lower hours of work per week than the other four groups, particularly the rapid cyclers, the stable employment group, and the full-time–wage-growth group. The full-time–wage-growth group reports a higher hourly wage than the other groups. The results of the analysis reported in table 2.1 confirm that the job pathways represented by each of the five cluster groups are typically quite durable over the course of the five years of the study.

Figure 2.5 Low-Wage–Full-Time Group

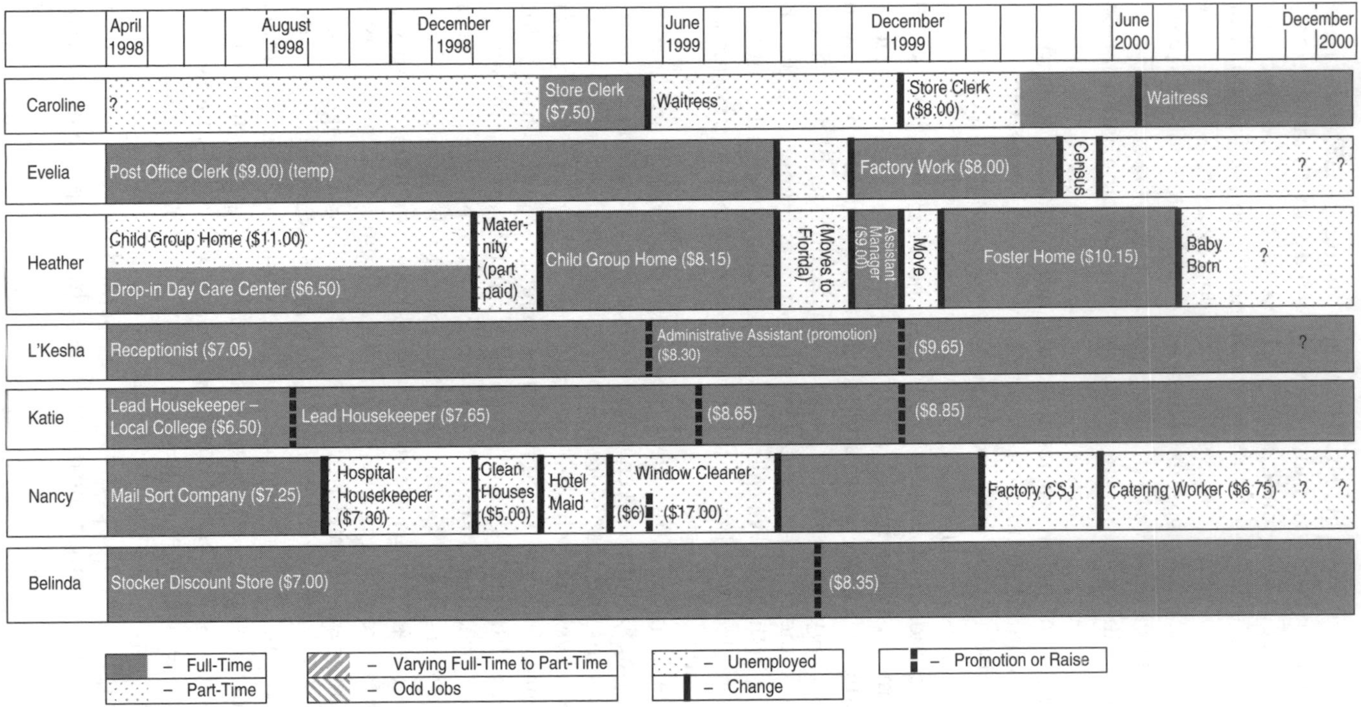

	April 1998	August 1998	December 1998	June 1999	December 1999	June 2000	December 2000

Caroline: ? — Store Clerk ($7.50) — Store Clerk ($8.00) — Waitress — Waitress

Evelia: Post Office Clerk ($9.00) (temp) — Factory Work ($8.00) — Census — ? ?

Heather: Child Group Home ($11.00) — Maternity (part paid) — Child Group Home ($8.15) — (Moves to Florida) — Foster Home ($10.15) — Baby Born ?
Drop-in Day Care Center ($6.50)

L'Kesha: Receptionist ($7.05) — Administrative Assistant (promotion) ($8.30) — Assistant Manager ($9.00) — Move ($9.65) — ?

Katie: Lead Housekeeper – Local College ($6.50) — Lead Housekeeper ($7.65) — ($8.65) — ($8.85)

Nancy: Mail Sort Company ($7.25) — Hospital Housekeeper ($7.30) — Clean Houses ($5.00) — Hotel Maid ($5.00) — Window Cleaner ($6) ($17.00) — Factory CSJ — Catering Worker ($6.75) — ?

Belinda: Stocker Discount Store ($7.00) — ($8.35)

Legend:
— Full-Time
— Part-Time
— Varying Full-Time to Part-Time
— Odd Jobs
— Unemployed
— Change
— Promotion or Raise

Source: Authors' compilation.

Table 2.1 Average Employment Characteristics at Sixty-Month Follow-up for Five Work Pathway Groups

	Low-Wage–Part-Time	Rapid Cyclers	Full-Time–Wage-Growth	Stable Employment	Low-Wage–Full-Time	Total	f	p
Job duration (months)	20.47	18.45	35.31	37.19	22.32	27.68	8.211	<.001
Weekly hours	33.83	39.53	37.51	38.37	36.52	37.37	3.387	<.01
Hourly wage	$8.82	$9.71	$11.56	$9.60	$8.48	$9.53	7.037	<.001
Wage change	$0.89	$2.37	$1.92	$2.11	$2.28	$2.03	0.742	ns
N	41	58	59	98	103	359		

Source: Authors' compilation.

WHY ARE THESE PATHWAYS SO DIFFERENT? THE ROLE OF PRIOR CHARACTERISTICS

The different pathways that low-income parents take through work may be related to other personal characteristics and characteristics of their families, their neighborhoods, and other social contexts. Iris, for example, had a husband, Juan, who did not want her to work. She recalled that the last time she worked full-time, at the local supermarket, Juan got upset not only because he could not manage her nephews but also because she was stressed and tired after getting home from work. In addition, he expected her to do all of the housework. The kids were acting out, Juan was complaining, and Iris, so stressed out that her hair was falling out in chunks, felt like she was going crazy. She also had health issues—arthritis, problems walking, and what appeared to be undiagnosed chronic depression—that kept her from working more. These health problems exacerbated the other influences on her work life, such as her partner; we heard in her story the toll that accumulated stresses can take on an individual's well-being.

Evelia reported a very different pattern of influences on her work pathway. Her child care needs in particular came across vividly in her story. Her youngest daughter, Karina, started a half-day preschool during the study, and her older children were in school but not old enough to walk home by themselves. Evelia's field-worker crystallized her struggles to balance work and family life:

The problems started for Evelia when classes began. Evelia doesn't have any problems with her three older kids because they go to school and come back home by themselves. The problem has always been with her youngest daughter. Her girl will start attending school and classes will begin at 7:45 A.M., but Evelia starts work at 6:45 A.M. and doesn't have anyone to help her to take her little girl to school. The school doesn't offer any form of transportation because Evelia lives near the school and her house isn't within the school's bus route. Also, her child is very small and couldn't stay home alone to wait for the bus, in Evelia's view. Evelia is trying to find a friend to help her to take her child to school. Evelia has a friend [with] a [fifteen-year-old] daughter, and the school is on her way to work. Evelia proposed to her friend that she could take her friend's daughter to school and in return [the friend] could take her youngest daughter to school. On the day that I was visiting she was waiting for her girlfriend's phone call to settle a deal. Evelia's girlfriend first had to talk it over with her own daughter to see if she agreed. Her girlfriend's daughter . . . has to be willing to wake up earlier and be at school fifteen minutes early before classes begin so that Evelia will have enough time to make it to work. Evelia says now everything depends on her girlfriend's daughter.

In many working families, child care arrangements are often balanced as finely and as precariously as a house of cards. But working-poor parents are at a further disadvantage: with low and unpredictable resources, they often find that their child care situations can collapse should just one card become unbalanced. Many have no extra cards to help keep the daily routine going. In this case, the point of vulnerability in the system was the fifteen-year-old daughter of a friend—or more specifically, her willingness to get up fifteen minutes earlier every day. (As any parent of an adolescent knows, a fifteen-minute period that could be spent sleeping at the beginning of the day is not trivial.) So one reason Evelia experienced job instability seems to have been her vulnerable child care supports, which were thin and barely flexible enough to respond to changing schedules over the school year. (Note that Evelia's problems started when the school year began; the summer class schedules of her children were compatible with her work schedule.) Recall that a major reason Evelia took the big risk of leaving her post office job was to work a shift that better fit her children's child care and school schedules.

What resources and contexts enabled Allison to have such a stable and upward-moving job trajectory? For one thing, she had access to job training classes that she "fought her way into" (since she was not a mother on welfare) at a crucial point in her work experience, just before she got her first job at a car dealership. She related that it was a long battle—she had to convince the state authorities that she needed this training for another job. She was grouped with the welfare mothers and received the six-week training in 1992. In 1993 she found a full-time job at a car dealership. Job training, at the right point in her career, resulted in her getting a job that she held for five years (the position she was in at the beginning of our ethnographic study).

Does Allison's job training story generalize to large-sample studies? Non-experimental studies of the effects of job training on later wage growth and job stability find that those who get on-the-job training do subsequently experience more wage growth (Bartel 1995). And it appears that school- or job-based training that is longer than one month has long-term effects on wage growth that are detectable even nine years later. This sustained job training effect appears stronger for lower-skilled workers (Lengermann 1999; Lynch 1992). But there are no long-term effects of training that lasts less than a month. These findings could be challenged, since there may be unobserved differences between those who pursued training and those who did not. Experimental evaluation, if carried out correctly, addresses such "selection bias." Randomized evaluations of government-sponsored training programs, such as the Job Training Partnership Act, have found a small earnings gain from classroom-based training across a thirty-month follow-up for both adult women and men (Bloom et al. 1997).

What family and personal characteristics are associated with the job pathways we identified in our sample? We searched for such characteristics in the survey sample, and indeed, clues already clearly appeared in our ethnographic stories. We examined the background characteristics in the twenty-four-month survey sample that predicted the full-time–wage-growth, rapid cycler, stable employment, and low-wage–full-time groups. We used the low-wage–part-time cluster as the reference group to which other groups were compared, because that group showed the lowest levels of work effort across the twenty-four months.[10] We compared the groups on age, race-ethnicity, work, welfare, family structure, education, transportation, and income variables, all measured at the outset of the study before random assignment. We also included the New Hope experiment variable to see whether the program affected the probability of being in a particular work pathway. Unfortunately, no data on children's behavior or school performance were available in the New Hope baseline assessment; we therefore could not test the association of parents' concerns about children with later employment patterns, a compelling theme in the stories of Iris and other mothers in the ethnography.

We found that the New Hope Project significantly increased the probability of being in both the full-time–wage-growth and rapid cycler groups, relative to the low-wage–part-time group. That is, the offer of the New Hope package of benefits increased a mother's probability of being in one of these groups by the time of the twenty-four-month follow-up. These data add substantially to results reported to date on the effects of New Hope on single employment variables. Those data showed that New Hope increased employment and earnings for adults not already working at baseline (Bos et al. 1999). In separate analyses that examined the effects of New Hope on each of the variables making up the cluster analysis (number of jobs, average job length, average number of hours worked per week, average hourly wage, and wage change), no significant effects were found at twenty-four months except for an increase in the number of jobs.[11] Thus, the cluster approach adds information beyond a single-characteristic approach about whether New Hope affected particular combinations of job variables. In this case, we found that *New Hope increased the probability of experiencing the combination of full-time work with wage growth, as well as the pattern of very rapid job cycling coupled with minimal wage growth.*

We also would expect that indicators of human capital would predict work trajectories. Not surprisingly, prior education and work effort were indeed significant predictors of group membership. Those in the low-wage–part-time group were less likely to have worked full-time previously than those in any of the other work pathway groups, and they were less likely to have a high school diploma or GED than those in the rapid cycler, full-time–wage-growth, and stable employment groups. The low-wage–part-time group was also more likely to be receiving government assistance than the stable employment group.

Mother's age was also predictive of group membership. Both the rapid cycler and full-time–wage-growth groups were more likely to be young (under twenty-five years old) relative to the low-wage–part-time group.

Finally, having access to a car distinguished the work pathway groups. Those mothers who reported having access to a car at baseline were more likely to be in the full-time–wage-growth and stable employment groups, relative to the low-wage–part-time group.

Our data suggest that job stability and wage growth are associated with access to a car or other reliable transportation. Wage growth over time seems fairly strongly linked to prior human capital (education and prior work experience). And the ethnographic data suggest that other factors impinging on the family lives of the working poor make a difference to their work pathways: the attitudes and influence of partners, interactions with government and institutions such as the welfare system, mental and physical health, and the existence of support networks that help reduce the risk of leaving a job for another one when a parent has few savings. We explore these additional factors in depth in later chapters of the book.

CONCLUSION

We found a great degree of heterogeneity in our working-poor sample. More importantly, we found that the heterogeneity was related to a variety of differences in experiences of work, as reported by the mothers in the New Hope Ethnographic Study.

For example, substantial numbers of NHES mothers, like Allison, experienced "good" job pathways characterized by wage growth and stable employment. These mothers were generally working full-time and started out the New Hope study with higher wages. Mothers in this group were the most likely to experience job mobility (job-to-job transitions) and to report taking jobs because of their positive characteristics. They were also the least likely to report being fired or suspended. Thus, voluntary job transitions were more common in this group. They were also the most likely to have access to a car at baseline, indicating the importance of transportation to the ability to hold down the better and higher-paying jobs that were outside the "Inner Core" of Milwaukee.

In contrast, other groups in our sample appeared more disadvantaged. One group—the low-wage–part-time cluster—reported lower levels of work than any of the others, coupled with low wages and little growth in wages. This group had lower levels of human capital—that is, less education and prior work experience—than the other groups. (They even had lower levels of human capital than the very small group in the sample who did not work at all over the two-year follow-up.) Both ethnographic and survey data from this sample confirmed that this pattern of largely part-time work at very low wages continued over the next three years of the follow-up. Moreover, the ethnographic data showed that this group experienced more mental health problems and higher levels of domestic violence than other groups.

Another group—the low-wage–full-time cluster—appeared to be stuck in low wages without much wage growth or promotions but differed from the low-wage–part-time group in their work hours, which were much higher. Evelia was characteristic of this group—"desperate" to keep working to feed her four children, she was stuck in a series of temp and entry-level jobs that resulted in very little wage growth over the three years of the ethnography.

One of the groups was characterized by very high levels of job instability. The rapid cyclers had an average of five jobs over the first two years of the follow-up and were some of the youngest members of the New Hope sample. Their high job instability was partly due to it being early in their work careers. They engaged in work at high levels, and experimental-group rapid cyclers were the most likely to take up New Hope's community service jobs (CSJs, or the jobs in nonprofit organizations provided to those participants who could not find work on their own). New Hope significantly increased the probability of being in this group, relative to the low-wage–part-time group. They continued to experience high job instability over the following three years, though they also experienced the highest absolute wage growth of the groups in our sample. The ethnographic data showed that the rapid cyclers were most likely to report being fired or suspended, relative to the other groups. They were also the least likely to report taking a new job because of a positive characteristic of it. Their very high levels of work effort, combined with their high job instability and higher percentage of problematic job transitions, suggest the possibility of negative effects on their own well-being and on their children's development.

Did New Hope change the probability of experiencing any of these work pathways? We found that New Hope increased the probability of being in both the full-time–wage-growth group and the rapid cycler group, relative to the group with the lowest levels of work effort (the low-wage–part-time group). These findings show cause for both encouragement and concern when it comes to the potential effects of these work pathways on parents' well-being and children's development. The full-time–wage-growth group matched the most important goal expressed by the mothers: wage growth in their jobs. The rapid cycler group experienced very high numbers of jobs across the two-year follow-up (an average of nearly five). In the next chapter, we see that being engaged in these two work patterns, in particular, did appear to have consequences for children's school performance and social behavior.

In sum, the variation in the New Hope sample in their work trajectories, as well as in their day-to-day experiences of job transitions, suggests a variety of possibilities regarding the effects of their work trajectories on both themselves and their children. We turn to these issues in the next chapter. In later chapters, we fill in remaining questions about how these work pathways relate to the complex web of supports and personal motivations in mothers' lives: marriage and relationship decisions, child care choices, agency- and policy-based services, and work- and family-related goals.

Chapter Three | Do Pathways Through Low-Wage Work Matter for Children's Development?

Hirokazu Yoshikawa, Edward D. Lowe,
Johannes M. Bos, Thomas S. Weisner,
Valentina Nikulina, and JoAnn Hsueh

WHAT DIFFERENCE DO the clearly varied pathways through work make for the children of the working poor? Concerns about how their work might be affecting their children were central to many of the parents in New Hope. In this chapter, we relate how mothers' work lives were often preoccupied with concerns or hopes about their children's prospects. Their worries (we heard mostly worries) ranged from concerns about their children's whereabouts or behavior after school and the quality of the attention they could provide to their children after long, often evening work hours, to worries that their work did not provide enough income to keep their children from being hungry.

The survey data, in turn, reveal that work pathways do appear to have consequences for children's development. We find that two of the work pathways we uncovered in the prior chapter—the rapid cycler and the full-time–wage-growth patterns—did show associations with these outcomes. Specifically, teachers of children in the rapid cycler group rated them as engaging in higher levels of aggressive and acting-out behaviors than were reflected in teachers' assessments of children in any of the other groups. In contrast, positive outcomes appeared to accrue to the children of mothers in the full-time–wage-growth group. Their teachers rated them as being more engaged in school and as acting out less than children in other groups.

In addition, mothers in the full-time–wage-growth group reported higher academic expectations, goal achievement, and monitoring of children than mothers in the other work pathway groups. These associations were found controlling for earlier levels of each of the child outcomes. Although the results could still be subject to some degree of selection bias, teachers in the study were not aware of the work patterns of their students' parents, so we can state with some confidence that work trajectories matter for children's outcomes.

HOW WORK AFFECTS CHILDREN: PERSPECTIVES OF THE NEW HOPE MOTHERS

What do the New Hope mothers say about how work affects their children? To explore this question, we assembled all of the field notes from the New Hope Ethnographic Study on the themes of work and children. We then examined these notes for themes that reflected how these mothers thought their work experiences affected their children.

We identified four major ways in which parents felt that their employment had an impact on their children's lives: child care, the provision of material resources, the monitoring of children and the quality of time spent with them, and parental stress. The field notes on child care were so extensive and varied that we decided to discuss that theme in a separate chapter (chapter 10). Here we describe the mothers' responses to the other three themes.

The Provision of Material Resources

The immediacy of the need to work so as to be able to provide for children is starker among the poor than the nonpoor. For mothers in the New Hope sample, relatively low earnings, particularly at times when money was tight or expenses were particularly high, raised the specter of not being able to feed their children. Marina, an African-American mother of three who worked for much of the ethnography at a child care center, experienced a housing and financial emergency at one point when her landlord moved and she had to move out of her apartment. Eventually she found an apartment, but she had to get a loan from the W-2 program and borrow money from her sister to cover the security deposit and the first month's rent. Between this expense and the moving expenses, and despite an understanding boss, she was left with almost no money:

> She said a low point came a few weeks ago, before she had moved out of her house but after everyone else who had lived there was already gone. She had

no money, and the only food she had left was a few sandwiches. She didn't even have enough money to go to work. She didn't really feel like that was an adequate meal for her children, and she started to cry because she felt like she wasn't a good mother. "I felt like I got to the point where I let them down."

For many of the New Hope mothers, the ability to meet their children's needs was a prime indicator of economic well-being (as well as psychological well-being; the different kinds of psychological well-being associated with different household expenditures are discussed in detail in chapter 8). As one field-worker put it in speaking about Alicia, a Nicaraguan immigrant mother with one daughter, "Regardless of the economic problems she has had since Rolando [her husband] doesn't work, they have not stopped spending on Beatriz [their daughter]. Alicia says that her daughter is primary and that she works a lot precisely so that her daughter doesn't lack anything."

Monitoring Children and the Quality of the Time Spent with Children

For the vast majority of working-poor mothers in our sample, time at work meant time away from their children.[1] They coped with this constraint by finding creative ways to squeeze in monitoring in the context of low-wage work schedules and settings and by altering the quality of the time they did spend with their children. By their own reports, these efforts were sometimes successful, sometimes not. Overall, the mothers who cited monitoring as a concern hated to leave their children unsupervised. Although all parents share this concern to some extent, for lower-income parents the trade-off between the limited, yet vital, income provided by a low-wage job and the risks associated with leaving their children unsupervised is often a difficult one. Marisa was a Latina mother of five, living on the South Side. She worked as a teacher's assistant during the course of the ethnography. She was explicit in telling the field-worker how far she was willing to go in terms of low wages, given that she would be leaving her daughters unsupervised: "Marisa explained to me that she wouldn't get an extra part-time job for less than $7.00 an hour. She told me that she doesn't like to leave her daughters alone, to spend gas, and to use her time just to go to work for $5.00 an hour."

New Hope parents monitored their children most often by calling home from work. Ana's field-worker reported that she called a few times a day to make sure that everybody was home. "She says that even though she is not at home, her kids know that she calls a few times a day to know what they are doing, and in general they obey her." Marisa provided another example: she hated leaving her children while she was at work in the afternoon, she reported, and "always calls at her break to see if everything is okay, if they have done their homework." She also enlisted her daughters to help her with cooking and housework.

When parents had flexibility at work to take time off, they often used it to monitor their children's school progress. For example, Dulce, a thirty-seven-year-old Latina, would maintain close contact with her children Maria, Tomas, and Alma by asking for time off during the week to talk to all of their teachers. She would make up the time the following Saturday.

Mothers in our sample most often reported wanting to be at home after school and at dinnertime, so as to monitor homework and make dinner. Being at home when children come home was a particularly important event to them. Maria made sure to work on an early shift "so that she can be home when they get home. This enables her to keep an eye on them." Faye similarly avoided the second shift at work because she wanted to be with her children for dinner and to help with homework. Many parents in the New Hope sample, however, were not able to work hours that permitted them to be home in the after-school and evening hours (see chapter 5).

New Hope mothers often made heroic efforts to respond to their children's pleas to spend more time with them. They reported trying to communicate that they could not spend more time with them because of their work demands. This example comes from field notes for Evelia, whom we introduced in chapter 2. A thirty-five-year-old mother of three who worked in a temp job at the post office for the first half of the ethnography, Evelia left that job and then had a variety of short-term jobs for the rest of the period:

> I asked Evelia if she knew what perception her kids have of their mom working so much and the children having to be home alone. She says that her children sometimes ask her if she feels tired because she has been working hard, but Evelia believes that her kids, like all children, if given a choice, would prefer that their mom didn't work, and stay with them all day long. Evelia replies that the children don't understand or they can't value the fact that their parents work so much. Evelia explains that a good example of this is when they ask for money and she has to say that there isn't any. Like yesterday, one of her kids asked her for $2.00, and she told him that she didn't have any money, and her son couldn't understand that she didn't have the $2.00. The oldest (thirteen years old), for example, told her to go to her job and ask for money. . . . Evelia is aware that her thirteen-year-old is getting at that age when he'll start understanding that there is not enough money at home. Even

more now that he'll start high school and will come across other kids that are in a better economic situation then he is.

The trade-off between time spent with children and time spent supporting them through work can be particularly painful for those in low-wage jobs, as this vignette from Evelia illustrates. Her children want her to spend more time with them, but they also want her to make more money; the only way she could do that—without a significant raise—would be to work more and spend even less time with them. One parent, Katie, a white mother of two children ages six and eight, worked in maintenance at a local college. She reported that she took the day off from work and volunteered in her son's classroom on his birthday because her son always told her, "You never spend any time with me."

When parents reported being able to make special efforts to spend "extra" time with their children, it was usually in the context of flexibility at work. Anna Marie was a Latina mother of two teenagers who worked in office manager and receptionist jobs during the study. Her field-worker noted:

> She said that she never was able to talk with her parents when she was young, like she does with her sons. Anna Marie said that she is trying to do the opposite thing. She said that a lot of people tell her that the three of them do a lot of good family bonding. She will leave work to be with them. She will take her to lunch, come in late, or leave early in order not to miss her sons' games, practices, school conferences, or anything pertaining to their school or health.

In contrast, when parents' work environments were less flexible, they were unable to be this involved with their children at school. Alicia would go on field trips with her children when she had a day off, but because she rarely had days off, she was not able to do this very often.

Parental Stress

Stress from family and from work, the reciprocal relations between these two forms of stress, and the impacts on parenting quality and child development are central topics in the research literature on maternal employment (Crouter and Bumpus 2001). However, most of the studies in this area are based on middle-class samples. Our ethnographic data highlight some sources of work-related stress that are not often discussed in the research studies, because they are more prevalent among low-wage workers. For example, the nonstandard hours that the majority of our sample worked were associated with particular forms of stress. Third-shift workers came home from work exhausted and with the additional burden of waking their children up and ensuring that they went to school:

> Belinda reported coming home from work at 9:30 and finding her son James still sleeping in bed. He was subsequently informed that he had to go to summer school to pass the tenth grade. On the other hand, when the field-worker interviewed James, he reported that "he thinks that his mother works too hard. He said that they used to have fun and do stuff together, but now all his mother does is work and they never do anything for fun. Now she is either at work or in the house asleep."

Samantha, an African-American mother of four children ages two to twelve, attributed her inability to manage her children, as well as her health problems, to the stress from her low-paying job at a video store. She felt that customers in this store took out their "bad mood" on the employees and that some of them treated her like a "black stupid woman"; she came home exhausted from this work. Her work stress, she believed, made it difficult to manage her children: "I'm stressed, and you know stress will kill you. That's why I tell my kids to stop frustrating me. . . . Little things like this [she points to crushed graham crackers on the floor], I try to keep off the floor now. They won't do it, so I just go around trying to pick up myself, and that stresses me out even more."

Fatigue from working nonstandard hours or extra jobs was cited often by mothers in the New Hope study. Alicia reported working more than full-time for much of the period of the ethnography, in the public school system and the foster care system and delivering newspapers. She reported that after coming home from working the third shift, she did not have the energy to run and check up on her daughter Beatriz. She was tired all the time and did not have the energy to do things with Beatriz if she wanted her to, saying, "My whole body is tired from work." When Leora was too tired, she would often just let her daughter Kim watch TV instead of playing with her.

Stress also flowed from the home to the workplace on occasion. Mothers' monitoring of their latchkey children from work often caused tremendous stress that affected their work lives, as illustrated in this excerpt from the field notes for Lynette, an African-American mother of two:

> When Pooh is home from school, he calls Lynette to tell her he is home and if he has a problem. When Pooh gets to clowning around, Lynette will tell him, "If you don't stop this shit, I'm going to fuck you up when I get home. . . ."

"I get crazy on my phone," Lynette says. According to the field-workers, she tells her son, " 'Go to your room, do your homework. I don't want to see you until I get home. I don't want to hear it from you.' Lynette said that she will walk around work frustrated, and then catch attitude with everybody."

Some mothers reported that their children's behavior problems had a direct impact on their work. In some cases, the disruptions even caused them to lose their jobs. Trisha was a mother who had great trouble during the ethnography holding on to a job because of the extreme behavior problems of her three teenage daughters. She lost one job because they called her two or three times a day, every day.

The qualitative findings, taken together, suggest links to both economic and psychological theories of how parental work affects children's development. From the economic perspective, the mothers were keenly aware of the opportunity costs associated with work. They tried to make up for the fact that they had to spend crucial after-school and early-evening hours away from their children by increasing the quality of the time they did spend with their children—for example, by volunteering in the classroom on their child's birthday. From a psychological perspective, stress permeated these mothers' feelings about work and family. Their stress often stemmed from factors, however, that have not been included in researchers' investigations of topics like the "spillover" of stress from work to family, or vice versa. What was stressful for some of these mothers was the daily need to put food on the table while coping with the vagaries of job instability and the low-wage labor market. The dynamic nature of stress, as mothers went from work to nonwork and back, was highlighted in these field notes.

What aspects of the effects of work on children are missing from these mothers' narratives? Surprisingly, some themes that are prevalent in the research literature on maternal employment and children's outcomes were rarely mentioned by the New Hope mothers. The theme of being a strong role model for children by working, for example, was brought up by only two mothers. Perhaps work was so much the norm and so much a necessity among this working-poor sample that the fact of working, by itself, was not associated with being a better parental role model. Moreover, the jobs that many of the women in the sample were able to get were not especially conducive to being a strong role model for working; temp work, rapid cycling, bouts of unemployment, and other conditions also made their low-wage work circumstances difficult.

THE IMPACT OF WORK PATHWAYS ON CHILDREN: EVIDENCE FROM THE NEW HOPE SURVEY SAMPLE

The New Hope study collected data on children right after the two-year period we used to estimate the clusters we described in chapter 2 (two years after random assignment), and then again three years later (five years after random assignment). At each of these points, both parents and teachers were surveyed. For children too young to be in school, only parents were surveyed. Parents and teachers were asked about both children's school performance and their behaviors (such as acting-out, or *externalizing*, behaviors and withdrawn, anxious, and depressed, or *internalizing*, behaviors).[2] We examined how children of parents from our five groups—representing the low-wage–part-time group, the full-time–wage-growth group, the rapid cycler group, the stable employment group, and the low-wage–full-time group—differed in their school performance and the two kinds of social behavior. In addition, we included the group of parents who reported not working at all during the two years (the no-work group).[3]

We also examined the associations of each of these work pathways with a set of parent and family factors that we felt might explain the effects of work on children's development. We chose three domains that the mothers themselves, as we have seen, spoke about: time pressure, parent well-being (parenting stress and depression), and monitoring of children. We also included both parent-reported and observed measures of parenting warmth, which can be an intervening factor between parenting stress and children's behavior.[4]

First, we compared the full-time–wage-growth group to each of the other groups (see table 3.1). We chose this group because its members most fully realized the New Hope parents' stated work goal of achieving wage growth; in fact, at sixty months, this group still had the highest wages of any of our work pathway groups. We saw in the prior chapter that this group was the most likely to make successful job transitions based on perceived positive characteristics of jobs, the least likely to report being fired from a job, and also the least likely to leave a job because of dissatisfaction with it. Among the work pathway groups, they were most likely to achieve job mobility (changes in jobs accompanied by wage growth), as indicated by the moderate number of jobs they held across the twenty-four months (an average of three) combined with the high levels of wage growth. All of these characteristics led us to hypothesize positive outcomes for children in this group and to expect those effects to occur through mediating factors such as lower parenting stress, time pressure, and depression, as well as through higher monitoring and parental warmth.

In our analyses linking employment cluster group membership to parents' and children's outcomes at two years, we adjusted for a wide variety of parent and family characteristics, such as education, prior work and income, family structure, maternal mental health, and perceived job quality, in order to avoid confounding the potential influence of work pathways with other kinds of differences among our families (which, as we have seen, do influence work patterns).[5] When we examined five-year

Table 3.1   OLS Regression Results Predicting Child and Parent Outcomes from Membership in the Full-Time–Wage-Growth Group

Outcomes	Contrast Group and Direction of Association	Unstandardized Coefficient (Standard Error) and p Level	Standardized Coefficient
Two-year child outcomes			
Teacher			
School engagement	No-work group higher	.59(.26)*	.12
School performance	No-work group higher	.53(.25)*	.11
Acting-out behaviors			
Withdrawn behaviors	No-work group lower	–.42(.18)*	–.13
Parent			
School performance			
Acting-out behaviors	Low-wage–part-time group higher	.30(.14)*	.14
Withdrawn behaviors			
Five-year child outcomes (controlling for parallel two-year outcome)			
Teacher			
School performance			
Acting-out behaviors			
Withdrawn behaviors			
Parent			
School performance	Rapid cyclers lower	–.37(.17)*	–.12
Acting-out behaviors			
Withdrawn behaviors	Stable employment group higher	.24(.10)*	.18

Two-year parent-reported
mediators

Parenting stress	Low-wage–part-time group higher;	.48(.21)*	.15
	rapid cyclers higher;	.45(.18)*	.16
	low-wage–full-time group higher	.36(.15)*	.16
Time pressure	Low-wage–full-time group lower	−.27(.15)†	−.14
Depression	Low-wage–part-time group higher;	5.12(2.46)*	.14
	rapid cyclers higher	4.82(2.34)*	.16
Self-reported warmth	Low-wage–full-time group lower	−.40(.20)*	−.13
Observed warmth			
Monitoring			

Source: Authors' compilation.

Notes: All analyses control for background characteristics gathered before random assignment, including those representing child's sex, child's age, parent's age, whether the parent has access to a car, whether the parent received AFDC as a child, parent's income, whether the parent graduated from high school or received a GED, whether the parent currently received AFDC, whether the parent worked full-time in the prior quarter, race-ethnicity, single-adult household, whether three or more children resided in the household, whether a child younger than two lived in the household, and the New Hope experimental variable. In addition, analyses control for maternal depression and perceived job quality, measured at twenty-four months. (These constructs were unavailable at baseline.)

*p < .05
†p < .10

outcomes, we adjusted for two-year child outcomes in order to reduce potential selection bias.[6]

What we found surprised us. Teachers of children in the full-time–wage-growth group reported *lower*, not higher, levels of school performance, when compared to the ratings of teachers of children in the no-work group. They also reported *higher* levels of internalizing behaviors than did teachers of children in the no-work group (for these associations, see teacher-reported two-year child outcomes in table 3.1). These teacher-reported associations occurred at the two-year follow-up point.

In contrast to the teacher-reported differences, mothers in the full-time–wage-growth group did not report lower levels of school performance or higher levels of behavior problems. In fact, these mothers reported lower levels of acting-out behaviors in their children than their counterparts in other groups. (This was statistically significant for the comparison to the low-wage–part-time group; see parent responses for two-year child outcomes in table 3.1.) When we examined the five-year outcomes, full-time–wage-growth parents again reported better school adjustment and lower levels of behavior problems than parents in other groups. (Specifically, they reported better school performance than did rapid cyclers, as well as lower levels of withdrawn behaviors than the stable employment group; see parent-reported five-year child outcomes in table 3.1.)

Why might teachers, but not mothers, have perceived children of parents who worked full-time and achieved wage growth as doing worse than their peers whose parents worked substantially less? The most obvious answer is that in our study teachers were "blind" to mothers' work characteristics in ways that mothers themselves were not. Perhaps there is a cost of full-time work, in terms of teachers' perceptions of children's development, that parents do not perceive because they are motivated to work (and particularly to work full-time). Teachers might have noticed behaviors that children of full-time workers displayed in school but that parents did not or could not see. Specifically, they might have picked up on the cumulative effect on children of parents' very high levels of work effort. The full-time–wage-growth group worked an average of thirty-two months total across the twenty-four months of follow-up (multiplying the average job length by the number of jobs), a higher total than for any of the other groups. These parents were therefore more likely to be working multiple jobs at once than the other groups. The combination of high number of hours, nonstandard hours, and rotating schedules is associated with lower child school performance and more acting-out behaviors (see chapter 5).

Mothers who work full-time and experience wage growth may not perceive higher levels of problematic outcomes in their children because they are achieving their work effort and wage-growth goals, ones that are shared by the majority of New Hope parents. Leora, a member of the full-time–wage-growth group, was a white mother who shared custody of her four sons with their father. She felt that work was important to her because it made her feel better and gave her the opportunity to go out every day. Her high level of attachment to work was accompanied by pride that she was providing for herself and her family. The field-worker reported:

> Work is more than just being able to get out of the house. It meant she could buy what they needed. It gave her "confidence, satisfaction, a sense of well-being and accomplishment," and it was a challenge she looked forward to. The kind of job she did in payroll, being responsible for everyone's check, gave her a sense of control in the office environment. She smiled and said, "I am not egotistical, but it makes me feel that I am in charge of everybody's check," and quickly [added] that a year and a half ago, "I was not even in charge of my own life." When she sets up four things to do at work during the day, she makes sure that she completes them, and it is a challenge to be able to finish it. She would call her boyfriend to pick up her daughter, but it is important to her that she completes the work.

Leora summed up the priorities in her life as "relationships, career, and children."

Mothers in the full-time–wage-growth group not only felt good about their children, relative to those with other work pathways, but felt better about themselves. They reported lower levels of parenting stress and depression and higher levels of parenting warmth than did mothers in the low-wage–part-time group, the low-wage–full-time group, and the rapid cycler group (see two-year parent-reported mediators in table 3.1). These three contrast groups share lower levels of wages and wage growth than the full-time–wage-growth group. Such career trajectories may lead mothers to experience higher levels of stress.

Which factor characteristic of the full-time–wage-growth group—relatively high hours of work, a moderate number of jobs, positive changes in wages—might be responsible for the differences ascribed to children in the group? Other analyses we ran have suggested that no one of these three factors alone turned out to be significantly associated with children's school performance or behavior problems (Yoshikawa et al. 2000). The *combination* of these factors appears to be key.

We were also interested in whether the rapid cycler group's very high levels of job instability, combined with relatively low wage growth (under $1.00 of growth over two years), might have influenced children's school performance or social behaviors. Recall from the previous chapter that ethnographic study members of this group were the most likely to report being fired and leaving a job because of a problematic aspect of the job. They were also the least likely to report taking a new job because of a positive characteristic of the job. We hypothesized that the children of rapid cyclers, because of the degree of flux in their parents' work lives, would exhibit more acting-out behaviors and lower school performance, and that the parents themselves would report higher levels of stress.

Here a clear pattern emerged in the teacher reports at five years. For these analyses, we again controlled for the parallel child outcomes at two years. At five years, teachers of children in the rapid cycler group reported the lowest levels of school performance, relative to all other groups. The differences were significant in the comparisons to the no-work group and at the trend level of significance in the comparison to the stable employment group (see teacher-reported five-year child outcomes in table 3.2). Teachers of the rapid cycler children also reported higher levels of acting-out behaviors in these children, relative to all the other groups. These differences were significant in the comparisons to the low-wage–full-time group, and at the trend level of significance in the comparison to the stable employment group. Finally, teachers of the rapid cycler children reported higher levels of withdrawn and depressed behaviors than did teachers of children in all the other groups. This difference was significant for the comparison to the no-work group.

What did parents in the rapid cycler group themselves perceive? Here the pattern in parents' reports was similar to that found among the teachers' reports. Rapid cycler parents reported lower levels of school performance than parents of any of the other groups. These differences reached statistical significance in the comparisons to the full-time–wage-growth and stable employment groups. And rapid cycler parents also reported higher levels of withdrawn behaviors in their children, relative to children in the stable employment group.

Other recent studies, using national datasets, have shown negative associations between job instability and academic outcomes for children from families in poverty (Kalil and Ziol-Guest 2005; Yoshikawa 1999; Yoshikawa and Seidman 2001). The rapid cyclers in the New Hope sample experienced particularly high job instability (an average of five jobs across two years), in combination with relatively low levels of wage growth, an indicator of stagnant earned income. These job characteristics may have resulted in these mothers' reports of lower well-being, which in turn may have led to their children doing less well on both academic and social fronts. Rapid cycler parents did report particularly high levels of stress—including consistently higher levels of parenting stress, time pressure, and depression— than parents in other groups (see two-year parent-reported routines, parent stress, and well-being, in table 3.2). They also were observed by

Table 3.2 OLS Regression Results Predicting Child and Parent Outcomes from Membership in the Rapid Cycler Group

Outcomes	Contrast Group and Direction of Association	Unstandardized Coefficient (Standard Error) and p Level	Standardized Coefficient
Two-year child outcomes			
Teacher			
School engagement	No-work group higher	.55(.27)*	.11
School performance	Low-wage–full-time group lower	−.35(.18)†	−.17
Acting-out behaviors			
Withdrawn behaviors	No-work group lower; stable employment group higher	−.33(.15)* .26(.10)**	−.10 .21
Parent			
School performance			
Acting-out behaviors	Low-wage–part-time group higher	.21(.13)†	.10
Withdrawn behaviors	Low-wage–part-time group higher	.27(.13)*	.12
Five-year child outcomes (controlling for parallel two-year outcome)			
Teacher			
School performance	No-work group higher; stable employment group higher	1.02(.38)** .41(.24)†	.19 .19
Acting-out behaviors	Low-wage–full-time group lower; stable employment group lower	−.38(.18)* −.37(.19)†	−.18 −.19
Withdrawn behaviors	No-work group lower	−.48(.24)*	−.14

(continued)

Table 3.2 OLS Regression Results Predicting Child and Parent Outcomes from Membership in the Rapid Cycler Group (Continued)

Outcomes	Contrast Group and Direction of Association	Unstandardized Coefficient (Standard Error) and p Level	Standardized Coefficient
Parent			
School performance	Full-time–wage-growth group higher; stable employment group higher	.37(.17)*	.11
		.46(.16)**	.19
Acting-out behaviors			
Withdrawn behaviors	Stable employment group higher	.21(.09)*	.16
Two-year parent-reported mediators			
Parenting stress	Full-time–wage-growth group lower; stable employment group lower	−.45(.18)*	−.13
		−.33(.17)†	−.14
Time pressure	No-work group lower; low-wage–full-time group lower	−.47(.28)†	−.11
		−.34(.12)**	−.18
Depression	Full-time–wage-growth group lower; stable employment group lower	−4.82(2.34)*	−.13
		−5.22(1.93)**	−.20
Self-reported warmth			
Observed warmth			
Monitoring	No-work group lower	−.33(.19)†	−.10

Source: Authors' compilation.
*p < .05
**p < .01
†p < .10

interviewers to show lower levels of warmth to their children than parents in the no-work group. The high levels of stress reported by the rapid cyclers may be an indicator of the general family stress and instability experienced by these children. Katrina, for example, a Filipina–African-American mother of four, in the rapid cycler group, experienced high levels of stress in her job as a shipping clerk at a bank. She told the field-worker, "I am not getting paid enough, not for what I do." Katrina resented the fact that the man who worked next to her, who was only a temp, made $12.50 an hour while she made $8.50 an hour, and she felt that she did more than he did in his job. She described her job as "basement work" and thought that people looked down on her and assumed that she was stupid. Katrina also related that working full-time left her exhausted and unable to control her children. One of her sons was taking Ritalin for his behavior problems.

The story of Trisha, a white mother of one son and three daughters, although an extreme example, shows how instability at work, instability in other aspects of family life, and difficulties in children's development combine to create chaos at home. Trisha was also a member of the rapid cycler group. She cycled in and out of jobs throughout much of the ethnographic period, owing to a particularly difficult combination of domestic violence, drug use (self and partner), and child delinquency and drug use. Her children repeatedly sabotaged her efforts to establish a work routine. One particularly harrowing sequence was described by the field-worker:

> The second day on the job her kids unplugged her alarm so they wouldn't have to go to school, but as a result she didn't get up in time. The third day she was supposed to go in for work, her son and some of his friends got into a fight with the gang members across the street. The police were called, and by the time they left, it was four in the morning. Trisha had to leave at five, so she thought she would just lay down and take a quick nap. But she fell asleep and missed going into work, although she brought in her police report and said that the employer was very understanding. The next day she was scheduled to work Nick unplugged her alarm again. Trisha said she felt like an "asshole" for not getting into work at all, and she called her employer, crying, to tell her she couldn't work. "I understand that this is a place of employment. You cannot keep waiting for me to come in. You gotta find someone who can make it on time and doesn't have such fucking assholes for kids."

On another occasion she began a job at a travel agency that lasted all of one day:

> She was going to get a ride with her neighbor each way. However, on her first day of work, she got a call from her son's school, saying that she had to get

down there right away. Unfortunately, there are no buses that go out that far. It would have cost her $9.00 to take a cab, but she decides to hitchhike instead. Her son had found a wallet at school and had been accused of stealing the money inside it. Her son swears he didn't steal it, and Trisha says that there is no way he could've, because not only did they search his locker, they also did a strip search on him (twice) and didn't find anything. But his stepfather had called Trisha at the job and told her that if she didn't come down right away, he would call the cops and have them come to her new job. She didn't really want that, seeing as how it was first day and everything. But because she had to leave that day, and because she was going to have to go to court in the future, they told her, "Don't bother coming in. We need someone every day."

Trisha's experiences highlight how difficult it is to disentangle the effects of multiple kinds of instability—in relationships, in jobs, and in children's behavior—on one another. The escalating reciprocal effects of these factors in Trisha's work efforts resulted in an extraordinary level of chaos in her life across the entire ethnographic period. The numbers in table 3.2 may reflect families under siege from stress in multiple domains.

We also examined whether the associations of rapid cycler group membership with less optimal child outcomes could be explained by the associations of this characteristic with the parent stress and well-being measures. We found little evidence of this. In statistical terms, once the parent stress and well-being measures were added to regressions in which rapid cycler group membership predicted child outcomes, the associations of being a rapid cycler with those outcomes did not change very much. This may have been because of relatively low levels of statistical power to detect mediation in our sample, relative to direct associations (MacKinnon et al. 2002).

New Hope mothers repeatedly stated that a steady job with wage growth and opportunities for advancement was what they wanted in their employment (chapters 7 and 9). None of the work pathways in the cluster analysis we conducted incorporated this particular combination of job qualities. In a last set of analyses, we examined the influence of the *combination* of wage growth and job stability on children's development (the same parent- and teacher-reported outcomes as before).[7]

The results we found were striking. The combination of wage growth and job stability was associated with higher levels of teacher-rated school engagement, and lower levels of acting-out behaviors, at the two-year follow-up. The combination of high wage growth and high job stability was associated with the highest levels of school engagement, while the combination of low wage growth and high stability was associated with the lowest levels (figure 3.1). Low wage growth and high stability were also

Figure 3.1   Interaction of Wage Growth and Job Stability Predicting
               Teacher-Reported School Engagement

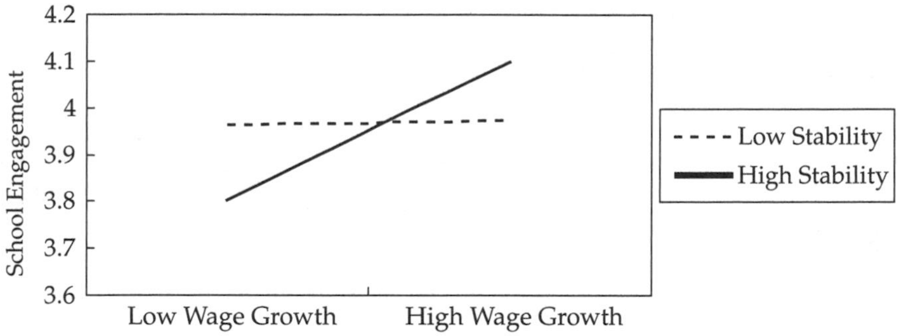

Source: Authors' compilation.

associated with the highest levels of acting-out behaviors (figure 3.2). So the benefits to children of the combination of these two "good" job dynamic characteristics that we had hypothesized were borne out. And being stuck in a low-wage job appears, not surprisingly, to leave children stuck with the lowest levels of adaptation both socially and at school.

What parent factors might explain these associations of wage growth and job stability with children's development? This positive job pattern was also related to higher levels of parent educational expectations and monitoring (figures 3.3 and 3.4). Those parents who experienced the combination of high wage growth and high job stability also reported the highest levels of educational expectations for their children and monitoring of their children. In addition, we found evidence for significant indirect associations linking the combination of wage growth and job stability to children's parent- and teacher-reported school performance and teacher-rated school engagement through parents' educational expectations. That is, the combination of wage growth and job stability predicted higher parental educational expectations, and those expectations in turn were related to higher school performance and engagement.[8]

CONCLUSION

We aimed in this chapter to examine how New Hope mothers thought their employment might affect their children and, from survey data, how their work pathways might have affected their children's school performance and

Figure 3.2   Interaction of Wage Growth and Job Stability Predicting
Teacher-Reported Externalizing Behavior Problems

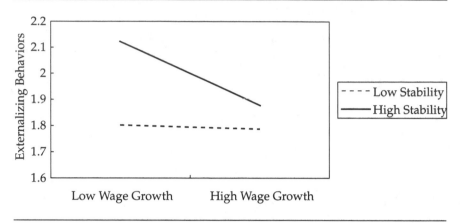

Source: Authors' compilation.

social behaviors. We found from our qualitative analysis that New Hope mothers reported several ways in which their work may have affected their children. They worried about their ability to monitor their children while they were away at work. Many of these mothers made heroic efforts to squeeze in quality time with their children, either at home or at school. They reported fatigue and stress from a huge array of day-to-day stresses, including nonstandard and shifting work hours, difficulty making ends meet, and children's behavior problems. Being able to work, finally, was a principal way in which these mothers felt able to provide for their children; this may be because informal supports in their lives were generally perceived as helpful but unreliable and costly in a variety of ways (see chapter 11).

In quantitative analyses, we observed that the different work pathways we uncovered in chapter 2 did appear to have consequences for children's development. We found reason for concern about possible negative effects of high job instability on children's school outcomes. That is, teachers of children whose parents were rapid cyclers reported that those children engaged in lower levels of school performance and higher levels of acting-out behaviors than did teachers of children in any of the other work pathway groups, even controlling for earlier levels these child outcomes. The parents of these children also reported higher stress and depression and were observed to be less warm toward their children than parents in other work pathway groups. So the children of the rapid cyclers appeared to be

Figure 3.3   Interaction of Wage Growth and Job Stability Predicting Parent-Reported Educational Expectations

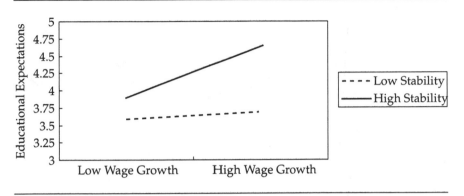

Source: Authors' compilation.

Figure 3.4   Interaction of Wage Growth and Job Stability Predicting Parent Monitoring

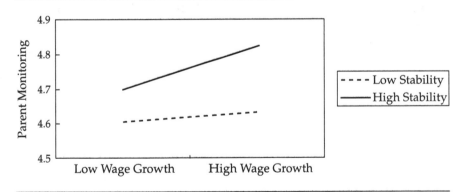

Source: Authors' compilation.

exposed to multiple family risks; this may have led in cumulative fashion to lower school performance and greater acting-out.

Who were the parents in the rapid cycler group? Rapid cyclers in this sample experienced a very high average of five jobs over two years. Our ethnographic data suggested that they were the most likely to experience problematic job transitions, such as being fired. Interestingly, in our long-term survey data, this group reported the highest levels of wage growth between the twenty-four- and sixty-month surveys (partly owing to the fact that they started out with some of the lowest wages among our groups). Although job instability is a feature of early work careers, parents in low-wage contexts endure higher levels of instability than those with higher wages (Johnson and Corcoran 2002; Royalty 1998; Topel and Ward 1992). Our results suggest that efforts should be made to provide jobs with opportunities for advancement at the lowest levels, replacing the temp jobs or the "basement work" that was described so vividly by Katrina, one of the rapid cyclers in our sample.

In contrast to this grim picture of revolving-door, low-wage jobs, the combination of wage growth and job stability appeared to be beneficial for children in multiple ways. Children whose parents experienced wage growth and job stability were rated by their teachers as exhibiting higher levels of school engagement and lower levels of acting-out. Their parents' expectations, goals, and monitoring were also higher than for those who did not experience this combination of job qualities. In chapter 9, we see that this combination is also associated with an unexpected consequence of New Hope: more marriages among single mothers. So the goal of many of the New Hope parents—a steady job, a sense of advancement made real through growing wages—appears, when realized, to have positive consequences in the schooling and social behavior of their children. In chapter 13, we discuss public policies that may facilitate this combination of wage growth and job stability among the working poor.

Chapter Four | Job Quality Among Low-Income Mothers: Experiences and Associations with Children's Development

Noemí Enchautegui-de-Jesús, Hirokazu Yoshikawa, and Vonnie C. McLoyd

NANCY, ONE OF the mothers in the New Hope Ethnographic Study, expressed that there is more to a job than its wages when she said she was looking for "work that makes me happy, not just the money." Thus far in this book, we have examined job characteristics mainly in terms of hours, wages, and stability or instability of work over time. In this chapter, we turn to job quality. Policymakers, researchers, and the public as a whole all have notions of what job quality is and why it matters, and scholarly and lay discussions on the topic of job quality suggest some common elements of a "good job."

Here we explore what job quality means to low-wage workers, the ways in which indicators of job quality vary among this population, and whether variation in job quality has consequences for family life and child development. Job quality is often measured in terms of structural characteristics of the job, such as hourly pay or the presence of employer-sponsored health insurance, paid sick and vacation days, and other benefits. But past research has also highlighted other characteristics that contribute to our understanding of what makes a good job (Clark 2005; Crouter and Bumpus 2001; Greenberger, O'Neil, and Nagel 1994; McLoyd et al. 1994; Menaghan and Parcel 1991;

Newman 1999; Raver 2003). These include job security, advancement opportunities, and the degree to which tasks involve enrichment and skill development. The New Hope survey included questions about all of these aspects of employment. But in the context of low-wage workplaces, such as those experienced by New Hope mothers, it is uncertain whether these indicators of job quality are meaningful or predictive of parent or child well-being.

In this chapter, we address this issue by examining the following questions. First, how do mothers in New Hope define job quality? What, in their view, distinguishes a good job from a bad job? Relying on the New Hope ethnographic data to answer these questions, we see that five dimensions of job quality were salient in the ethnographic data: the duties and complexity of the job, the adequacy of the pay, the formal job benefits, flexibility, and the quality of relationships at work. Second, we turn to the survey data to examine two questions. Is job quality related to the dynamic work pathways discussed in chapters 2 and 3? And does job quality influence parents' well-being and their children's school performance and social behavior? These survey analyses showed that occupational complexity, perceived job quality, and job stress were related to parental psychological well-being and child behavior outcomes.

HOW DID NEW HOPE MOTHERS DEFINE JOB QUALITY?

To examine the question of how New Hope mothers defined job quality, we used the NHES data because our interest was in capturing mothers' spontaneous comments about job quality rather than collecting their answers to predetermined survey questions. We wanted to understand jobs from these workers' point of view, using their own language and their own categories. The qualitative interviews and the many conversations with these mothers about their jobs provided this evidence. We compiled all of the field notes having to do with the quality of the jobs held during the period of the ethnography, and then coded them to examine what dimensions of quality emerged. Five dimensions—the duties and complexity of the job, the adequacy of the pay, the formal job benefits, flexibility, and the quality of relationships at work—were most often mentioned by the New Hope mothers. We also examine survey data, when available, on each of these five qualities.

Job Duties: Content and Complexity

Over the course of at least two years of ethnographic data collection, the forty women in the NHES held approximately 107 jobs, mostly low-paying positions in the service industry, such as child care (nine jobs), clerical-receptionist (eight), food preparation (six), factory assembly line (four), nurse's aide (five), and cleaning-maintenance (five). Less common occupations included waitress (three), post office worker (two), teacher or teacher's aide (two), cashier (two), case manager (one), transportation (one), and librarian (one). Several aspects of these occupations and positions are striking. First, as one would expect from Milwaukee's transition from a manufacturing to a service economy, most of the jobs were in service industries. Second, many of the jobs held by the NHES mothers in the service industries were in the lowest-paying occupations (child care, food preparation, entry-level clerical, nurse's aide). Finally, the few jobs they held in traditionally stable sectors of civic employment, such as the post office, were often temp jobs without the benefits and job security associated with these jobs in the past. Both of the mothers who worked in a post office, for example, were in a temp job.

The New Hope mothers had a great deal to say about their job duties. They wanted jobs that offered variety and challenge rather than routinization and tedium, development opportunities, and demands that could be fulfilled. The varying workloads in the 107 jobs they held created feelings that ranged from boredom to burnout and exhaustion. Although some of the women complained about excessive demands, including the physical demands of moving heavy boxes or dealing with patients or children, others complained about not having enough to do to keep them busy. Job duties were quite frequently reported to be tedious. Nine of the mothers (23 percent) reported feelings of boredom from having a routinized job. Tedium was most often expressed by mothers in clerical jobs, who were three times more likely to express boredom than mothers in other jobs; for some of them, having to sit all day in an office doing highly routinized work was difficult. Faye's absenteeism, for example, was related to the boredom she felt in her job. She said that she found office and technical jobs the most boring. Katrina was another mother who was bored with her job, which consisted of finding computer mistakes that rarely occurred. She described herself as "bored to death. My boss tells me that I am getting paid to be bored. And okay, that's fulfilling? Like I said, I would just as soon be making less money doing something that I like."

Tied to the continuum between tedium and exhaustion lies what economists and sociologists have described as the problem of low-wage jobs with regard to skill requirements and development. Such jobs require limited or low skill levels and offer poor opportunities to learn new skills. When we turned to the New Hope survey, however, we found that 287 of the mothers—about two-thirds of them—thought their job offered them opportunities to learn skills that would be valuable for getting a better job.

Unfortunately, these survey data do not include information on exactly what it was about these jobs that the mothers perceived as providing opportunities. For this information, we turn again to the ethnographic data. Eight women in the NHES (20 percent) mentioned that they could take classes or that their job offered them training opportunities, which they valued because extra training helped in getting raises, being promoted, learning more aspects of the current job, and applying existing skills to new tasks. Some of these mothers also reported that these educational and training experiences helped them get a better job elsewhere. The source of information for such opportunities was most often the supervisor. Carla, for example, was a Latina mother who worked in a factory for the bulk of the ethnographic study period. She began work at the factory counting parts for quality control, then switched to operating machines directly. (She was one of the only women in the factory working directly with the machines.) She was hired initially as a temp and then transitioned to a permanent position. Carla said that her job made her feel smarter and better about herself. She reported that she had learned a lot of vocabulary by working there. Inez's job provides a good example of the opportunity to exercise existing skills. She felt that she learned more than she ordinarily would have learned about many aspects of her customer service job because of her bilingual skills, which were valued because many of the customers were Spanish-speaking.

Both routinized work and skill development are aspects of what researchers call job complexity, by which they mean the level of skill and education, control, repetitiveness, creativity, and abstraction involved in or required by job duties. The construct has been operationalized using indicators of occupational characteristics found in the *Dictionary of Occupational Titles* (DOT) (Ganzach 1998; Parcel and Menaghan 1994b). According to studies using the DOT to describe the complexity of job duties, occupational complexity predicts a slew of positive outcomes in families, including more stimulating home environments and ultimately better child cognitive and socioemotional development (Menaghan and Parcel 1991; Parcel and Menaghan 1990; Parcel and Menaghan 1994a). However, relatively few of these studies have focused on low-wage workers. In the New Hope survey, participants described the duties in their current or most recent jobs. This information was coded using the DOT to classify the jobs. Although more recent classification systems exist, we chose this occupational classification system in order to compare our scores on occupational complexity to those in prior studies that also examined occupational complexity in relation to parent and child outcomes. In addition, the job descriptions for the vast majority of low-wage jobs in our sample have not changed drastically since the time of the last revision of the DOT system we use (see U.S. Department of Labor 1991).[1] The codes for each occupation include one-digit scores for the level of complexity of the occupation in functions related to data, people, and things. Based on these scores, the level of complexity of the jobs of mothers in the survey tended to be very low (on a scale from zero up to seven or eight). Each score is associated with a description of the level of complexity of the functions of the job.

Eighty-eight percent of the jobs (382) reported by the survey sample at the five-year follow-up occupied the bottom three levels of complexity with respect to people: 0 (taking instructions or helping), 1 (serving), or 2 (speaking or signaling). The other 12 percent involved persuading, such as telemarketing (level 3), supervising (4), instructing (5), negotiating (6), and mentoring (7). The average level of complexity was between levels 1 and 2, or between the level of serving and the level of speaking and signaling. The jobs that involved functions with people included waitress, telemarketer, nurse's aide, case manager, child care worker, crossing guard, food preparer in a cafeteria, dishwasher, sales representative, coat attendant, clerk, cashier, receptionist, and librarian. As we noted in chapter 2, very few New Hope mothers held even the lower-level supervisory or managerial positions associated with more complex job duties.

Categories of job complexity with respect to data ranged from 0 (comparing) to 6 (synthesizing). The average level of complexity with respect to data in the jobs reported in the survey was level 2 (computing, involving simple calculations). In the New Hope sample, the kinds of jobs that involved work with data included payroll, mortgage applications, and bank positions. Thirty-nine percent of the jobs described in the survey were coded at the even lower level (0) of simply comparing data. Nearly one-third (32 percent) of the jobs were coded as ones that required compiling (level 3). Only 11 percent were at the highest levels of coordinating and synthesizing data—levels 5 and 6, respectively—and only one person in the survey sample held a level 6 job.

Jobs that involve working primarily with objects include those in dry cleaning, post office positions, custodial (janitorial) work, assembly-line jobs, and positions in stocking and packaging, driving, and benchwork or machine work. These levels of complexity range from 0 (handling things) to 7 (setting up). Over half of the jobs (54 percent) involved handling, the lowest level of complexity, which is described in the DOT as involving "little or no latitude for judgment with regard to attainment of standards or in selecting appropriate tool, object, or materials."[2] Close to one-quarter (23 percent) of the jobs involved a higher level of complexity, up to level 5 (operating and controlling); most of these jobs (87 percent) were clerical. Another 14 percent of the jobs involved manipulating functions (level 3) and were mostly represented by occupations as attendants in hospitals and other health services.

Overall, these findings show a tendency for the jobs of mothers in the New Hope survey to be low in complexity, in contrast to the reports of the majority of the women that their jobs offered opportunities to learn new skills. The jobs described by the women in the ethnographic study paint a picture more in line with lack of complexity and limited opportunities for skill development. Lack of challenge and tedium reduce these women's sense of satisfaction and fulfillment and, in turn, their motivation and commitment to do the job. These effects have implications for absenteeism, turnover, and productivity that are important to consider as the labor market continues to absorb working-poor mothers without necessarily offering the intrinsic rewards that come from working.

The Adequacy of Pay

Perhaps there are no more salient objective aspects of a good job than the next two we consider: good pay and good benefits. Beyond objective measures of wages, scholars have found evidence of the importance of subjective measures of pay in studies of job quality and job outcomes, such as job satisfaction and job separation (Clark 2005). In chapter 8, we discuss the adequacy of mothers' pay for covering household expenses, but here we are concerned with the perception of whether the pay was good for the kind of job done. The New Hope survey asked whether the mother thought the pay was good at her job for the type of work she had to perform. Only about half of them (205, or 49 percent) thought the pay was good for the type of work involved in their job. Eighteen percent thought this was not true at all of their jobs.

The majority of women in the ethnographic sample thought that the *amount* of their pay was inadequate. Those who worked for less than $8.00 an hour were more likely to express dissatisfaction with their pay. Faye, for example, had not completed high school. Her job trajectory fit the rapid cycler pattern, and true to that pattern, she had nine jobs over the two and a half years of the ethnography. She also cycled on and off welfare during these years. She complained about the pay in her job in a school kitchen because it "paid minimum wage for the hardest duties working at the deep fryer five hours per day and lifting heavy boxes." When Faye moved to another kitchen job, this time in a nursing home, she still found that the pay was "not very good." At one point, she found work part-time in a catering business making $8.00 an hour, but this was short-lived. Twice during the ethnography she engaged in "workfare"—a W-2 community service job at no pay in exchange for a monthly cash grant ($649 in Faye's case); it is thus, in reality, a job that pays less than minimum wage.

Other NHES examples illustrate the mothers' perception that wages were inadequate for the jobs they were likely to get. Katie worked as a head housekeeper at a local college; though she was interested in getting another job, she realized that she couldn't "get this good pay" [$8.85 an hour] and benefits anywhere else doing cleaning. Nancy's experience bears out Katie's observation. Nancy, a housekeeper at a hotel making $5.00 an hour, said that "her cleaning job does not pay well." Eventually, she got another job as a window cleaner in which she was "very happy with the pay"— $17.00 an hour for twenty hours' work per week. However, only nine months later she found herself again in a job whose pay she perceived as inadequate: her new catering job paid $200 a week, or $6.75 an hour.

Despite the tendency to be unsatisfied with their pay, some mothers had positive things to say about it relative to their job. For example, Tiffany commented that she knew she had to take a particular job when she saw that it paid $9.50 an hour, the kind of pay for which she had been waiting. Maria could not believe that she was paid for doing very little work looking after the children of the parents who came to the agency where she worked.

Besides the amount, the *frequency* with which mothers were paid was an aspect of job quality for some of them. This construct does not appear in the literature on job quality, but it may be especially important for low-wage workers, whose financial crises can occur more frequently than those of higher-wage workers. For Nancy, being paid weekly was a positive aspect of her job. Rose expressed a similar view: even if the pay was not good, she said, it was good to be paid quickly. These comments suggest that mothers in the sample needed a stream of income flowing more frequently than monthly if they were to take care of family needs. Very few of them had enough savings to "tide them over," much less investments or other kinds of equity or financial resources on which to rely.

Another kind of job perceived by the mothers in the ethnographic study as being of good quality was the *salaried* position. Michol was happy because she was salaried, an indicator of a better-status job with benefits. When L'Kesha became salaried, she noted, she gained other job benefits, such as vacation days. And Inez commented that her wages had a higher equivalent when she switched from a temp job to a salaried one at a mortgage company. However, as we reported in chapter 2, raises and promotions were relatively rare; they were reported by about one-third of the ethnographic sample.

In general, women in the study did not refer to jobs in specific occupational sectors as paying better than others. It is possible that with a restricted range of labor market opportunities, they simply did not perceive higher-paying sectors as being within their reach. However, many of the mothers felt that jobs were better outside the Milwaukee area. Several women moved to suburbs of Milwaukee during the ethnography and found jobs there. The findings reported here suggest that what they wanted was adequate and frequent pay, especially if in a salaried position, and that salaried jobs were valued because of the benefits that came with them.

The Paramount Benefits Concern: Health Care

Although a variety of benefits were mentioned by the New Hope mothers, including sick days, vacation days, and pension plans, the benefit mentioned most often by far was health care coverage. Data from the New Hope survey sample showed that 68 percent (315 mothers) had health insurance coverage at least for themselves that was sponsored by their employer at the last place they were working.[3] This proportion is roughly comparable to recent national data on low-income African-American and Latino parents (Ku and Waidmann 2003). When New Hope mothers in the ethnography talked about benefits, their hopes were mostly about health care coverage, preferably for themselves and for their children. Katrina put it bluntly: "Without health insurance, I will die."

Even when health care coverage was available, the premiums were onerous to the mothers in our sample. As a single mother with two children, making $9.00 an hour, Anna Marie had to pay a relatively high premium for health care coverage: $230 a month, nearly one-fifth of her salary. She explained to her field-worker that the premium was what she liked least about her job. When premiums were very high, mothers could not afford health care. Four mothers in the ethnographic sample of forty (10 percent) reported having to drop coverage for their children, or not getting any coverage at all, owing to high premiums. Inez, for example, could not afford to pay $320 per month in health insurance premiums and banked on the hope that her children would not need the coverage: "My kids don't get that sick." Julie also had to make a choice. She left a job with health insurance she could afford for one that paid slightly more in wages but left her unable to afford the $250 monthly payment. L'Kesha had to drop health coverage for her children when the premium increased to $400 per month (one-third of her salary). She kept it for herself, left two daughters uninsured, and obtained coverage for her son through other assistance. Yet she reported liking the job in other respects (for example, it provided vacation days).

Other benefits were often mentioned as enhancements of the more basic need for health coverage, especially paid leave in the form of sick and vacation days. Being able to take time off was a critical need for mothers in the ethnographic study, but it would come at a price for some. Our analyses of New Hope survey data showed that 270 of the mothers (57 percent) reported having paid sick days as a benefit. This is roughly in line with other studies of lower-income parents. The analyses by Jody Heymann, Alison Earle, and Brian Egleston (1996) of the National Longitudinal Survey of Youth (NLSY) show that 38 percent of parents living in poverty lack sick leave and that parents of color are more likely to be lacking this benefit than European-American parents. Other analyses by these researchers (Heymann and Earle

1999) show that 36 percent of mothers previously receiving public assistance have lacked sick leave for the entire time they have been employed.

From what women in the ethnographic study had to say about leave, it is clear that sick days would have enabled them to take care of themselves and, more often, of their children when they were sick and to take care of other needs of their children, such as chaperoning on field trips. All families with children need some kind of paid leave, or at least job flexibility, but that need is particularly important for those in poverty and of ethnic minority status. Parents in these families need to be available to take care of their children when they get sick. Over one-third of the mothers in another study sample whose children had chronic conditions lacked sick leave (Heymann, Earle, and Egleston 1996). In our study, Carla had medical coverage and reported getting paid sick days only if she was sick for more than seven days. Others did not have even this restricted form of paid sick days.

The process of getting a sick day approved as a paid one was onerous to some parents. Lisa, for example, worked at a furniture plant, on the third shift, making $10.50 an hour. Despite what was, in the context of the sample, a good job with above-average pay and benefits, one of the only ways in which she could get a paid day off to attend to events involving her children was to use a sick day; she had no flextime or personal day benefits. Lisa reported having to go to an emergency room for ten hours to get a doctor's note so that she could miss a day of work and make sure that her son would be able to go on a school field trip. Lisa also said that "her supervisor is not a nice person and tries to make people feel bad for taking a day off of work." Indeed, three mothers (8 percent) mentioned losing their job because they needed a leave. One was Nancy, who was fired because she took four days off owing to her physical condition after a domestic violence incident. A second one was Rhonda, who was fired for, among other reasons, missing three days of work with a respiratory infection. The third one, Heather, was fired when she missed work because she did not know the exact date she was expected to return from her maternity leave.

Another kind of leave that parents find useful is vacation time. About two-thirds of the mothers in the survey (310, or 66 percent) reported having paid vacation days. Again, with few other work-based benefits, they frequently used this benefit not to take actual vacations but to address pressing needs in their often turbulent family lives. Alicia, for example, generally saved her two weeks of vacation per year for family emergencies.

Finally, a pension plan, specifically one paid for by the employer, is another indicator of job quality. Trends from 1979 to 1993 in the provision of pensions by gender and educational attainment showed that as educational attainment decreased, so did the likelihood of having a job that provided a pension plan (Houseman 1995). In 1993, 28 percent of women who had not completed high school had a job with a pension plan, in contrast to 51 percent of those who had completed high school and 56 percent of women with some college education. In the New Hope survey, 54 percent (251 of the mothers) said their employer offered a pension plan. Karen, for example, said that her employer put $100 into the new retirement fund at her job for each month that she worked full-time.

As these findings suggest, traditional fringe benefits were far from widespread in the jobs held by the women in the New Hope study. They perceived benefits as desirable aspects of jobs, but unfortunately, even when benefits were offered, these women were not always able to enjoy them, for different reasons. One reason was lack of affordability, as with high health insurance premiums; also holding them back were the restrictions that employers and supervisors placed on using paid leave.

A related aspect of job quality, flexibility, was described by some women as another benefit, even when this was not formally the case.

Flexibility as a Characteristic of Supervisors, Not Jobs

The mothers in our study had a great need for flexibility in scheduling (see chapter 5). In the survey, 68 percent (286 of the mothers) said their job was flexible enough to allow them to keep track of their kids while at work and to handle emergencies. (The survey did not ask about formal flextime or other leave benefits.) But we found in the ethnographic data that this flexibility was rarely provided as a formal benefit (such as flextime). Three of the mothers (8 percent), in fact, had no days off at all at their jobs. Flexibility was an informal benefit.

In the absence of formal flextime or leave policies, supervisors were the key to flexibility. When mothers in the New Hope ethnography talked about time flexibility, it was most often in the context of what their supervisors allowed or did not allow them to do: coming early to work on some days so they could leave early; leaving to attend to family emergencies; calling in sick; or getting personal or vacation days approved. When flexibility was allowed, mothers referred to their supervisors as "understanding." For example, Katie mentioned that "her supervisor is very understanding and supportive," her field-worker noted,

about her calling in sick if her child is sick, or taking a vacation day. She mentions that she rarely takes a sick day. When she does take a sick day, it is usually because one of the kids is sick, or she has to take them to the doctor. Today, she took a vacation day in order to spend time with her son for his birthday. She said that her son is always saying, "You never spend any time with me," so she thought she would take the day before his birthday off. This afternoon she is going to volunteer in both of his classes. Last month when Katie went to the free clinic to get her foot checked out, she ended up being there for hours waiting for her time to see the doctor. She called in that afternoon, and asked her supervisor if it was okay if she didn't come in because she was just leaving the doctor's clinic and her foot was sore. Her supervisor said, "No problem," and told her to fill out a sick slip when she came in. Her previous experience in a nursing home was very different; she was not allowed to go home with a bleeding tooth or if she had a child sick at home.

Similarly, Anna Marie told her field-worker that her supervisors usually cooperated when she asked to leave work early or come in late to attend something with her children (sports events, school conferences, and the like). Inez said that her boss understood that she had another job and a family and was good about scheduling her when she asked to be scheduled. She reported that some of the other workers complained because she always got the hours she wanted, but she told them that her boss knew that if she was scheduled for a time when she could not make it, then she just would not come in. She was confident in telling her boss, for example, that she would take two hours off to go to her son's school. This degree of discretion, however, was rare in the working lives of the other mothers in the ethnography.

Some women described jobs in which supervisors did not allow them such flexibility. Rhonda told her field-worker: "I had to take too many days off work, and they sent me a letter in the mail that said I was fired. But before I got the letter, I never seen the letter. I had went on to work for two more weeks before the letter came." Rhonda reported to work, but her name was not on the schedule. However, the supervisors let her work for the two weeks, figuring it was a mistake. She said, "Well, that was a very good job to lose. I guess when you have kids, that's the breaks."

Two mothers in the ethnography were fired for getting too many personal calls at the workplace from or about their children. One was Trisha, who reported that she had to leave the cash register to answer the phone, while the other, Caroline, lost several jobs for the same reason. Another mother, Frida, got sick and left to go see a doctor after her supervisor said she could not. She reported that even after the physician called her supervisor, the supervisor was upset about her leaving work. She described her supervisor as unfair to her, and in many visits with the field-worker she described how inflexible, even cruel, her supervisor was. He suspended her for three days because she was absent when her daughter was sick. As mentioned before, three mothers were fired or suspended for missing days.

For the nineteen women in the ethnographic study who brought up the issue, flexibility was a characteristic of their supervisor's disposition more than a benefit built into their job. Very few women (two in the entire ethnographic sample) had access to formal flextime. Not surprisingly, Leora, one of the mothers who enjoyed this benefit, was a clerical manager, a job with higher-level responsibilities than was the case with the jobs held by most of the ethnographic sample. She was able to come in early twice a week so that she could be with her daughter in the afternoons. Other women in the study who did not have such a position or formal benefit were left with the hope of having a supervisor that would be understanding and supportive of their need for flexible work time.

The Quality of Workplace Relationships

The quality of jobs—and more specifically, the level of satisfaction with which the mothers in the study described their jobs—was heavily dependent on the quality of their relationships with supervisors and coworkers and the support derived from them. Karen, for instance, hated her new job chiefly because she did not like the people with whom she was working. The mothers valued almost entirely different aspects of their workplace relationships with supervisors as with coworkers. Those aspects included issues of respect, effort recognition, social respite, and information networks.

Relationships with supervisors again took center stage over all other relationships, for these were the people who controlled so much of when and how the women did their jobs. Earlier, we mentioned the importance to these mothers of their supervisors' understanding of their family needs. Here, we discuss other types of support they sometimes received from their supervisors. For instance, Maria said that her supervisor was wonderful and always asked her if she needed things. Of the twenty-three women who mentioned the quality of their relationship with their supervisor, eight (35 percent) volunteered positive remarks about them. These eight women consistently reported valuing their supervisor's trust in them. Trust and respect were reflected in the level of autonomy or discretion afforded to employees by these supervisors. For example, Shaquita reported that her supervisor "know[s] you're grown and [can] do what you're supposed to do."

These women also valued being treated with respect and fairness by their supervisors. Some of them reported that their supervisors encouraged professional or career development, a signal to them that their work and effort was acknowledged and valued. Edith shared that her supervisor asked her if she felt ready to have an interview to be promoted to be a supervisor herself. Katie shared a similar experience: she thought her supervisor was trying to get her ready to take over a supervisor position in a few years. Moreover, her supervisor wrote a letter praising her and recommending a pay increase. Nancy was also happy with the recommendation letter she received from her boss, which allowed her to receive raises. Julie's employer sent her to take computer courses, training that she appreciated because she thought it would give her marketable experience. These examples show that the mothers in our sample appreciated supervisors who showed they cared about the overall growth and development of their employees.

In contrast, fifteen of the twenty-three mothers who spoke about their supervisors (65 percent) made negative remarks about them. Most common were statements about feeling unrecognized for contributions at work, a lack of autonomy, and personal disposition factors, such as rudeness, disrespect, or outright discrimination. L'Kesha highlighted the impact that supervisors could have on these mothers' perceptions of their job quality when she said that her supervisor was "the job aspect that stresses [her] out, because otherwise the job is easy and has real good benefits."

For workers at the bottom of job hierarchies, not being recognized for contributions at work hit particularly hard. Heather said she felt "blue" in her daytime job because some days earlier her supervisor had a meeting with the staff asking for their opinions. When she expressed her opinion, he replied that she always wanted things her way. She felt offended. She said that she had to continue working at this job for a while (three more months) because of the money. Belinda said that her "manager acts like he doesn't care about [her]." She complained about the lack of acknowledgment or gratitude from her managers after she stopped a shoplifter from stealing hundreds of dollars in merchandise.

Evaluations were a key dimension of being recognized. As mentioned earlier, three mothers reported getting supportive letters of recommendation from their supervisors or evaluations indicating that their supervisors wanted to promote them. On the other hand, three mothers reported not being happy with how their supervisors assessed their performance. These mothers felt that their work went unnoticed, or that they did not receive acknowledgment when they went beyond the call of duty to do things right. One mother said that she and her coworkers had to "kiss ass" to be promoted. In the chapter on discrimination (chapter 6), we explore in detail perceptions of inequality in access to promotions.

Very close supervision was problematic. Katrina, for instance, wanted "a job with a little more freedom"; in her job she was monitored very closely and constantly told what to do. Karen complained that she had a different supervisor every day in her new job: each one would tell her what to do, but none agreed on the directions to be given. On the other hand, insufficient supervision could also present a problem. Tiffany, for example, needed more direction in a new job and did not get it because her supervisor was too busy.

Some workers reported rudeness and even abuse on the part of supervisors. In an extreme case, Frida described multiple incidents of her supervisor's abusive behavior. It escalated from pressure and mistreatment to make her work faster in the kitchen, which caused her to get injured, to physical abuse when her supervisor threw an object at her. Some New Hope mothers in the ethnography understood the exploitative structure of low-wage jobs. Evelia, for example, expressed the feeling that she was an "instrument of exploitation" in a meatpacking factory job. She was responsible for supervising the line of workers taking apart carcasses. Although she herself worked under harsh conditions (a ten-hour day with only one fifteen-minute break), she felt that the line workers, mostly undocumented Mexican immigrants, had an even harder time. She quit after three weeks. Such critiques of the social structure of jobs and the oppressive environment it can create were also made by several women concerned about the racial or gender makeup of their workplaces (see chapter 6).

Qualities perceived as important in relationships with coworkers were often quite different from those mentioned in relationships with supervisors. Lillian Rubin (1994) describes women's relationships with coworkers as spanning beyond the work sphere, through phone contacts, outside socializing, and mutual support.[4] Nearly equal numbers of women expressed positive and negative remarks about their coworkers. (Seventeen made positive remarks, and fifteen made negative ones.)

Women in the ethnography were pleased with their jobs when relationships with coworkers were smooth. One field-worker wrote that the first reason Maria cited for liking her current job was not having to contend with difficult coworkers. The relationships with coworkers follow some of the lines expressed about supervisors. Most common in comments about coworkers were statements about reliability and ethics, contrasted with exploitation and gossiping. Reliability, for example, was more valued as a characteristic of coworkers than of supervisors. This characteristic is a neglected aspect of social capital assistance (Smith 2005). Reliability may be particularly important for low-income working parents because, with less child care, transportation, and other resources than higher-wage workers, they often rely on their coworkers to fill in when other personal networks fall short. Reliability is important when a mother needs to leave in an emergency and someone else has to fill in. In Belinda's estimation, when coworkers are reliable, they look out for each other.

Conversely, the New Hope mothers were quick to denounce gossiping, cheating, and dishonest behavior in coworkers. They said that they felt exploited by such behavior, especially because they had to do more work when others did not show up for work or did not fulfill their duties. For example, Karen felt stressed because she was being called from her job to cover for a coworker who was not showing up for work, and this created a lot of instability in her life.

Respect for the quality of one's work was also salient for a few of the mothers. Michol reported, for example, that she would regularly receive compliments from coworkers about how good she was at her job as assistant director of a child care center. Tiffany felt respected by coworkers because she did a good job. In contrast, she quit one of the several short-term jobs she held during the course of the ethnography because she didn't like her coworkers' attitude. She verbally fought with another woman who she felt always tried to tell her what to do. Similarly, Marina endured such conflict with a coworker that she asked to be transferred because she felt it would end in a physical fight.

Coworkers' sociability was more salient for New Hope mothers than supervisors' sociability. Shaquita said that she had many friends at work and that her friendships with her coworkers were the most important part of the job. Thus, when coworkers were not friendly, many of these mothers felt like Faye, who cited unfriendly coworkers as the primary reason she did not like her job.

Finally, jobs provided an important opportunity for New Hope mothers to enter another world outside of their family (and often their neighborhood). Jobs provided an opportunity to meet and talk to other people. Relationships from work provided social support and opportunities to socialize outside of work and even opened possibilities for women. For example, through job networks, they learned of other jobs, available resources, and better ways to cope with life situations. Leora felt that work was important because it made her feel better and gave her the opportunity to go out every day. Maria said that working exposed her to many different ways of living. She credited the exposure to people's ideas and ways of living for helping her leave an alcoholic and abusive man. She felt that she learned at work that she could be independent and take care of herself. In fact, one of the unexpected consequences of some recent employment programs aimed at increasing work effort among low-income mothers has been a decrease in reported domestic abuse.[5]

In general, relationship quality made an enormous difference in mothers' overall experience of their jobs. Among the relationships, the supervisor-worker relationship was paramount because of the relatively low degree of autonomy these mothers experienced in their jobs. Being recognized by the supervisor for their work was critical to these mothers' well-being; because almost none of them were in a supervisory position themselves, they relied on supervisors almost exclusively for evaluations of how they were doing.

Among coworkers, however, the most highly valued aspects of the relationship were reliability, honesty, respect, and friendliness.

THE IMPACT OF JOB QUALITY ON PARENT AND CHILD WELL-BEING AND ITS RELATIONSHIP TO PREVIOUS EMPLOYMENT DYNAMICS

We started our quantitative analysis by examining whether the dynamic work pathways recorded in the first two years of the New Hope study were related to the quality of jobs held five years after baseline. We did not find such associations, perhaps because those work dynamic pathways were specific to the first two years of the follow-up.[6]

In addition to the potential linkages between job quality and employment clusters, we were interested in whether job quality could have affected mothers' well-being and their children's development. To examine that possibility we explored survey items connected to the five job quality dimensions described in this chapter, structured as four predictor variables—number of benefits, complexity of functions with respect to data and people, overall perceived job quality, and job stress—in relation to two sets of outcomes. The first set was children's cognitive and socioemotional outcomes— specifically school performance and both problem and positive behaviors. The second was maternal well-being, which our ethnographic data suggested might explain the link between job quality and child outcomes. The measures of maternal well-being included assessments of levels of depression, parenting stress, and time pressure.

The work described here reinforces and expands the extant literature by including additional aspects of job conditions that have not been examined in relation to child outcomes. In addition, we use a change-score approach in our analyses, a relatively stringent technique that rules out selected threats to causality by accounting for confounding variables that might bias our estimates of the association between job quality and our outcomes.[7] We now turn to the four dimensions of job quality available in the survey data, provide a brief overview of relevant findings from previous studies, and then use those findings to provide a context for the findings from our analysis of New Hope data (summarized in table 4.1). Notably, the significant associations we found were above chance levels.[8]

Fringe Benefits

Although employment benefits, such as health insurance, paid sick and vacation days, and a pension plan, constitute an important marker of job quality, very few studies have attempted to link them to children's cognitive

Table 4.1 OLS Regression Coefficients for Job Quality Dimensions Predicting Change in Child and Parent Outcomes Between the Twenty-Four-Month and Sixty-Month Follow-up Assessments

Outcome	Occupational Complexity			Perceived Job Quality			Job Stress		
	b	SE_b	β	b	SE_b	β	b	SE_b	β
Child behavior									
School performance (parent report)									
School performance (teacher report)									
Externalizing (parent report)				−.16	.05	−.19**			
Internalizing (parent report)									
Externalizing (teacher report)									
Internalizing (teacher report)							.20	.08	.23*
Positive behavior (teacher report)	.06	.03	.10*						
Positive behavior (parent report)									
Parent well-being									
Depression							1.31	.76	.11†
Parenting stress	−.08	.05	−.11†						
Time pressure				−.16	.09	−.12†			

Source: Authors' compilation.
Note: b = unstandardized coefficient; SE = standard error; β = standardized coefficient. All outcomes are change scores representing change in the construct from twenty-four- to sixty-month assessment points; nonsignificant coefficients are not reported in the table. The number of job benefits does not appear as a predictor in the table because there were no statistically significant associations between that variable and the outcome variables of interest.
†p < .10; *p < .05; **p < .01

or socioemotional outcomes. One such study is Ariel Kalil and Kathleen Ziol-Guest's (2005) analysis of job quality in terms of wages as well as employer-sponsored health insurance. They found that adolescents whose mothers were more consistently employed in higher-quality jobs, as represented by these indicators, reported better self-esteem and mastery outcomes. In our analysis, we did not find a relationship between the number of fringe benefits (ranging from zero to four) offered in the most recent or current job and any indicators of maternal well-being or child cognitive or socioemotional outcomes.[9] There are two possible reasons for our lack of significant associations. One is the fact that we examined the unique contribution of benefits to the outcomes of interest, rather than combining it with other job aspects. Second, it might be that there is a distal relationship mediated through other elements, such as the consistency of benefits availability to parents and children, as well as the extent to which parents are able to use such benefits to enhance their own well-being and their children's. In addition, we do not have benefit data directly from employers, but rely on mothers' own reports.

Occupational Complexity

As mentioned, occupational complexity describes the extent to which a job involves routinized and repetitive tasks or autonomy and higher-order thinking. This critical aspect of a job has important implications for parent and child well-being, as previous studies have confirmed, although that work has not necessarily focused on low-income parents and children. Toby Parcel and Elizabeth Menaghan (1990) found that the occupational complexity of mothers' jobs was related to their children's verbal facility, as well as to enriching characteristics in the home environment that were conducive to the child's cognitive development (Menaghan and Parcel 1991). In another study, they found that the effects of mothers' cognitive skills, age, education, part-time or overtime work, and non-employment on young children's verbal facility and behavioral problems differed, depending on occupational complexity (Parcel and Menaghan 1994a). For example, the positive effect of the mother's cognitive skills on her children's verbal facility was greater if she worked in a highly complex occupation. Les Whitbeck and his colleagues (1997) examined occupational complexity in relation to adolescent self-efficacy, as well as parenting behaviors, but did not find linkages between these mother-child constructs in their sample of white rural families. They suggested that the limited variability in the job characteristics of mothers in their sample might have accounted for the lack of findings. Occupational complexity was examined in relation to parenting style in a study by Ellen Greenberger, Robin O'Neil, and Stacy Nagel (1994). They found that parents with greater occupational complexity in functions having to do with people expressed more optimal parenting behaviors toward their sons.

All of these studies examined national and mixed-income samples; no studies have examined whether these complexity factors are associated with parent or child outcomes in a low-income sample. One of the few studies that did so was Cybele Raver's (2003); in a sample of low-income mothers and their children, she analyzed occupational prestige as a proxy for whether a job was considered menial. She found that mothers' employment in lower-prestige jobs was associated with the use of more coercive and angry parenting styles. Hers was one of the few studies linking job quality to parenting that used high-quality observational measures of parenting.

Very few studies have examined the relationship of occupational complexity to parenting stress, a powerful predictor of the quality of parenting and often a mediator between socioeconomic factors and the quality of parenting. We found that a composite variable of occupational complexity in functions having to do with people and data was related to lower parenting stress.[10] Moreover, we also found that this indicator of complexity was associated with higher levels of positive child behaviors, as reported by parents (see "Occupational Complexity" in table 4.1). These findings are important because they underscore that there are linkages between parents' job duties, how they feel at home in their role as parents, and their children's behaviors.

Perceived Job Quality

To our knowledge, the composite indicator of perceived job quality that we have included here—the extent to which workers perceived that their jobs offered good pay and job security, opportunities for promotion and learning new skills, and flexibility to attend to emergencies—has not been examined in previous studies in relation to child outcomes.[11] One exception is a study by Whitbeck and his colleagues (1997), who studied mothers' job flexibility in relation to parenting style and adolescent outcomes but found no statistically significant relationship. Other researchers have examined objective measures of pay in relation to child outcomes, but not satisfaction with pay, as we do here. Another study worth noting is that of Maureen Perry-Jenkins and Sally Gillman (2000), who assess perceived conditions of work using Moos's work environment scale (WES) in relation to children's reports of hassles, negative well-being, and restraint (that is, impulse control and repression of aggression). Using a sample of working-class dual-earner parents and single mothers, they found that children of single mothers with more positive work environments reported more restraint. This finding is in line with our own.

We found that the composite measure of perceived job quality in our analysis was related to lower levels of children's externalizing behavior problems, as reported by mothers (see "Perceived Job Quality" in table 4.1), as well as to lower levels of parental time pressure. These findings point to the importance of considering not just the structural elements of jobs, such as wages or hours, but also their psychosocial aspects, which have implications for the well-being of working parents and their children.

Job Stress

Our last indicator of the quality of job experiences is job stress: at the end of the workday, to what extent did mothers feel drained of energy and often angry with people at work?[12] To date, we have not found studies directly linking job stress and child outcomes. However, there is some work that links job stress to parent psychological well-being. For example, Rena Repetti and Jennifer Wood (1997) found that middle-class mothers withdrew from interactions with their preschool children on stressful workdays, that is, days when they experienced more negative social interactions at work and higher workload. Ann Crouter and Matthew Bumpus (2001) reviewed the literature on job stress and children and concluded that a number of family processes, such as parental withdrawal from interactions with children and less acceptance of the child, could link job stress with indicators of child development. For example, they summarized a study they conducted with colleagues in which they found that maternal work pressure predicted feelings of overload, which were related to elevated mother-adolescent conflict. Conflict, in turn, predicted lower psychological well-being in the adolescent (Crouter et al. 1999).

In our analysis, we found that mothers' job stress was related to higher levels of internalizing problem behaviors in children (being anxious, withdrawn, depressed), as reported by their teachers, as well as higher levels of parent depression. This finding is notable in that a parent-perceived measure of job stress predicts teachers' reports of children's social behaviors. Teachers are certainly less aware of parents' job stress than parents themselves, and therefore we can have somewhat higher confidence in the causal nature of this association. The importance of the indicators of job stress examined in our quantitative analysis was underscored in the ethnographic data. In the ethnographic study, the women reported on whether lack of support and respect characterized their relationships with people at work and on the degree to which they felt absolute boredom, exhaustion, or burnout.

CONCLUSION

Our goals in this chapter were to use the ethnographic data to define job quality from the point of view of mothers in New Hope, and then to use the survey data to link job quality to parent and child well-being. In their own words, women expressed wanting a job that they liked, not just one that paid okay. In the field notes, the New Hope mothers reported what made a job good or bad. Our findings point to five salient elements: (1) health insurance that covers both mothers and their children and is affordable at their low wages; (2) a flexible, supportive, and fair supervisor who understands and supports the need for time flexibility, allows the use of sick leave, accommodates changes in schedules to attend to family and personal needs, allows some autonomy but provides good direction regarding time and task completion, acknowledges good effort, and promotes the growth of workers; (3) reliable and sociable coworkers who maintain a good work ethic, are prepared and willing to assist a colleague, and share informational resources in an atmosphere of civility; (4) a variety of tasks, so as to avoid tedium and repetitiveness; and (5) adequate compensation for the job done and the effort made. Despite their desire to experience these positive aspects and benefits of work, substantial percentages of the mothers reported not having access to them. For example, about one-third reported not having vacation days, and a similar percentage reported a lack of sick days and health insurance coverage at work. In the absence of formal policies for flexibility, supervisors often held the key to whether a mother would be excused from work to attend to a child-related emergency or whether she would be castigated for it.

We also examined whether job quality mattered for children's academic or social outcomes and for parental well-being. Using a change-score approach to adjust for unobserved confounding variables that do not change over time, we found relatively few associations between job quality and parental or child well-being. However, the ones we found were above chance and in the expected direction. Better job quality, as measured by overall quality, job stress, and occupational complexity, was associated with lower levels of children's acting-out and withdrawn behaviors, as reported by parents and teachers, and with higher levels of parental well-being (lower levels of depression, parenting stress, and time pressure). These associations are among the first to be found between job quality and parent and child outcomes in a study of low-wage work. They suggest that parents' perceptions of job quality may indeed matter, though more strongly for socioemotional outcomes and well-being than for academic ones.

Our findings have implications for organizational and public programs and policies aimed at improving the quality of the jobs available to low-income families. As the findings suggest, job quality enhancement may lead to better parental well-being. Where we found evidence of a relationship with child outcomes, it appears that similar benefits may accrue for children's socioemotional development. In addition to the importance of better wages and benefits, there are psychosocial aspects to consider that could improve significantly the work experience of mothers like those in the New Hope study. For instance, work could be structured so as to allow for more variety, less tedium, more autonomy, less burnout or exhaustion, and more skill development without having to compromise the quality of the work being done. Supervisors should have clear guidelines and incentives to support family needs and not penalize workers who need flexibility and time off to balance life, family, and work. (More details about policies related to time flexibility and paid leave will be discussed in the concluding chapter.) Perhaps as important as the workload and the job duties are the relationships at work. Thus, organizations and communities may foster the ability of workers to develop supportive and respectful networks in the work environment and create strategies for workers to derive extrinsic and intrinsic rewards from their job experience, from information sharing to a sense of fulfillment.

We wish to acknowledge the research assistance of Jessica Lobenherz of the University of Michigan, and Catelin Blowers, Julie Fitt, Ashley Goldstein, Myra Gorostiaga, Naoko Hoshimoto, Min Ying Li, Amanda Metcalf, José Pizarroso, and Molly Siegel, of Syracuse University. Noemí Enchautegui-de-Jesús is with the Department of Psychology at Syracuse University. Vonnie C. McLoyd is with the Center for Developmental Science and the Department of Psychology at the University of North Carolina, Chapel Hill.

Chapter Five | Mothers at Work in a 24/7 Economy: Exploring Implications for Family and Child Well-Being

JoAnn Hsueh

IN THE UNITED STATES, according to data from the 1997 Current Population Survey (CPS), approximately 46 percent of all employed adults regularly work variable shifts (different hours on different days) or at nonstandard times, defined as work mostly in the evening, at night, or on the weekend (Presser 2003). Estimates from the 1991 CPS show that, because the demographic portrait of these workers is strikingly similar to that of low-income parents, working-poor parents are overrepresented among American workers who are employed on alternative schedules (Presser and Cox 1997). Fifty-five percent of New Hope parents worked schedules with nonstandard hours or variable shifts at the twenty-four-month follow-up interview (Hsueh and Yoshikawa, forthcoming). This chapter extends the discussion of job characteristics from the dynamics of work across months and years (chapters 2 and 3) to the dynamics of work across days and weeks. Although, as those chapters showed, the characteristics of work at the longer time scale could have cumulative effects on children, work schedules at the daily and weekly level could have substantial immediate effects. Indeed, the results from this chapter show that work schedules are associated, in both predicted and surprising ways, with children's development. We will see that, in the New Hope sample, working a combination of nonstandard and variable shifts places children at higher risk for school-related difficulties and behavioral problems. Yet working fixed shifts during nonstandard hours or variable shifts during daytime hours does not appear to represent a risk to children. In addition, the ethnographic data show the importance of predictability and flexibility of work schedules for managing work and family. Working nonstandard schedules and variable shifts proved to be one of the ways in which some working-poor mothers managed the daily demands of work and family life to care for their children.

Research examining the consequences of nonstandard and variable schedules among low-income families is rare. Most existing research on the effects of work on child development has assumed that parents work fixed nine-to-five weekday schedules (Presser 2003). However, as the 24/7 economy continues to shape low-wage labor markets and demands for work on alternative schedules, it is important to know how these societal changes affect low-income families. This chapter seeks to fill this gap in the literature by examining how low-income parents and children experience nonstandard schedules and variable work shifts. We explore two questions: First, what are the developmental consequences for children in low-income families of maternal employment on nonstandard schedules or variable shifts? Second, given not only the constraints faced by these mothers but also the opportunities available to them, why do some, but not others, choose to work nonstandard hours or variable shifts?

THE NEW HOPE ETHNOGRAPHIC STUDY: THREE STORIES

Three stories drawn from the NHES illustrate the varied work experiences of low-income mothers in the 24/7 economy.

Carla

Carla, a Latina single mother of seven children in her early thirties when the ethnographic study started, worked full-time at $8.00 an hour as a mechanist for an automotive shop. She found the job through a temp agency. Being a temp was difficult for Carla because she never knew when she was going to work or how much money she would make. In 1998 she was relieved when she was hired full-time at the automotive shop. When possible, Carla worked extra hours. She needed to pay her bills, and she wanted to take her kids out. There were times she worked up to twenty hours in overtime a week. Even so, she thought about getting a second job to stay on top of her bills and buy her children clothes.

When her father fell ill, she cut her hours back to care for him. Soon thereafter, her company instituted a new policy limiting the number of overtime hours any one person could work. After her father became ill, she cut her overtime hours from twenty to five a week. Already at the limit of her finances, however, Carla was left with no money and a mounting stack of unpaid bills. Later that year, during the summer, her situation improved slightly when she took on some double shifts. She worked from 6:00 A.M. to 10:00 or 11:00 P.M. The overtime helped, but her situation remained precarious because she never knew when she would get the extra hours she needed.

Despite the hardships, Carla took great pride in her successes on the job. She was drawn by the possibilities of making extra money if she were to take on a second job. But she readily acknowledged the costs of working so many hours. Scheduling school visits, doctor appointments, and WIC appointments was a constant struggle because she worked during the day. She felt that her children became difficult to control, and she worried about spending so much time away from them. Carla was torn. She said, "I have tried to look for [a second part-time job], but then I think no. 'Cause then I won't see my kids at all." But "[my kids]," Carla continued, "are going to have to deal with what I deal with right now until I pay whatever off." At the end of the ethnography, Carla was saddened by her circumstances and upset at herself for not getting her act together. Her children depended on her, but she had little prospect of getting them everything they wanted or needed.

Katie

Katie, a thirty-six-year-old white mother of two children at the beginning of the ethnographic study, worked in the cleaning department of a local college earning $6.50 an hour. She worked the second shift from 5:00 P.M. to 1:00 A.M. on weekdays.[1] During the summer, she worked a bit earlier, from 3:00 to 11:00 P.M. or from 2:00 to 10:00 P.M.

There were opportunities for overtime hours, but Katie was not interested. Early on, she realized that working extra hours made little difference to her financially. Working at night, Katie said, gave her great flexibility. Her brother, a licensed W-2 child care provider, watched her children at night. Moreover, because she worked at night, she rarely needed to use her vacation or sick time, even though her daughter had chronic health problems. With her days free, she could take her daughter to the doctor or run other errands with relative ease. She also liked the seclusion that came with working the night shift. She felt that this was her time to relax and unwind from her hectic days. Even though Katie preferred working at night, she worried about all of the time that she spent away from her children. Now and then, her son complained about not seeing her. Katie said that her work never allowed her to volunteer at school or go on school trips with her children. In reality, she only saw her kids on weekends and in the mornings before they went to school. Katie often said that this was not enough time.

Leora

Leora was a white single mother in her thirties with one daughter who lives with her and four sons who live with their father. She was employed as a manager in the payroll division of a hospital processing paychecks, administering health benefits, and helping out with accounts payable and accounts receivable. Leora's job gave her a sense of "confidence, satisfaction, a sense of well-being, and accomplishment."

In prior years, Leora had felt like her life was out of control. Her life as a single parent had been difficult. She was tired after eight hours of work and wished that she could share the responsibility of raising her daughter Kim with someone. Life was not easy; it was difficult for her to find the physical and emotional strength to do all the things that needed to get done. During the ethnography, Leora found a job in the payroll department of a local bank. She worked from 8:00 A.M. to 5:00 P.M. and was home by 5:30 P.M. Compared to her last job, the pay was better, her commute was easier, and both she and her daughter received health benefits.

Despite the marked job improvement, Leora felt depressed. Overwhelmed by her domestic workload and full-time work hours, she began seeing a psychiatrist. When her daughter started elementary school, Leora changed her work schedule to accommodate Kim's school hours. The bank offered flextime hours, so two days a week she got into work at 7:00 A.M. Early in the morning, only the janitors were in the office, but she felt safe and did not mind working on her own. On these days, she left work early and was home by 3:30 P.M. when her daughter returned home from school. In the evenings, Leora was able to spend more time with Kim working on her homework. On the days when Leora did not leave work early, her boyfriend Stan was home with her daughter. Leora liked this work arrangement and felt that both she and her daughter were doing much better as a result.

Carla, Katie, and Leora are three of the many working-poor mothers in the United States who negotiate work in a 24/7 economy. Their work schedules are diverse, often requiring nonstandard hours, variable shifts, or both variable *and* nonstandard shifts. Carla, for example, frequently worked at night with overtime hours, although she was unable to predict when she would be working overtime hours. Katie steadily worked at night. Unlike Carla's schedule, Katie's hours did not fluctuate. Leora worked a standard nine-to-five weekday schedule. Like Carla, Leora had some daily variations in her work schedule, although she had much more discretion over the hours she worked.

NONSTANDARD SCHEDULES, VARIABLE SHIFTS, AND CHILD DEVELOPMENT AMONG LOW-INCOME FAMILIES

How might maternal employment on different schedules affect children in low-income families? Using the New Hope survey data, we explored independent and combined associations of nonstandard schedules and variable shifts with children's school and behavioral outcomes.[2] Using survey data collected at the twenty-four-month follow-up interviews, families were divided into four groups according to the schedules that mothers worked: fixed daytime schedules, fixed nonstandard schedules, variable daytime schedules, and variable nonstandard schedules. A standard work schedule was defined as any schedule in which more than half of the hours worked on the job fell between 8:00 A.M. and 4:00 P.M. on weekdays (Monday to Friday). A nonstandard schedule was defined as any schedule in which at least half of the hours worked on the job fell outside of 8:00 A.M. and 4:00 P.M. on weekdays and anytime during the weekends.[3] Among working mothers, approximately 45 percent worked fixed standard schedules, 26 percent worked fixed nonstandard schedules, 15 percent worked variable standard schedules, and 14 percent worked variable nonstandard schedules.[4] In an initial analysis, we also considered whether the New Hope program affected the type of work schedule the mothers reported; however, no evidence emerged that it did.[5]

In the analyses exploring the consequences of work schedules for children, those whose mothers worked fixed, daytime, weekday schedules were compared to children whose mothers worked fixed nonstandard schedules, variable standard schedules, and variable nonstandard schedules.[6] We also investigated aspects of the mothers' perceived stress and time pressure and the regularity of family mealtimes, which might account for the associations of work schedules with child development.[7] The results of these analyses are summarized in table 5.1.

In the first set of analyses, comparing fixed daytime hours to fixed nonstandard hours (see "Fixed Nonstandard Schedule" in table 5.1), maternal employment on fixed nonstandard schedules showed little association with any child outcomes in this sample of low-income families. And one unexpected association emerged: mothers who worked fixed nonstandard schedules reported that their children showed fewer depressive symptoms than those who worked fixed standard schedules. This finding was surprising. Prior studies, conducted mostly with married couples and mixed-income families, suggested that children whose parents work at nonstandard times (which includes nonstandard hours and variable shifts grouped together) are at developmental risk for less favorable outcomes than those whose

Table 5.1 OLS Regression Coefficients for Work Schedules Predicting Child and Parent Outcomes at the Twenty-Four-Month Follow-up

Dependent Variables	Unstandardized Coefficient (Standard Error) [Standardized Coefficient]		
	Variable Standard Schedule	Fixed Nonstandard Schedule	Variable Nonstandard Schedule
Teacher-reported child outcomes			
School engagement	.21[†]	−.03	−.44*
	(.11)	(.15)	(.23)
	[.11]	[−.01]	[−.12]
School performance	−.01	−.12	−.42*
	(.18)	(.15)	(.20)
	[−.00]	[−.05]	[−.12]
Externalizing behavior problems	−.11	−.10	.45*
	(.14)	(.12)	(.24)
	[−.04]	[−.04]	[.14]
Internalizing behavior problems	.23	−.09	.11
	(.17)	(.09)	(.12)
	[.08]	[−.06]	[.05]
Parent-reported child outcomes			
School performance	−.21	.07	−.31
	(.17)	(.14)	(.20)
	[−.06]	[.03]	[−.07]
Externalizing behavior problems	.06	−.01	.15
	(.13)	(.17)	(.17)
	[.03]	[−.01]	[.05]
Internalizing behavior problems	−.08	−.22[†]	−.28[†]
	(.12)	(.12)	(.16)
	[−.03]	[−.12]	[−.10]
Aspects of family functioning			
Maternal stress	−.11	−.24*	.01
	(.10)	(.10)	(.16)
	[−.04]	[−.12]	[.00]
Regularity of mealtimes	−.45**	−.07	−.29
	(.14)	(.14)	(.18)
	[−.17]	[−.03]	[−.09]
Maternal perceived time pressure	−.07	.25[†]	.11
	(.14)	(.14)	(.19)
	[−.02]	[.11]	[.03]

Source: Authors' compilation.
Notes: The reference category for work schedule comparisons is the group of low-income mothers who were working fixed standard schedules in the prior week.
[†]p < .10; *p < .05; **p < .01; ***p < .001

parents work fixed daytime weekday schedules (Presser 2003; Han 2005). In addition, studies have shown that parents who work at nonstandard times have more difficulty scheduling family activities and are more likely to use informal child care arrangements, such as self-care, relative care, and home-based care, than parents who work fixed, daytime, weekday schedules (Presser 2003). These differences, in turn, are expected to relate to less favorable outcomes for children. In the New Hope sample, although mothers who worked fixed nonstandard schedules reported feeling slightly more time pressure, they also reported feeling *less* maternal stress, with significant differences in the reported regularity of family mealtimes. As we see from the ethnographic data reported later in the chapter, some mothers choose to work nonstandard schedules, and our associations may reflect this.

When maternal employment on fixed versus variable shifts during standard hours was compared in the second set of analyses, a striking pattern appeared (see "Variable Standard Schedule" in table 5.1). Teachers reported that children were more engaged in school when their mothers worked variable, as opposed to fixed, shifts during standard work times. This is the first study to show that variable shifts during standard times can have beneficial implications for children. However, these results did not line up with associations of variable standard shifts with the aspects of family functioning we examined. Interestingly, mothers who worked variable standard shifts reported less regularity in their family's mealtimes than mothers who worked fixed standard shifts. No other significant differences on indicators of family functioning were found.

Finally, children whose mothers worked a combination of variable and nonstandard schedules were compared to children whose mothers worked fixed standard schedules. Drawing on cumulative risk models of child development, children whose parents worked both nonstandard and variable shifts were expected to be at a particular developmental disadvantage. For example, parents who work variable nonstandard schedules may report heightened levels of stress, experience more extreme hardships in juggling family routines, and feel more stress and time pressure than parents who work either nonstandard schedules or variable shifts alone. Consequently, children might show lower school achievement and more behavior problems than children whose parents work either nonstandard or variable shifts, but not both.

The results were generally in line with these hypotheses (see "Variable Nonstandard Schedules" in table 5.1). Teachers reported that children whose mothers worked variable nonstandard schedules were less engaged in school and showed lower levels of school performance and more externalizing behavior problems than children whose mothers worked fixed standard schedules. However, none of the indicators of family functioning we tested appeared to explain the associations between variable nonstandard work schedules and children's schooling outcomes and externalizing behavior problems as rated by teachers; working variable nonstandard schedules was not significantly associated with differences in maternal stress, perceived time pressure, or the regularity of family mealtimes.

So in our results the associations of variable nonstandard schedules with mother-reported outcomes did not always align with their associations with teacher-reported outcomes. In contrast to teachers, mothers felt that their children showed fewer internalizing behavior problems when they worked variable nonstandard schedules, as opposed to fixed standard schedules.

These quantitative associations begin to paint a nuanced picture of the relationships between maternal work schedules and child development. Work schedules appeared to pose a risk for children only under certain conditions. Only when mothers worked schedules with *both* variable shifts and nonstandard hours did their children show lower school engagement and performance and more externalizing behavior problems, according to teachers' reports. And when examining variation among daytime schedules, children whose mothers worked variable shifts appeared to fare slightly better than children whose mothers worked fixed shifts, in terms of their teacher-reported school engagement. However, these findings did not always align with mother-reported child outcomes. Indeed, mothers who worked variable nonstandard schedules reported that their children showed fewer depressive behaviors than were reported by their counterparts who worked fixed standard schedules about their children. Moreover, the aspects of family functioning we tested did not appear to reduce the strength of associations between work schedules and child outcomes. Although maternal work schedules predicted scattered differences in maternal perceived time pressure and regularity of family routines, these differences were not strong predictors of child outcomes. Therefore, these quantitative analyses introduce novel findings to the literature but raise a number of questions—most notably, what factors account for the pattern of associations between work schedules and child outcomes? And what factors account for the discrepancy in the pattern of associations between work schedules and teacher- and mother-reported outcomes in this sample of low-income families?

WHY DO SOME LOW-INCOME MOTHERS CHOOSE TO WORK NONSTANDARD SCHEDULES OR VARIABLE SHIFTS?

Thus far we have discussed children's responses to different work schedules. Missing from this discussion, however, are the factors that drive some low-income mothers to work nonstandard schedules or variable shifts. As we saw in the stories of Carla, Katie, and Leora, working nonstandard schedules or variable shifts can yield both costs and benefits, and these may shape children's responses to their mothers' alternative work schedules. Yet little is known about how low-income mothers view the trade-offs of work at either nonstandard times or on variable shifts. Here we explore the work-family conflicts that low-income mothers struggle with when making the decision to accept (or stay in) a job that requires employment at nonstandard times or on variable shifts.

Turning to the ethnographic data, we examined how low-income mothers in Milwaukee viewed work on nonstandard schedules or variable shifts. We were particularly interested in how these mothers talked about the challenges and benefits of particular work schedules in relation to their families' functioning, their own sense of well-being, and the well-being of their children. Our analysis is one of the first to examine choices concerning nonstandard and variable schedules in a low-income sample from a qualitative perspective.

From the ethnographic field notes for forty NHES families, we selected excerpts with keywords relating to work and schedules.[8] We then developed a list of the costs and benefits of nonstandard schedules or variable shifts. Once this coding scheme was finalized, we could calculate the prevalence of each theme for the entire NHES sample (see table 5.2).[9]

Of the forty mothers interviewed in the NHES, thirty-five (88 percent) worked either nonstandard times or variable shifts at some point during the ethnography. The analysis of mothers' experiences and perceptions of work on nonstandard schedules or variable shifts gives a detailed description of the work-family tensions facing working-poor mothers. They cogently weighed what work on nonstandard schedules and variable shifts would mean, not only for themselves, but for their children.

NONSTANDARD SCHEDULES: POTENTIAL BENEFITS
Financial and Material Gains

Like many people who work at nonstandard times, many of the New Hope mothers had done so because they worked multiple jobs or overtime hours. Restricted to low-wage labor markets and jobs that offered only hourly wages, these mothers' total earnings were intimately tied to the total number of hours they worked. Twenty (50 percent) of the mothers supplemented their regular work hours with overtime work or second jobs because their low-wage jobs seldom left them better off than those receiving welfare.[10] More often than not, these hours fell during nonstandard times. Mothers talked about wanting and needing extra work hours so as to earn additional

Table 5.2   Prevalence of Themes Relating to Perceived Costs and
             Benefits of Working Nonstandard Hours and Variable
             Shifts in NHES Sample

Perceived Costs and Benefits of Working Nonstandard Hours and Variable Shifts	Prevalence of Themes in NHES Sample
Benefits of working nonstandard hours	
Financial and material gains associated with working overtime hours, multiple jobs, or nonstandard hours	50.0
Ability to maintain financial independence from others and governmental assistance when working overtime hours, multiple jobs, or nonstandard hours	35.0
Working overtime hours, multiple jobs or nonstandard hours because of stigmas associated with welfare use	17.5
Easier work requirements and demands during nonstandard hours	10.0
Mothers work nonstandard hours because their partners prefer that mothers are home during daytime hours	10.0
Ease of balancing work and family demands when working nonstandard hours	35.0
Use and preference for informal child care arrangements	30.0
Costs of working nonstandard hours	
Fatigue and stress	42.5
Time away from children and home during evenings, nights, and weekends	50.0
Nonstandard schedules result in mismatch in work schedule with partner and time away from partner	10.0
Unsafe work conditions during nonstandard hours	5.0
Transportation difficulties during early morning or late night commute	7.5
Difficulties arranging child care during nonstandard hours	32.5
Lack of financial gain associated with working overtime hours, multiple jobs, or nonstandard hours	7.5
Lack of employment opportunities that do not require nonstandard hours	10.0
Costs of working variable shifts	
Dislike of inconsistent and unstable work hours and schedules	27.5
Benefits of working variable shifts	
Preference for flexibility in work schedules and ability to manage family demands and emergencies when necessary	55.0

Source: Authors' compilation.

income to provide food, shelter, and clothing for their families. Carla, for instance, overburdened with bills and expenses, such as loan payments for her van, worked overtime hours to pay off her debts and make ends meet.

In other cases, mothers worked extra hours or additional jobs because they wanted to have "a little extra" to give their children "nice" things and experiences that they believed every child should have while growing up (on the importance of little extras in the lives of the working poor, see chapter 8). To these mothers, being able to respond to their children's requests for things would prevent them and their children from feeling poor or deprived. Early in the ethnography, for instance, Heather, a single African-American mother in her midtwenties, described working two jobs. Although often exhausted, she tried to give her children everything they wanted. She said:

> I just like to be comfortable in knowing that if I need anything, or if my kids need anything, I'm not just sitting there with no money at all. That is just like the worst feeling to me, because I can imagine how my mother felt. My mother raised four kids by herself. . . . She was working part-time and going to school part-time. And my brothers were not understanding at all. It was hard enough trying to study to be a nurse, plus she's trying to work so they can have a decent Christmas, Easter, whatever. I know that she had a hard time and, I don't know, I think that I can avoid that situation.

Alicia, a married Latina mother in her midthirties with one daughter, held similar financial goals. She worked as a teacher's assistant and was scheduled to get off work at 3:30 P.M. Early on, she took up opportunities for overtime hours, sometimes working until 8:30 P.M. on weekdays, because the extra money paid the bills and bought her daughter "nice" things. Later she described her precarious financial situation when her husband lost his job. Consequently, she took on an additional part-time job from 5:30 to 9:00 P.M. at a local motorcycle factory. Alicia was fatigued, but afraid to turn down the work.

> Alicia said that regardless of the economic problems she has had since Rolando [her husband] didn't work, they have not stopped spending on Beatriz. Alicia said that her daughter was primary and that she worked a lot precisely so that her daughter didn't lack anything. Alicia said that she didn't like that her daughter felt bad because she didn't have things that others had.

Unlike Alicia, who consistently worked overtime hours or multiple jobs over the course of the ethnography, other mothers only occasionally increased their work effort in order to fulfill short-term goals or pay off unexpected expenses and debts. Anna Marie, a Latina mother in her midthirties with two sons, worked full-time at a drug treatment center and occasionally transported patients to and from the center outside of business hours to buy a washer-dryer and new beds for herself and her son. Similarly, Inez, a twenty-one-year-old Latina mother of two who had been working full-time at a music store, took on a second part-time job at a gas station from 5:00 to 9:00 P.M. on weekdays and alternate weekends to pay for her mother's move from Puerto Rico to the United States. She worked at the gas station for about three months. Inez reported being "pretty tapped out," but as she summed up her situation, "You gotta do what you gotta do."

Some mothers took on overtime hours or additional jobs in response to changes in formal assistance and agency-based services. As the New Hope intervention ended, for example, many mothers in the experimental group worried about what this change would mean for their families. Anna Marie, at first, talked about finding a small part-time job to bring in extra money when she no longer received the earnings supplement from New Hope. A few months later, she was working more hours by transporting patients in the early morning and evenings for the drug center where she worked.

Maintenance of Financial Independence

Beyond actual material and financial gains, thirteen (41 percent) of the mothers who worked nonstandard schedules at some point over the course of the NHES did so because they felt that working overtime hours or additional jobs allowed them to be independent from formal or informal assistance. Self-esteem and confidence increased when they did not depend on others. Heather, who worked at a day care drop-in center from 9:00 A.M. to 5:00 P.M. and a group home from 11:00 P.M. to 7:00 A.M., struggled with her finances throughout the ethnography. She repeatedly talked about how she worked two jobs so she would not have to depend on government support or welfare. When she began to feel burned out by her hectic work schedule, her fiancé offered to help her out financially. She briefly took him up on the offer, but ultimately she decided to continue working two jobs. She hated feeling like she owed him something or had to depend on another person. Heather was proud of being able to take care of her family herself.

Like Heather, Maria, a Latina mother in her late twenties, felt that her financial independence was one of her greatest accomplishments. Maria ardently believed that she should be able to take care of her family without a man. Working full-time at a day care facility from 6:00 A.M. to 3:00 P.M., she was tired and sometimes wanted nothing more than to be home in the mornings with her children. She earned very little and did not receive New Hope,

AFDC, TANF, or food stamps. Yet she worked tirelessly and stretched her finances to provide for her family on her own.

Similarly, some mothers expressed extreme dislike of welfare agencies and the stigma associated with welfare receipt and chose to work extra hours or jobs to avoid receiving assistance. Susan, an African-American single mother, worked at a nonprofit agency during the day and as a nursing assistant two nights a week from 11:00 P.M. to 7:00 A.M. She briefly received welfare when she first moved to Milwaukee, but she had not received assistance since then. She said her welfare experiences were humiliating. Caseworkers asked "the most nosy and personal questions." Susan felt that the caseworkers interfered in her personal life, and when she received her welfare checks, she was "embarrassed" by her lack of work effort. Not much later, Susan applied for New Hope but was assigned to the control group. That was when she decided to get a second part-time job. In a sense, she "felt even better" about herself, knowing that she had made it on her own. She was better off than a lot of other people she knew and felt "good about myself."

Ease of Balancing Family and Work Demands

Most American parents face the struggle of balancing work and family, but the conflicts faced by low-income mothers, particularly those who are single parents, can be difficult.[11] Wanting both to be home for their children and to earn enough to meet their children's needs, low-income mothers in the NHES often had few resources and choices. Working nonstandard schedules often eased these tensions. Of the twenty-two mothers who reported working nonstandard schedules for most of the ethnographic period, eleven (50 percent) thought that balancing family and work was easier on such schedules.

Like the mothers highlighted by Anita Garey (1999) in her qualitative study of nurses working the night shift, many NHES mothers felt that working nonstandard schedules allowed them to maximize their time with their children. They valued being at home to monitor their children in the mornings and late afternoons, critical times when, they believed, their children were likely to get into trouble. Marina, an African-American mother in her early twenties with two sons, illustrated this point nicely when she talked about her work as a temp in a post office. According to her field-worker, she said that

"It is not an ideal job," but she [also] said that "it got her foot in the door" and it was the only thing available. . . . The pay [is] good [$9.81 an hour]. However, she [doesn't] have benefits, because she is not a "regular." . . . The one thing she liked about the job was that she was not missing any time with her children—she can work while they [are] sleeping. . . . Marina works from 11:00 P.M. to 5:00 A.M. every night, seven days a week. She gets home at about 5:30 in the morning and watches the news until 6:30 A.M., when the kids get up. Then she gets up with the kids and gets on the bus with them to take them to day care or school. Then she tries to get some sleep during the day before she turns around and picks them up again at about 4:00 P.M.

Many mothers also felt that nonstandard schedules gave them the flexibility to tend to family emergencies and errands during the day. Marina, for example, said that she did not have to worry about missing work when one of her children got sick. She was able to spend the entire day with the sick child and still go to work while her children slept at night. Similarly, Katie turned down a first-shift position because of her daughter's health (she had gotten a lot of ear infections over the last months).[12] Katie wanted to keep her daytime hours free to take her daughter to the doctor and run other errands.

Informal Child Care Arrangements

As most urban working mothers know, many child care centers are not open after 6:00 P.M. or on the weekends (Kreader, Piecyk, and Collins 2000; Siegel and Loman 1991). Informal arrangements are more flexible in this respect than child care centers. Even so, the stories of the NHES mothers suggest that their work schedule choices were also driven by their child care preferences. This is echoed in the findings of Harriet Presser and her colleagues (see, for example, Presser and Cox 1997), who found that single mothers with low levels of education worked alternative schedules because such schedules allowed for better child care arrangements.[13]

In the New Hope ethnographic sample, eleven (34 percent) of the mothers who worked nonstandard schedules said that they preferred informal child care arrangements. These mothers talked about not trusting strangers to take care of their children. They told stories about when they had picked up their children from child care centers only to find that their children had not been fed or changed for hours (Lowe and Weisner 2004). Not surprisingly, these mothers were reluctant to place their children in such arrangements unless absolutely necessary. Heather and her fiancé, for example, talked about hating child care centers. Indeed, Heather once said that she preferred working the third shift because she could bring her children to work with her.[14] On other occasions, her children spent the night with her mother (their grandmother). Like Heather, Katie preferred to have her brother watch her son. In the past, she had used private child care centers, but she was never satisfied with the care her son received. She found that they did not feed or play with him or change his diapers.

Many of these mothers relied on relatives to care for their children, and others relied on their partner. Mothers and their partners often worked different shifts to meet their child care needs at low cost (Edin and Lein 1997). Dulce, for instance, felt terrible about leaving her children in day care. She also did not want to leave her children at home by themselves. So she and her husband worked different shifts in order to care for their children. As a cashier at a discount supermarket, she had great flexibility in her scheduling. Her husband worked during the day, while she worked on Saturdays and Sundays for a total of sixteen hours per week. There was a lot of juggling of schedules, but they coordinated their schedules and organized their routines so that someone was always home with the children. For Dulce, this was an ideal arrangement.

Although distrust of formal child care arrangements was prevalent across this entire sample of NHES mothers (see also chapter 10), such feelings were particularly salient among mothers with young children. Susan said she would never send her child to someone she did not know, especially before her child could speak. "After four years of age," she added, "when your child can talk, you can think about placing them in outside day care, because at least your child can tell you what is going on in the day care center." Some of these mothers said that they would rather be unemployed than place their children in formal child care arrangements. Sometimes mothers chose to work nonstandard schedules to ensure that a friend, family member, or partner would be able to take care of their young children. Like Susan, Shaquita, an eighteen-year-old single mother of African-American descent, had strong concerns about placing her son in formal child care before he was able to talk. So she and her boyfriend worked different shifts; she worked at night, and he worked during the day. That way, someone was always available to take care of her son.

The developmental literature has overwhelmingly identified the negative consequences associated with work at nonstandard times, but the stories of the working-poor mothers in the NHES identify a number of key benefits associated with work on nonstandard schedules. This qualitative evidence suggests that work at nonstandard times had beneficial effects on maternal psychological well-being and on these mothers' ability to balance work and family demands. This may be one of the reasons why we were unable to identify overall detrimental associations of fixed nonstandard schedules with child development in our quantitative analyses, even though prior research suggests that nonstandard schedules should have negative consequences for family functioning and child development. This may also explain why teachers and mothers perceived children's behavioral adjustment in different ways when mothers worked nonstandard schedules.

NONSTANDARD SCHEDULES: POTENTIAL COSTS

Despite these perceived benefits of work on nonstandard schedules, mothers also described the costs of such work. Fatigue, time away from children, and problems finding child care were some of the downsides of nonstandard schedules. After exhausting job searches, some felt that they had no choice but to take second- or third-shift jobs.

Fatigue and Stress

Alicia was exhausted from working three jobs. She delivered newspapers in the early mornings and on Saturdays and Sundays, worked a day care job during the day, Monday through Friday, and worked with foster parents in the evenings and on Saturdays. She was tired by and tired of her overloaded routine. On weekdays she would arrive home at 8:00 P.M. and go directly to sleep because the next day she had to wake up at 3:30 A.M. to deliver newspapers. She worked Saturdays from 1:00 to 5:00 P.M. The only day she had to rest was Sunday, but the day was never long enough to recoup all the energy she had spent during the week. Nineteen of the thirty-two mothers who worked nonstandard schedules over the course of the ethnography said that these schedules were exhausting.

The mothers working these schedules reported that sleep was a rare event. For example, Lisa, an African-American mother of three children, worked from 11:00 P.M. to 6:00 A.M. at a wood manufacturing company. She went to sleep at about 5:30 P.M. and then tried to sleep until 10:00 P.M. But her house was noisy and she did not get much sleep. She would have preferred to work the first shift because working the third shift left her with little energy or time to check up on her children.

Observing their own stress and fatigue led mothers to worry about how their work might be harming their children. Mothers talked about having difficulties dealing with their children. Karen, a white mother in her midthirties, told her field-worker that she was sick of "always working shit," so she refused to pick up work on the weekends or any overtime hours. She felt that her kids became out of control when she was working so much. She said, "You know now, when I have a little more time, I keep tabs on them the way it's supposed to be. I can make them act right." She later said, "You know, I was so tired. By the time I came home, I didn't want to hear [the kids] or anything. I was tired, you know?"

Time Away from Children and Home

The time they spent away from their children, particularly in the mornings before their children went to school and in the evenings, was unbearable for half of these mothers: 50 percent (twenty) of the mothers in the NHES sample believed that the time they spent away from home would have severe costs for their children's well-being. Belinda said that she hated the third shift for this reason. Although she liked having easier work requirements, she hated not being able to see her children at night or in the morning before they went to school. She desperately wished that she could work from 11:00 P.M. to 7:00 A.M. so that she could at least see her children off to school.

Children became more difficult to handle when mothers worked nonstandard schedules. Inez worked a second part-time job at a gas station from 5:00 to 9:00 P.M. on weekdays and alternate weekends. She found the schedule tiring, but was upbeat about her situation. However, she ended up quitting this job because her youngest son started acting out and she did not feel that the job was worth it. She was not quite ready financially, however, to leave her job; she would have liked to work the part-time job for another three weeks. But she ultimately felt that her son was more important than the money. Faye, an African-American mother working the second shift in catering, liked her job duties. But not being home at night made her uncomfortable because she was unable to keep an eye on her children and do things around the house. She often left her oldest son, thirteen-year-old Erik, in charge of the household chores and child care duties for his four-year-old brother Baylor. While she worked, usually from 4:00 or 5:00 P.M. to 11:00 P.M. or midnight, the kids' dinner and bathing and the laundry and housekeeping were not done.

Evelia felt that her four kids were happier when she was home more often. Over the course of the ethnography, we observed her working a variety of schedules. When she worked the first shift, she was able to pick up her daughter by herself; she felt that when her work schedule matched her children's schedule, it was easier. The only bad thing about working the first shift, she said, was that her paychecks were small, because there were few opportunities for overtime. Later in the ethnography, Evelia said that she hated working weekends, as she often had to do in her job at the post office. She thought her work schedule was especially difficult for her daughter, who was not even three years old. Even though Evelia hated the hours of her job, she felt that she had to stay at it. Even if she found another forty-hour job, she said, she probably would not make enough money to pay all of her bills, including rent and car payments. She felt that her work schedule was literally hurting her children. Sometimes, when she was at work, she thought that it was a mistake to work all day without enjoying her children, but she had no choice because she needed the money.

Difficulties Arranging Child Care During Off Hours

For some mothers, working nonstandard schedules required that they overcome nearly insurmountable barriers to employment. In this ethnographic sample, eleven (34 percent) of the mothers who worked at nonstandard times had no way of caring for their children during the "off hours." For Nancy, a Latina mother in her late twenties with three daughters, the logistical difficulties of arranging child care prevented her from taking a job as a nurse's aide at a local hospital because she did not know what shift she would be offered. Later in the ethnography, when she moved into a new neighborhood, she felt that she was in a position to reapply for the job. She now lived next door to her sister, her uncle and aunt lived across the street, and her father lived down the street. She knew that even if she came home late, someone would be able to keep an eye on her children.

Informal care arrangements were often experienced not as flexible but as unstable. When these informal arrangements fell apart, mothers who were working nonstandard hours were left with few alternatives. Evelia's case exemplifies the precarious child care circumstances under which mothers were able to work nonstandard schedules. She relied heavily on her mother to take care of her children when she was frequently working the second and third shifts. But this arrangement became problematic when her mother was unable to take care of her children. As a backup, she turned to her brother to provide child care, but she felt that it was too much to ask of him because her daughter would cry uncontrollably. So she frequently relied on her oldest son, who was about fourteen, to take care of his younger siblings in the afternoons and evenings. He disliked being expected to babysit, however, since he wanted to go out and play. Left with few other options, Evelia was forced to take her youngest daughter to a day care center, despite her intense dislike of such care.

Lack of Employment Opportunities

Several of the mothers talked about not having any choices when it came to the hours of their job. Lisa, who worked as a temp in a post office, felt that she had few employment options. When her children said that they did not see her enough and they did not get to talk to her, she changed her schedule from the second to the third shift to appease them. Even so, she did not spend a lot of quality time with them because she was always tired. Although she hated her job, she kept it for two and a half years because the labor market, she said, was "tight." Faye was looking for a full-time, nine-to-five job because she did not want her children to be alone if she worked evenings. But the only job in catering she found had part-time and evening hours. She took the job even though she did not really like the hours, saying, "I gotta do what I gotta do right now, you know?"

Thus, even though work at nonstandard times was associated with a number of perceived benefits, it is also clear that it presented hardships for many working-poor mothers. Work at nonstandard times increased fatigue and stress levels, a finding that is in line with previous survey research. Working nonstandard schedules also often interfered with the time that mothers spent with their children and created unanticipated difficulties in making child care arrangements and maintaining well-run households. Mothers often struggled with these costs, but felt that they needed to take jobs with nonstandard schedules because they had few other employment options. Despite these hardships, it is noteworthy that their mothers' nonstandard work schedules, particularly on fixed shifts, did not have overall negative consequences for the children in our survey data. It is possible that the benefits and costs of working nonstandard schedules offset each other in our quantitative analyses. Future survey work should incorporate questions about whether mothers choose to work nonstandard hours; as Harriet Presser (2003) has noted, virtually no national surveys do so.

VARIABLE SHIFTS: COSTS AND BENEFITS

Kathryn Edin and Laura Lein (1997) have suggested that the variability in work hours among the working poor is an adverse consequence of the low-status and often temporary jobs available at the lowest rung of the labor market. We found, surprisingly, that variability in work schedules benefits working-poor families and even their children's development under certain conditions. Why might this be the case? To the extent that mothers are able to choose their own start and end times, variability in maternal work schedules may buffer against potential adverse effects of employment on child development in low-income families. However, to date, we know almost nothing about how working-poor mothers experience variability in their work hours on a week-to-week basis.

Almost all of the NHES mothers experienced variability in their work schedules at some point during the course of the study. Some mothers worked variable shifts while putting in the same overall number of hours each week. All too often, however, mothers had little control over their work hours; the variability in their schedules was the result of unforeseen instability in their total number of work hours. Eleven of the forty mothers in this ethnographic sample disliked this type of inconsistency in their work hours. In addition, unwanted variability in work schedules was more common among mothers who worked nonstandard hours (31 percent) than among those who worked exclusively standard hours (13 percent), though this difference was not statistically significant. Mothers frequently talked about needing to work more hours than their jobs allowed. They questioned whether they could get the hours they needed to make ends meet for their families. Carla was one such mother. As discussed in the beginning of the chapter, she hated not knowing where she was going to work or what amount of money she was going to earn.

For those using public programs, variability in hours meant variability in eligibility due to fluctuating income. Transitions over and under the eligibility line resulted in repeated recertification. For every year since the start of the ethnography, one single African American mother with four children had worked at the local fairgrounds while she was on hiatus from her job as a teacher's assistant in the Milwaukee public schools. During the summer she put in about eighty hours per week. Her hours fluctuated from week to week, and she worked a lot of nights and weekends. As the summer came to an end, however, she knew that she would be working fewer hours. That was both good and bad, she said. She appreciated working less, but she also foresaw the hardships that would come with less money. In the fall, when her hours at the fairgrounds decreased, she found it difficult to make ends meet. The fairgrounds was paying her less, but she was not yet getting paid from her teacher's assistant job. She did not use many forms of government assistance because she was sure that her earnings over the summer pushed her over the limits, but once her hours decreased, she became eligible for assistance once again.

The constant recalibration of family routines required split-second changes in work supports, like child care, and made for difficulties in planning much of anything ahead of time. Rose had a hard time managing unexpected work, especially in the evening or at night. She worked for a temp agency an average of fifteen to twenty hours a week as a nursing assistant. She rarely worked over thirty hours a week, but she usually made enough to pay her bills. However, she frequently had to turn down jobs because she needed time to arrange child care. Other mothers felt that it was difficult to plan their daily routines and family activities, even doctor's appointments. Like Samantha, who worked part-time at a local eatery for about twenty hours a week, many mothers found that variability in their work schedules heightened the tension between wanting to spend time with their children and earning enough money to meet basic needs.

Samantha said that the way her job at the local restaurant schedules work periods makes it really hard for her to plan things for her kids, specifically scheduling doctor appointments. The schedule at work is made every Sunday, so you are supposed to call Sunday night to find out if you are working Monday morning. Then on Monday you can find out the rest of the [week's] schedule. Samantha said that [her schedule] is not regular. Sometimes she opens and works from nine to three. Other times she works from ten-thirty to four. Sometimes she works at night until closing. She never knows what her schedule will be from one week to the next. You can ask not to be scheduled for a particular day because you have something planned, but what happens then is you end up being scheduled very little, if at all. Samantha said that she asked for Thursday off, and had her mom fill in for her. She ended up not getting scheduled for four days straight. She cannot let that happen because she needs the money. She said that her paycheck is small enough. She brings home between $150 and $200 a paycheck (which is every two weeks).

The qualitative evidence suggests that variability in work schedules could exacerbate the negative aspects of nonstandard work schedules. Such work hours were often dictated by the nature of the job rather than the worker's choice or family needs. As a result, mothers who worked these schedules often experienced greater difficulties in making child care arrangements and maintaining family routines and stable household incomes. Such variability, particularly when not expected, may have led to the higher levels of depressive symptoms we found among children whose mothers worked variable nonstandard schedules.

Even though variable work schedules often presented difficulties, about half of the NHES mothers (twenty-two out of forty) strongly preferred work schedules that gave them the flexibility to manage household chores, accommodate their children's daily routines, and tend to family emergencies. These mothers explicitly sought out jobs that allowed them to change their hours. Dulce, for example, said that she chose to stay at a low-paying job because it had very flexible shifts. She was able to arrange her schedule to accommodate her children's school schedule, with no interference or problems. Similarly, Ana disliked her job on a nonstandard schedule but kept it instead of taking another one that would have required that she work from 9:00 A.M. to 5:00 P.M. on a fixed schedule; the difference was that her current job had flexible hours. For these mothers, it is evident that flexibility in work schedules played a crucial role in the logistics of balancing family and work. Compared to Ana and Dulce, L'Kesha, who worked full-time as a receptionist at a homeless shelter from 8:00 A.M. to 4:00 P.M., had little flexibility in her work schedule. She found it extremely difficult to take care of her daughter while working full-time. If her daughter was sick, she always had to fight to take a day off. If she did take a day off, her supervisor lectured her about her responsibility to work. L'Kesha once took a day off because her daughter had the flu. When she called in to tell her boss that she was going to have to take the day off, her boss told her with a negative attitude, "You *need* to be at work, and the child *needs* to be at school." L'Kesha said that her supervisor was always trying to make her feel bad, as though she was not a fit employee, when she needed to take time off because of her daughter.

Single mothers in the sample needed flexibility in their work schedules because they had few external sources of support. One such mother was Katrina, who struggled with the dilemmas of family and work as a sole caregiver. At the end of the ethnography, she said that she desperately wanted flexibility in her work hours. She had been getting off work late and could not get dinner together until 8:00 P.M., which she thought was too late for her children to eat. She said, "I'm tired of being the only one responsible. I want to have choices." She felt that she did not have any options because she was the only one responsible for her children.

Although 55 percent of the mothers in the ethnography appreciated flexibility in their work schedules, the ways in which they were able to achieve flexibility showed great heterogeneity. Only two of these mothers worked for an employer that sponsored programs, such as flextime, that gave workers the option of changing their starting and ending hours of employment. When Leora, one of those two mothers, worked a fixed standard schedule from 8:00 A.M. to 5:00 P.M. on weekdays, she found it difficult to work an eight-hour day and then come home and take care of her daughter. Later, when Leora took advantage of her employer's flextime policy and left work early (3:30 P.M.) a couple of days a week, she found that she was less stressed and could spend more quality time with her daughter in the afternoons and evenings. Only three out of forty mothers were able to use sick days or vacation days to tend to family emergencies, such as a family member's illness. Katie, for example, could accumulate her sick days and vacation days and then take off work with pay when necessary.

Not having access to these benefits, the majority of mothers used less traditional approaches to sustain flexibility in their work schedules. Many preferred to work in temp positions, despite the lack of formal benefits. For example, Shaquita said that she preferred working for an agency because she had flexibility in determining when she would work. Like Shaquita, Rose, an African American mother in her early twenties, said that she preferred temp work; she worked for a nursing placement agency as a temp rather than in a permanent position on staff at a nursing facility. She said that taking a job on staff somewhere might force her to work regular hours and that such a work schedule might or might not coincide with other things in her life. Nevertheless, later in the ethnography Rose acknowledged that being a temp had its costs. She said that sometimes she found it difficult to get good placements and hours consistent enough to meet her family's needs. Moreover, as a temp, she lacked health benefits and had few opportunities for advancement.

Some mothers preferred to work split shifts in order to have one or two weekdays free to run errands, do household chores, and care for children. For example, early in Dulce's time in the ethnography, she kept her job as a crossing guard, even though she felt the job was dangerous, because her work hours were 8:25 to 9:15 A.M., 11:55 A.M. to 1:05 P.M., and then 3:35 to 4:30 P.M., Monday through Friday. She felt that this was one of the only jobs with a work schedule that would allow her to pick up her children from school. Alma, her youngest daughter, went to kindergarten from 8:00 to 11 A.M. Maria and Tomas went to the same school from 8:00 A.M. to 5:00 P.M. Dulce picked Alma up from school on her way to work at 11:55 A.M. Alma would then go to work with her until 4:30 P.M., when Dulce picked up her other children from school. Similarly, Marina contrasted her experiences working two different schedules at a child care center. She used to work four days a week, for ten hours a day. Then her boss wanted her to come in every weekday for eight hours. Marina said that she did not want to do that, because she liked having that day, not only to run errands that she was unable to do during the week but also to renew her energy. She was eventually suspended from this job for seven days without pay, because her W-2 (welfare) appointment ran late and she returned to work late from her lunch break and did not clock back into work.

Finally, other mothers preferred to be self-employed. They felt that this allowed for maximum flexibility in balancing work and family demands. For Wendy, running a day care facility out of her own home was an ideal situation. An African American single mother in her midthirties, she felt that self-employment gave her a greater degree of flexibility than she had experienced when she was working for other employers. Like many who are self-employed, she frequently worked all hours of the day and evening and found this exhausting. But running her own child care center allowed her to fulfill her main goal, which was to be at home for her sons.

The ethnographic evidence suggests that variable shifts can offer low-income mothers flexibility in their work schedule to help them manage the dual demands of work and family. Such a schedule allowed mothers to tend to family emergencies as needed, manage household chores, run errands, and make welfare and doctor appointments during the day so that they were able to spend more time with their children at night and on weekends. These forms of involvement in their children's lives may help explain why variable work hours, particularly during the daytime, did not show negative effects on child development in our survey data. Some women selected this kind of schedule as the best adaptation for them (given that their other work options were not very generous), and these were the women who reported more positive routines and parenting experiences.

CONCLUSION

The complex schedules of low-income families are perhaps no different from those of higher-income families. They occur, however, in the context of fewer resources and opportunities for choosing hours or flexibility. The stories of working-poor mothers in the New Hope study make it clear that employment at nonstandard times came with both costs and benefits. In some cases, nonstandard schedules or variable shifts allowed mothers to resolve many of the hardships associated with low-wage work and single-parenthood. These mothers found it easier to work on nonstandard schedules than exclusively during daytime weekday hours. They felt that they were able to earn money to support their families while maximizing the amount of quality time they spent with their children, particularly before and after school. Indeed, the majority of working mothers in the full New Hope sample (68 percent of working respondents at the sixty-month follow-up interviews) said that their current job gave them the flexibility to handle their children and family emergencies (see chapter 4). For mothers who could rely on a network of informal child care arrangements provided by relatives, partners, or friends, and who preferred to use such care, child care did not pose a barrier to work on nonstandard schedules. Working overtime hours or multiple jobs gave some mothers a sense of pride and accomplishment from maintaining financial independence without the help of others or the government.

On the other hand, working-poor mothers remained keenly aware of the costs of working nonstandard schedules. Chronic stress and exhaustion were rampant among those who worked nonstandard schedules, and some of these mothers felt that their fatigue made them less effective as parents. Such feelings were particularly common among mothers who worked overtime hours or multiple jobs. New Hope mothers also expressed concerns about spending too much time apart from their children, particularly during the afternoon and evening hours. Working at nonstandard times could be an extraordinary hardship when there was no one to care for children in the evening, at night, or on the weekend.

Similarly, work on variable shifts benefited some parents but was a hardship for others. The difference between liking and not liking variable schedules tended to come down to whether a mother worked these hours by choice. The mothers in the NHES sample disliked unforeseen variability in their work schedules. They said that instability in their work hours made it difficult to plan their finances and family routines and arrange child care.

At the same time, the majority of mothers preferred flexibility in their work schedules to manage household chores, accommodate their children's daily routines, and tend to family emergencies. These mothers sought out jobs that allowed them to tend to their families as needed. However, almost none of the mothers had access to flextime benefits at work that might have allowed them to take some days off to tend to family needs.

Taken together, this ethnographic evidence provides critical insights into the pattern of quantitative findings from the survey data. We found that maternal employment on nonstandard schedules per se did not pose a developmental risk for children. Although we found that mothers who worked fixed nonstandard schedules felt more time pressure than mothers who worked fixed standard schedules, mothers who worked fixed nonstandard schedules also experienced less stress. Here the ethnographic evidence identifies several factors that may help explain this pattern in the quantitative findings. For some working-poor mothers, the benefits of nonstandard schedules outweighed the costs. For other mothers, the costs of nonstandard schedules were much too difficult to endure. However, in the quantitative analyses, the benefits and costs of working nonstandard schedules may have offset each other.

What about the consequences for children of variable shifts? We found effects in opposite directions, depending on whether the variable shifts occurred in combination with nonstandard hours. When mothers worked variable shifts during daytime hours, their children appeared to be more engaged in school, according to teachers' reports, than when mothers worked fixed daytime hours. In contrast, when mothers worked variable shifts at nonstandard times, their children appeared worse off. These two factors, when experienced together, appear to have had a synergistically negative effect on children. Those whose mothers worked these schedules showed less engagement in school, lower school performance, and more externalizing behavior problems than children whose mothers worked fixed standard schedules.

The qualitative evidence also helps us interpret this contrary pattern of results. For those mothers who work variable shifts at nonstandard times, the variability in their work schedule could potentiate the negative aspects of its being nonstandard. Such work hours were often dictated by the nature of the job rather than the worker's choice or family needs. As a result, mothers who worked these schedules often experienced greater difficulties in making child care arrangements and maintaining family routines during the "off hours" when formal child care was less available. Variation in hours could make earnings fluctuate and cause repeated crossings of eligibility thresholds for federal forms of assistance, resulting in uncertain financial situations. In addition, mothers often had to make sudden adjustments to child care arrangements when brief changes sent their family income above mandated income limits and they lost support from child care subsidy programs (Lowe and Weisner 2004). Such changes, particularly when not expected, may have led to the higher rates at which withdrawn and depressed behaviors were observed among children whose mothers worked variable nonstandard schedules.

In contrast, mothers who worked variable shifts during the day appeared to be better able to manage the demands of family and work than those mothers who worked fixed schedules. The ethnographic evidence suggests that variable shifts can offer low-income mothers flexibility in their daytime work schedules. Such schedules allowed mothers to tend to family emergencies as needed, manage household chores, run errands, and make welfare and doctor's appointments during the day so that they were able to spend more time with their children at night and on weekends. These forms of involvement in their children's lives may help explain why the survey data showed positive effects of variable work hours during daytime hours.

The flexibility of work schedules was important for family processes and children's well-being in both the survey and ethnographic data. Yet national estimates indicate that a much smaller portion of low-wage and low-income workers are likely to have control over their work schedules. In data from the 1997 National Study of the Changing Workforce, researchers at the Families and Work Institute found that only 26 percent of low-wage and low-income workers reported getting paid time off to care for sick children; 32 percent reported being able to choose their start and end times on the job, and 57 percent said that if they took advantage of flextime benefits they would be less likely to advance on the job. In contrast, among their higher-wage and higher-income counterparts, 57 percent received paid time off to care for sick children, 49 percent had discretion over their start and end times on the job, and only 37 percent reported that they would be less likely to advance if they used available flextime benefits (Bond 2003).

In our study, the ethnographic data highlight the following strategies that could be explored to promote flexibility in low-income parents' work schedules: (1) employer-sponsored programs, such as flextime, that give workers discretion over their start and end times on the job; (2) benefits, such as sick or vacation days; (3) split shifts; (4) self-employment. However, the ethnographic evidence also highlights the need for work schedules to be predictable in nature. We explore these workplace and policy strategies in more detail in chapter 13.

In sum, the data presented in this chapter show that the majority of mothers in the New Hope program and control groups experienced nonstandard and variable work schedules, that negotiating the trade-offs of low-wage work and single-parenthood in a 24/7 economy is a struggle, and that issues of control and choice over such schedules are crucial for low-wage workers. Variable shifts appeared to matter for children's well-being, although associations were in opposite directions depending on whether they were experienced during the daytime (with some suggestion of flexibility) or during nonstandard hours (with the suggestion of cumulative stresses). The findings suggest that predictability and flexibility in work schedules can ease the hardships associated with low-wage work and single-parenthood. These results also support the finding reported in chapter 4 that in their perceptions of job quality, mothers in our sample highly valued flexibility as a job characteristic.

Chapter Six | Discrimination in the Low-Wage Workplace: The Unspoken Barrier to Employment

Amanda L. Roy, Hirokazu Yoshikawa, and Sandra Nay

WE TURN IN this chapter from the dynamic nature of work trajectories and overall job quality to a more specific domain of work experience: discrimination. We were struck by the scope and depth of workplace discrimination experienced by the New Hope mothers. Again and again they spoke of being treated unfairly at work owing to their race, ethnicity, or sex. These experiences affected their well-being not only as workers but as parents.

Discrimination in the workplace is important not only because of its harmful effects on well-being and health (Krieger 2003; Krieger, Sidney, and Coakley 1998; Schneider, Hitlan, and Radhakrishnan 2000), but also because of its particularly potent function as a barrier to employment. For example, a recent longitudinal study of welfare recipients in Michigan found that, after adjusting for a variety of work experiences, education, skills, family backgrounds, and other factors, experiences of discrimination strongly predicted lower work effort (Danziger, Corcoran, et al. 2000; Kalil, Schweingruber, and Seefeldt 2001). The association of discrimination with work effort, in fact, was as powerful as that of having less than a high school education or having few job skills.[1] Experiences of workplace discrimination are also related to problematic health and mental health (Fitzgerald et al. 1997; Schneider, Swan, and Fitzgerald 1997). These parent factors, in turn, can harm children's well-being (Downey and Coyne 1990; Mistry et al. 2002). Thus, workplace discrimination may have negative effects on employees and indirect effects on their children.

Most of the research on discrimination in the workplace has been conducted with middle- and upper-class workers. We know very little about how low-wage workers experience discrimination, or how these experiences affect future work or well-being. In this chapter, we take an in-depth look at the effect of workplace discrimination on low-wage workers and their employment experiences. Specifically, we examine the reports of New Hope mothers about their experiences of discrimination of two kinds: racial-ethnic and sexual. We also assess the relationship between these experiences of discrimination and different dynamic patterns of employment. And finally, we investigate the individual and contextual factors related to discrimination. In this way, we begin to answer the questions of how low-wage workers experience discrimination in the workplace and how it is related to their employment decisions.

Answering these questions is particularly important given that the federal welfare reform enacted in 1996 has now brought hundreds of thousands of new entrants into the workforce. Also, many of these workers are at particular risk for experiencing discrimination because of the "multiple jeopardies" they face being women of color working in low-status jobs. Given the lack of information on experiences of discrimination in low-income work environments, particularly for women workers of color, we have yet to fully understand experiences of the workplace post-1996. Additionally, by considering experiences of workplace discrimination in relation to patterns of employment, we aim to identify characteristics of the workplace that might be associated with experiences of discrimination. We will see that nearly half of this sample reported experiences of discrimination at work. About one-quarter of those who reported discrimination cited both sexual and racial-ethnic discrimination, suggesting that low-wage workers who are women of color may be particularly at risk of experiencing discrimination. Finally, we explore the relationships between discrimination, employment patterns, and individual characteristics. The results suggest that experiences of discrimination are related to membership in the low-wage–part-time or rapid cycler employment clusters. We explore why these work pathway patterns are more commonly associated with experiences of discrimination.

As we explore the workplace discrimination experiences of the New Hope sample, it is important to keep in mind the context. In 1960 only 8 percent of Milwaukee's inner-city population were people of color. Over the next twenty-five years, the city underwent massive suburbanization of the white population. Discriminatory housing practices made it nearly impossible for blacks to settle in the suburbs, forcing them into inner-city areas to an even greater extent than was the case in other cities of comparable size. By 1985, 87 percent of Milwaukee inner-city residents were African American. This division in patterns of residence continues today and has made Milwaukee one of the most segregated cities in America (Orum 1995; Rury and Cassell 1993). In this context, it is important to examine how race- or ethnicity-based discrimination is experienced by workers of color in Milwaukee, such as those who make up the majority of the New Hope sample.

CONCEPTUALIZING DISCRIMINATION

Workplace discrimination includes a variety of behaviors and actions, many of which can be subtle, depending on the perceiver. There is no one way to define these experiences. From a legal perspective, workplace discrimination is defined as any behaviors that inhibit employment opportunities based on race, color, religion, sex, or national origin (U.S. Equal Employment Opportunity Commission 2004). Harassment is usually defined as a subtype of discrimination that includes verbal or physical conduct based on race, color, religion, sex, or national origin that creates a hostile working environment. Harassment is considered to have occurred when submission to or rejection of this conduct explicitly or implicitly affects an individual's employment, when such conduct unreasonably interferes with an individual's work performance, or when it creates an intimidating, hostile, or offensive work environment (U.S. Equal Employment Opportunity Commission 2004).

Researchers, on the other hand, have used a huge array of definitions of workplace discrimination that do not coincide exactly with legal definitions. For example, measures of workplace discrimination often include perceptions of unfair treatment, negative interactions with supervisors or coworkers, or hearing hostile comments about particular groups. Although differences in the conceptualization of discrimination exist, the majority of the research done on workplace discrimination recognizes the role of power differences. Two power-related models are commonly used as frameworks for understanding discrimination. The organizational power model argues that institutions have vertical power structures that contribute to the occurrence of discrimination (Fain and Anderton 1987; Tangri, Burt, and Johnson 1982). According to this model, workplace discrimination is motivated by differences in occupational status, with those in the lowest standing experiencing the majority of the discrimination. Because women and minorities tend to occupy the lowest positions in the vertical power structure, they are most likely to experience discrimination. The patriarchal power model proposes that sexual discrimination is a manifestation of the power imbalances between men and women (Farley 1978; MacKinnon 1979). This model assumes that discrimination occurs between men and women regardless of the position they occupy in the organizational structure of the workplace. The patriarchal model can also be applied to racial-ethnic discrimination, driven by the power imbalance between majority- and minority-group members. Understanding the role that power plays in discrimination is essential when considering the experiences of a low-income population. Not only were the women in our sample subject to inequities in power based on their sex and race-ethnicity, but they also tended to occupy low-status jobs, a factor that can also contribute to an imbalance in power.

To explore the prevalence and forms of discrimination experienced by the mothers in the New Hope sample, we relied on the ethnographic data. These data consist of their accounts of their work experiences; the field-workers did not ask the mothers' employers or other employees at their workplaces for their accounts. Because limited work has been done on workplace discrimination in low-income populations, the analysis of the field notes did not rely on predetermined definitions of discrimination. We deemed an experience discriminatory if it met all of the following conditions: (1) it occurred in the workplace; (2) it resulted in differential treatment or experiences; and (3) it was based on personal characteristics such as race or sex.

The proportion of women who mentioned experiences of discrimination was quite high.[2] Of the forty women in the ethnographic sample, seventeen (43 percent) reported having encountered discrimination in the workplace at some time. Of these seventeen, eleven reported discrimination that occurred during the period of the ethnography. The examples of workplace discrimination fell into two primary categories, sexual and racial-ethnic.

SEXUAL DISCRIMINATION

Although many employers in the United States have attempted to reduce sexual discrimination in their workplaces, it continues to be something that many working women experience. Approximately one of every two women will experience some form of sexual discrimination at some point during her working career. This estimate has not significantly changed since sexual discrimination gained visibility in the early 1980s (Fitzgerald and Shulman 1993). Of the seventeen women in our sample who reported some form of discrimination, nine (53 percent) described discrimination that was sexual in nature.

Iris was a white woman whose work history was characterized by low work hours. Her work experiences had not been positive, and although she believed that having a job was important in terms of providing for the household, she often found working to be stressful. These feelings were compounded by a variety of health problems that limited her ability to work long hours and the types of jobs that she could hold. Despite the challenges that Iris faced in the workplace, she still viewed herself as someone who stood up for herself at work. She described a situation in which she experienced sexual discrimination while working at a factory temp job. The field-worker wrote:

> One of the first few days she was working, [when] she was sitting at a table by herself, a coworker threw a penis at her made out of tinfoil. She was very upset and told the manager that she wanted something done about it because this was sexual harassment. The manager told her to relax, that it was just joking around and it was meant in jest. Iris was very offended by the actions and did not think it was fair that she should be treated this way while the manager looked the other way. She said that she created a fuss because it was not right to do that to her. The next night, [when] she returned to the job, they did not have an assignment for her. Everyone else on her bus was placed in an assignment but her. She had to take the bus home without an assignment. Iris was angry because she knew that she was not placed because she stood up for herself.

Iris was very offended by the sexual discrimination she experienced and responded by bringing it to the attention of her manager. Her manager did not feel that it was a problem, and Iris's complaint resulted in the loss of her job. Although the temp agency where she was employed offered to find her another job, she chose to leave the agency because she no longer wanted to work for them.

Iris's experience shows how the organizational context of sexual harassment can exacerbate its effects on well-being and work motivation. The factory manager to whom she reported her experience downplayed the episode, and ultimately Iris left both the temp placement and the agency. Although it is difficult to disentangle the many potential reasons for her low levels of work effort during the ethnographic period, Iris herself viewed this episode as contributing to her reluctance to find a new job outside the home. She ended up working at home, becoming certified as a foster parent for her two nephews.

The sexual discrimination that women experience at work can come in many forms. Louise Fitzgerald and her colleagues have identified three categories: *sexual comments and gestures,* which include hostile, offensive, and misogynist remarks and behavior; *unwanted sexual attention,* that is, sexual attention that is not desired and not reciprocated; and *sexual coercion,* in which job-related outcomes are made contingent on sexual cooperation (Fitzgerald, Gelfand, and Drasgow 1995; Fitzgerald et al. 1988). These categories were established by drawing largely on the experiences of white, middle-class women. We sought to determine whether they also captured the experiences of low-income women in the New Hope study.

On the whole, the three categories did capture the experiences described by the women in our sample. The instances of sexual discrimination fell into two groups, sexual comments and gestures and unwanted sexual attention. None of the women in our sample mentioned instances of sexual coercion, though there may certainly have been some that were not reported. The lower base rates for this form of sexual discrimination may also explain the lack of reports in our sample. The instances of sexual discrimination reported by this sample were thus coded for only the two categories of sexual comments and gestures and unwanted sexual attention.[3]

Sexual Comments and Gestures

Of the nine cases of sexual discrimination, five fit the category of sexual comments and gestures. In the case of Iris, we saw how one woman experienced both sexual comments and gestures and unwanted sexual attention. Like Iris, Allison, an African-American woman who worked in the automotive industry during the course of the ethnography, experienced sexual comments from her coworkers. She linked her experiences with sexual discrimination to working in a male-dominated field. According to her field-worker,

> Allison knows that there are a lot of gender issues in the auto industry, but she has learned to cope with it. Most of the time she ignores the sexist comments and shakes it off by saying something like, "Freako," or, "Sicko," and moves on. "I ignore men saying stupid things," she announces and reassures me that it does not bother her. She pauses for a moment and adds, "That's a new term I have learned, 'freako'," and smiles. Other women have problems, and her manager asked her to have a chat with one of them—he asked Allison to explain to the other woman how Allison handles men in her job. Allison says it with obvious pride that she can cope with harassment and does not let that bother her. She feels that she is quite an anomaly in her workplace. Typically women who work in these jobs are big, burly women. Allison is petite and looks "like a girl" and yet can still manage the work perfectly. That sometimes surprises people.

Allison felt that she did not fit the stereotypic expectations about a woman working in her field and that this motivated many of the sexist comments she received. It is clear from this excerpt that she learned to cope with the discrimination she encountered from her coworkers. Allison was proud of the fact that she did not let the sexual discrimination at her workplace interfere with her ability to do her job.

Unwanted Sexual Advances

Of the nine women who reported sexual discrimination, four mentioned unwanted sexual advances (and as mentioned earlier, Iris reported being the object of both sexual comments and gestures and unwanted sexual advances). Trisha was a white woman who worked for a short period of time during the ethnography at a scrap yard. Trisha's boss on this job made sexual advances toward her, telling her that she could come to his house and take a shower. Unlike Allison, who was harassed by her colleagues, Trisha was harassed by her boss. Trisha remained at this job for only a short period of time before quitting.

Rhonda, an African-American mother of two, experienced unwanted sexual advances while working as a home health aide during the ethnography. The discrimination was not initiated by her boss or coworkers but rather by her patients. The field-worker wrote: "The amputee male patients (5:00–7:00 P.M.) occasionally ask if they can touch her breasts. She just ignores it. She knows that other home health aides will occasionally supplement their income with accepting money for such favors." Rhonda did not let the sexual advances of her patients interfere with her job. She coped with the situation by ignoring their advances.

These stories show that the level of the social hierarchy at which discrimination is experienced makes a difference in its effect on well-being. Trisha's experience of discrimination was instigated by her boss, while Rhonda's came from a patient. This difference in position in the workplace hierarchy may explain why Trisha had to leave her job while Rhonda stayed at hers. Harassment from someone who has a higher position in the workplace may have more of a negative effect than harassment from someone in a lower position. This may be particularly true for women who already occupy low-status jobs. Very little research has examined the differential effects of discrimination from different levels of low-wage workplaces.

RACIAL-ETHNIC DISCRIMINATION

Like sexual discrimination, racial-ethnic discrimination continues to be a problem in the American workplace. In 2003 the U.S. Equal Employment Opportunity Commission (2004) filed 6,180 racially motivated discrimination charges, a number significantly higher than those received based on sex (4,906) or national origin (2,365). The racial-ethnic workplace discrimination described by the women in our sample took place in the context of extreme racial-ethnic segregation. The two neighborhoods selected to take part in the New Hope Project were two of Milwaukee's poorest. The majority of the South Side neighborhood residents were Latino, and the majority of the North Side neighborhood residents were black (Bos et al. 1999). Although both neighborhoods were economically depressed, the North Side neighborhood had been particularly affected by Milwaukee's long history of racial-ethnic segregation and discrimination. It had been part of the "Inner Core" of the city, and subject to increasing segregation, since the 1950s. According to 2000 U.S. census data, about half of the North Side neighborhood's census tracts were over 70 percent African American, and about one-quarter were over 85 percent African American (U.S. Census Bureau 2004).[4]

Of the seventeen women in our sample who reported experiences of workplace discrimination, thirteen described discrimination that was racially or ethnically motivated. Lynette was an African-American mother of two whose pattern of work was characterized by rapid movement through a number of jobs. She enjoyed being employed, not only because it allowed her to buy her sons things she would otherwise not be able to, but also because it energized her and provided her with a purpose. Her employment history was diverse: her prior jobs had ranged from working in fast food to being employed by an insurance agency. Throughout the ethnography, Lynette continued the same cycling pattern, rotating through several jobs. At the start of the study, Lynette was seasonally employed at an insurance agency doing tax preparation work. Although she found the job personally rewarding, she continued to look for another job that would provide her with higher wages and medical benefits. When she did in fact receive a more lucrative job offer and told the insurance agency she might leave to take the full-time position, her boss agreed to make her a full-time employee at the agency, with a substantial increase in wages and full medical benefits.

Lynette was happy with the stability she gained from her promotion. She also felt that she was very good at her job and served as a role model for the other employees. However, there were negative aspects of her work environment as well. Fewer than half of the employees in her office were people of color. The employees of color represented a variety of different racial-ethnic groups, including Indian, African American, and Latino. Lynette felt that some of the supervisors were prejudiced. She described one supervisor's offensive jokes and refusal to stop making them even when asked to. She also saw differences in how white and minority employees were treated. Lynette's field-worker wrote:

> Lynette told me that one way in which they are prejudiced is how they [the white supervisors] will give minority employees a hard time about things but

not the other employees. For example, she explained that her (African-American) friend had a troubled son and had to regularly go to court with him every other week or so. She would come in during the morning, leave, and then return at the end of the day. The management gave her a very hard time about this, but didn't bat an eye when another (white) employee regularly came in sobbing and unable to work, and was called away to handle her truant son despite the fact that her husband was home. Lynette said that the management has perceptions that favor the white workers. Similarly, they will put her (African-American) supervisor on probation, but not discipline other workers.

Lynette responded to experiences of discrimination by standing up for herself when she felt that her ability to do her job was brought into question. She said, "Whatever he sees me doing, if he don't say nothing, it ain't nobody else's place to say anything. And if they don't like it, they can kiss my butt, and if I ever hear them come my way, I will pull them into the boss's office and tell them what I got to say to them and I'm done. Leave me alone." After more than two years of employment, Lynette was fired from her job at the insurance agency. She felt that her termination was not fair. Although she was told that she was being let go because she was not able to keep up with the workload, she felt that the real reason was her refusal to "kiss ass." She believed the management was just looking for something to pick on her about. Lynette's supervisor, who was also African American, was fired at the same time. Lynette hoped that their stories, along with the story of another African American who had been fired shortly before Lynette, would make the discrimination apparent. She intended to file a lawsuit charging wrongful termination.

Lynette's story weaves together several themes that emerged in other material on racial-ethnic discrimination in the ethnography, including the racial makeup of the workplace, differential treatment by race, verbal comments with racial content, and coping with and responses to discrimination. Past research on racial-ethnic workplace discrimination has categorized discriminatory behaviors into two groups: verbal conduct with a racial-ethnic component and unequal job treatment (Schneider, Hitlan, and Radhakrishnan 2000). These categories encompass the experiences described in our sample, but a third dimension emerged from those descriptions as well: perceived imbalance in workplace racial-ethnic composition. Many of the racial-ethnic discrimination experiences fell into multiple categories. The majority of the thirteen women who reported experiencing racial-ethnic discrimination were women of color. Six were African American, five were Latina, one was African American/Filipina, and one was white.

Unequal Access to Opportunities and Resources

The most common form of discrimination reported by the New Hope mothers was unequal access to opportunities and resources. Eight of the thirteen women reported experiences that fell into this category. For instance, as discussed earlier, Lynette described how her African-American coworker was hassled for leaving work to take care of her son while nothing was said to a white coworker with the same problem. Like Lynette, Katrina, a half-African-American, half-Filipino woman who worked at a bank, perceived unequal access to opportunities in her workplace. During the ethnography, Katrina was steadily employed leasing credit card machines. She commented that although she valued working and would rather be working than staying at home, she found her job boring and lacking in variety. Additionally, she felt that there were differences in treatment and opportunities for white and African-American employees. The field-worker wrote:

> Katrina thinks that race is an issue at her job, even though she has never experienced it firsthand. She said that in the six months she has been there, she has watched lots of white people get promoted but no black people. Apparently, a black employee wrote a memo about this, and within a day a black person got a promotion, one that she hadn't applied for. They also had their group employee meeting, and seven white people got promotions. Her boss told the group, though, that the reason these people were getting promotions was because they "gave 110 percent" and they deserved it. Katrina said she lost all desire to work there after that. She felt like her boss was insulting the black employees, implying that they did not give 110 percent. Katrina feels like the white management people see what they want to see, and they don't look at the effort that the black people are putting forth. Katrina said it didn't really affect her anyway, since she has to wait until they are "ready to promote yellow people" (she's half-Filipino, half-African-American). . . . She also noticed that when her old boss had meetings, he would group the whites with the whites, and the blacks with the blacks. Her boss asked her if she thought that this was racist, and she said it could be. Racism, however, was not the reason she was leaving her job—"it's just boring."

Although Katrina felt that her boss was partially responsible for the discrimination she witnessed at her job, it is clear that she thought it was part of a larger issue, that racism was pervasive throughout her workplace. Katrina's comments suggest that the promotion practices at her job had created a general climate of hostility, including unequal opportunities for advancement.

Marisa, a Latina mother of five children, described being a target of the hostile climate and inequities at her workplace. At the start of the ethnography, Marisa was employed as a teacher's assistant in a public school. Even though Marisa had worked full-time at this job for eleven years, she did not like it because she felt that she had no opportunities for advancement. Additionally, she described the management at the school as "white, and racist against Latinos." Marisa provided an example of how school resources were not made equally available to all employees. The field-worker wrote:

> Marisa says there is much racism in this society. For example, when she started working at the school, the Hispanics were segregated. The school depended on funds for the bilingual programs, but the Hispanic teachers could not use the photocopy machine. One day, Marisa was denied the key code for the photocopy machine. All this changed when one day, in a loud voice, in the presence of a school counselor, she said there was racism against Hispanics because they were not allowed access to some resources. Marisa started spreading the word to the students that they were being discriminated against. Within a week, the problem was resolved because they did not want this idea to be spread amongst the students.

Marisa's experience of discrimination was closely linked to her perception of a racist climate at the school. Although she experienced the inequity in resources firsthand, she did not hold one person responsible; rather, she attributed the inequity to the racist management in general. Both Katrina and Marisa responded to an experience of discrimination with confrontation, and in both cases a confrontational response produced immediate change, confirming their sense that the discrimination had been real.

Samantha, an African-American woman, linked her experience of discrimination to broader inequities in job opportunities. For a short period of time during the ethnography, Samantha was employed at a video store. One evening while Samantha was working the night shift, the store was robbed at gunpoint. She thought that one reason the police were slow to respond to the crime scene was because the employees were black. She said, "You know that if it was the middle of the day when all the white people work up in here, the police would have been right over. But no, they know it's late at night, when only the black people work, and this little, skinny white manager. They don't care about us, and they are in no hurry to protect us, you know." Samantha felt not only that the slow police response to the robbery was racially motivated, but also that the neighborhood employment patterns were discriminatory. She pointed out the racial-ethnic division in the hours that the white and black employees worked at the video store and other local stores. Samantha felt that this inequity was putting her safety at risk, and as a result she quit the job.

Although these cases of racial-ethnic discrimination appear to demonstrate unequal access to opportunities and resources among coworkers, some of the mothers also tie these experiences to their sense of inequity at higher organizational and institutional levels. This may reflect their higher levels of critical consciousness, which Paolo Freire (1971) and others have characterized as central to the organizing of marginalized people. The critically conscious observer can perceive patterns of discrimination by generalizing from individual incidents involving particular people. Both Katrina and Marisa linked the unequal access to resources and opportunities in their jobs to what they described as the "white management." Additionally, Samantha felt that the patterns of employment in her entire neighborhood were discriminatory and put her at risk of crime. Although the specific instances of discrimination they described involved individuals, these mothers perceived a general climate of discrimination that coincided with a lack of diversity in the workplace and in the neighborhood. Studies have in fact found that the race and sex composition of workplaces is related to the occurrence of discriminatory behaviors and to employee well-being. Women and racial minorities report more stereotyping and negative evaluations in work settings in which their group is underrepresented (Reskin, McBrier, and Kmec 1999). Tyrone Forman (2003) has demonstrated a negative relationship between perceived racial segmentation and overall psychological well-being in both a national and a local probability sample of African Americans. This association remained significant after controlling for perceived workplace discrimination as well as sociodemographic and workplace characteristics.

Derogatory Racial-Ethnic Comments and Gestures

Seven women (half of the group that reported racial-ethnic discrimination) described situations in which racial or ethnic slurs were made. For example, Evelia is a Latina woman who had worked as a temporary employee for the post office for over two years. She was very frustrated in the job because she had the same duties as the permanent staff but was paid less and was not provided with benefits. Although Evelia liked some of her coworkers at the post office, she also felt that there were a lot of racist people working there as well. The field-worker wrote: "She told me about a 'white man who doesn't like the blacks, but he dates black women and then he says very bad things about them.' " On another occasion,

> Evelia told me that one of the guys opened the refrigerator in the lunch room and said loudly: "This seems like a fucking welfare refrigerator." Evelia got

really angry and thought to herself, What is a fucking welfare refrigerator? The refrigerator was full of food, what kind of mind does that man have? I was really angry, and I wanted to tell him: "Let's hope your refrigerator looks like that, because that has a lot of food, maybe your refrigerator doesn't look like that." Evelia says that he is a white man who spends all his time saying bad things about black people. Evelia and a lot of employees are angry because a few days ago he was promoted to supervisor.

Evelia was very upset by the discrimination that she experienced at her job, particularly by the comments made by her racist coworker. Work by Martin Gilens (1999) has demonstrated that the cash assistance component of welfare is by far the most stigmatized government program, owing to its close association with racialized stereotypes of black mothers on welfare. In several national datasets, he showed that the association of disapproval of cash welfare assistance with lack of support for government spending was almost entirely explained by stereotypes of African Americans as lazy. Evelia's perception that the "welfare refrigerator" comment was racially motivated is thus supported in the research on this topic. Evelia's negative feelings toward her coworker were exacerbated when he was promoted to the position of supervisor; meanwhile, she had stayed at the job for over two years without achieving permanent staff status. Some New Hope mothers did appear to link episodes of discrimination to the more general organizational contexts they faced.

Not all of the instances of racially motivated comments and gestures were as blatant as those described by Evelia. Belinda was an African-American woman who worked full-time at a discount store. Although she enjoyed the work, she had difficulty relating to her white coworkers and customers:

Belinda said that she is always on her guard when she is around white people. She said that some of them are fine, but you never really know if you can trust them. She said that is true for all people, and all colors, but she gave examples of the attitudes and experiences she had with white people. Belinda said that her bosses at (the discount store) always act funny. Belinda said that one minute they will get an attitude with her. For instance, when she called in sick because she had to go to the hospital for her daughter. Belinda said that those folks acted like she was lying and didn't believe her. They just said to her with a serious attitude, "Sure, yeah, whatever." Belinda said that she always is sure to get a doctor's note so that she can bring it into work so they know that she is not lying. Belinda said that when she brought in the doctor's note to work and showed the supervisor, they would act all apologetic and nice. Belinda said that most of them are so phony. She said, "They don't act real, you know?" Belinda said that most of her coworkers are white, and they always act funny too. Belinda said they will be nice to your face and in front of other coworkers, but then she will turn around and hear them talking about the same people they were nice to like a dog. Belinda said that you just can't really trust them, that is why she just keeps her distance. Belinda said that she used to go out to lunch with them, but once she realized the way they talked about people, she figured they could be talking about her the same way, and she didn't want to hang around people like that.

Although the behaviors that Belinda described were not as clear-cut as those Evelia experienced, Belinda felt that she was treated differently because of her race-ethnicity. The situation involved only Brenda's supervisor, but it was clear from the field notes that she mistrusted both the white managers and her coworkers.

Racial Distribution of the Workplace

In a city as segregated as Milwaukee, we might expect that the racial distribution of workplaces might also be highly segregated. In fact, six of the thirteen women reporting racial-ethnic discrimination described the skewed racial composition of their workplace. As was suggested in the discussion of unequal access to opportunities and resources, perceptions of imbalance in the racial distribution of the workplace tended to occur alongside other forms of racial-ethnic discrimination. Allison, the African-American woman who worked in the auto industry during the ethnography, was not only one of the few African Americans working in a mostly white workplace but one of the few women in a male-dominated environment. The field-worker wrote:

> Allison mentioned that she was comfortable being in a white and mostly male environment at her workplace. Her mother had taught them that they have to "mix and fend" for themselves. She does stand out in her workplace environment, but she is happy at her work. Sometimes she suspects that she is not getting the right salary raises. She is comfortable with people of other races, and she has always had friends who were not black.

Although Allison was aware of the unequal distribution of minority and women employees, she claimed to be comfortable with these inequities. She mentioned the fact that she got along well with people of different races to highlight the fact that she was comfortable with the racial-ethnic distribution of her workplace. However, she also suspected that she was not advancing in her job because she was an African-American woman. As in the situations described by Katrina and Marisa, Allison drew a connection between the racial-ethnic distribution of her workplace and unequal access to opportunities.

Michol was an African-American woman who worked as a teacher at a child care center during the ethnography. She described "racial tensions" in her workplace, driven by a division between the managers and the teachers. She stated that none of the managers were African American, while the majority of the teachers and children were African American or Latino/a. She added that at one time the company had hired an African-American male in a managerial position. He was considered a double minority because he was a male in a female-dominated company. However, he quickly "figured out he didn't want to be the token" and quit. Michol saw a lack of opportunity at the center for employees of color to advance. Michol never mentioned that she was directly affected by the racial inequities in her workplace. After working at the day care center for over two years, she was eventually promoted to the position of director.

Unlike the cases of sexual discrimination, women who perceived racial-ethnic discrimination perceived it in multiple forms, particularly with respect to instances of inequity in the racial-ethnic distribution of the workplace. Many of the women who described a specific encounter with a discriminatory behavior also mentioned the general inequity of the workplace. Similarly, while experiences of sexual discrimination tended to be linked to specific harassers, experiences of racial-ethnic discrimination were more often attributed to the general "management." These patterns may be linked to Milwaukee's historical lack of diversity in management-level positions. The 1990 index of managerial diversity for the nation's fifty largest metropolitan areas listed Milwaukee as the worst city in the United States in terms of black representation in management positions and forty-fourth in terms of female employees. These numbers had improved only slightly by 1999: the index for that year demonstrated that Milwaukee was ranked forty-eighth in managerial diversity for black employees and thirty-ninth for women employees (University of Wisconsin Center for Economic Development 2001).

THE OVERLAP OF SEXUAL AND RACIAL-ETHNIC DISCRIMINATION

Because women of color may be exposed to both sexual and racial-ethnic discrimination, they are at double risk of experiencing negative work and health-related outcomes as a result of discrimination (Puryear and Mednick 1974). In a diverse sample of U.S. military personnel, Mindy Bergman and Fritz Drasgow (2003) found significant differences in rates of perceived sexual discrimination by race-ethnicity. White and Asian-American women reported the lowest levels of sexual harassment, while Latina and African-American women reported the highest. Latina and African-American women also reported significantly higher levels of racial-ethnic discrimination in the workplace than European-American women (Corbie-Smith et al. 1999).

The overlap between sex- and race-based discrimination for women of color is partially supported by the findings in our study. Four (23 percent) of the seventeen women who discussed any form of workplace discrimination described a work situation in which both sexual and racial-ethnic discrimination occurred. All were African American or Latina. For these four, it appeared that the experiences of racial-ethnic and sexual discrimination were closely related. For instance, the comments made by Evelia's coworker made her feel uncomfortable not only because they were racist but also because they were misogynistic.

The co-occurrence of racial-ethnic and sexual discrimination can also take place in the same job but come from different sources. This was the case for Samantha, who experienced racial-ethnic discrimination while working at the video store in her neighborhood. She felt that the unequal employment patterns in her neighborhood contributed to the lack of safety at her job. When the store was robbed while she was working, Samantha felt that the police failed to respond quickly because of the race-ethnicity of the employees. Additionally, Samantha felt that the store manager was sexually discriminating by only hiring men. Unlike Evelia, who experienced both racial-ethnic and sexual discrimination from the same source, Samantha experienced both types of discrimination from multiple sources within the same job.

It may be that exposure to one type of discrimination, such as workplace discrimination, increases critical consciousness (Ward 1996; Freire 1971). For example, African-American and Dominican parents who report experiences of perceived discrimination are more likely in their child-rearing to prepare their children for bias (Hughes 2003). An experience of discrimination may increase an individual's sensitivity to future instances and other forms of discrimination. For example, Evelia linked her experience of discrimination to multiple inequities in society. She recognized that this behavior is embedded in societal attitudes toward race-ethnicity, gender, and class. She related multiple critiques, for example, of the welfare system in addition to her reports of sexual and racial-ethnic discrimination in her workplaces. She also maintained, "I prefer to be poor instead of subjected to a man's fist for the rest of my life." Some of the overlap between racial-ethnic and sexual discrimination in our sample may be a result of increased attention to multiple forms of discrimination.

EMPLOYMENT PATTERNS AND DISCRIMINATION

As highlighted in chapter 3, patterns of employment over time can have effects on mothers' well-being and the development of their children. Additionally, the stories of discrimination recounted in this chapter suggest that workplace discrimination can affect an individual's decisions about employment. Could experiences of discrimination be associated with different work dynamics? For example, according to the organizational-power model of discrimination, women with lower levels of education or less work experience would be exposed to higher levels of discrimination. Experiences of discrimination and overall job quality might then affect a woman's decision to stay in a job, cycle through several jobs, or stay out of the workforce altogether. Although our data do not make it possible to examine causal relationships between discrimination and employment patterns, we can explore associations between these experiences as a first step toward understanding the interactive effect that they might have on the lives of low-wage working women.

Using the employment clusters found in chapter 2, we considered this relationship by first identifying the pathway (cluster) membership of each of the forty women in the NHES.[5] We then examined the distribution of reports of discrimination across the cluster groups. Within the ethnographic sample, there were six women we identified as rapid cyclers. Of these six, five reported at least one episode of discrimination. A similar pattern emerged for the six women assigned to the low-wage–part-time group: four of them reported discrimination. For each of the three other clusters, one-third or fewer of the women reported discrimination (see figure 6.1). The percentages who experienced discrimination were as follows: rapid cyclers, 83 percent; low-wage–part-time group, 67 percent; low-wage–full-time group, 29 percent; stable employment and full-time–wage-growth groups, 33 percent.[6] Based on these patterns, experiences of discrimination in the rapid cycler and low-wage–part-time groups were compared to instances of discrimination in the other three groups. This comparison revealed that women who reported discrimination were significantly more likely to be in the rapid cycler or low-wage–part-time group compared with the other three groups.[7] Although this finding indicates an association between cluster membership and discrimination, the nature of the data makes it impossible to determine the direction of the relationship. It may be that women who are more likely to report experiences of discrimination have similar patterns of employment.

Figure 6.1   Discrimination Cases, by Work Pathway Group

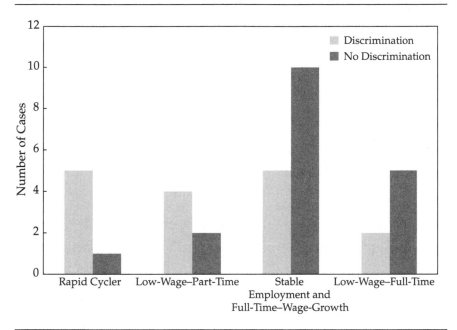

Source: Authors' compilation.

Conversely, it may be that women who share these patterns of employment are more likely to experience discrimination.

In an attempt to untangle this relationship, we examined why women in these two work dynamic patterns might have been more likely to report discrimination. Past work has shown that individual characteristics, such as age, education, marital status, and overall feelings toward the job, can influence an individual's likelihood of reporting workplace discrimination (Forman, Williams, and Jackson 1997; Kessler, Mickelson, and Williams 1999). These factors might influence both employment dynamics and perceived discrimination. For example, women who have less job experience and fewer resources may be forced into patterns of sporadic (low-wage–part-time) or unstable (rapid cycler) employment and may work at the lower levels of workplace hierarchies, where discrimination is more frequently experienced from a position of lack of power. To better understand the relationship between cluster membership and reported discrimination in our sample, we compared women with these two work dynamic patterns to the others on their baseline characteristics. We found that women in the low-wage–part-time group had the lowest levels of work experience (full-time work) and education relative to all the other work pathway groups. In addition, the rapid cycler group was likely to be particularly young relative to the other groups. Members of both the low-wage–part-time group and the rapid cycler group were less likely to have access to a car than other groups. Thus, the relative lack of work experience, education, and resources among members of these groups may have led them to be working in particularly low-status jobs, where experiences of discrimination can be more frequent. In addition, given that the rapid cyclers moved quickly through multiple jobs, this group may have had more opportunities to encounter discrimination and as a result may have become more likely to report it in their current jobs.

CONCLUSION

Experiences of racial-ethnic or sexual discrimination were reported by nearly half of the New Hope ethnographic sample. Of those, the majority occurred during the period of the ethnography. This suggests relatively high levels of prevalence and incidence of discrimination in low-wage workplaces in Milwaukee. In addition, about one-quarter of those who reported discrimination reported both race- and sex-based discrimination. The African-American and Latina women who made up the majority of the New Hope sample may have been at particular risk for both kinds of discrimination.

The cases of sexual discrimination fell into two categories: unwanted sexual advances and sexual comments and gestures. These categories mirror those used in past research on sexual discrimination. Unlike other work on sexual discrimination, our research did not reveal any cases of sexual coercion, possibly because of lower base rates for this form of sexual discrimination. Three types of racial-ethnic discrimination were reported: unequal opportunities, derogatory racial-ethnic comments, and skewed racial distribution of the workplace (including low percentages of workers of color in higher positions). Perceptions of skewed racial distribution of the workplace are new to the research literature, but among our sample they were not surprising given Milwaukee's status as one of the most highly segregated cities in the United States, at both the neighborhood and workplace levels.

The cases of discrimination varied not only in form but also in source. In our sample, discriminatory behaviors were reported to have been initiated by supervisors, coworkers, clients, and customers. Assuming that power differences are a motivating factor in workplace discrimination, it is likely that the source of the discrimination influenced the perceived severity and effects on employee well-being. Our ethnographic data suggest that discrimination coming from a superior has greater effects on well-being and satisfaction with work, and that discrimination coming from a client or patient is not as severe on these dimensions. Future work needs to continue to explore the source of the discrimination when considering its effects on well-being.

Our study also suggests that there is a relationship between employment patterns over time and discrimination experiences. Women who were characterized as rapid cyclers or as low-wage–part-time workers were more likely to report discrimination than women who followed the other three patterns. The low-wage–part-time group had lower levels of work experience and education than all the other work pathway groups, suggesting that they may have occupied the lowest-status positions in workplaces and therefore may have been more likely to experience discrimination. The rapid cyclers were younger on average than those in the other work pathway groups; their age may have placed them at greater risk for discrimination as well. Members of both groups were less likely to have access to cars, a key work support resource in Milwaukee. Although it is impossible to fully understand the relationship between discrimination and employment patterns given the nature of our data, these findings suggest that those with low levels of work experience, education, and resources may be at particular risk of experiencing discrimination in the workplace.

Taken as a whole, these findings demonstrate that sexual and racial-ethnic discrimination may be a relatively common experience in the low-wage workplace. However, before the results presented in this chapter can be generalized to other groups of low-wage workers, future research needs to consider the occurrence of discrimination in less segregated cities. This will allow a more comprehensive understanding of how workplace discrimination affects the lives of low-wage workers.

As a result of the mandates for employment in the Personal Responsibility and Work Opportunity Reconciliation Act (PRWORA) of 1996—mandates that may increase in the welfare reform reauthorization currently under consideration—more workers are entering the low-wage workforce. It is likely that many of these people will be exposed to workplace discrimination and the negative effects on well-being that it can have. Employers and policymakers need to acknowledge workplace discrimination as an important part of the employment experience of low-wage workers and address this issue when implementing job creation, retention, and advancement programs.

Many employers now offer some type of diversity training to their employees (Rynes and Rosen 1995). However, simply providing a single training may not be sufficient to effectively combat racial discrimination. That effort requires institutional approaches so as to change demographic makeups as well as many aspects of workplace policies and climate. Important steps identified in prior work include written policies, managers who observe employee behavior and intervene if necessary, and the fair and just implementation of human resources practices (Deitch et al. 2003; Hicks-Clarke and Iles 2000).

Research has shown that there are a number of steps that employers can take to reduce sexual harassment. First, organizations with leadership that is seen as proactively addressing issues of sexual harassment have fewer problems than organizations with indifferent leadership or leadership that encourages such behavior. Second, organizations that use multiple methods for addressing sexual harassment have had more success in reducing harassment than those that use few methods or none at all. Methods for addressing sexual harassment can include alerting staff to the issue by distributing posters and/or pamphlets, creating official complaint procedures within the organization, and providing employees with sexual harassment training. Proactive methods, such as creating complaint procedures and conducting training, are related to the lowest levels of harassment (Gruber 1998). The literature on workplaces and discrimination thus suggests the steps that employers can take to combat a problem that appears endemic in low-wage workplaces.

Part II | Work and Family

Chapter Seven | "I Want What Everybody Wants": Goals, Values, and Work in the Lives of New Hope Families

Thomas S. Weisner,
Hirokazu Yoshikawa, Edward D. Lowe,
and Faye Carter

IN THE FIRST part of this book, we considered New Hope mothers' experiences of work over time and the associations between those experiences and their children's development. In the second part, we turn to the relationship between work and family. Since the 1950s, aspects of the work-family interface have been considered important mechanisms that link parental employment to children's schooling and social development (Hoffman 1961). In part 2, we examine work and family from relatively understudied perspectives—goals and values, household budgeting and what earnings buy for children, and marriage and relationships. In this chapter, we consider an important—and even controversial—characteristic that mattered to the work pathways in particular and to women's family lives more generally: parents' goals and values for their work and family life.

We show that goals in fact did influence work trajectories, holding other influences constant. Women who reported higher educational goals for themselves at twenty-four months, for example, experienced greater wage growth between the twenty-four- and sixty-month follow-ups. We also show that goals and values were quite widely shared across the sample, rather than differing dramatically for women in the different employment pathways. How these broadly shared goals are put into practice is what appears

147

to matter most in how goals influence women's membership in one of the five employment groups. A close examination using ethnographic evidence shows that the effective *deployment* of goals (turning them into specific plans and tactics for improving income and balancing work and family) is the characteristic that differed across the women in the various employment clusters. Wage growth and growth in work hours, for instance, are associated with a pattern of making more strategic and concrete plans linked to one's goals. For women engaged in highly unstable and sporadic patterns of work, in contrast, short-term goals are thwarted by events, even as women remain hopeful that they are on the way to achieving their long-term goals of family and job stability and higher income. The patterning of goals and plans differed among the mothers in the different employment clusters, largely in the quality of the specificity of goals linked to their plans and in some women's practice of taking intermediate, modest steps to find and keep jobs that met their goals.

Then we turn to how the mothers in the sample talked about their work goals and families. They spoke in very instrumental ways ("I want to get a GED so I can improve my income from jobs"), but also in playful and ironic ways, such as spinning fantasies, making humorous commentaries, and critiquing the system. They also talked about potential goals and values that, at least so far in their lives, had not been realized.

GOALS, VALUES, PLANS, AND INTENTIONS

Values are our generalized understandings about what is good in life. Achieving economic success and being a spiritual person are values. Goals are the directions we decide to take in order to live life according to those values. Obtaining a certain job with benefits and high wages or planning to take the family to church each week are goals associated with those values. Plans and intentions are the chains of specific actions linked to goals that are valued and meaningful for a person in a particular cultural community (Weisner 2001, 2002; Weisner et al. 2005). In this view, positive change could occur in the lives of the women and families in our sample if they held values that were consistent with their goals and that could be turned into specific plans and intentions.

The women in our study talked about their values related to work and planned tactics and strategies to try to reach their goals. For some of them, goals and planning proceeded in proactive, linear ways. For example, Leora (from the full-time–wage-growth cluster) held a position as a payroll manager for a hospital at the beginning of the ethnography. She then spent three months unemployed before taking a better position in payroll at a bank, which offered her better pay and benefits. She strategized about how she could get benefits and, more importantly, get into a place with upward mobility and some kind of career ladder. Wendy (also in the full-time–wage-growth cluster) held a position as a machinist early in our study. She was unemployed for four months after getting married and then spent three months working part- and full-time as a telemarketer. For the final two years of the ethnographic study, she provided in-home day care, work that offered her autonomy and higher wages—and met her goals. By the end of the ethnography, Wendy was running her own day care center and trying to get her own building and increase enrollment. Maria (stable employment cluster) was a teacher in a day care center as the ethnography began. She continued to provide child care throughout the ethnographic portion of the study, and her wages increased over time. She got her GED and did other training for a job in day care, but her goals—less hassle in her job and more autonomy—were yet to be met by the end of the study. These women were active agents who made decisions about work, parenting, and family adaptation in response to the constant changes in their personal circumstances, their social and resource network, their child care needs, and their work contexts. Proactive, rational planning to attain goals in a linear fashion was one kind of goal direction we saw.

But there were other ways in which parents' values and goals had meaning for them yet were not so instrumental. Many of the women were consistently thwarted in their job goals; they would attempt to reset and redeploy those goals in order to confront their difficulties and get back on track, although many of them were reactive, reflexive, and angry in response to these difficulties. These mothers discussed their values not only in instrumental terms of achieving their goals but also in emotionally charged critiques of the world of work, fantasies about what might have been, and ironic comments on the world and their own often thwarted efforts to attain their goals. These projective and reflexive ways of discussing their goals and plans reflected their long-term experiences and their beliefs about work, family, and the fairness of the economy.

Both of these ways of talking about goals—instrumental and projective/reactive—involved agency, which women brought to their work and family situations. Whether they were more instrumental or more reactive, they incorporated their goals, plans, and values into their thought and behavior in their work and family lives. Since these working-poor parents were engaged in chains of both proactive and reactive decisions and choices, their goals and values certainly had the potential to influence their work trajectories, even in the resource-poor contexts and difficult job markets they faced.

GOALS AND STRUCTURAL CONDITIONS

Some have confused a focus on the values and goals of individuals with blaming those individuals for their circumstances (Valentine 1968). But taking seriously the values and goals of the poor does not preclude the study of the structural and institutional constraints that they face. Dividing their goals from their circumstances is not a useful analytic approach. To the contrary, goals, values, and agency are of self-evident importance to working-poor mothers, just as they are for all social and cultural actors in every community. In fact, taking cultural goals seriously in understanding employment does not preclude the consideration of other factors but rather complements them, and such an analysis is an integral part of a holistic understanding of these women's lives. Considering values and goals as an influence on employment trajectories is also entirely consistent with recognizing that poverty is embedded in the structural conditions of low-wage work, dangerous neighborhoods, class and race discrimination, poor educational backgrounds, and so forth; this recognition is essential for a multivariate view of human behavior in context. Parents strategize and change their work lives in the context of structural circumstances, and they use their goals and values to help make decisions and understand what is happening.

There is good reason for both theory and empirical evidence to consider structure (low-resource communities and labor market conditions), goals (intentions to seek more stable work, higher wages, more education, closer families), and agency (locally rational choices to work toward goals and reflexively adapt and change) as jointly influencing employment trajectories and family circumstances. Several recent studies using data from experimental welfare policy demonstrations, for example, have found that parents' goals at baseline (for pursuing work and education) not only predict later employment but also interact with employment policies to influence earnings, income, and their own well-being (Yoshikawa et al. 2003).

Furthermore, as the ethnographic data on families in our volume amply show, there is enormous variation of all kinds (age, family and household circumstances, ethnicity, life experiences) in the low-income people we portray, as well as in their employment clusters. As Rebecca Blank writes in It Takes a Nation (1997, xv): " 'Poverty' is not synonymous with 'single mothers and their children on welfare'; in fact, the majority of the poor are in other types of households and have traditionally had little access to direct cash assistance. . . . The poor are an extremely heterogeneous group of persons."

Knowledge about work and family always exists in a specific local context. The New Hope mothers, using local or bounded rationality, took into account the diversity of their complex environments and multiple and often conflicting goals. Yet with all that diversity and local or contextual rationality, many of these mothers had values and goals that are widely shared by all Americans. Tiffany, quoted in the title to this chapter, said, "I want what everyone wants—a steady job, a house, a husband, and a family."

With regard specifically to work commitment among the poor, our data, covering three years of close ethnographic work with low-income families, generally support the view of Katherine Newman (1999, 61) in her study of low-wage food service workers in Harlem, New York, that the great majority of the nation's working poor continue to "seek their salvation" in the labor market, in spite of all the difficulties that entails. Similarly, Kathryn Edin and Laura Lein (1997, 230), in their study comparing the income generation and budgeting strategies of low-wage working mothers to those of welfare-reliant mothers, found that, "all else equal, almost all mothers said they would rather work than rely on welfare. They believed work had important psychological benefits and welfare imposed stigma costs." Belief in the necessity of work was nearly universal among the women in the New Hope sample as well. Variations in their work goals were accounted for by the pull of *other* goals (to be with their children, to improve their poor health, to further their training and education, to find a partner to assist them), as well as by other life experiences and, in some cases, health limitations. These mothers had a very rich set of goals and personal beliefs about work in their lives, and typically quite reasonable goals for stable work. It was the vagaries of the low-wage job market—not any lack of goals and values—that led to their work struggles and the thwarting of their goals.

THE VALUES OF HARD WORK AND FAMILY RESPONSIBILITY

A General Commitment to Work Goals and Values

Values and goals like Tiffany's (who wants what everybody wants) were widely shared among most of the women in our study. In the sixty-month survey, respondents were asked about a number of personal, interpersonal, and family circumstances that might have influenced their *desire* or *ability* to work for pay in the preceding year. Included among these was a question that specifically addressed values regarding work by asking how three factors influenced their desire or ability to work: feeling good about oneself for bringing home a paycheck; wanting to be a successful role model for one's kids; and feeling good about oneself for hard work and doing a good job. Each respondent was asked to rate these items on a five-point scale from "a big *negative* influence" (1) to "little or no influence" (3) to "a big *positive* influence" (5).

Overwhelmingly, the respondents reported that these three items were a big positive influence on their desire and ability to work for pay. A higher-than-expected 79 percent (based on a chi-square test with standardized residual = .3) reported that feeling good about hard work was a big positive influence, with an additional 13 percent reporting that it was a small positive influence (standardized residual = .1). Eighty-two percent reported that being a role model for the kids was a big positive influence, with an additional 8 percent reporting that it had a small positive influence. Results of a chi-square analysis indicate that there was a higher-than-expected positive influence of being a role model (standardized residual = .2) and a higher-than-expected small positive influence (standardized residual = −.1). Seventy-four percent reported that feeling good about bringing home a paycheck was a big positive influence, and 12 percent reported that it was a small positive influence. Both proportions are what we would expect according to a chi-square test (standardized residuals = .1 and .0, respectively).

These data suggest that the virtues of work, at least as represented by these three items, were important for nearly all of the members of the sixty-month survey sample. Ninety-two percent reported that feeling good about hard work or a job well done was a positive influence, and 86 percent felt that bringing home a paycheck was a positive influence. With so little variation in the pattern of response, the values associated with the virtues of working for pay cannot really predict employment characteristics at sixty months.

Conflicts Between Work, Family, and Care Values and Goals

Although the women in our study nearly universally valued work, there were other values they broadly shared that, if pursued actively, could conflict with and even contradict their values and, by extension, their ability to work for pay. Of particular interest were those values associated with being personally responsible for the care and well-being of their children and the management of their household. Values can and do conflict with each other when parents are faced with very difficult choices and an often unforgiving job market.

These values regarding care and family and their complicating influence on many women's desire or ability to work for pay are reflected in the same set of sixty-month survey items already discussed. The New Hope mothers were asked three questions that capture the extent to which their concerns over the management of their household and their concerns over the well-being of their children may have influenced their desire or ability to work for pay: To what extent did they feel "stressed when there is too much to do in too little time"? How concerned were they "that work will disrupt family life"? And to what extent were they concerned "that [their] absence from home could be harmful to [their] kids"?

Overall, a substantial group of women reported that these concerns were a *negative* influence on their desire or ability to work for pay. Forty-five percent reported that feeling stressed was a negative influence (24 percent reported it as a small negative influence, and 21 percent reported it as a big negative influence, both of which are higher-than-expected proportions according to a chi-square test; standardized residuals = .2 and .3, respectively). Thirty-six percent reported that their concern that work would disrupt family life was a negative influence (an expected 20 percent reported that it was a small negative influence (standardized residual = .1 based on a chi-square test), and a higher-than-expected 16 percent reported that it was a big negative influence (standardized residual = .3)). Forty-six percent reported that their concern that their absence from home would be harmful to their children had a negative influence (25 percent reported a small negative influence, and 21 percent reported a big negative influence; of which both proportions are higher than expected based on a chi-square test; standardized residuals = .2 and .4, respectively). In prior work on an earnings-supplement program in Minnesota, concerns about being absent from home were in fact associated with lower work effort over a subsequent three-year period (Yoshikawa et al. 2003).

These data suggest that, for some women in our sample, their concerns for the well-being of their children and the management of their household negatively affected their desire or ability to work for pay, even when work was a positive value and a goal they did want to implement. But putting a high value on family could lead to paying *more* attention to the goal of getting and keeping jobs, as well as to paying less attention to that goal. Supporting a family often *meant* working, even though it produced conflicts, hardships, and strain for so many. Parents said that they had to work in order to sustain their families and households, and so their narratives often were about the blend of work and family and the ways in which they monitored and cared for their children in spite of having to work. Family and work goals may be analytically separable in survey responses, but from the points of view of these parents, they were linked in practice.

The Negative Impact on Work and Earnings of Balancing Work and Family Goals

Did these concerns actually affect these women's work for pay? Work is necessary, but it also can produce conflict, in the form of work-family trade-offs that may lead to fewer work hours or less income. To examine this possibility, we created an index variable from the three items dealing with concerns over the management of the household and the well-being of the children; we then correlated this variable with some of the characteristics of each woman's current or most recent job (such as job duration, hourly wage, weekly hours, and wage growth between the twenty-four-month and sixty-month surveys). To create the index variable, we added together each respondent's values on the three items. The resulting index had a value between zero (no influence or only positive influences) and six (only big negative influences on all three questions).

Using ordinary least squares (OLS) regression with a comprehensive set of covariates entered into the equation,[1] we found that the index of concerns for home management and the well-being of children was in fact associated with lower wages (b = −$0.25, β = −.16, p < .01) and lower weekly hours (b = −0.54, β = −.13, p < .05) at the sixty-month point. The measure also predicted significantly lower estimates of total income for the fifth year, based on administrative records of reported employment earnings, food stamps, and estimated earned income tax credit (EITC) receipt (b = −$705.85, β= −.14, p < .01).

Summary

The women in our sample overwhelmingly endorsed the mainstream American values associated with hard work and economic self-sufficiency. In fact, so little variation exists in our measures of this value that it cannot possibly predict the variation in these women's employment characteristics. Rather, our evidence supports the view that many women find the two mainstream American values associated with parental work (valuing paid work, if necessary, to support the household financially, and valuing unpaid work to manage the household duties and care for the children) very difficult to jointly put into practice. Even though most of the women in the study greatly valued paid work, the higher their level of concern over work's effects on the well-being of their children and household, the lower their pay and hours. The difference in income can be considerable for a low-income working parent. According to the estimate derived from our regression analysis, women who scored six points on the influences of family concerns on the desire to work for pay index (recall that this means that respondents reported big negative influences on all three questions) would have $2,100 less annual income than women who scored three points, controlling for other demographic and baseline characteristics.

THE GOALS OF NHES MOTHERS FOR WORK AND FAMILY ECONOMIC WELL-BEING

Goals as Reported on the Survey

When the participants in our study had the opportunity, in an open-ended format, to discuss the important goals and plans they had set for them-

Table 7.1   Goals That Respondents Reported Pursuing
at the Twenty-Four-Month Follow-up

	Number of Respondents	
Educational goals	214	55%
Complete or continue education	202	52
Upgrade job skills	20	5
Learn to speak English	5	1
Job goals	165	43
Obtain specific or better job	134	35
Start or improve own business	37	10
Have more flexible work schedule	1	0
Financial goals	122	32
Buy a house	63	16
Improve housing situation	36	9
Improve financial situation	33	9
Buy a car or other costly item	16	4
Family goals	63	16
Provide for family	37	10
Children to do well	19	5
Get married or have baby	8	2
More time with spouse or children	1	0
Personal goals	39	10
General personal growth	29	8
Solve an immediate problem	6	2
Volunteer or be a role model	3	1
Control weight	2	1

Source: Authors' compilation.
Note: N = 386. Number of respondents varies owing to missing data for the wage-change measures.

selves at the time of the twenty-four-month survey, many mentioned getting a GED or finishing a twenty-four-month or four-year college degree program. Others mentioned getting a new and better-paying job or a promotion from their current employer. Others described financial goals, like getting their bills under control, saving more for their retirement, or improving their family's financial condition. Still others mentioned goals like helping their children do better in school. The various goals were coded into five categories: educational, job, financial, family, and personal (see table 7.1).

The most common goals mentioned were educational goals related to completing or continuing an educational training program (52 percent of respondents). The second most frequent set of specific goals (35 percent) was job-related: obtaining a specific job (such as working in a hospital) or a better job (such as gaining a permanent position with better pay and benefits). The third most frequently mentioned set of goals was financial: buying a house (more rarely a car) or improving their current living or financial situation (32 percent). Fourth were family goals, such as being a provider or making sure that their children do well in life (16 percent). Finally, about 10 percent described more personal goals, such as becoming more organized, getting off of probation, being a better role model in the community, or losing some weight. Since personal goals, though important, were only rarely mentioned in the survey context, we did not examine these further. For the analyses that follow, we focus on educational goals, job goals, financial goals, and family goals.

Were Goals Related to Personal Characteristics or to Employment Clusters and Work Outcomes?

Since there was a reasonable amount of variation in the goals mentioned by the NHES mothers, we wondered whether particular kinds of goals might be related either to personal and household characteristics (age, ethnicity, and so on) or to particular patterns of work (the employment clusters). We found that only rarely did demographic or household variables predict that respondents would mention particular goals. Using logistic regression, we did find that people younger than twenty-five were 2.6 times more likely to mention education goals than respondents over the age of thirty-five ($p < .05$). But no other demographic characteristics were associated with the likelihood of mentioning any of the four major goals. Furthermore, none of the five employment clusters (calculated between baseline and the twenty-four-month follow-up) were significantly associated with the mention of particular goals.

In the survey methodology, however, respondents were asked about their goals in the form of questions, not about the past, but about their directions and plans for the future. Thus, we can determine whether the goals mentioned at twenty-four months predicted the relevant job and family characteristics at sixty months.

Rather specific and measurable ends were associated with the general goals that respondents described at twenty-four months: improving one's education and training, ostensibly to improve one's employment opportunities; getting a new or better job; improving the household standard of living or finances; and better providing for the family and making sure the children were on a positive track in life. To see the degree to which these goals led to related outcomes, we used OLS regression to examine the relationship between these twenty-four-month goals and sixty-month outcomes such as education, specific job characteristics, and family financial characteristics. These analyses controlled for a comprehensive set of baseline covariates.

Goals at Twenty-four Months and Job Characteristics at Sixty Months

We began by examining the relationship between the goals measured at the twenty-four-month follow-up to a host of employment characteristics at sixty months and the change between the two follow-ups. The particular job characteristics at sixty months that we included as dependent variables in our models were hourly wage for the current or most recent job; wage change between the last job at twenty-four months and the current or most recent job at sixty months; current or most recent job duration, hours, and number of benefits (paid sick days, paid vacation, health insurance, and/or a pension plan); and change in the number of benefits between the last job at twenty-four months and the sixty-month reference job.

In general, we would expect that job improvement goals would have the greatest impact on work characteristics. But educational goals could also be of some benefit, since greater levels of education can improve an individual's marketability on the job market and improve his or her chance of getting better employment than would be the case at a lower level of education.

We used OLS regression to test the relationship between these variables and the goals at twenty-four months (coded in the survey simply as present or absent). We included the standard set of baseline controls, as well as the analogous twenty-four-month measure to the dependent variable at sixty months. Finally, we included all four goal categories as variables in the same model so that we could be sure that the association of any particular goal with the dependent variable was independent of associations with other goals. The results of these analyses are summarized in tables 7.2 and 7.3.

What we found with regard to job characteristics only partly confirmed our expectations. Those who were pursuing *educational* goals had greater levels of wage growth than those who did not mention pursuing educational goals.[2] Those who reported pursuing family goals had jobs with better *benefits* than those who did not report pursuing family goals at twenty-four months. However, our expectations for job improvement goals were flatly contradicted: those goals were associated with *lower* hourly

Table 7.2 OLS Regression Coefficients Predicting Job Characteristics at Sixty Months from Stated Goals at Twenty-Four Months

	Education Goals	Job Improvement Goals	Family Financial Goals	Other Family Goals	N R^2 Adjusted R^2
Hourly wage	Ns.	−0.72 (0.36)* −0.12	Ns.	Ns.	281 .25 .20***
Wage change between two and five years	0.98 (0.50)[†] 0.13	−1.10 (0.47)* −0.15	Ns.	Ns.	318 0.14 0.08***
Job duration	Ns.	Ns.	Ns.	Ns.	291 0.22 0.17***
Weekly hours	Ns.	Ns.	Ns.	Ns.	286 0.10 0.04[†]
Job benefits	Ns.	Ns.	Ns.	Ns.	295 0.23 0.17***
Benefits change between two and five years	Ns.	Ns.	Ns.	0.41 (0.24)[†] 0.08	317 0.39 0.35***

Source: Authors' compilation.

Note: Coefficients are presented as unstandardized (standard error) with standardized coefficient on the second line. All models include DV (dependent variable) at twenty-four months and these measures at baseline: age; education (high school degree, GED, or better); ethnicity (African-American, Hispanic); single-adult with children in household; three or more children; youngest child age two years or younger; ever worked full-time; receiving AFDC, general assistance, food stamps, or Medicaid; income in the past year under $5,000; access to a car; in an AFDC household as a child; New Hope experiment. "Ns." is not statistically significant.

[†]$p < .10$; *$p < .05$; ***$p < .001$

Table 7.3 OLS Regression Predicting Personal and Family Characteristics at Sixty Months from Stated Goals at Twenty-Four Months

	Education Goals	Job Goals	Financial Goals	Family Goals	N R^2 Adjusted R^2
Financial worry	Ns.	Ns.	0.26 (.13)* 0.10	Ns.	339 0.32 0.28***
Happiness with standard of living	Ns.	Ns.	−0.24 (.11)† −0.11	Ns.	338 0.17 0.12***
Worsened housing condition between two and five years	−0.23 (0.11)* −0.09	Ns.	Ns.	Ns.	311*** 0.66 0.64
Total income change between three and five years	Ns.	−$1,266 ($656)† −0.08	$1,161 ($661)† 0.07	Ns.	402 0.45 0.42***
Highest grade	Ns.	Ns.	Ns.	.74 (.22)** .17	311 .37 .33***

Source: Authors' compilation.

Note: Coefficients are presented as unstandardized (standard error) with standardized coefficient on the second line. All models include DV (dependent variable) at twenty-four months and these measures at baseline: age; education (high school degree, GED, or better); ethnicity (African-American, Hispanic); single-adult with children in household; three or more children; youngest child age two years or younger; ever worked full-time; receiving AFDC, general assistance, food stamps, or Medicaid; income in the past year under $5,000; access to a car; in an AFDC household as a child; New Hope experiment. "Ns." is not statistically significant.

†$p < .10$; *$p < .05$; **$p < .01$; ***$p < .001$

wages and a negative wage change value between two and five years. It may be that educational goals indicate a beneficial and unobserved motivation to achieve higher human capital that is not reflected in job improvement goals. In addition, those who reported higher job improvement goals may have shared unobserved characteristics that are associated with difficulty in the labor market.

Different Goals and Strategies for Success

The two most frequently cited types of goals (educational and job improvement) led to very different outcomes. When we compare those who were pursuing job-related goals to those who were pursuing educational goals, we find that educational goals led to greater wage growth and income growth than job-related goals.

This comparison is demonstrated in figures 7.1 and 7.2. Figure 7.1 shows wage change for the first two years of the study and wage change between years two and five of the study for those who reported pursuing either educational goals or job improvement goals in the twenty-four-month survey. Those who were pursuing educational goals experienced accelerated wage growth between the twenty-four-month and sixty-month surveys. On the other hand, those who were pursuing job-related goals experienced modest levels of wage growth between the two time points.

Figure 7.2 shows a comparison of change in total personal income, based on estimates from records of reported earnings and welfare receipt from the state of Wisconsin, for those who reported pursuing educational goals and job improvement goals at the time of the twenty-four-month survey. While those who reported pursuing educational goals at twenty-four months experienced substantial income growth between years three and five, those who reported pursuing job improvement goals actually experienced a modest decline in income between years three and five.

Those who were pursuing educational goals enjoyed much greater wage growth and growth in personal income than those who were pursuing job-related goals at the time of the twenty-four-month survey. Often, in the low-income employment literature, these two avenues are referred to as pursuing either human capital (such as education and skill development) or labor force attachment ("finding and keeping work") (Hamilton et al. 2001). This analysis suggests that, for those women in our sample who were already employed, pursuing more education and skill development was a better strategy for improving their wages and income than simply trying to find a better job in the rather difficult, low-wage job market they faced in their Milwaukee communities. Other recent work on

Figure 7.1 Comparison of the Association Between Job Improvement and Education Goals and Subsequent Wage Growth

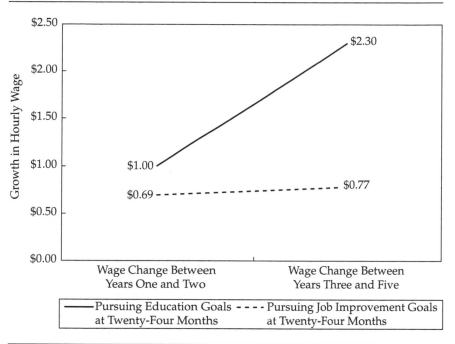

Source: Authors' compilation.

this topic supports our findings here. For example, data from the National Evaluation of Welfare-to-Work Strategies (NEWWS) suggest that placing a high value on one's education, combined with a welfare policy mandate to pursue education or job training on the way to a job, has particularly positive effects on one's earnings and school attainment for one's children. This is not true for high levels of valuing work over family (Yoshikawa et al. 2006).

There is also some evidence from the New Hope data that the type of goal that mothers expressed at twenty-four months was related both to their own educational expectations at that point and to their children's educational expectations (also at twenty-four months after the New Hope program started). Maria Ramos and Hirokazu Yoshikawa (2005) have found that educational goals (but not work-related ones) are associated with higher levels of both parents' and children's educational expectations and that indirect

Figure 7.2   Comparison of the Association Between Job Improvement and Education Goals and Change in Total Annual Income, Years Two to Five

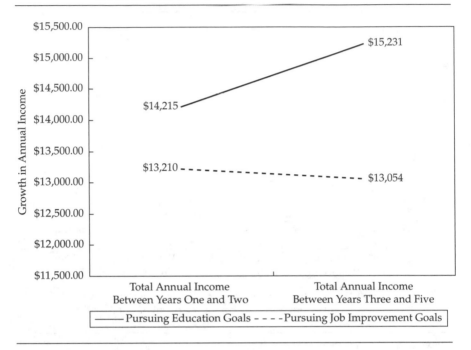

Source: Authors' compilation.

associations of parental goals with children's self-reported expectations through their parents' reported expectations are significant.

Overall, there were some parents whose goals led to somewhat improved job circumstances at sixty months, net of demographic background and controlling for their employment trajectory at twenty-four months. Goals are a relevant influence in employment trajectories, but not the dominant one, and the magnitudes of associations with outcomes are in line with those of non-goal variables. Goals did not seem to lead independently to changes in wages, but they did affect benefits and job length.

The connections between family goals and working for longer periods of time (as with the stable employment cluster) suggest a pattern we now turn to in the ethnographic data: some parents saw their work and family goals as reconcilable, though often difficult to achieve.

ETHNOGRAPHIC DATA ON PARENTS' WORK GOALS

Goals related to work had meanings for the NHES women that went beyond hopes of finding and keeping jobs and perhaps improving their economic circumstances. Many of the topics they brought up when they talked about employment goals had to do, not with their concrete plans or immediately attainable job results, but with their wishes, frustrations, and hopes. Looking more closely at the ethnographic cases shows that these mothers' goals were often thwarted by events over which they had little or no control.

The Multiple Functions of Goals

One of the reasons that goals influence, but are certainly not determinants of, employment patterns is that they are not just statements of instrumental strategy or tactics. When parents are working in low-wage jobs, their comments about work goals are also about personhood, fantasies, position in society, and feelings, in addition to (or instead of) a strictly instrumental, strategic calculation of job prospects. Values and goals have many functions in addition to the instrumental one of organizing an individual's attention and efforts to work and parent (D'Andrade and Strauss 1992).

For example, thinking about goals helps to make sense of the world and what it means. Allison commented to a field-worker that "work . . . is about much more than just making money." Allison was in the stable employment cluster. She worked in the auto parts industry for the entirety of the ethnography and realized steady wage increases over the three-year period.

Goals also guide one's attention and appraisal of events and provide rationales for what one does and critiques of what others are doing. Rose commented that she "doesn't believe in just sitting in the house doing nothing all day, collecting a state check and watching TV . . . but I know people who do." Faye talked about "starting small" as a job search plan: "You can't expect to go out there and get a job earning $11 to $13 an hour immediately. . . . It happens for the lucky few, but it is not going to start with most people. . . . You got to be willing to start small." This helped her to make a near-term decision about finding a job in spite of the fact that she was not going to get her hoped-for ideal job right away.

Goals and values surrounding work also helped define our participants' social identities. Heather talked to her field-worker about the gap between her work goals and her real hopes for the future. "Heather said that what she would really like to do is volunteer work. Volunteer at the school, help out at her church, run a youth choir, or develop and run a support group for teens. She said that she would really like to do something like that, just as long as it wasn't a job. It would be something that she wanted to do, not something she had to do." Samantha, who struggled to get steady work, remarked that she was not a "fast-food person. . . . Believe me, I don't want to work in fast food. I want a real job where I could look nice and go regularly every day." Maria was in the steady employment cluster and worked in child care; she also commented on her hopes to change her job because she wanted to be treated "like a human": "It's not human to order adults around like that. . . . They treat you like you are nobody."

When the goal of having a job meets the actual experience of dead-end, low-wage work, that goal can become both a blessing and a curse. It keeps families afloat, but sometimes it also keeps them from moving up. To some extent, society defines low-wage work (such as working at a fast-food restaurant) "as something akin to the untouchable status of the Indian low castes" (Newman 1999, 297). Although there is no shame in that game, as Newman puts it, imagine the ambivalence and mismatch with their broader goals and values that so many of the women in our study experienced when they found themselves working at jobs with no benefits, little chance of an upward path, and little chance of controlling their future. Yet even such jobs hold the promise of finding a better life and greater respect by moving up into a better job. Nancy's field-worker described a conversation with her about work and personal happiness:

> Nancy says, "I want to find work that makes me happy, not just the money." She described her high-wage job as a window cleaner with an hourly wage of $10. Her eyes *shone* when she mentioned the $10 figure, since it was clearly much higher than her previous job. Besides, she worked thirty-five hours a week at that job, as opposed to the twenty-five hours a week she was given in the earlier job.

Many of the comments about work and job goals and about overall goals regarding money also provide humorous or ironic commentaries on the world or reflect fantasies. Evelia was in the full-time, low-wage cluster and had a steady job for much of the ethnographic portion of the study, but she was unemployed for several months, and her salary decreased by $1.00 an hour during year two. Evelia smiled when talking about her income and family goals, saying, "I want to be a millionaire . . . win the lotto . . . and get married, all in the next year." Belinda just said that "Wal-Mart is getting on my nerves." Hence, narratives about goals ranged beyond the instrumental in many ways. These mothers' narratives about their work and family goals were connected to other cultural schemas about themselves, about their communities and families, and about what they wanted in life. Thus, what they said and felt about their work and family goals was not necessarily unidirectional from goals to specific intentions and plans, and then directly to jobs.

FAMILY VIGNETTES: GOALS AND WORK EXPERIENCE BY EMPLOYMENT CLUSTER

The largest number of values and goals statements in our field notes, compared to any of the other field-note domains (including family, children, spirituality, politics, marriage, and fathers), were about employment. This emphasis on work and employment goals no doubt was due in part to the New Hope focus on work-based supports. Nonetheless, parents were constantly concerned about making ends meet, budgeting, and work. Their work values and goals were no different in overall content from what most American workers talk about. For example, they described good jobs (those that were stimulating and offered autonomy, benefits, stability, and respect), strategies for getting work, stress at work, types of work, and the kind of worker they were or wanted to be (someone with a good work ethic, more experience, or good references; someone able to enjoy the job).

Some general observations about these mothers' work trajectories are relevant to appreciating goals in the context of employment clusters. The wages they earned were low, averaging around $8.00 an hour, and benefits were few. Only a few were able to move up in wages or job stability—but some succeeded. It should be apparent that regardless of their values and goals, the range of jobs and incomes open to them was rather limited, *including* the often long stretches when they were working. Few of these mothers were ever doing dramatically well by any means.

The No-Work and Part-Time, Low-Wage Clusters

Prior to the ethnographic study, all of the women in these two clusters had primarily been caring for their children at home. They had little prior experience in sustained employment. Many of them had strong parenting goals, while others had health problems that prevented them from doing steady work. Iris and Elizabeth were in committed relationships with their partners for the entire study period, and they relied on these men as the major source of household income. Iris, a long-term recipient of public assistance, tried to work briefly in early 1999 at the W-2 offices and held a few part-time temporary positions prior to the ethnography, but these jobs never lasted. She eventually gave up public assistance and came to rely on the foster child payments she received for caring for her two nephews, in addition to the income her husband brought home.

Iris had a criminal record, had been fired from a job at baseline, and reported serious health problems. In other words, several significant barriers kept her from working—or certainly made it difficult to find work that fit her circumstances. She wanted things for herself, but she did not want to do what she needed to do to get them. That is, she wanted a good job, but she was not willing to go out and apply for jobs or take a job that was not great now but would give her opportunities to move up. Iris compared herself to her family members, usually her sisters and mother. For example, she thought that her sister who had attended college and become a medical secretary was quite successful. Such comparisons to the work trajectories of friends and relatives play an important role in shaping the schemas that connect values to goals and to plans and action. Regardless of her current circumstances, Iris recently had accomplished an important goal: she completed her GED, while working a full-time job. She would spend four hours in the morning at GED class and then eight hours working at the second-hand store. She said that she would get home at 11:00 P.M. just exhausted, but was so proud when she walked across the stage to get her GED, with the spotlight on her.

Elizabeth, a U.S.-born Latina mother of six children ages one to eight, relied on partners for support when her children were young. She tried a few temp jobs, but nothing lasted very long. She eventually gave up her efforts to find work and settled for full-time homemaking as a career choice. Staying home and taking care of their children was particularly important for Elizabeth, Iris, and others in these clusters. For example, in early 2000 a fieldworker was discussing with Elizabeth whether she had any plans to work and whether her husband, Victor, wanted her to do so. She said, "Victor doesn't understand. He thinks I should work, but I've decided that I should stay home with the kids. Who else will treat my kids well? . . . Who else will deal with all this?" (Elizabeth pointed to the children running around through a maze of toys.) "You just don't know about people nowadays. . . . The main thing I need to do with myself is take care of my family—of my kids." These data corroborate other recent findings from samples of low-income families suggesting that putting a high value on taking care of family and children at home over working full-time indeed predicts later employment behavior (Yoshikawa et al. 2003).

Elizabeth wanted to become a parole officer for juveniles or perhaps a police officer, but she had only a vague idea about what it would entail to get either of those jobs. Mostly, she reported wanting to get her GED. She said that she was tired of staying home all the time. She "didn't want to work at Taco Bell for five years and then look back to see that she hadn't accomplished anything." She wanted an education and a "good job." "The first thing I want to do is finish my GED." She only had to pass the math and social science parts of the test and thought that she might take a class for those sections or just study on her own.

Elizabeth said that she would have liked to work, but that she really wanted to get an education so that she could get a good job. She said that when she started with New Hope she liked the idea of working, but that she wanted to go to school. She thought getting an education should be a priority, and New Hope really didn't help her in her efforts to reach that goal. Elizabeth said that her husband's brother had recently gotten a college degree. She smiled and said, "He thinks he's really something. I can't wait to go to school too."

Parents in the part-time, low-wage cluster elected to care for their young children, did not have much work experience, and, in some cases, had partners to assist them. Parenting and family caretaking goals were especially important to many in this group. They encountered significant barriers to regular employment, such as uncertain mental and physical health, unstable child care, and for many of them a partner who did not want them to work. Their goals, such as pursuing their own education or becoming a foster parent, often had been achieved without wage work. Their work goals were often clear and focused on upward mobility, but they rarely had the intermediate goals to achieve them, nor the supports.

The Rapid Cycler Cluster

Heather and Evelia had personal and domestic relationship problems and concerns that affected their employment. For example, Heather, an African-American mother of two at the start of the ethnography, stopped working twice during the study because of the births of two more children. She also moved for several months to Florida with her children and her fiancé before returning to Milwaukee in January 2000. These moves were planned: she had intended to join her fiancé there and was counting on family in Florida to help her with the children and with getting a job. But Heather also had quit her nursing home job (a job she hated, she said) after getting 401K money cashed out from a former job, and she was fired from another job for not returning to work immediately after the birth of her second baby. Evelia also lost a job, in part because of problems with her boyfriend.

The goals expressed by many of the mothers in this group were not unrealistic. Rather, the jobs available did not match their otherwise reasonable goals. Evelia's main goal was to find a secure and stable job, not a job that, as a field-worker wrote, would be stable today, "but maybe tomorrow they will move the company and she will lose the job. 'My goal is just to have a stable, good job, a job that I like.' " But she did not manage to find such a job and remained stuck in a post office temp job without benefits for much of the ethnography. When she finally left to take a job as a line supervisor at a meat-packing plant, she discovered that it did not provide stability either. Evelia did not like to be responsible for so many people, and liked even less the working conditions in the meatpacking job. She said that never in her life had she seen people work so much, so fast, in such bad conditions, for so low a wage. Evelia did not think that the salary she earned ($8.79 per hour) was right, because it did not reflect the great responsibility her job entailed. She had to enforce the sanitary requirements that the law demanded, and she also had to look after the quality of the meat that was being packaged. Evelia also worked at obtaining a regular position with the U.S. Post Office and worked there as a part-timer for long periods. But according to her report of how hiring was done, she said that she was "never going to get a regular job" at the post office.

Heather's long-term goal was to open her own child care center. She explained that she already had all the child care certifications she needed to open a child care center of her own. All she had to do was renew her license. She took all the early childhood development certification classes. Heather said that she did not mind working, but that she wanted to work on her own terms; she didn't want to be *obligated* to work. Further, her goals changed and cycled along with her employment patterns. Heather said that she would have liked to go back to school and finish her college degree—but how could she? She was thinking about returning to school in the winter and majoring in a medical assistant field. She was also thinking about getting training in medical terminology, which her mother would be able to help her with. Her mother was a registered nurse; family contacts and work comparisons and connections—social capital—help explain the connections between goals and plans. Heather, it turned out, was not able to do this training and still work enough hours to make ends meet.

If jobs had allowed for some flexibility, some of their goals could have been met. For example, one participant got a community service job (CSJ) through New Hope to work at a shelter for homeless men. After working the CSJ for a while, she was hired as a regular employee by the shelter and worked as a receptionist. One of the things she liked about this job was that it afforded her the flexibility she needed to take care of sudden family concerns, such as the times when her children or her partner's children got sick. She was also supported by her partner in managing the household. In addition to being employed and contributing to the household finances, he attended to the children's needs when she could not take time off and provided some help with household chores. The relationship was stable throughout the study period, as was her job; she eventually moved from cycling or not working to steady work.

Tiffany, the mother who simply wanted "what everyone wants," still did not want "just any job, she wants a high-paying job and a nice, decorated house so that all she has to do is move her furniture in." She did not want to become satisfied with a $7.50-an-hour job. She saw too many people in her neighborhood who settled for too little. They "just get a job, get a house, have kids, but never really make much of themselves." Tiffany had high goals and expectations and wanted to get the education to achieve them—yet she did not succeed. Her goals were admirable, but she was thwarted by not only her immediate job situation but by her inability to take all the intermediate steps, to write a script for attaining her goals.

These women's goals included work, but they were often derailed from their jobs by other concerns and problems in their lives. They continued to try to meet their work goals, and the goal remained salient, but events overtook their plans. This pattern was common among those mothers who cycled from one job to another that did not provide income gains or improvements in skills.

Medical or drug/alcohol problems prevented some rapid cyclers from working regularly, and others had family problems, had to move, and experienced other non-work-related disruptions. For example, Katrina had both an education and job skills, and she did find steady work for most of the ethnographic study. However, she was in a relationship with an abusive boyfriend, whom she eventually left, and one of her four children had severe emotional problems. She herself, she said, had problems with depression. It was no wonder that she sometimes struggled with working and taking care of her children.

A number of mothers could not keep steady work because their jobs simply came and went in spite of their intentions and plans. The ethnographic data also revealed non-work-related life changes that affected work, such as residential moves, partner relationships, health concerns, job harassment, and transportation glitches. The goal of staying employed was strong in this group, but many other concerns, such as child care problems or their own health problems, often thwarted mothers' work intentions.

The Stable Employment and Full-Time– Wage-Growth Clusters

About one-third of the mothers in the ethnography found more stable work, and their incomes often went up. This was clearly an important group of parents for policy. Parents in the stable employment and full-time–wage-growth clusters gave us a window into what mattered most in attaining work and family goals. Their jobs provided them with both networks of contacts and skill sets (such as computer skills and accounting) that led to more regular employment and growth in income. These mothers worked at auto dealerships and county agencies, in their own child care businesses, and in financial services, computers, and similar industries in which one could move into a job based on experience in the last job held in that same industry. The women in these clusters had some control over their work schedules, and many had good employment histories that allowed them to get better jobs in the same industry. Not surprisingly, job mobility was most common in these two clusters. Leora's field-worker gives us a glimpse of one such situation:

> Leora comments about her current job at a bank in the payroll office, that being responsible for everyone's check gave Leora a sense of control in the office environment. She smiled and said, "I am not egotistical, but it makes me feel that I am in charge of everybody's check," and quickly [added] that a year and a half ago, "I was not even in charge of my own life."
>
> Leora's mother-in-law has been looking for an entry-level position in a real estate agency for Leora. She told Leora a few days back that an agency was looking for an assistant who could do basic clerical work. They would pay at least as much as Leora is making in her current position and pay health benefits as well. Leora can join such an agency and then work her way up. In her current job, there is no job ladder.

Alicia was an immigrant from Nicaragua whose goals included learning English, obtaining a higher education, and thereby steadily enhancing her career chances. She worked as a teacher's aide and as a teacher at a day care program and then took on another job, delivering newspapers, to try to make ends meet. Maria, another mother in this cluster, was proud that she had obtained her GED and finished several training programs. Her child care center job remained stable for four years.

> She likes her work and described her experience as one in which she has progressed through the ranks. She is currently the employee who has been there the longest. She started the position as a teacher's assistant and now has her own classroom. It took her a while to feel that she wanted the responsibility of her own classroom. She turned down the offer the first time that it was made to her. As the most senior employee, she has a good amount of leverage with her supervisor and the other employees.

Wendy similarly worked at her own day care center. Her goals included opening the center, expanding it to eight kids, and getting her own building for it. She reached all these goals. Her next goal was to buy her own house.

Allison got steady raises by staying in the same niche industry—auto service and sales—and by working out a very clear strategy: if she did not get a raise where she was, she would look for a higher-paying job at another company. Each of these job changes was facilitated by a coworker from a former job. Allison had computer skills and worked in an industry that provided opportunities for job mobility. Her field-worker commented:

> Allison is aware that having computer skills is an asset in the job market and therefore it was important she practiced that set of skills for future jobs. Allison has always worked since her teenage years. She thinks it is important to work and everyone should work. It was more for her than just making money.

Allison had both goals and social capital (social networks, prior work experience, access to industries) and made use of both.

The goals of mothers in the stable employment and full-time–wage-growth groups were often concrete, intermediate in their difficulty of attainment, and characterized by short-term objectives that were part of a chain of plans and intentions (get a modest raise; plan for a new job before leaving another; make a move to a new apartment, but do not change jobs yet). Their goals and plans fit better with their non-work-related circumstances: for example, their partner was also working, so they could take time off; their child care arrangements fit their work hours; their health was good; someone in the household had a car; their education and training efforts fit into their work schedules and complemented their existing skills. These mothers usually did not face what other working-poor parents in other employment clusters often did: cascading problems that arose unpredictably and sometimes all at once, thwarting their high-level goals and thus preventing them from being realized. Their overall daily family routines were more *sustainable*—that is, their routines fit with the available resources, were relatively more balanced, created less conflict among family members, and were more predictable and stable (Lowe and Weisner 2004; Lowe et al. 2005). Thus, their employment goals were less often thwarted.

CONCLUSION

Most NHES mothers' goals for work and family were not unrealistic, and they sometimes achieved their goals. If low-wage work conditions were improved, good transportation was made available, and New Hope–type supports were more routinely offered, many working-poor parents would be ready with goals to fit those conditions. Though it may be analytically useful to distinguish goals for work from other kinds of goals, in these parents' minds educational and family goals were closely intertwined with work goals. We in fact found mixed evidence concerning the associations of work and educational goals with work trajectories. For example, educational goals measured at twenty-four months predicted higher wage growth between twenty-four and sixty months, but job improvement goals did not. Mothers in the New Hope program group did earn more income, work more hours, were less often in poverty, and their children's school achievement and well-being was higher than the control group (Duncan, Huston, and Weisner 2007). The mothers in the Stable Employment and Full-Time Wage Growth clusters suggest some pathways through which income and employment gains are related to values, goals, and plans. These parents linked values (a better job, more income, more education and training, success for their children) to attainable intermediate goals and plans. Their daily routines, though hardly easy to sustain, fit better with those goals and plans.

But the realities of low-wage jobs often did not fit what were the fairly reasonable job goals of the New Hope parents. Their work goals were also thwarted by cascading family problems and insufficient resources. These mothers sometimes worked less than full-time, or only intermittently, in order to achieve their goal of staying home with their children, or because of health concerns. Others had children with significant developmental and behavior problems that sometimes constrained their ability to work (Bernheimer, Weisner, and Lowe 2003). Job instability, flat wages, and churning from one job to another were work conditions that often had an impact on their parenting obligations. Their goals and beliefs about parenting, family, and good work sometimes limited their ability to work steadily or to take better jobs. These included, for example, the notions that good parents do not leave young children with strangers, that health comes first, that children need their mother when they are very young, or that no one should have to work under certain exploitative job conditions. Indeed, some women who experienced little improvement in their employment trajectories actually described this intermittent work pattern as a step on the way to a goal that was merely *deferred* for a while.

Chapter Eight | What Earnings and Income Buy—The "Basics" Plus "a Little Extra": Implications for Family and Child Well-Being

Rashmita S. Mistry and Edward D. Lowe

A FUNDAMENTAL WAY in which work and family are linked is economic—through the income and resources that earnings bring to families and children. Chapters 2 and 3 demonstrated that the dynamics of work across time predicted parents' psychological well-being and children's school and social outcomes. However, those chapters did not investigate whether in fact work resulted in higher income and improved financial standing. Nor did the earlier chapters examine how families negotiated across competing expenditure demands to make ends meet and the impact of negotiations related to income and expenditures for family and child functioning. These questions are central to understanding whether or not work translates into one source of meaningful difference in the lives of low-income families—that is, economic security. The combination of survey and qualitative data provides us with a unique opportunity to not only investigate what the New Hope women thought and felt about their income but also to use this information to conduct a quantitative exploration of some of the *family processes* through which income affects children's academic and social outcomes.

Welfare reform in Wisconsin and elsewhere did not necessarily lead to greater economic well-being. For many low-income mothers, increased work effort did not always lead to escape from poverty. For example, national studies of welfare "leavers" in the first years after welfare reform

showed that low earnings in combination with reduced government benefits and increased work-related costs left some families financially worse
off than when they had been on welfare (Brauner and Loprest 1999). On
the other hand, findings from two post-1996 studies—one conducted in
Michigan and the other in Boston, San Antonio, and Chicago—indicated
that women who were able to leave welfare for work experienced greater
economic gains (and in one study, greater increases in hourly wage) than
did women who either combined welfare and work or remained on welfare and were not working (Danziger et al. 2002; Danziger, Corcoran,
Danziger, and Heflin 2000; Danziger and Wang 2004; Moffitt and Kinder
2004). Although the magnitude of the economic gain is still being debated,
both studies report a substantial number of working women continuing
to live in poverty and experiencing some degree of material hardship.

Experiencing economic hardship despite work is also not limited to families making recent exits from the welfare rolls. The researchers Kathryn Edin
and Laura Lein (1997), in their seminal book *Making Ends Meet,* document
the near-impossibility of surviving off either public assistance or low-
wage work during the early 1990s. Based on interviews with over 350 low-
income women in Chicago, Boston, San Antonio, and Charleston, their
results demonstrate that surviving welfare and low-wage work requires
that women pool resources across multiple sources (family, friends, partners, off-the-books jobs, community resources) to supplement their meager
income from formal sources (public assistance and formal-sector jobs). Even
with creative juggling of this array of supports, women reported a great deal
of financial strain.

More recent evidence suggests relatively little change in the economic circumstances of many low-income families. As part of a longitudinal study of
the experiences of federal welfare reform, seventy-five women residing in
Cleveland and Philadelphia were interviewed in 1997–98 and again one year
later. Researchers observed that very few women managed to secure stable,
full-time work and that overall average incomes at follow-up were extremely
low. Only 17 percent worked for more than six months without receiving
welfare. Of these, only a small minority (7 percent) managed to hold on to
the same job for the entire six months. The more common experience was
instability in both work and income. For most, work meant low-wage jobs
with no benefits and frequent turnover. Struggling to balance work and
family demands, including finances, was a common experience among the
study participants. Most women reported relying extensively on family
members and others to make ends meet or to defray the costs of child care
(Scott et al. 2004).

These studies also include some discussion of how women's experiences
around work and income made them feel about themselves, their families,

and their children. For example, women in the Cleveland and Philadelphia samples mentioned having more income to do and buy more for their children as one of the greatest benefits of working. Women reported purchasing items and doing things that made their children feel better about themselves, such as buying expensive clothes or going to the movies. But working, especially when it entailed working multiple jobs or shift work, left many women feeling physically as well as emotionally drained. In such cases (see chapter 5), women lamented feeling stressed and not being able to do much with their children or enjoy their company (London et al. 2004).

In this chapter, we focus on the role that household income, a primary by-product of employment, played in the daily lives of the women and children in the New Hope sample. We do so in three parts. First, we investigate whether a systematic link between work and income was evident among the Child and Family Sample (CFS) families. We do so by comparing both absolute levels and changes in income across the study period of women in the various job pathway clusters described in chapter 2. Our analyses demonstrate that, on average, more stable and progressive work histories brought about more rapid increases in families' earnings-related income over time. We also observed significant variability across individual participants in terms of both absolute levels and changes in income over time, suggesting that whereas some CFS families experienced more sustainable incomes over time, a sizable percentage continued to struggle financially.

In the second part of the chapter, we explore this issue more closely through the ethnographic data. Specifically, we examine how women in the NHES sample managed their household economies—that is, how, where, and what their income was *spent* on as well as decisions surrounding expenditure patterns. Unlike Edin and Lein (1997), our goal was not to do an exact accounting of the sources of income the women relied on or to detail where they spent their income—our data did not lend themselves to such an analysis, and in any event, this was not our primary interest. Instead, we explore how women in the NHES sample negotiated between income levels and expenditure demands and the psychological and emotional ramifications of such decisions. We will see that NHES mothers reported different kinds of satisfaction in conjunction with three kinds of household expenditures: keeping up with bills, spending directly on children, and spending on big-ticket durable items. Keeping up with bills was never associated with anything better than feeling "okay." On the other hand, spending on children directly was associated with more positive feelings, and spending on big-ticket items was associated with pride, longer-lasting satisfaction, and feelings of independence.

Third, we build on the findings from the qualitative analysis and test the consequences of income and expenditure patterns for children's behavioral adjustment using data from the CFS five-year survey. Income is one of the primary pathways through which employment has systematically been shown to influence children's development. Studies have shown that income effects on children are due in part to whether or not parents perceive that income as being sufficient for meeting their needs (Conger and Elder 1994; Elder 1999; McLoyd 1990). When income is perceived as inadequate, this is typically referred to as "economic pressure." Surveys capture such perceptions of financial adequacy by asking questions having to do with the level of material hardship the family has recently experienced (for example, being behind in the rent or having utilities shut off) or the degree of concern with making ends meet on a monthly basis. Much less attention has been paid to understanding how parents, regardless of economic status, negotiate income-expenditure patterns and deal with the burdens of trying to make ends meet. Even less is known about how children factor into parents' decisions about income and expenditures. Our results both confirm findings from the qualitative analysis and extend them to impacts on children's academic and social adjustment. Finally, in the last part of this chapter, we discuss the policy implications of our findings, particularly concerning work-support policies such as the earned income tax credit (EITC) and basic supports (food stamps, housing assistance, and so on).

DOES WORKING LEAD TO ECONOMIC GAINS?

A central question of our analysis was whether *changes* in income over time could be predicted by the work pathway groupings. Establishing this link was crucial to our analysis of how and why income matters for children and family functioning. To do so, we assessed whether the work pathways, calculated over the first two years of the follow-up, were systematically related to changes in income over the same time period (contemporaneously) and subsequently across the study period (years three to five). We did so by comparing the income trajectories of women in two of the clusters (full-time–wage-growth and rapid cyclers) to those of the remaining groups (low-wage–part-time, stable employment, and low-wage–full-time). We also included the small no-work group (only twenty-two women) as an additional comparison group.

Prior analyses, based on administrative data from the state of Wisconsin, had already documented that on average the earnings of New Hope primary caregivers increased over the study period and were accompanied by significant, offsetting reductions in public assistance income (Huston, Mistry, et al. 2002).[1] The resulting net effect was a modest overall increase in total income across five years as families traded earnings-related income (earnings, EITC payments, and New Hope income supplements for program participants) for welfare income, a pattern that reflected the national trend of declining welfare rolls evident during the mid to late 1990s.

The observed pattern of income composition changes was similar for participants in both the New Hope program group and the control group. Experimental impact analyses indicated a similar rate of decline, and no significant difference, in the receipt of public assistance (AFDC and food stamps) across program and control group participants over the study period. Where evident, differences in earnings-related and total income across the program and control group were concentrated in the early years of the study, when the New Hope program was in effect. Such findings are not unique to the New Hope sample: citywide, Milwaukee observed a reduction of more than 50 percent in its welfare caseload from 1995 to 1997.[2] The dramatic drop in welfare caseloads was not unique to either Milwaukee or Wisconsin. Data from a longitudinal study of welfare recipients in Michigan also show dramatic decreases in welfare cash assistance between 1997 and 1999 (Danziger, Corcoran, Danziger, and Heflin 2000). And national estimates indicate that the number of families applying for and receiving welfare cash assistance dropped significantly from 1995 to 2000. In 1995 approximately 4.7 million families were receiving welfare assistance in any given month. By 2000 this number was slightly more than 2.2 million families—a greater than 50 percent reduction (U.S. Department of Health and Human Services 2001).

These earlier findings clearly demonstrate that, on average, families experienced little change in their overall levels of economic sustainability during the study period. Such "average" results, however, mask individual variation across sample members' income dynamics. For example, close to half of all sample members experienced an overall decline in income over the five years, while 10 percent experienced average increases of $400 or more per quarter. Understanding the source of such variation has important implications for understanding family well-being. Given the aforementioned differences in income composition (declining public assistance, increased earnings-related income) over the study period, it would appear that work effort probably contributed to differences in both the level and the changes in income experienced by individual participants across time. We now turn to the results for our first research question: do the work pathway groups from chapter 2 predict changes in income over time?

As shown in chapter 2, women in the full-time–wage-growth group had high average work hours (almost forty hours per week) and average hourly wages ($8.00), and they reported the greatest average increase in their hourly wage (nearly $4.00) over the first two years. We were interested in determining whether women in this group also experienced greater increases in their overall income over the two years, and whether this trajectory was sustained over the final three years of the study. We observed this to be the case. Table 8.1 shows that after adjusting for baseline covariates, assignment to New Hope, and initial income levels, women in the full-time–wage-growth cluster experienced significantly more rapid increases in their incomes over the first two years than did women in each of the remaining clusters, except those in the stable employment group.[3] These positive increases in income over the first two years are also reflected in the higher average annual incomes for the full-time–wage-growth group ($17,099) than for all of the remaining clusters—again, except for those in the stable employment cluster, who had comparable incomes ($17,248).

The other employment cluster of interest was the rapid cyclers group; women in this cluster were distinguished by the number and length of jobs they reported during the first two years of the study. Although employed consistently during the study period (and for close to full-time hours on average), women in this cluster changed jobs more than four times on average, with each job lasting an average of five months. These job changes, however, were not accompanied by significant changes in wages. The average wage growth was less than $1.00 in two years, suggesting that these women were making lateral job shifts. Our analyses indicated significant income differences between women in the rapid cyclers cluster and each of the remaining employment clusters (except the no-work and low-wage–full-time groups) across the first two years of the study period. As shown in table 8.1, women in this group experienced more rapid increases in their incomes over the first two years than did women in the low-wage–part-time group, but slower rates of increase than women in the full-time–wage-growth and stable employment groups.[4] However, this pattern of income changes was different when we examined the last three years of the study period. During these years (between the two- and five-year follow-ups), women in the rapid cyclers group experienced more rapid increases in income than women in the no-work group, the full-time–wage-growth group, and the low-wage–full-time group (see bottom panel of table 8.1).[5]

Also included in table 8.1 are the average annual income estimates for years one and two and for years three through five, by cluster. First, we notice substantial differences in annual income across the work pathway groups. As expected, the no-work and low-wage–part-time groups show much lower annual incomes than the other groups. The stable employment and full-time–wage-growth groups show the highest, and the rapid cyclers and low-wage–full-time groups are in between. A comparison of the income estimates across the two time points (two-year and five-year follow-ups) suggests modest changes in income across these two time frames. Across clusters, women experienced an average net economic gain ranging from $500 and $950 between the early and latter study years. (Women in the

Table 8.1 OLS Regression Coefficients Predicting Income and Rates of Change in Income from Work
Pathway Group Membership

Comparison Group	Average Annual Income Estimates, Years One and Two[a]	Rate of Change in Income, Years One and Two b (SE)	Average Annual Income Estimates, Years Three to Five[a]	Rate of Change in Income, Years Three to Five b (SE)
Comparing full-time–wage-growth group to all other Pathway Groups				
No-work	$10,874	−.15*	$10,346	−0.02
Low-wage–part-time	9,868	−.29**	10,398	0.04
Rapid cyclers	13,277	−.18*	15,039	0.16*
Stable employment	17,248	−0.03	18,190	0.13
Low-wage–full-time	13,142	−0.22**	13,806	0.01
Comparing rapid cyclers to all other Pathway Groups				
No-work		−0.05		−0.11+
Low-wage–part-time		−0.14*		−0.10
Full-time–wage-growth	17,099	0.16*	17,961	−0.14*
Stable employment		0.20**		−0.07
Low-wage–full-time		0.00		−0.19*

Notes: The top panel summarizes the analyses comparing the significance of the estimated average rate of change in income (slope) across years one and two and years three through five, and the estimated average income at quarter nine for women in the full-time–wage-growth group to all other groups. The bottom panel summarizes the results for women in the rapid cycler group versus all other groups. The coefficients are interpreted as the rate of change in income in any given cluster membership in comparison to the reference group. A negative coefficient reflects a slower rate of change than that experienced by members in the reference group; a positive coefficient reflects a more rapid increase in income as compared to that experienced by the reference group.

[a]Estimated marginals, adjusted for baseline covariates and experimental treatment group membership.

+p < .10; *p < .05; **p < .01

no-work group actually experienced a net loss in their total incomes across these two time periods; however, recall that this was a tiny group of twenty-two mothers.) Once again, the one exception was the rapid cyclers group, whose average annual incomes increased by over $1,700 across the final phase of the study; this increase was not surprising given that this group was also the only one that continued to experience significant income growth over the latter part of the study period.

To summarize, the results of our first series of analyses confirmed that work and income trajectories were related. As expected, women in the two most upwardly mobile and stable employment clusters—the full-time–wage-growth group and the stable employment group—experienced more rapid increases in their total income, especially during the first two years, than did women in less stable groups.[6] Interestingly, the rate of increase in income (primarily earnings) for the rapid cyclers during the final three years of the study exceeded that of the full-time–wage-growth group. These findings are in accordance with those reported in chapter 2 demonstrating that, in year five, the rapid cyclers worked more hours than women in the remaining clusters and also had the greatest increase in wages between the two- and five-year surveys ($2.37). In contrast, women in the full-time–wage-growth group reported working slightly fewer hours and experienced less wage growth (an average increase of $1.92). The combination of higher-than-average hours and a greater increase in hourly wage probably contributed to the difference in the rate of income increases observed between women in these two clusters over the final three years of the study period. The age of the participants may also have contributed to the relations between employment dynamics and economic growth. From earlier analyses (see chapter 2) we know that the rapid cyclers group tended to be younger and consequently earlier in their work careers than those in the full-time–wage-growth group. A normative pattern in the early career years is relatively rapid increases in income as people move up from the lowest-rung jobs. Younger workers also change jobs more often. One possibility is that as the rapid cyclers continued to gain work experience across years two to five, they started to display the signs of upward mobility, including increases in their overall income comparable to those of women in the more stable and work-ready groups during the first two years of the study period.

WHY INCOME MATTERS

Our first set of analyses confirmed a connection between women's work histories and their concurrent and successive income trajectories. Women with more stable and progressive jobs had greater earnings and total income than did women whose work histories were more precarious. We also learned that the income trajectories of individual participants in the CFS sample were quite variable over time: while some experienced overall net increases in income (and presumably greater economic security), for others income declined, sometimes steeply. Although instructive, the analyses fall short of informing us about the consequences of variability and changes in income on child and family functioning. Is it the case, for example, that families with greater economic resources experienced less material hardship and financial stress, or that those with higher and more rapidly increasing incomes were better able to negotiate and balance their family's expenditure demands? What are the psychological consequences to New Hope participants of managing their household economies? And finally, what are the implications of all of this for children's school performance and social behaviors?

In this section, we address the issue of why income mattered for family functioning—how, where, and on what it was spent, and the implications of such allocation decisions for adult well-being. To do so, we turn to a qualitative analysis of data from the ethnographic study. The qualitative data are well suited to answering these questions. Our analysis revealed two broad themes: the women meaningfully distinguished between various categories of expenditures (the "basics," "extras," and big-ticket durable items such as a car or furniture); and the women attributed different subjective meanings to the various expenditure categories and exhibited distinctly different affective responses to their (in)ability to afford these expenses. Figure 8.1 is a schematic representation of the major expenditure patterns reported by the women in the NHES sample, including prevalence rates and brief descriptions of the various expenditure categories and affective responses observed.

Categories of Expenditures

As we see in figure 8.1, the first major distinction the women made was between expenses that they expected or desired and those that were unexpected or due to an emergency. The field notes were particularly detailed about expenditures related to expected or desired needs. Entries pertaining to unexpected emergencies were less common, despite the fact that a majority of the women (thirty out of forty) reported such an expense at least once during the ethnography. Unforeseen expenses included emergency or unexpected home repairs and car repairs, emergency medical expenses, legal fees and fines (such as speeding tickets), and emergency loans to family members. A common strategy for dealing with such crises was to rely on family members and friends. Expenses were often owed until tax time, when tax refund checks helped the women catch up on outstanding

Figure 8.1 The Organization of Expenditures for the Forty Women in the NHES Sample

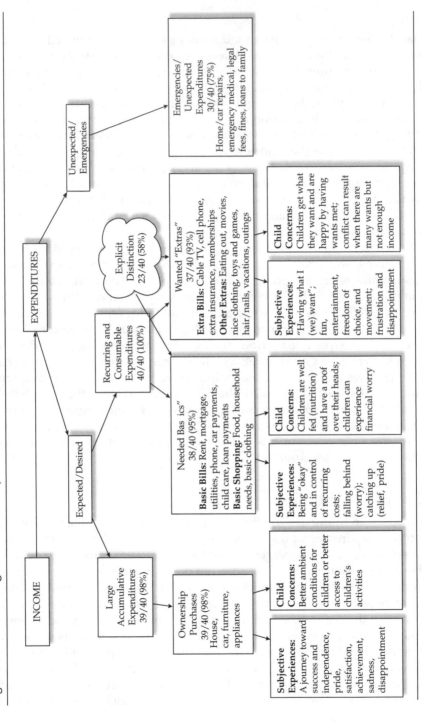

Source: Authors' compilation.

expenses (Romich and Weisner 2001). Although reported by a majority of the women, there is far less description in the field notes of the subjective experiences surrounding unexpected expenditures. Because we were primarily interested in women's psychological reactions to their expenditure demands, we concentrate here on the experiences surrounding the expected and desired expenditures. Such expenditures could in turn be differentiated between *nondurable* expenditures that occurred on a regular basis and *durable and accumulative* expenditures, which occurred less frequently.

Recurring and Nondurable Expenditures   This category of expenditures included payments for monthly household services like electricity and gas, rent or mortgage payments, food, clothing, toys for the children, and also occasional evenings out to the movies or to a restaurant. Also included were less frequently occurring expenses such as trips to the zoo, the summer fair, or travel. Such expenditures were universal in our sample.

Within this category, most of the women (58 percent) often made an explicit distinction between those expenditures that were needed or that they viewed as "basic" and those that were wanted or desired but not absolutely necessary for survival. Recurrent expenditures like payments for phone service, electricity, gas, and other monthly expenditures that involved the receipt of a paper bill or a formal agreement for monthly payment were often organized into a more general category called "the bills," as the following quote demonstrates: "Samantha mentioned some of *the bills* that take up her money. She explained that her child care bill is now $65 per week. Samantha also pays the rent, the telephone bill, the lights, and gas" (emphasis added). References to such items were often lumped together in the field notes with food and basic clothing and labeled "the basics" or "basic needs." The following field note is an example: "Ana makes $11.00 an hour. She says that now she's a bit better than when I first met her; even so, she lives day by day. [The] money is barely enough for the *basic things of the family*, like rent, bills, gas for the car, food, and clothing for her four children" (emphasis added).

Non-essential items were often described as "extras" by the women themselves and were desired for the way they conveyed a sense of well-being and satisfaction with everyday living. These expenditures included the purchase of personal items like nicer clothes and toys for the children, having one's hair or nails done, and dining out and entertainment. Extras also included household items such as a premium cable or satellite TV service or the purchase of more expensive foods, like a good steak or colored bell peppers. The following field note is an example of the use of the term "extras": "Heather said that the reason she works two jobs is so she does not have to struggle to make ends meet, and her kids won't have to struggle with her. She said that she wants to have enough money not only to pay the bills but also to *get the extras* that her kids and she need and want" (emphasis added).

Durable and Accumulative Expenditures   Big-ticket items like cars and furniture, as well as expenditures like buying a home and/or moving, were either actually purchased or mentioned as desired future purchases by nearly all members of the sample. (Thirty-three mentioned housing and furniture/appliances; thirty-four mentioned cars.) Among those who mentioned housing, a majority (58 percent) *wanted* to buy a house. Fewer participants referred to either owning or purchasing a house during the study period. Of the thirty-four women who mentioned a car, all but three mentioned owning or buying a car during the study period. None of these women, however, purchased a brand-new car. Finally, all but one of the thirty-three participants who mentioned furniture or appliances and discussed owning or purchasing them actually did so during the study period.

We refer to housing, cars, and furniture and appliances as accumulative rather than simply durable because of the way the women described the importance of accumulating these items over time. As we show in greater detail in the next section, many of the women in the ethnographic sample felt that their ability to purchase better housing or a car and to accumulate nice furniture for their house symbolized their independence and success.

The Subjective Experience of Meeting Recurring Nondurable Expenditures

When reading the field notes, we were struck by how often women described their *subjective experience* of different kinds of expenses, including their psychological experience. We limit our discussion here to how they described their own and their children's subjective experiences. Husbands or other male partners also figured prominently in the story of expenditures for many of these women, but they will be discussed in chapter 10.

Meeting Basic Needs Each Month   Sixteen mothers (40 percent) described their experience of meeting basic needs. Nine of them described feeling "okay" when they were able to pay their bills each month in full. Being okay indicated that the participant was achieving a certain minimum level of well-being. But being okay did not reach the level of being happy or fulfilled in terms of expenditures. For example, consider the following excerpt for Rose: "I guess I'm doing something right. I'm *okay* so far. At least I have a roof over my head, and stuff like that. And food in the house for kids and whatever" (emphasis added).

The recurring nature of basic expenditures was important to their meaning. When Karen described her finances, she spoke of how paying off her basic bills each month was important to her sense of being okay:

> You know, I'm doing *okay*. I was used to having the extra money, but I know bills are still going to be there no matter what. As soon as I pay them off, another month they're here again. Nothing I can do about it, so don't see the need to worry about it. The bills are under control. I'm not behind in anything. (emphasis added)

Families in the ethnographic sample frequently were unable to meet all of their basic expenditures in a given month. Naturally, such experiences were often described as creating anxiety and worry or feeling "stressed" economically. The following field note for Faye is an example:

> Faye said that she is feeling very stressed about being behind in her bills. Losing her job in May and not being able to find one again has really set her back. She owes electricity ($450) and is three months behind in rent ($800). While I was there her phone rang, and it was the gas company—she owes them about $250. She said that it has been difficult—she feels she needs to catch up and she will feel better.

One strategy for dealing with falling behind on the "basics" was to prioritize which bills got paid first and which were allowed to lapse. The women in the sample complained often about their inability to pay all of their basic bills, including rent, food, utilities, and child care. In such cases, housing (rent or mortgage) and food expenses most often had the highest priority. For example, after being laid off from her job as a temporary health care worker and subsequently falling behind in her bills, Rose told her field-worker: "I was really worried about paying the bills on time and stuff, but at some point you just change and think, okay, so what, bills are late. The most important thing is that my kids have something to eat." Once families had paid off their outstanding bills, they reported feeling "in control" and feeling "good" or "trying to stay calm" as a result. Those who were eligible to receive the earned income tax credit as a lump sum each year found it to be a great help in this regard (Romich and Weisner 2001). For example, Wendy's field-worker noted that "she thinks it is a really good thing that she got caught up on all of her bills when she was getting paid. Wendy said, 'When the county did send the last check [for her W-2 child care clients], we took care of some bills. . . . That's good. That's why I am just trying to stay calm." The field-worker also recorded Janet's report that "she has finally paid off all the late bills that had accumulated from the time when she was not being paid on time. She was pleased to have gotten everything paid off."

In sum, we see that meeting basic needs each month was not necessarily a source of much positive affect or an enhanced sense of well-being. Rather, meeting basic needs conveyed a sense of being merely "okay." Falling behind on basic expenditures was a source of stress, worry, and anxiety, while the experience of catching up with late bills provided a temporary sense of relief. Feeling just okay at being able to cover basic monthly expenses is not unique to the women in the NHES sample. Such feelings probably resonate with many parents and working adults. One difference, however, between the experiences of low-income adults and those of their more affluent counterparts is the consistency with which they were able to meet their basic needs from one month to the next. Studies also show that covering the basics consumes a significantly greater proportion of low-income families' resources as compared to those of middle-class families (Institute for the Study of Homelessness and Poverty 2001).

A dominant theme of our analysis was the constant struggle and flux faced by many women to ensure that their family's basic needs were met. This contributed in part to their lackluster response to meeting their basic expenses: they recognized the temporary nature of the reprieve. The constant struggle also mattered for their sense of well-being, since it created anxiety, worry, and concern that at some point in the near future they would once again be faced with tough choices about which bills to pay and which ones to let lapse. Many of the women spoke of trying to save a little every month, but few were able to do so, or to do so on a regular basis.

Consuming Desire: The Subjective Experience of Buying "Extras"   The subjective experience of purchasing "extras" was described by eighteen of the women (45 percent). Extras were typically described as items that the individual *wanted* but that were not absolutely necessary. For example: "Belinda said that at one time she used to have a little money left over at the end of the month, that she did what she *wanted* to do with it. Sometimes she would get her hair done or her nails. Just a little something for herself" (emphasis added). In a similar vein, extra spending, such as purchasing nicer clothing and jewelry, helped some of the women project an image of economic success for themselves and their children. Allison, for example, "likes to dress well, and she explains that she does not mean jewelry and diamonds and all that. But she wants a decent outfit and shoes. She wears uniforms at work, which is good, but she has a meeting at the Hospitality Inn and she wants a nice outfit to attend it. She says, 'If you look like you got something, or are going somewhere, you are going somewhere.' "

The ability to purchase nondurable extras was important for the women in our study because it conveyed to them and to their children a sense of fulfillment, enjoyment, or happiness with everyday life. Some even felt that it was important to spend a little extra because it was important to feel fulfilled and not deprived, at least at some modest level. For example:

> Lynette said that she does not believe in denying herself cravings. . . . She explained she doesn't believe in not getting things because you are worried about money. It doesn't matter what kind of job she has, if she wants a good steak she will go to the store and buy one. She said that everyone is always low on money, and if you deny yourself things, then *you'll never be happy or enjoy life.* (emphasis added)

The New Hope mothers were also concerned about providing things that their children wanted. The ability to do so helped them feel like they were good mothers. When money was tight, many felt strongly about sacrificing their own desires so that they could meet their children's desires. Being able to buy extras for themselves or for their children made these women feel good:

> Lisa said that she spends most of her money getting things for her children. She rarely buys things for herself. She said that one of the reasons she probably splurges so much money on them is because she never had that advantage when she was a child. Her parents never took them to movies or out to eat. Lisa said that she is trying to show some things that she never got to experience as a child. . . . Lisa said that it feels good to go shopping and buy her kids stuff. It gives her a natural high.

Purchasing the extra goods and services that the women and their children wanted conveyed a sense that their families were not deprived. For example, Heather "said that for a while she tried to work only one job, and that was just not enough money to do everything that she wanted to do. She said she doesn't consider herself poor and doesn't feel that she and her kids should live like they are, so she works the two jobs."

Extra spending also gave these mothers a sense that their families could enjoy activities that they understood to be typical of a middle-class American lifestyle. For example:

> Faye said that if she could have money left over she would really like to do something with it for [her teenage son] Eric. She said she would like to enroll

him in something so he has something to do besides hanging out. She said she would like to enroll him in a basketball league, karate class, or music, or something that he could do and like. She said she would also really like to buy bikes so the whole family could throw a backpack of food on their backs and go bike and picnic together. Faye said in a nostalgic manner that she really would like to do that.

Many women could not spend anything extra on their children, even if they wanted to, because their income was simply too low.[7] This proved to be a source of disappointment and tension in their parent-child relationships and led to feelings of lower self-worth:

> Faye said that Eric knows that they don't have money, but he really doesn't understand how lacking in money they are. He is always asking her to buy him clothes or get cash, and she has to tell him that she doesn't have it. Faye said that kids really don't understand the stress parents go through in providing for them. . . . He knows that things are tight, but it doesn't really have any meaning for him. He would easily allow her to spend all the money they had on clothes if she let him. Faye does feel bad and really low when Eric makes comments about their economic situation.

Women in Faye's position wanted to shield their children from feeling deprived as much as they could. Often their self-sacrifice for the sake of their children made them feel good, even gave them a "natural high." But being unable to buy things occasionally for their children made some women feel poorly about themselves as mothers. And constant self-sacrifice could be depressing, particularly on special occasions like a mother's own birthday, when she might expect to have her desires indulged, at least a little. Samantha's experience of her birthday was an occasion for sadness, not celebration:

> Samantha also seemed a little stressed or sad thinking about her birthday that was coming up in the next week. She said that she wanted to get her hair and nails done, and maybe go out and celebrate it, but she doesn't have any money to do that. . . . She knows she looks a mess, but she puts all her time and money toward making sure her kids look together. She said that nobody can say that her children don't come first.

Their children's desire for new purchases seemed endless to many of the mothers. Some reported helping their children to understand the importance of limiting their desires and learning how to save a small weekly allowance to purchase things on their own. For example,

> Susan said that she is really trying to save money and control her spending on "unnecessary stuff" for Mary like clothes, nail polish, etc. . . . She has told Mary that if she wants these things, she will have to use up her allowance to buy them and cannot keep asking for them from her mother. It was okay to ask for these things once in a while, but Susan has noticed that Mary's demands were endless.

As we can see, rather than promoting a sense of worry and anxiety, as the inability to meet basic expenditures did, an inability to purchase wanted extras led to a sense of sadness and frustration. It also added to tensions between family members when only some of the family members' desires were satisfied. In general, mothers willingly sacrificed their own desires for those of their children in order to prevent their children from feeling deprived. But occasionally constant self-sacrifice generated feelings of disappointment.

In our reading of the field notes, we were struck by the relative absence of one major category of recurring expenditures especially related to children's development. A large body of research points to the importance of early and continued exposure to educationally oriented activities and materials for children's positive adjustment, particularly with respect to cognitive and academic outcomes. Children who have access to high-quality child care and after-school programs, participate in supervised extracurricular activities, are read to frequently, and have stimulating experiences at home and outside (such as visits to the library and to museums) show greater competency across a number of developmental domains than do children with limited experiences in these areas (Bradley and Corwyn 2004; Brooks-Gunn, Klebanov, and Liaw 1995; Duncan and Brooks-Gunn 2000; Guo and Harris 2000; Yeung, Linver, and Brooks-Gunn 2002).

When describing their regular expenditures, women in our sample rarely referred to their children's participation in academically oriented activities or talked about purchasing items that would be likely to stimulate their cognitive development. Almost three-fourths of the women made at least one mention of a child-related purchase. Of these, the most frequent purchase were toys, including media equipment (for example, video games), which were mentioned by twenty-two women, followed by clothing (seventeen women). Extracurricular activities were mentioned relatively infrequently (seven). Televisions were rarely mentioned as new purchases. Although we do not have frequency counts for the number of NHES families who owned a television set, there is reason to suspect that almost all of them owned at least one. Results from the Department of Energy's 2001 Residential Energy Consumption Survey indicate that 99 percent of American households own a color television. Among low-income households (less than $15,000 annual income), 64 percent also report having cable or satellite service, and 74 percent own at least one VCR (U.S. Department of Energy 2004). For NHES families, televisions may have figured more prominently when they discussed either getting a better television or home entertainment center or making family purchases rather than child-specific purchases. Any such purchase was thus more likely to be classified as a durable and accumulative expenditure.

Although women frequently mentioned buying toys and media equipment for their children, these items were typically purchased for entertainment rather than educational purposes. For example, they frequently mentioned X-Box and Nintendo games as both desired and purchased gifts for their children's birthdays and for Christmas. The one exception was computers: three reported purchasing a computer during the study period, and several more spoke of wanting to purchase one. Women reported purchasing a computer so that their children could complete homework assignments and have access to the Internet. They also talked about the importance of computer skills for future job success. They were keenly aware that computer literacy was essential for securing a well-paying job.

Our findings are more meaningful in light of what we know about the desire expressed by many of the women in our sample to shield and protect their children from economic deprivation. Their efforts in this regard appear to have focused primarily on social participation, leading to an emphasis on the purchase of toys, electronic equipment, clothing, and accessories. These mothers reported a variety of strategies to ensure that their children did not feel deprived during the holidays or on their birthday. For example, one year Evelia was strapped for cash until her tax refund check arrived, so she told her children that Christmas would be delayed. The field-worker noted that "her children have also been told not to expect any Christmas gifts, that they would have to wait till Día de los Reyes (Three Wise Men Day in January), and then they would get some money or a small present." The women also made sure that other family members would buy the children presents, even if they themselves could not afford to do so. For example, "Karen had not bought any Christmas presents yet because she doesn't have any money. Karen said that she plans to go to Toys for Tots again to get something for the kids. She said that her family will also give the kids gifts so they will have something under the tree." They voiced less concern about their children's academic progress, but it is impossible to know from these data why this was the case. Our findings that whenever possible women chose to spend a portion, if not all, of their extra income on their children is consistent with other analyses of low-income families' experiences around work, income, and family life (London et al. 2004).

The Subjective Experience of Meeting Durable and Accumulative Expenditures

Durable purchases (such as housing, cars, or furniture) seem to signify something quite different from nondurable expenditures. In particular, the women in our sample viewed these expenditures as signifying progress on a journey of accomplishment. As they were able to improve their housing, their mode of transportation, and the furniture and appliances they collected for their homes, they gained a sense of having made steady improvements in the quality of their lives and their children's lives. Moreover, being able to buy nicer or better-quality items also mattered.

Housing: A Bigger, Nicer House in a Better Neighborhood When discussing nondurable purchases, quality issues rarely came up (with the exception of clothing). But issues of quality came up frequently in the context of discussing durable expenditures. For instance, fourteen women (35 percent) described aspects of housing quality that mattered to them.

The most commonly discussed feature of housing was size, in particular the adequacy of the home given the size of the family. Housing size, given the cost, was a primary concern of these women, in terms of both coming up with the money for moving to a new rental and discussing the sort of house they would like to buy. A larger house often signified a "move upwards" for these families. Consider the following excerpt from field notes about Heather:

> She said that if her fiancé gets them a house, then maybe she will move. She said that she wants her next move to be a move upwards. She said she doesn't want to move just into another small apartment. She told him that she would like to move to Arizona. She said that she wants a big beautiful house, with a swimming pool for her babies.

One reason for finding a larger home was to accommodate children of the opposite sex, since many women felt it was inappropriate for brothers and sisters to share a room. For example: "Belinda complained that their apartment is really too small for seven people (the four kids, her husband Joe, his son, and her). The boys are old now and should have their own space where they can go and be by themselves. Belinda also said that her daughter, Joella, is starting to develop and will become a woman soon enough, so she also needs to be away from the boys."

In addition to size, the New Hope mothers described the importance of having a house that was well maintained and of adequate quality. For example, when Maria and her husband decided to look for a new place, her husband said that their "main reason for moving was because the other house needed maintenance and was infested with cockroaches and rats." The quality of the neighborhood was also mentioned often (35 percent of the ethnographic sample). In general, these women were looking for a neighborhood that was quiet and well maintained and that offered more opportunities for their children. Many of these themes can be heard in Leora's account of her family's prospective move: "She is happy that the move would mean living in a better house in a nicer neighborhood. . . . Bannerville is a much nicer and quieter neighborhood. Leora is also enthusiastic about the school district and is happy that Kim could go to a different school district and will not have to go to the Milwaukee Public School District."

Finally, crowding and crime were major concerns. For example, "Maria's husband likes the area where he lives, but maybe they'll go and live at Thirtieth or Thirty-fifth Street. Their current neighborhood has a lot of people on drugs."

Homeownership   Nearly all of the ethnographic participants (91 percent) either discussed wanting to buy a house or actually owned their house during the period of ethnographic study. Homeownership was associated with greater feelings of control and a sense of happiness, pride, satisfaction, and accomplishment. These themes are reflected in the following field note about Elena:

> She changed addresses because she finally bought her own house. She was very happy and she wanted me to visit her so I could see the new place where she lives. She told me that the house was small but that she was very happy. The seller of the house was her own brother, so that made all the procedures very easy. Elena says that now she feels a lot more control over her life.

One reason for the feeling of greater control with homeownership was that those women who owned their home felt independent of bad neighbors and bad landlords and believed that the money they spent each month for the mortgage was an improvement over "throwing away" their money in rent payments. Katie, for example, was finally buying a house. "She has been thinking about buying a house for a few months now. She said she is sick of living next to people, having 'slum lords,' and paying all this money towards rent that just goes out the window."

Homeownership also conferred a sense of accomplishment, as exemplified in Marisa's experience of owning her own home:

> She had always wished to have her own home. There are more responsibilities to owning a home. In total, she paid $18,000 for her home. She considers that it would have been impossible to find a home for that price in a better neighborhood. She felt satisfied when she got her own home. Now that she has a home and a car, her next goal would be to retire.

The accumulation of the American dream, in the prototypic sequence of family, car, home, and leisure, is evident here, but with one major deviation: leisure is limited to the end of one's career. The implication is that for Marisa, resting and leisure cannot occur during her work life, with its constant pressure to meet the "basics."

Cars: Practical Transportation and an Important Symbol of Achievement   We found in chapter 2 that having access to a car was one of the stronger predictors of being on an upward job trajectory (membership in the full-time–wage-growth or stable employment group). Of the forty participants, fifteen discussed what owning a car meant to them. Of these, ten discussed cars as a practical resource, particularly when their children needed to be transported to different locations. Considering the many places that they and their children had to go (work, church, shopping, multiple schools, child care locations, child activities, and so on), they viewed owning a working car as an invaluable resource, particularly during Milwaukee's harsh winters. Owning a working car seemed to make life "easier":

> Faye believes that having a car will make things a lot easier in her life. She said running round looking for a job, taking her preschool-aged son, Baylor, to school, going shopping—all will be easier with a car. Faye said that she probably won't come home as tired by the end of the day because she has a car. She said that having a car is so much easier and faster than depending on the bus.

Faye was not alone in comparing transportation by car to Milwaukee's bus transportation system. Of the seventeen women who mentioned the buses in Milwaukee, just over half spoke about their unreliability, their tardiness, and the fact that they simply did not go to many of the places where they needed to go (particularly places where better jobs were located). The commutes described by the New Hope mothers were substantially longer when taken by bus (typically sixty to ninety minutes) than by car (typically twenty to thirty minutes).

Car ownership was also an important indicator of economic success for many women. For example, "Nancy did not have a car, and that did come up in the conversation several times in different contexts. In her mind, possessing a car was an indicator of success." Nicer cars, those that were in better condition and looked fashionable, were especially significant in creating a sense of pride and accomplishment, particularly for those women who were able to purchase the car with their own earnings. Michol's experience was typical:

As we walked out the door, Michol looked through her purse for her sunglasses. Then she said she had to get them out of her car. She walked around to a freshly waxed, dark green Dodge with a spoiler (early '90s model?), saying proudly, "This is mine." . . . She said that this was the first new car she's ever gotten, explaining that it's not new, but it's the first non-junker, non-bought-from-a-friend car.

In the following, particularly telling excerpt, an NHES mother, Rose, literally pats herself on the back as an indication of her feelings of financial independence (particularly from men), pride, and accomplishment: "Rose bought a car, the car she was going to buy last time we met. She said that she didn't get any money from her partner, Roland. . . . In any case, she proudly claimed, while she tried to literally pat herself on the back, that she bought that car all by herself."

Cars, however, also brought on additional expenses and troubles. Seven of the women in the sample described a breakdown of their car at some point during the ethnography; only two of the seven reported being able to afford to fix the car.

Furniture and Appliances: Markers of Progress   Close to half of the women (eighteen) discussed the significance of purchasing and accumulating furniture, appliances, and other durable items for their homes. As with housing and cars, some discussed the importance of buying higher-quality furniture and other durable items for the home. Others discussed the importance of having nice furnishings for being able to enjoy their home. A number of women described their experience of collecting or accumulating nice furniture as conveying a sense of accomplishment, particularly a sense that all of the hard work was worth the effort and hassle.

Iris once talked about the importance of buying better-quality furniture that would last longer:

> The one piece of furniture that Iris does not have but would really like is a hard-wood bed. She could get bedroom furniture from First American, but they do not have hardwood furniture, usually only pressed wood, and it breaks too easily. She much prefers sturdy, real wood furniture to pressed-wood furniture. She said that when she has enough money she will look for a new bed at a used furniture store.

Having better-quality furniture was also important for keeping a "nice" home, one that family members could enjoy. Some women even discussed taking extra steps to protect and preserve their furniture so that it would last longer.

> Belinda said that she really likes to keep her house looking nice. She said she likes to have nice furniture for her and her family to enjoy. She pointed to the living room and pointed out the furniture. She told me that she spent about $2,000 on that living room set. She said that she is planning on getting plastic covers for the furniture, but doesn't know where to get them and knows it is going to be expensive.

For these women, collecting furniture and other nice durable items for the house was about more than conveying a sense of enjoyment of their standard of living or feeling as though they were more accomplished than other family members or neighbors. For many of them, the accumulation of nice furniture was a powerful symbol of their achievement as financially independent adults. Several women independently described the accumulation of furniture as conveying a sense of moving away from having nothing. Accumulating nice things for the house gave them a feeling of well-being and pride in having accomplished so much given their years of effort and sacrifice in the low-wage labor market:

> Rose said that it is important for her to have her house set up and filled with nice furniture. She said that she couldn't stand it when she moved in and they were living in practically an empty house. It made her depressed. She said that buying the furniture and making her house look nice makes her feel good. She

said that the furniture gives her something that shows what she is working for. Rose said that she likes to have something to show how hard she is working. "It gives me something to work for."

In the field notes for Heather, we see that the things she had collected for her home made her feel good as well; they also helped her to feel better about some of her current financial difficulties:

Even though things are stressed and Heather feels things in her life are out of balance right now, she feels good when she compares to where she used to be. Heather explained, "Oh, if you could have seen me then. I moved into this apartment with nothing. I had some old wicker furniture my mother gave me. Two chairs that were broken and you couldn't sit on, and one bed frame. Now look, I have all of this. I've worked really hard to get where I am and I am blessed."

In summary, there was a different relationship between the NHES participants' sense of well-being and their acquisition of durable goods over time than was observed for nondurables. These women reported feeling proud when they were able to acquire pieces of the American dream—owning a car and a home that they were able to furnish. They viewed the accumulation of such goods as evidence of their accomplishments. Beyond acquisition, however, women also made distinctions in terms of the quality of the goods they owned. Size, safety, and location concerns dominated their discussions of housing and their decisions to move. They also expressed great satisfaction at being able to furnish their homes and relished the opportunity it gave them to reflect on how far they had come.

INCOME, EXPENDITURES, AND CHILDREN'S ACADEMIC AND BEHAVIORAL OUTCOMES

In the final section of the chapter, we build on findings from the qualitative analysis using five-year survey data collected on the larger sample of CFS families. Our goal was twofold: first, to replicate findings from the qualitative analysis with a larger sample of CFS families; and second, to test a mediated model, following the ethnographic findings, of how earnings and other sources of income affect children's development through multiple dimensions of parental well-being.

The link between economic hardship, family processes, and child outcomes was informed by a large body of mostly survey-based research.

For low-income families, or those facing income loss, economic hardship appears to lead to increased economic pressure and disruptions in the daily routines of family members. The link to children's well-being and functioning is through the disruptions in parenting behaviors associated with parents' emotional distress, which, in turn, place children at risk for adjustment problems. It is the parents' perceived *adequacy* of income, above and beyond absolute levels, that is a critical determinant of children's adjustment, particularly with respect to their social behavior (Conger et al. 1994; Elder 1974/1999; Gutman and Eccles 1999; McLoyd 1990; Mistry et al. 2002).

There is little evidence from evaluations of New Hope's experimental effects that it had long-term effects on the key mediating constructs of interest in this chapter (Huston, Richburg-Hayes, et al. 2003). Five years after the implementation of New Hope, program and control group members reported similar levels of material and psychological well-being. (One exception was that program group members reported fewer depressive symptoms and greater awareness of the resources available in their community than did control group members.) Furthermore, few differences were evident between program and control group members with respect to parenting behaviors. It appears therefore that while New Hope had a significant impact on the economic well-being of families in the program group as compared to the control group, this impact did not filter through to the set of family processes of interest in the current investigation. The findings shed little light on the pathways by which income matters for children's adjustment, irrespective of program group status. Although the experimental impact analyses suggest that family processes are not the primary pathway by which New Hope influenced children's outcomes (results point to systematic differences in the use of formal child care and structured activities), they do not negate the possibility that income matters for children in part because of its influence on the family system, irrespective of program group status.

Our qualitative analysis, however, went one step further in informing us about the link between the economic resources of our families and the mothers' mental health. Despite limited finances, over time many of the women in the ethnographic sample were able to accumulate such assets as a car, a house, and decent home furnishings. Ownership of such items provided them with something tangible by which to assess their economic and social progress. They reported a sense of pride and accomplishment at being able to accumulate assets and greater satisfaction with their standard of living. Such feelings did not, however, occur in isolation. While expressing satisfaction with their current overall standard of living, women also lamented the precariousness of their financial security and their constant struggle to meet their monthly financial obligations—the "basics" plus a little "extra."

Understanding how and why economic hardship matters for children and their families is clearly influenced by both sources—asset accumulation and material hardship. But research has focused almost exclusively on the latter. Our qualitative analysis clearly shows that in the face of ongoing financial difficulties, especially in meeting the "basics," the acquisition of material possessions denoting status has an influential impact on women's sense of well-being and may affect their children's well-being as well. In light of these findings, we conducted a quantitative analysis that examined how both dimensions of families' economic experiences affect parents and children. Using path analysis, we were able to test whether individual changes in income over the study period predicted how well children were faring at the end of the study period.[8] In addition, we included mediators of the link between income change and child outcomes, informed by the results of our qualitative analysis and prior research.[9] Before presenting our results, it is important that we mention one caveat to our analysis—the incomplete representation in the survey of all of the important constructs identified in the qualitative analysis. This could not be helped given that all data were collected prior to our analysis, both qualitative and quantitative. For example, within the domain of durable goods, we were only able to include assessments of car and home ownership. Survey questions about home furnishings and appliances were not included in the five-year survey. Likewise, with respect to nondurable goods, we were unable to do a formal test of the effect of "extras" on maternal mental health. Nevertheless, we believe our analysis approach represents an important advance in thinking about the processes by which income matters for children living in poverty.

We estimated separate models for children's academic[10] and social adjustment,[11] assessed at the five-year follow-up (see figures 8.2 and 8.3). All analyses controlled for initial levels of income at the beginning of the study period and included an extensive set of individual and family covariates assessed either at baseline or at the time of the five-year follow-up.[12] As with child outcomes, all potential mediators were assessed during the five-year follow-up survey. We included pathways from income (initial level and individually estimated rate of change) to women's reports of material hardship and home and car ownership.[13] Questions about car and home ownership were included as representations of the accumulative (durable) expenditures mentioned by women in the ethnographic sample. To capture recurring (nondurable) expenditures, we included an index of material hardship that assessed survey respondents' difficulty in meeting their financial obligations for such recurring expenses as rent or mortgage payments.[14] Reports of material hardship and ownership were hypothesized to influence three indicators of perceived economic well-being and pressure: expressed satisfaction with overall current standard of living and with current housing, and a mea-

Figure 8.2   The Relations of Changes in Family Income over Five
            Years to Family Processes and Children's Academic
            Outcomes, Assessed at the End of the Five Years

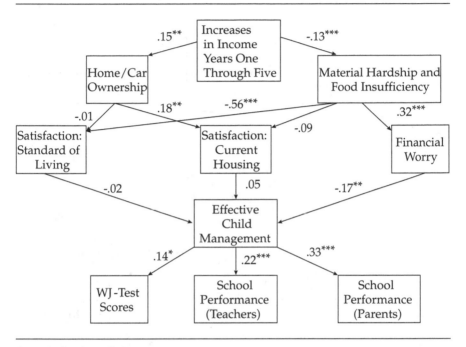

Source: Authors' compilation.
Note: Model fit: $\chi^2(25, N = 328) = 38.526$, p < .05; CFI = .991; RMSEA = .040; low 90% = .008; high 90% = .06. Analyses control for demographic, human capital, and maternal characteristics (including maternal depressive symptoms) and for initial income at the beginning of the study period (quarter one).
* p < .10; ** p < .05; *** p < .01

sure of financial worry.[15] Based on the larger literature on economic stress and its relation to child well-being, we expected that economic well-being (pressure) would influence parents' capacity to discipline, control, and monitor their children's behavior.[16] That capacity, in turn, was hypothesized to have an impact on children's school-related performance and behavioral outcomes.

Overall, the results were generally consistent with our expectations, although there were a few notable exceptions. Figure 8.2 presents the results predicting academic outcomes, and figure 8.3 presents those for behavioral outcomes. First, as expected, mothers whose incomes increased more rapidly over the study period were more likely to report owning a car or house and

Figure 8.3   The Relations of Changes in Family Income Over Five
Years to Family Processes and Children's Behavioral
Outcomes, Assessed at the End of the Five Years

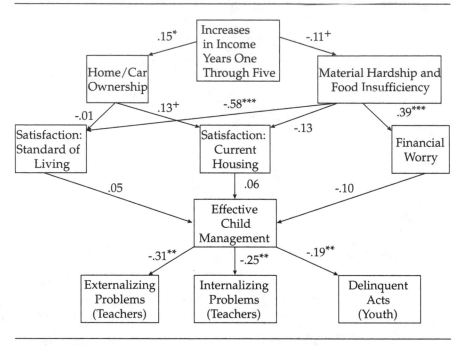

Source: Authors' compilation.
Note: Model fit: $\chi^2(25, N = 222) = 25.413$, ns.; CFI = 1.00; RMSEA = .009; low 90% = .00; high 90% = .05.
The reduced sample is due in part to the delinquency items being asked of only the older children in the
sample (ages nine and older). Analyses control for demographic, human capital, and maternal
characteristics (including maternal depressive symptoms) and for initial income at the beginning of the
study period (quarter one).
[+] p <.10; [*] p < .05; [**] p < .01; [***] p < .001.

experiencing less material hardship at the five-year assessment than those
who experienced less rapidly increasing or declining incomes. Ownership
was unrelated to how satisfied the women reported feeling about their overall standard of living. But women who owned a car or home by the end of
the study period were more likely to be satisfied with their current housing
than those who did not. Ownership and overall standard of living were
unrelated in the survey data; this was inconsistent with the ethnographic
data, in which mothers' satisfaction with their current status was related to
their ownership of durable items such as a car or a house. One possibility is
that the difference in results reflects the restricted range of the ownership

items assessed in the survey, relative to the ethnography. Although home and car ownership represented important milestones for the women in our sample, they were also the most difficult to acquire and maintain compared to items like furniture and appliances. For example, the cars that women in our sample purchased were exclusively secondhand models that often required frequent maintenance and repair to keep them functional. Finally, the owned items most frequently mentioned by mothers in the ethnography, furniture and appliances, were not measured in the survey and could not be included in our ownership measure.

The findings with respect to the link between material hardship and women's perception of economic well-being were generally consistent with our expectations (see figures 8.2 and 8.3). Material hardship was unrelated to their expressed satisfaction with their current housing, but women who reported experiencing greater material hardship indicated less satisfaction with their overall standard of living and said that they were more worried about their finances. This mirrors the findings from the qualitative analysis, which showed that the constant struggle to meet basic needs took a toll on the women's mental health.

The next link in the chain is from perceptions of economic well-being to parenting behavior, and in turn to children's adjustment. Of the three indicators of economic well-being (satisfaction with standard of living, satisfaction with current housing, and financial worry), only financial worry was related to parenting behavior.[17] As expected, women who reported being more worried about their financial situation also reported feeling less competent when disciplining and monitoring their children's behavior. The children of women reporting less effective parenting strategies scored lower on a standardized test of achievement and were rated as faring less well academically by teachers and parents (see figure 8.2). Parenting behavior was also related to children's social behavioral outcomes: higher perceptions of effective parenting predicted lower youth-reported delinquency, as well as higher teacher-reported internalizing (withdrawn) and externalizing (acting-out) behaviors (see figure 8.3).

The results presented thus far provide initial support for our thesis that family income and expenditures influence children in part through their impact on the family system—particularly parents' mental health. To evaluate more formally whether family processes *mediate* the relation of family income and expenditures to child outcomes, we calculated the magnitude and statistical significance of the *indirect* effects of income and expenditures on children's adjustment through the set of family processes—perceived economic well-being and parenting behavior.[18]

As hypothesized, income mattered for children's academic adjustment, in part because of its impact on each of the intervening indicators of family well-being. Controlling for the covariates and for income level at the study outset, more rapid increases in income over time had a positive (albeit modest) indirect influence on all three indicators of children's academic adjustment.[19] Further, this effect was observed to exist primarily as a consequence of how much parents reported worrying about their finances, which indirectly affected children through parenting behavior.[20] Neither of the satisfaction variables was significantly related to children's academic behavior. And there was no evidence that either of the two expenditure sources (ownership and material hardship) influenced children's academic well-being indirectly through economic pressure and parenting behavior.

The pattern of relations between income, expenditures, and children's social behaviors differed from those observed for academic outcomes. As a consequence of income's impact on family functioning, children whose families experienced more rapid increases in income reported less delinquency and were rated by teachers as showing fewer internalizing and externalizing problems.[21] It was not possible, however, to determine the precise pathway through which income affected social behavior.

In sum, the results of our quantitative analyses provide some confirmation of the links between income, expenditure patterns, and mother's mental health observed in the analysis of the NHES study, but with a couple of exceptions. Ownership and perceived satisfaction with one's standard of living were not as consistently predicted by or related to the other measures in the model. This may have been due in part to psychometric issues (both were less reliable than either material hardship or financial worry). Future research should include more reliable measures of these two constructs. Lastly, family processes partially mediated the influence of income on children's academic outcomes, but not their behavioral adjustment.

CONCLUSION

At the beginning of this chapter, we stated that we were driven to answer three primary questions. First, did work translate into greater economic stability for the women in the CFS sample? The results of our quantitative analyses comparing the income trajectories of women in the five job pathway groupings suggest that it did, at least contemporaneously. Women who were able to achieve stable employment and full-time work with decent wages experienced more rapid increases in their incomes during the first two years of the study, and these income gains translated into higher total incomes at the end of the two years compared to the incomes of women in less secure and lower-paying jobs. An interesting pattern was observed across the final three years of the study for women in the rapid cycler group, who showed the highest levels of wage growth. (They had shown only moderate wage growth in the first two years of the study.) Analyses of the income trajectories also revealed that, even though a majority of CFS families were successful in trading welfare income for work-related income, on average, families experienced little net gain in their overall level of economic well-being. Furthermore, families varied dramatically in their levels of economic security and changes in their economic standing over the study period—such that while some CFS families experienced more sustainable incomes over time, a sizable percentage continued to struggle financially.

Our remaining research questions picked up on this theme of economic variability and assessed the ways in which mothers in the NHES sample negotiated income-expenditure demands and the consequences of such negotiations, for both their own psychological well-being (using data from NHES and the five-year follow-up survey of CFS families) and that of their children (using data from the five-year follow-up survey). Qualitative analyses of the forty NHES participants revealed the complexity of feelings associated with different kinds of expenditures. The field notes were full of examples of the unrelenting psychological strain and burden that accompanied the economic hardship endured by many of our families. Women reported feeling anxious, tired, and worried about being able to make ends meet. Particularly telling were their reports of feeling just "okay" for being able to stay on top of their monthly bills, in part because they were acutely aware that the reprieve was short-lived. These mothers expressed concern about being able to provide for their children and a strong desire to try to shield them from some of the economic hardship. Many of them talked about sacrificing some of their own needs so that they could meet the needs (and wants) of their children.

An equally revealing theme in these women's experiences was the balance between struggling to meet basic needs and making progress in achieving the American dream of owning a car and a home and acquiring nice things to put in it. The longitudinal nature of our data was critical for revealing the satisfaction that participants experienced in accumulating big-ticket items over time. The women expressed a sense of pride in ownership and viewed their accomplishments as evidence that they were slowly but surely moving up. Further, our analysis demonstrated the importance to their sense of well-being of having just a little "extra" left over to spend on nonessential material items. In contrast to their ongoing struggles to meet basic needs, being able to purchase the extras as well as durable items made the women feel less on the margins of American society, and for some it made the toil of working multiple jobs tolerable. Finally, the results of the qualitative analysis clearly illuminate the difficult and complex budgeting decisions that these women faced on a daily basis. They balanced opposing needs, such as their own personal needs versus those of their child, or the desire to purchase extras at the cost of forgoing some of the basics.

Building up from the qualitative analysis, the survey-based quantitative analyses confirmed the link between family income, expenditures, and multiple indicators of maternal psychological well-being. In addition, we extended these links to include indicators of parenting practices and children's academic and social outcomes. We observed that income mattered for child outcomes in part through its influence on degree of material hardship, which was associated with increased financial worry and less-than-optimal parenting behavior. Both the qualitative and the quantitative analyses confirmed that mothers who experienced greater difficulty in making ends meet spent considerable time worrying about their finances. The quantitative analyses showed that worrying about their finances also affected women's parenting behavior, and ultimately their children's adjustment.

Overall, the pattern of results from our combined qualitative and quantitative analyses demonstrates that income matters for children's development because of its influence on low-income mothers' ability to meet not only their basic needs but also broader instrumental and emotional needs that foster a feeling of belonging and participation in U.S. society. Indeed, we observed that the pure physicality of material items often helped to remind these women that their hard work was worth the effort; however stressful and difficult to manage their day-to-day concerns became, their material accomplishments helped to convey a sense that it was all worth it in the end. This sentiment is nicely captured in the following field note from a visit with Rose:

> Rose expressed again that she felt that she had come a long way in the past few years. Rose said that when she moved into her apartment two years ago last December, she had hardly anything in it. She said that it feels good to finally get things in it. . . . Rose said that she knows it's just material goods, but it makes her feel good. That all her hard work is getting her somewhere. The *fact that she can actually see with her eyes and feel with her hands* the stuff she worked and paid for makes her feel good. That it is all not for nothing. (emphasis added)

Several policy implications can be drawn from the pattern of results presented here. First, our findings point to the significance of maintaining and increasing funding for work-support policies such as the earned income tax credit. EITC has been shown to be the single most effective U.S. work-support policy for alleviating family-based poverty. Among our sample of families, many reported using EITC as their primary savings mechanism. In accordance with this view, most elected to receive their EITC refund as a lump sum payment, despite the knowledge that refunds could be received on a quarterly basis.[22] Participants were also strategic about how they spent their refunds. For many, this was the only means by which they were able to acquire the more durable big-ticket items, such as cars and home furnishings and appliances. For others, EITC refunds provided a respite from the constant struggle to meet everyday expenses, enabling them to afford modest extras and to catch up on past bills.

A second policy recommendation is for continued support for policies targeting low-income families' basic needs around food and shelter. Surveys of American adults show greater support for the provision of in-kind benefits to the poor than for cash assistance (Heclo 1997). This includes programs such as food stamps, energy assistance, housing assistance (for example, Section 8), the Women, Infant, and Children (WIC) program, and the federal school lunch and breakfast program. The need for such support is well documented. Despite the strong economy during the late 1990s, many low-wage workers continued to struggle to secure what the women in our sample deemed the "basics" (Shipler 2004). A recent report by America's Second Harvest (2001) noted that even for those receiving food stamps, food stamp allocations, on average, covered only about three-fourths of a family's monthly food budget. As we have shown in our analysis, to the extent that mothers faced difficulties paying for the basics, their well-being was jeopardized. They reported feeling more anxious and worried, and those feelings, in turn, negatively influenced their interactions with their children and ultimately their children's academic and behavioral adjustment.

Programs that target families' basic needs around food, shelter, and the like could alleviate some of the material hardship experienced by not just the sample of families in our investigation but also scores of low-income, working adults in the United States. For example, given the geographic location of the New Hope Project, it was not surprising that participants' discussions about the basics often included references to their need for energy assistance. Of course, a family's needs extend beyond food and shelter. It is important to note that during the same period that welfare reform took place, funding for child care subsidies, Medicaid, and the Children's Health Insurance Program increased dramatically (although more recent estimates are beginning to show declines in such funding sources). In addition, eligibility requirements were relaxed, making such benefits available to greater segments of the working poor. Such policies make sense in light of the evidence presented in this and other chapters in this volume.

Chapter Nine | Can Money Buy You Love?
Dynamic Employment
Characteristics, the New
Hope Project, and
Entry into Marriage

Anna Gassman-Pines,
Hirokazu Yoshikawa, and Sandra Nay

So FAR IN part 2 of the book we have been generally silent about the role of
partners in the lives of the New Hope mothers. It is clear from numerous
studies that partners and relationships are inextricably intertwined with the
work experiences of low-income women and represent a central aspect of
how work and family influences together shape children's development.
Partners can not only provide love and emotional support to mothers and
children but also bring a vast array of supports or barriers relevant to work,
including extra household income, child care, coparenting, pressures to
work or not to work, conflict and domestic violence, and their own children
from prior relationships (Carlson and Furstenberg, forthcoming; Gibson-
Davis, Edin, and McLanahan 2005; Nelson, Clampet-Lundquist, and Edin
2002; Scott, London, and Myers 2002).

Partners—or more specifically, male partners suitable for marriage—are
also a major current focus of U.S. policy related to single mothers. Rates of
entry into marriage are low and declining among never-married mothers
living in poverty. The trend is clear: compared to their higher-income counterparts, low-income individuals are less likely to marry and have marriage
rates that are declining more rapidly (Edin and Kefalas 2005; Fields and

Casper 2001; Seefeldt and Smock 2004). Policymakers and researchers are concerned about this trend in part because of research on the relationship between marriage and adults' and children's well-being. Research shows that, compared to single adults, both men and women who are married have fewer physical and mental health problems and greater financial well-being (Nock 1995; Waite and Gallagher 2000). Also, children in two-parent families have higher levels of academic achievement and fewer behavior problems than children in single-parent families, and children in married two-parent families exhibit fewer behavior problems than children in cohabiting two-parent families (McLanahan and Sandefur 1994). The bulk of the relevant research in this area, however, has been conducted on mixed- or upper-income samples and thus may not be generalizable to low-income populations. Only recently have researchers begun to examine marriage among low-income individuals.

To fill these gaps in the literature, this chapter examines marriage and partner relationships among the New Hope survey and ethnographic samples. Our main finding is that women's economic circumstances matter both in their decisions to marry and in the quality of their relationships. First, we show that, consistent with other ethnographic studies, women in our ethnographic sample stated that financial security was an important prerequisite to marriage. Second, we present data showing that both wage growth and the New Hope program itself—which increased both employment and income—appear to increase rates of marriage among never-married mothers. Finally, because relationship quality is such an important facet of marriage and other relationships, this chapter concludes by examining relationship quality in depth. We see that over time the women in the ethnographic sample experienced improvements in relationship quality and that this pattern was strongest for those with more wage growth. We find overall that the economic context of low-income, single mothers' lives, particularly wage growth and income, matter for both marriage and relationship quality.

HOW DO LOW-INCOME ADULTS THINK ABOUT MARRIAGE?

While marriage rates are declining among low-income individuals, the symbolic significance of marriage remains strong for low-income mothers, as well as for the country as a whole. For instance, one recent study conducted in Florida found that 92 percent of adults agree or strongly agree that "a happy healthy marriage is one of the most important things in life." Similarly, 65 percent of unmarried adults reported that they would like to be married at some point in the future. Despite the disparity in relative marriage rates between low- and higher-income individuals, low-income adults expressed a stronger preference for being married in the future than did higher-income adults (Karney, Garvan, and Thomas 2003). Similarly, many low-income parents expect to cohabit and marry immediately after the birth of a child (Edin and Kefalas 2005; Waller 2001). When two people have a child together, they both agree that they see marriage in their near future. Data from a variety of sources clearly demonstrate that low-income individuals and the population as a whole agree on the importance of marriage.

If low-income individuals respect and desire marriage, why then are their rates of entry into marriage so low? Some qualitative studies provide an answer to this question. One study, conducted by Christina Gibson-Davis, Kathryn Edin, and Sara McLanahan (2005) as part of the Fragile Families project, found that low-income individuals have a number of prerequisites for marriage, including financial stability and asset accumulation as well as interpersonal stability and trust. Rather than facilitating marriage, these prerequisites may serve as a barrier because it may be difficult for low-income individuals to satisfy each one. For poor couples, the desire for high levels of financial stability and interpersonal stability may set the bar for marriage too high. Poor couples may feel that they are never reaching their goals and therefore are not ready to marry.

While studies reveal that low-income couples identify many requirements that they want to meet before marrying, the same conditions seem not to exist for cohabitation. Cohabitation, which is more informal than marriage, is not viewed with the same level of importance, and the same prerequisites do not apply. Parents sometimes describe cohabitation as a first step to marriage, but they do not make lists of requirements for cohabitation in the same way that they do for marriage (Gibson-Davis, Edin, and McLanahan 2005).

What did mothers in the New Hope Ethnographic Study say about their prerequisites for marriage? Did they describe prerequisites that were similar to those found in other ethnographic studies of low-income parents? In short, the answer is yes. The ethnographic study participants had a clear idea of what they wanted to accomplish before getting married. Although they were not explicitly asked about their plans to marry, all of the participants talked about relationships, and many of them described plans to marry and barriers to marriage. Of all the barriers to marriage identified by sample members, economic issues were discussed most often (about 50 percent of the time). Many sample members thought about financial concerns and relationships simultaneously and described economic stability as one goal they needed to achieve before they could marry. For instance, a field-worker described what Inez had to say about financial stability and her decisions about marrying: "I asked her if they were planning to get married anytime soon, and she said that she wasn't ready to get married yet—maybe in a couple of years. She said that they wanted to be more financially secure before they got married, and they also wanted the boys to be a little bit older." Another field-worker made this report on Rose: "She said that she can't see getting married anytime soon. She said that she would like to be more financially secured before she got married. . . . She said she would have to have a regular check that was the same every two weeks, and knows where her money is coming from before she ever thought about marriage."

While financial stability was by far the most frequent prerequisite for marriage, it was not the only goal cited by participants. NHES sample members, like the mothers in the study done by Gibson-Davis and her colleagues, also talked about wanting an overall sense of stability and a reduction in the chaos in their lives before marrying. For example, Inez planned to resolve some personal issues before becoming involved with a man. She said, "I wanna get my life together, spend some time with my kids, and that's it." Similarly, Lynette expressed a strong interest in getting married but said that she felt that her life and her partner's life were too complicated to plan a wedding.

It is also clear that the NHES participants—like participants in other studies of low-income parents—attached more significance to marriage than to cohabitation. They believed that marriage requires a major commitment. For example, Heather's field-worker noted that "Heather said that marriage tells you that this commitment is for real and is not just for show for right now," and also that "she said that they got married to make their commitment to each other more permanent." The NHES sample's patterns of cohabitation and marriage over the study period also reinforce this notion. Many women moved in and out of cohabitation with relative frequency, sometimes from one field-worker visit to the next. Transitions into cohabitation seemed to happen with little advance deliberation. Marriages, in contrast, took place much less frequently, and when they did occur, they were preceded by serious consideration.

THE LITERATURE ON THE RELATIONSHIP BETWEEN ECONOMIC CIRCUMSTANCES AND MARRIAGE

If low-income parents talk about a need for financial stability before marriage, then how do work and economic indicators actually relate to marriage? Quantitative research in economics and sociology has depicted a shift in economic predictors of marriage in recent decades. While men's earnings have always been a strong predictor of marriage, the relationship between women's earnings and marriage seems to be changing. From the late 1800s through the 1980s, theoretical work has predicted that the more women earn, the less likely they will be to marry, because they will not need to depend on a male partner for financial support (Becker 1981; Durkheim 1893/1960; Parsons 1949). This theory is based on a specialization model in which women are assumed to specialize in care for children and the home and men are assumed to specialize in work outside the home. A more recent review of the literature suggests that the relationship between women's earnings and marriage may in fact mirror that of men's earnings and marriage (Oppenheimer 1997). As women earn more, they are more likely to marry. This may be because they have more resources to contribute to a potential partnership. A recent empirical study supports this recent shift in the relationship between women's earnings and marriage. Although for women born in the 1930s and 1940s earnings and marriage were negatively related, the opposite was true for women born in the 1950s and 1960s (Sweeney 2002).

In addition to examining women's earnings, prior work has also explored the relationship between women's *employment* and marriage. Overall, the pattern of results is mixed, but most studies find that compared to women who are not employed, women who are employed are more likely to marry (Blau, Kahn, and Waldfogel 2000; Ellwood and Jencks 2004; Oppenheimer 1997; Smock and Manning 1997). This prior work, however, has some limitations. First, these studies focused on upper-income or mixed-income samples, ignoring the fact that processes may be different for low-income adults in low-resource systems. Second, they simply asked whether a person was employed or not. This is problematic because employment experiences vary in stability, hours, and wages, among other things. The characteristics of individuals' employment *over time*, rather than employment per se, may make a difference in their decisions to marry.

What role do policies that increase financial stability play in women's entry into marriage? Policymakers are proposing and enacting programs to encourage marriage because they are worried about low marriage rates among low-income individuals. Marriage promotion is one of the primary pieces of current welfare reform efforts. Marriage promotion programs have two key approaches. The first is to focus on the context of the relationship itself. Programs typically provide counseling to couples to encourage them to marry and stay married or training in relationship and communication skills (Dion and Devaney 2003; U.S. Department of Health and Human Services 2002). The other type of program aims to affect the economic context by altering tax policy to remove financial disincentives to marriage (Seefeldt and Smock 2004). Marriage promotion programs have not utilized other economic approaches or tried to alter other aspects of the economic context. For example, marriage promotion efforts have not emphasized direct antipoverty measures that might increase financial stability.

While there may be a role for antipoverty or other economic policies in marriage promotion, relationship quality remains a vital element of relationships. What makes relationships positive or negative for low-income couples? And how do those features of relationships play out over time? Although the New Hope participant survey did not collect data on relationship quality, the ethnographic data give us the ability to observe the ways in which low-income women defined quality in their relationships and changes in relationship quality over time.

DO DYNAMIC EMPLOYMENT CHARACTERISTICS AND THE NEW HOPE PROJECT PREDICT ENTRY INTO MARRIAGE?

It is evident that for the women in the New Hope ethnographic sample, financial considerations were central to their approach to marriage. Like participants in other ethnographic studies of low-income parents, the New Hope mothers described wanting both financial and overall stability before marrying. If these were important prerequisites, then what happened if women's employment helped them be met? Are women whose employment includes more financial and overall stability more likely to get married than those whose employment is less stable or provides less financial support? This is the first question we consider in this chapter.

To answer the question of whether dynamic employment characteristics relate to marriage, we conducted analyses using the survey data. Recall that in chapter 3 we examined the relationship of the combination of wage growth and job stability to children's outcomes. This combination was associated with a variety of positive developmental indicators. Here we considered job stability, wage growth, and the combination of stability and wage growth in relation to marriage. We chose these variables because of their links to the ethnographic sample members' prerequisites for marriage. We examined only the women in the sample who reported at baseline that they had never been married and who were still not married at the two-year follow-up survey, because we believe that the process for entering into marriage for the first time is likely to be very different from the process of getting remarried.[1] We considered women's employment characteristics during years one and two of the follow-up period and examined whether those employment characteristics were related to marriage at year five, using logistic regression.

Our results show that the more wage growth women experienced during years one and two, the more likely they were to be married at year five.[2]

These findings do not change even when adding a number of potential con-founds to our analyses, including assignment to the New Hope program, demographic characteristics, family characteristics, job quality, children's behavior problems, and mothers' mental health and self-esteem.[3] Therefore, the finding that the more women gained in wages in years one and two the more likely they were to marry between years two and five remains after controlling for a number of alternative explanations. Our data suggest that the more wage growth women experience, the more likely they are to marry. We do not find a relationship between job stability and entry into marriage. Given that financial concerns were the single most commonly reported barrier to marriage among our sample, it is not surprising that wage growth emerges as the strongest predictor of marriage.

Among sample members who reported at the beginning of the study that they had never been married, the New Hope program increased wage growth, as well as total income, over years one and two of the follow-up period.[4] On average, over the first two years of the follow-up period the con-trol group's wages increased \$0.77 while the New Hope group's wages increased \$1.22. During the same time period, control group members had an average yearly income of \$6,629, while New Hope group members had an average yearly income of \$7,177, a difference of \$548 a year.[5]

Because our previous analyses indicated that the more wage growth women experience, the more likely they are to marry, and because financial stability is a central prerequisite for marriage, we might expect that the New Hope program—which increased wage growth and income—would also increase marriage rates among participants. Did New Hope increase the percentage of sample members who got married over the follow-up period? To answer this question we again examined all women who reported at baseline that they had never been married, using logistic regression. Overall, the percentage of these women who were married by year five is fairly low, 16 percent. However, when we compare New Hope group members to con-trol group members, differences emerge. The New Hope program did indeed affect the likelihood that women would marry. About 21 percent of the New Hope group were married by year five, while only 12 percent of the control group were married, a statistically significant difference.[6] This program impact is displayed in figure 9.1. Thus, New Hope appears to have increased the marriage rate among never-married mothers by 75 percent. This constitutes one of the only examples of an experimental increase in mar-riage due to a program that increased employment and income.

When discussing cohabitation relative to marriage, the ethnographic study members clearly regarded marital and cohabiting relationships differently and believed that marriage requires a greater commitment. Therefore, it is not surprising that the patterns for cohabitation and marriage in our quantitative analyses look different. A relationship exists between

Figure 9.1　The New Hope Impact on Marriage at Year Five for Never-Married Mothers

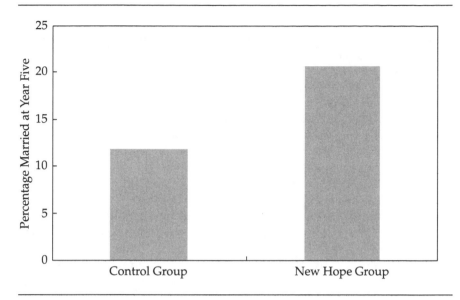

Source: Authors' compilation.

wage growth and marriage, but this is not the case for cohabitation. Neither wage growth nor job stability was related to cohabitation. Finally, the New Hope program did not affect women's entry into cohabitation. There seems to be something special about marriage that sets it apart from more informal cohabitation. The women in our sample approached marriage and cohabitation very differently, and the results of our quantitative analyses support the notion that the processes leading to these types of relationships differ.

In addition to wage growth and income, other factors might explain why New Hope increased marriage rates among never-married mothers. We explored the mothers' perceptions of goal achievement, because the ethnographic data suggested that stability and wage growth were important goals related to the decision to marry for these women. The large literature linking well-being to current marital quality (see, for example, Fein et al. 2003) led us to explore other indicators of well-being as well. Higher levels of depression, parenting stress, and material hardship have all been linked to lower levels of marital quality (Conger, Rueter, and Elder 1999; Cox et al. 1999; Vinokur, Price, and Caplan 1996). We in fact found that, among never-married mothers in the New Hope sample, higher levels of material hardship were related to a lower likelihood of entering marriage.[7] However, since New Hope did not affect material hardship among never-married mothers, this association does not explain the New Hope impact on marriage.

Given that research consistently finds that children of married parents fare better than children of single parents, an additional question to ask is whether the increases in marriage found in this sample made a difference for children's outcomes. Did the children of the mothers who got married have higher school achievement and fewer behavior problems than those whose mothers stayed single? To answer this question we examined whether having a mother who got married between year two and year five was related to children's school achievement and behavior problems in year five.[8] We found that when mothers got married, their children's behavior improved. Teachers reported that children whose mothers had gotten married acted less sad and withdrawn than children whose mothers stayed single.[9] And the mothers themselves reported that their children had fewer aggressive and acting-out behavior problems.[10] Change in marital status was not related to children's school achievement. There is a considerable literature showing that the relationship between family structure and children's outcomes differs for boys and girls (Cherlin et al. 1991; Hetherington and Stanley-Hagan 1999; Krein and Beller 1988). Our results, however, were the same for both boys and girls: improvements in children's behavior did not differ by their gender.

A CLOSER LOOK AT RELATIONSHIP QUALITY

Another factor that might explain the New Hope impact on marriage is a change in relationship quality. Relationship quality—what makes relationships good or bad for certain people—is an important element in the success of relationships. People aim to be in relationships that they consider high-quality and try to avoid relationships that are low in quality. The ethnographic data provide an opportunity for closely examining aspects of relationship quality in a low-income population. Although they were not specifically asked about relationships or plans to marry, all of the women in the ethnographic sample spontaneously talked about their relationships. They readily described things they liked and did not like about their current partners, told stories about relationships from the past, and discussed what they were looking for in future relationships. The richness of the women's stories allows us to learn about the quality of their relationships, even though they were not specifically asked about that in the survey. We also can examine how relationship quality might be associated with indicators of economic well-being that the New Hope mothers value, such as wage growth.

To observe relationship patterns in the ethnographic sample, we first analyzed separately each relationship described during the ethnography. We coded specific aspects of each relationship and applied two general codes, one describing the quality of relationships overall (as "positive," "negative," or "mixed") and one describing the quality of the current or most recent relationship. In this section, we first describe patterns of relationship quality and how they changed over time, and then we explore whether relationship quality was related to wage growth and/or the New Hope program.

Positive relationships are those that were defined primarily by positive interactions between the sample members and their partners, including the partners' involvement with the children of the household, help with child care and other household tasks, financial contributions to the household, and emotional support. Negative relationships are those that were defined primarily by negative interactions and partner characteristics, such as partners' draining of household resources, lack of involvement with the children, failure to help with household responsibilities, jealousy or stalking, infidelity, domestic abuse, drug use, and involvement with the criminal justice system. Mixed relationships are those that included both positive and negative interactions with partners, who were engaged in both positive and negative behaviors.[11]

Alicia was in a positive relationship with Rolando for the entire ethnographic study. At the beginning of the study, they were dating and living in adjoining apartments. Although this arrangement provided them with more space, supporting two households instead of one made it difficult to pay the bills. A few months after the study began, Alicia and Rolando got married. She said that they loved each other so much and wanted to stay together, so they decided to get married. After their marriage, Alicia was happy with Rolando. She said, "He makes me happy. He supports me." After getting married, they moved into the same apartment and agreed to pay all of their bills together. This arrangement made Alicia feel considerably less distressed about her financial situation. Not only was Rolando helpful in paying for household expenses, Alicia asserted, but he was also very good with her kids from a previous relationship. He helped provide discipline, and Alicia felt that the children really listened to him. At the end of the study, Alicia reported that the only problem with her relationship with Rolando was that they rarely had time to spend together alone because they were both working so much. She wished that they could see each other more.

Marina was a single African-American mother of three who was looking for a husband and a father for her children. Her field-worker noted: "Because her kids all have different fathers, she would like someone they could all call Daddy." She expressed interest in companionship, affection, and help with parenting and disciplining her children, as well as financial assistance for her household. During the course of the ethnography, she met Jack through her job. She was working at a day care center, and he was driving the van for the center. They became involved. Marina's relationship with Jack was positive. She enjoyed their relationship and described Jack as a "good provider" who helped her financially when needed. Marina appreciated the fact that her children loved him and he spent a great deal of time with them, playing games, reading, and just hanging out. She also praised him for helping with household chores like cleaning and cooking and for providing child care. By the end of the ethnography, their relationship had progressed, and she and Jack were considering getting married.

While some relationships, like Alicia's and Marina's, were primarily positive, others were very negative. Some of the most negative relationships that participants described included serious cases of domestic abuse. Although we did not initially seek to examine domestic abuse in this chapter, it was difficult to ignore the stories of abuse that some sample members recounted. Domestic abuse was common among sample members. Twenty-three of the forty women in our ethnographic sample revealed that they had been abused in at least one romantic relationship, an overall rate of 58 percent.[12] Although high, this number is very similar to estimates of lifetime domestic abuse for women in the welfare population.[13]

Leora was one of the participants who described a boyfriend in very negative terms after suffering both physical and emotional abuse. Her field-worker reported:

> He was controlling and tried to monitor whatever she did. He seemed insecure and did not want her to work full-time and meet other people. He was afraid she would meet someone else. She picked up a job in the liquor store next door, and that way he could keep an eye on her. He was also a few years younger [than] her. He was abusive and would tell her unkind things, like she was an "old hag," with stretch marks; she had five kids, [so] which guy would take her? He would spend the nights at drug houses and be there all night. When she complained about it, he said that if she did not like it, she can get out. He was also physically abusive and hit her. One day he threatened her with a knife when she was getting ready to leave. The physical abuses started showing, and she would go to work at the liquor store with her bruises. Her coworkers started asking her why was she still hanging out with him. She stayed with him even though she didn't want to, mainly because of financial reasons.

Leora eventually ended this destructive relationship, but she continued to be plagued with low self-esteem and trust issues even after she found a secure relationship with the man who would become her fiancé. She attributed these feelings to her experiences with her abusive ex-boyfriend. According to her field-worker, "Leora said, 'I carry a lot of baggage from my relationship with Kim's father.' She is still afraid that he will come back in her life—

she has nightmares about him. Stan keeps telling her that he is a cowardly man and would do nothing. But Leora's previous experience of abuse with him has left a permanent scar. It is hard for her to trust men, and it is hard for her 'to open up.' "

Although many of the women in our sample described experiences with domestic violence, not all negative relationships involved abuse. Sample members also talked about partners who had problems with drugs or alcohol, who were severely jealous, who drained household resources, or who were not involved with their children. Carla's relationship for the entire ethnographic period is an example of a relationship that was negative but did not include domestic violence. Although she never experienced any domestic abuse with Jorge, she was very unhappy with him for many reasons, including his treatment of some of her children, his alcohol use, his lack of financial contributions, and his jealousy. And there was another aspect of Jorge's behavior that troubled Carla. According to her field-worker:

> One thing is that he will act very differently towards the children he fathered and the three oldest. Carla said that he will tell the older kids not to touch something because it belongs to "his" daughter. He will be mean at the oldest kids, and will say things to them about them not being his. Then he will dote, and do everything for the youngest children that are his. He will buy them clothes, or give them treats and ignore or say mean things to the oldest three. Carla said that his outward favoritism causes the kids to start fighting not only with him but also among themselves.

Carla was very unhappy that Jorge treated the children he fathered differently from her other children who were living with them. This type of conflict is common among low-income parents who have had children with multiple partners (Gibson and Edin 2004). Carla was also unhappy because Jorge did not work regularly and did not contribute financially to the household. As she described it, Jorge "has done nothing but bring her down." He also drank a large amount, so that even when he did have money, he spent most of it on alcohol. Additionally, Carla said that Jorge was jealous of her coworkers, most of whom were men:

> She said that Jorge gets angry about the guys at work. She said that he liked it when she got the job and started bringing home money. She said he still really likes that part, but he started getting angry and fighting with her when he realized that she was getting along really well with the people from her job, especially because they are almost all men. Carla said that Jorge complains that she tells people from work too much of her business, but she tells Jorge that she gets so sick and tired of the things he says sometimes that she feels she

has to tell somebody. He also complains that the people from her job don't like him. Carla said, "What does he expect? He comes to my job and isn't even nice, he doesn't even say hello." She tells Jorge that it isn't that they don't like him, it is just that they don't care about him.

When her field-worker asked her why she stayed with Jorge if she was so unhappy with him, Carla replied that she thought she stayed with him because he watched the children sometimes while she was at work. This was a valuable form of support for her even if it did not happen frequently. She stayed with him because of this assistance with child care, even though she did not like most of his other behaviors.

In a striking example of how relationship quality and women's financial situations are intertwined, most of the women who described very negative relationships (about 85 percent of them), whether abusive or not, said that they stayed with the person for financial reasons. Sometimes the partner provided occasional financial support or took care of the children from time to time. Providing child care was often considered a form of financial support because it allowed the women to work and not have to pay for child care. Although the women were very unhappy in these negative relationships, they often talked about staying because of the economic support that the relationships provided, even if this support was neither consistent nor stable. These women faced the impossible choice between continuing a relationship that they knew was very negative while receiving irregular financial support and ending both the negative relationship and their receipt of their partner's financial assistance.

Although some women described relationships that were very positive or very negative, the majority of relationships overall were mixed in quality. We found that most of the women—thirty-one out of forty (78 percent)—had a mixed overall relationship quality, with eight women having a negative overall rating and only one woman having a positive overall rating (overall ratings averaged across each woman's relationships over the course of the ethnography). Mixed relationships were the most common and featured significant positive and negative aspects.

Karen's relationship with her boyfriend during most of the ethnographic study is an example of a mixed-quality relationship. Although she relied on him to help care for the children, she was unhappy about the fact that he did not work and seemed not to have any motivation to do so.

Karen is not satisfied with her current relationship with Robert. Karen described a dream she had about relationships and marriage when she was young. When she was young she said that she always imagined getting married and being with a man who went out of the house to work and take care of her. Her job was to take care of the house and the kids. To be sure there was a nice meal on the table when her man got home. Karen said that dream has fizzled. Karen said that with Robert, although he does help her out, he really doesn't do anything and she can't stand that. She said that he is always just hanging around the house doing nothing. Karen said it's like Robert doesn't have any motivation to do anything. Karen said that Robert's big task of the day is picking up Jasmine after school gets out. Then he will play with the kids after school and during the evenings. He will watch TV with them, watch movies, play cards. Karen said that she doesn't know that she can live with Robert's lack of motivation to do anything. Karen said she can't stand him being around the house all day like a log. She said that he does help her out. That he does watch the kids when she needs him to, and he will entertain them in the evenings if she is helping her mom out. Also, his SSI money does help with the household expenses. But Karen is not sure if that help outweighs the things that she does not like. She said that she wishes that Robert would go to school or find a job. Something, anything.

Although she found Robert's involvement with her children and his contribution to household expenses helpful, Karen was disappointed in Robert's lack of motivation and perpetual state of unemployment.

Faye was also in a relationship for most of the study that was mixed in quality, including both positive and negative elements. Like Karen, she appreciated the fact that her boyfriend helped her with the children. He also assisted the household financially, which was a significant source of support for Faye. At the same time, however, he was very jealous and controlling.

Faye said that as soon as he moved in, his behavior towards her changed. Faye said that he was literally crazy. For instance, she would be sitting on the front porch and he would accuse her of trying to pick up guys. She said they went to the supermarket and he would say that she was trying to make eyes with a clerk, while she is checking the eggs. They go for a drive, and he would say she was trying to pick up a cop. Faye said that he would always accuse her of trying to pick up a guy.

Although she was very unhappy with this level of jealousy, Faye continued the relationship with her boyfriend because of his involvement with her children and the financial support that he provided.

Like Karen and Faye, most of the women who were in mixed-quality relationships tended to endure a variety of negative behaviors in their partners because of significant positive contributions they made to the household, particularly with respect to the children: help with child care, other involvement with children, or financial contributions. The mothers in this study felt that it was very important for their children to have male role models and men in their lives. They were willing to endure men's jealousy, drug use, and other negative behaviors if it meant that they had someone to help with the children. In their view, helping with children included providing child care and discipline or simply being a playmate.

The mothers in our study also were keenly aware that having a partner in the household who contributed financially could be very useful. They were often willing to stay with partners who engaged in negative behaviors because of the financial support they provided. Faye's boyfriend was extremely jealous, but he bought her things and contributed to the household expenses. Many of the mothers who were in mixed-quality relationships were in situations similar to Faye's. Despite the fact that their partners were significant negative influences in their lives, they recognized and greatly appreciated the importance of having financial support and a partner who was willing to contribute.

As we have seen, partners' level of financial contribution was an important factor in these women's assessment of their relationship quality. Sample members often talked about their partners' assistance or lack of assistance with household expenses. In fact, only two out of forty sample members *never* mentioned a partner's financial contribution. Because the partner's financial contribution was mentioned so often as a key component of relationship quality, we decided to examine it systematically. We reviewed the relationship quality ratings to determine how the women described financial contributions to the household for each relationship, and we assigned each participant an overall rating based on whether she described her partner primarily as contributing or not contributing. We rated relationships as neutral when partner contributions were not discussed, and as mixed when no clear pattern of contributions could be discerned. Across all relationships experienced or described during the ethnography, the majority of sample members' relationships (twenty-eight out of forty, or 70 percent) were rated as mixed in terms of partner's level of contribution. Over the course of the study, these women were sometimes in relationships with men who were primarily drains on household resources, but at other times their partners contributed to expenses. As discussed in the next section, there was a clear pattern in how this aspect of relationship quality changed over time.

Figure 9.2   Improvement in Relationship Quality for Sample Members
with More Than One Relationship over the Study Period

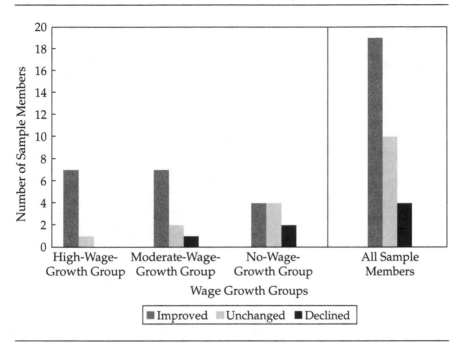

Source: Authors' compilation.
Note: The number of sample members in the wage-growth groups does not equal the number of all
sample members because some sample members were missing wage-growth data.

HOW DOES RELATIONSHIP QUALITY
CHANGE OVER TIME?

One advantage of the availability of longitudinal ethnographic data is that
we can observe relationships as they develop and change over time. A
clear pattern emerges as we look at the dynamics of relationships in the
New Hope ethnographic sample: the quality of the women's relationships
improved. Of the thirty-three women in the ethnographic sample who
described more than one relationship over the course of the study, we found
that nineteen of the women (58 percent) experienced an improvement in
relationship quality over time (see the bars on the far right of figure 9.2).
Twelve of those women entered into a positive relationship, while seven
moved from a negative relationship into a mixed-quality one. The story of

Tiffany demonstrates one way in which a sample member's relationship quality improved over the course of the study.

Near the beginning of the ethnography, Tiffany, an African-American mother of two, ended a difficult relationship with her children's father. Her ex-boyfriend was physically abusive: he often beat her up and even once threatened her with a gun until a family member intervened. He never assisted with the family's expenses and did not provide financial support for their children. "He never bought diapers, he never helps buy clothes for school, nothing!" she said. When he visited her house occasionally after the breakup—ostensibly to see the children—she felt that he did not pay much attention to them and did not take an interest in their lives. He repeatedly pursued her romantically, trying to convince her to become involved with him again, but she refused. She was happy to have liberated herself from the relationship and preferred not to associate with him anymore. Her field-worker noted, "She says that the thing she regrets most in life is that he is the father of her children."

After this disastrous experience, Tiffany was cautious about dating again and vowed to find a better man than her ex-boyfriend. "As things in her life started to fall into place recently, Tiffany started praying to the Lord for a husband. She says she heard that you should be specific, so she asked for a dependable man, with a good job and a strong faith. She also wanted a handsome man." In describing her goals, she stated, "I want what everyone wants—a steady job, a house, a husband, and a family."

Tiffany soon began a relationship with a new man. She saw this boy-friend as a measurable improvement over her children's father. She appre-ciated the fact that he was very supportive of her and encouraged her to continue pursuing her goals. He helped her by picking her up from work every day and had a good relationship with her children. He was gener-ous financially and also supported two children from a former marriage. Tiffany was also glad that he was involved in his church. She and her new boyfriend considered getting married, but she was concerned about rush-ing into marriage. She resolved to settle her outstanding bills and accu-mulate some savings before getting married because she did not want to enter marriage as a dependent person. Despite several positive aspects of this relationship, it eventually ended.

Several months later Tiffany met her future husband. She considered him to be more mature than her previous boyfriends, and she valued his ability to communicate effectively and constructively even when they were angry with each other. He enjoyed her children and helped provide discipline in the household. He also contributed to the household in other ways, such as doing most of the cooking. He was generous in assisting with their house-hold bills and also paid child support for two children of his own from a previous relationship. At some point after their marriage, Tiffany's husband began supporting the entire household with his salary while she was unemployed. When asked, several months after the wedding, how she enjoyed being married, she told her field-worker, " 'It's fun.' She says that they have a lot of fun together."

Tiffany was one of many sample members who moved into more positive relationships over time. Despite the fact that her ex-boyfriend was the father of her children, she chose to end the relationship with him because he was physically abusive, did not take an interest in their children, and did not contribute financially to the household. After some dating, she was able to enter into a more positive relationship with a partner who contributed to household expenses, supported her emotionally, and was involved with her children. Ultimately, Tiffany chose to marry this boyfriend because of all the positive aspects of their relationship. Unlike Tiffany, most of the NHES participants did not get married over the course of the study, but they did move into more positive relationships.

As discussed earlier, a significant number of women in our sample disclosed a particularly negative relationship experience—domestic abuse. In addition to examining changes in the overall quality of relationships over time, we were also interested in observing whether experiences of domestic abuse changed over time. Similar to the overall improvement pattern, the women in our study left abusive relationships much more frequently than they entered them. To determine whether there was a pattern of change, we differentiated between those women who described abuse only in previous relationships, only in their current or most recent relationship, or in both. Twelve of these nineteen women who described any abuse (63 percent) reported domestic abuse only in previous relationships, while only four women had entered abusive relationships for the first time in their current or most recent relationship. The remaining three reported abuse in both previous and current relationships. Thus, it appears that over time many of the women in our sample who reported domestic abuse tended to move out of those relationships.

Because of its clear importance to the participants in our study, we also investigated changes in partner financial contribution over time. The results of this analysis also mirror those for overall relationship quality. About half of the women who reported on more than one relationship experienced improvement in partner financial contribution (fifteen out of twenty-eight). That is, over time sample members tended to move into relationships with more partner contribution. Few women (three out of twenty-eight) moved into relationships that involved less partner contribution. The remaining ten experienced no changes in partner financial contribution.

Shaquita's relationships during the ethnography illustrate the pattern of moving into relationships with partners who contributed more financially. At the beginning of the study, Shaquita was dating Shaun, whom she described as a "freeloader."

> Shaquita was long tired of Shaun. "It got so that his living here was just a drain on me. He didn't contribute at all." He has been out of work for over three months. She ticked off her expenses, $555/month for rent, about $60 each for gas and lights, phone bill, plus the expenses for the kids. Then there are miscellaneous expenses, like fixing her washer. Shaun would give money sporadically from his "hustles." "He'd give me $100 or $150, but other times I'd ask and he'd say, 'Next week.' And when he did give me money, who knows, it could be from selling drugs," she snorted. This was not acceptable to her. "I can't go to my landlord and say, 'Well, maybe next month.' I can't tell the gas company that I can't pay now, they'll cut off my gas, they'll cut off my lights."

After a huge fight about breaking up, Shaquita pulled a knife on Shaun, and in the resulting tussle she was stabbed in the leg. Although she told the police the truth about what had happened, Shaun was arrested. After the incident, they did not see each other again. Rather than being upset about what had happened, Shaquita was relieved. She said, "I feel free. I feel like a weight has been lifted off of me."

Soon after her relationship with Shaun ended, Shaquita became reacquainted with an old high school boyfriend. They began dating, and Shaquita immediately noticed a difference. When comparing John to Shaun, she said, "That's good that he a working man. He ain't lazy, that's for sure." John had a regular job in construction and helped Shaquita out with her bills. Because he was able to help out financially, Shaquita was able to cut back her work hours, allowing her to spend more time with her children. By not having to work as many hours, she described feeling more relaxed and less stressed about her life.

Overall, participants described relationships that varied greatly in quality. When looking at these relationships over time, we see a strong pattern of improvement emerging. This can be seen when examining overall relationship quality as well as the specific issues of domestic abuse and partner financial contribution. Although this pattern is clear, exactly why this occurs is less obvious. Two hypotheses are related to the pool of potential partners. Did the partner pool change over time, with women being exposed to more positive men? Or did the partner pool remain the same over time but the men within that pool change, becoming more positive?[14] Another hypothesis is generated from theories of life-span development. Did the women in the sample simply become older and wiser, following a developmental trajectory of learning from their past mistakes?[15] Any and all of these changes may have played a role in the improvements in relationship quality over time among these women. Unfortunately, we are not able to fully explore these changes, in part because we did not systematically talk with the partners of the women in our sample. Without the partners' perspectives, we are unable to fully understand the reasons for improvements in relationship quality over time.

HOW ARE RELATIONSHIP QUALITY, WAGE GROWTH, AND NEW HOPE RELATED?

Having described the patterns of relationship quality in the ethnographic sample, we can now return to the question of whether relationship quality is related to wage growth or to exposure to the New Hope program. Although the quantitative findings indicate that wage growth and entry into marriage are related, the questions of *how* and *why* they are related are still unanswered. To better understand these findings, we compared ethnographic sample members with different levels of wage growth and focused on each group's relationship quality. It could be that women who experienced greater wage growth were more likely to be in high-quality relationships than women who experienced less wage growth. With increased wage growth, perhaps they were able to spend their time and money in different ways and to meet and become involved with men who were more supportive and helpful. As discussed earlier, the field notes provide a great deal of information about relationship quality and therefore allow us to examine this hypothesis.[16]

To determine the relationship between wage growth and relationship quality, we compared three groups of ethnographic sample members: those who experienced at least $1.00 of wage growth during years one and two (the high-wage-growth group); those who experienced less than $1.00 of wage growth during these years (the moderate-wage-growth group); and those who experienced no wage growth or a decline (the no-wage-growth group). The wage-growth groups are based on the wage growth of sample members before the ethnographic study began.

While the overall trend for the ethnographic sample was one of improvement in relationship quality over time, this was especially true for those women who experienced the most wage growth. As shown in figure 9.2, nearly all of the women who experienced high wage growth also experienced improvements in relationship quality. None of the women with high wage

Figure 9.3 The Quality of the Current or Most Recent Relationship for All Sample Members

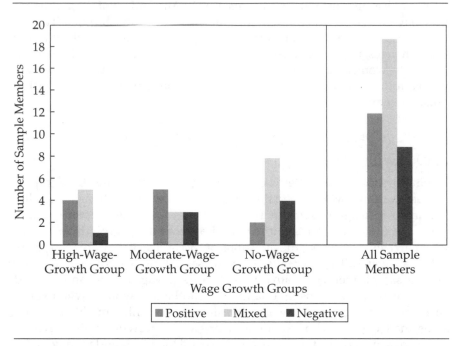

Source: Authors' compilation.
Note: The number of sample members in the wage-growth groups does not equal the number of all sample members because some sample members were missing wage-growth data.

growth experienced a decline in relationship quality over time. Similarly, among those who experienced a moderate amount of wage growth, the majority experienced improvements in relationship quality. In contrast, the pattern of improvement was much more mixed for those women who did not experience wage growth. Fewer than half improved in relationship quality, and a small group experienced a decline in quality. Although overall the quality of the ethnographic sample's relationships tended to improve over time, this improvement in relationship quality appears to have been accelerated for those with the highest levels of wage growth.[17]

The improvements in relationship quality for those who experienced higher wage growth seem to be explained in part by the fact that these women were less likely to be in negative relationships by the end of the study (see figure 9.3). When looking only at sample members' current or most recent relationships, only one out of ten women who experienced high levels of wage growth was in a relationship rated as negative in quality, three out of eleven women who experienced moderate wage growth were in negative relationships, and four of fourteen women who experienced no wage growth were in negative relationships.[18]

We also explored partners' contributions to household expenses to see whether women who experienced higher wage growth were more likely to be involved with partners who contributed financially to the household. The overall trend of sample members moving into relationships with partners who contributed financially does not vary by wage-growth group. Regardless of the wage growth that women experienced, over time they were more likely to be involved with partners who contributed financially. Experiencing wage growth does not seem to increase the likelihood that women will enter relationships with partners who participate in paying for household expenses.

The qualitative analyses reveal some relationships between wage growth and relationship quality, though the size of the sample and its subgroups makes us cautious about this finding. Relationship quality increased over time for all sample members, but especially for those who experienced the most wage growth. Those with the most wage growth were the least likely to be in negative relationships by the end of the ethnographic study. Although wage growth does appear to be related to moving out of negative relationships, it is not necessarily related to moving into positive relationships. Women at all levels of wage growth were equally likely at the end of the ethnographic study to be in a relationship with a partner who was contributing financially to the household. And women with the highest wage growth were only slightly more likely to be in a positive relationship at the end of the study. Experiencing high levels of wage growth may have increased these women's belief that they could take care of themselves and may have empowered them to end negative relationships. However, it should be noted that the direction of the association is not clear. It could also be that the women who were moving out of negative relationships were then more likely to find higher-paying jobs and to experience wage growth.

Although those sample members who experienced more wage growth also experienced more improvements in relationship quality over time, it is difficult to determine whether this helps to explain the association between wage growth and entry into marriage. Because marriage rates were so low, there were only a few cases of entry into marriage among the ethnographic sample members. Too few NHES participants were married during the course of the study to allow us to explore whether improvements in relationship quality provide a link between wage growth and marriage. However, our results suggest that such a link may exist.

Figure 9.4   Improvement in Relationship Quality for Sample Members
with More Than One Relationship During the Study Period
by Research Group

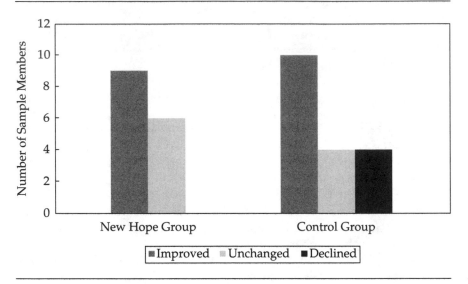

Source: Authors' compilation.

In addition to examining whether women who experienced different
levels of wage growth also differed in terms of their relationship quality,
we wanted to examine whether changes in relationship quality helped to
explain New Hope's impact on marriage. To do this we compared the relationship quality of those ethnographic sample members in the New Hope
group and those in the control group.

In terms of overall relationship quality, the New Hope and control groups
did not differ. The majority of women in both groups had relationships that
were mixed in overall quality (fifteen of nineteen New Hope group members; sixteen of twenty-one control group members). Differences between the
New Hope group and the control group did emerge when we looked at
change in relationship quality for those women who experienced more than
one relationship. Compared to controls, a slightly larger percentage of New
Hope group members experienced improvements in quality (nine of fifteen
in the New Hope group; ten of eighteen in the control group) (see figure 9.4).
Also, none of the women in the New Hope group experienced declines in

relationship quality, while four of the eighteen control group members experienced declines in quality. The quality of the ethnographic sample's relationships tended to improve over time, and the majority of sample members in both the New Hope group and the control group experienced improvement. However, women in the New Hope group appeared to avoid moves into more negative relationships. Finally, New Hope group members were less likely than their control group counterparts to be in a negative relationship by the end of the study. The current or most recent relationship of only three of nineteen New Hope group members was rated negative in quality, while six of twenty-one control group members were in a negative relationship.[19]

Why might the New Hope and control groups differ in their change in relationship quality over time? It could be that those women who experienced increases in income because of New Hope felt more independent and were less likely to stay in very negative relationships. Or perhaps, by working, more women in the New Hope group felt a sense of control over their own lives that prevented them from entering into negative relationships. We caution, however, that the size of the ethnographic sample precludes our confidence in these differences as statistically significant (Gibson-Davis and Duncan 2005). However suggestive, they cannot be interpreted as experimental impacts.

CONCLUSION

A great deal of research has examined marriage and its correlates, but relatively little of this research has focused on low-income populations. This chapter adds to the growing body of literature on marriage and relationships among low-income individuals by showing the importance of the economic context of women's lives. The economic context matters for their decisions to marry, for how they describe positive and negative relationships, and for improvements in the quality of their relationships over time. Both our quantitative and qualitative analyses clearly reveal that the economic and relationship contexts of women's lives do not operate independently. Economic and relationship contexts are intertwined: women who experience improvements in their financial situation are more likely to get married, and the quality of their relationships is more likely to improve over time.

Theorists who have written about the association between women's financial circumstances and their likelihood of marrying have disagreed about the direction of that association. Some propose that women's earnings should be negatively associated with marriage, while others argue that women's earnings should be positively associated with marriage. The results of this study clearly align with the latter argument: women's wage growth during the study period was positively related to their entry into marriage, and participation in the New Hope program nearly doubled the likelihood that women would marry. Taken together, these findings reinforce the importance of *employment* and *income* contexts in never-married women's decisions to enter into marriage.

These findings have implications not only for theory but also for public policy. If policymakers are concerned about increasing marriage among low-income individuals, the results described in this chapter indicate that they should consider broadening the focus of their attention beyond the dyadic to the economic contexts of low-income women's lives. Policymakers should focus not only on the relationship context but also on the employment context. Perhaps efforts to increase low-income women's income and wage growth would be as effective in promoting marriage as current efforts to improve communication between partners. Current random-assignment experiments to promote marriage do not test efforts to increase both employment and income through earnings supplements like the one offered by New Hope (Hershey et al. 2004). The evidence presented in this chapter suggests that they should.

Relationship quality is an important facet of relationships that has been underexplored in the research. This chapter took an in-depth look at what low-income women consider positive and negative aspects of relationships. Like the quantitative findings, these qualitative results reinforce the importance of economic considerations. Most of the ethnographic sample described the financial contribution of partners as one of the key aspects of relationship quality: they praised partners who contributed and bemoaned those who did not. Our analyses also revealed a developmental trend in relationship quality: ethnographic sample members tended to find their relationships improving in quality over time. These improvements were especially concentrated among those women who had also experienced wage growth, providing further evidence for a link between economic circumstances and relationships. Wage growth might facilitate the end of negative relationships marred by factors such as domestic violence.

Relationship quality might also explain how New Hope increased marriage rates among never-married mothers. No prior studies have examined relationship quality as a mediator of program impacts on marriage. Compared to their control group counterparts, New Hope group members had slightly higher rates of improvement in relationship quality over time. They also were much less likely to be in a very negative relationship at the end of the follow-up. Just as wage growth might have facilitated the end of negative relationships, the New Hope program, which increased both wage growth and income, might have facilitated the end of such relationships. New Hope group members' higher levels of goal efficacy might also have helped them set and achieve goals such as avoiding negative relationships.

Research has typically explored whether and how partners support or undermine women's employment experiences. This chapter has looked at employment and relationships in another way by examining whether and how women's employment affects their relationships. Taken together, the findings in this chapter indicate that when employment is coupled with increases in wage growth and income, low-income women are more likely to marry and are more likely to move into positive relationships.

Part III | Supports for Work

Chapter Ten | Child Care and Low-Wage Employment

Edward D. Lowe and Thomas S. Weisner

THUS FAR, IN parts I and II of this book, we have considered how employment trajectories and work-family issues are experienced by low-income mothers and how these experiences influence children. In part III, we turn to the question of how parents find support, from both informal and formal sources, for their efforts in the low-wage labor market. We consider three types of support: child care; informal social support from family, friends, and coworkers; and formal work support services.

We begin part III with the topic of child care, high on every working parent's list of concerns and high on the research agenda as well. The New Hope Project offered child care supports for those parents working thirty or more hours a week, and parents' use of that benefit was second only to their use of the income supplement. This is not surprising when we recall from chapter 3 that child care was the concern most frequently mentioned by mothers in the ethnographic sample about the impact of employment on their children's lives (mentioned by twenty-four of the forty mothers).

In this chapter, we explore two questions. First, how did child care arrangements affect the work pathways of the New Hope sample? Second, what factors determine the fit between child care and a family's work and other routines? Our focus here is not on the isolated or independent effects that the various components of the family ecology might have on the relationship between child care and employment. Rather, we are more interested in the dynamic relationship among the elements of the family ecology as they are woven together by family members, who each day must make and remake the family's routine activities.

We examine data from the two-year survey to understand how problems securing child care affected the New Hope mothers' employment. This survey asked a number of questions about the family's child care arrangements over the first two years of the study, and specifically about whether the survey respondent quit a job or failed to start a new job owing to child care problems. The data from this part of the two-year survey also have the advantage of referring to the same time period as the employment data used to construct the work pathway clusters. As a result, we are able to use these data to get fairly good estimates of the extent to which child care problems have played a role in the work pathways of the women in our study up to the time of the two-year survey.

Neither the two-year nor the five-year survey asked respondents about the specific problems they had in arranging their child care. So we are unable to answer our second question using the survey data. However, there is a good deal of material available from the ethnographic study concerning child care arrangements and the type of concerns the women in that sample had in negotiating the demands of employment while arranging acceptable child care for their children. In the second section of this chapter, we turn to these ethnographic data, which overlap with the ending period of New Hope, through the five-year survey data. Owing to the limitations of the small sample size, the ethnographic data do not allow us to estimate which child care concerns most frequently created problems for women's employment overall, but we can use the data inductively to identify the major concerns of the women in the ethnographic sample.

We will see that these women's concerns were about the fit between child care and the other aspects of their work and daily routines. The fit of child care costs, for example, with the overall budget of economic and material resources in the home was important, rather than its fit with any particular single resource. Other aspects of the interface between child care, work, and family that came up in the narratives included the fit of the child care choice with multiple members of the family, its temporal fit within the daily routine, and its fit with mothers' goals for their work, family, and children's development. The main message from our analysis of these materials is that multiple aspects of a family's circumstances must work together if a particular child care arrangement is going to work. Having adequate financial resources or social supports is not always enough; other features of family life—particularly strongly held beliefs and values regarding the best care for one's children—and the spatial and temporal organization of family routines also matter.

CHILD CARE ARRANGEMENTS AND
EMPLOYMENT TRAJECTORIES

The following field-note excerpts for Katrina, L'Kesha, Katie, and Lisa convey many of the struggles of the families in our study who had to negotiate the demands of employment and the care of their children. Their situations are similar to those of many working parents in the United States today who must decide whether to place their children in nonparental care so that one or both parents can find work or work more to improve the family's material conditions. The decisions that these and other parents make about the care of their children can have profound consequences for their ability to organize their daily routine, their success in improving their family's material well-being, and their children's social, emotional, and cognitive growth and development. This is particularly true for low-income families, for whom access to reliable, high-quality child care may improve their children's chances for future success as well as support the parents' ability to remain engaged in work (Besharov and Samari 2001; Chaudry 2004; Crouter and Booth 2004; Fuller et al. 2002; London et al. 2004; NICHD Early Child Care Research Network 2006; Scott et al. 2001; Shonkoff and Phillips 2000; Vandell and Wolfe 2000).

Child care is something that drives a lot of Katrina's [rapid cycler group] life. It is the main reason that she couldn't hold down a job for very long, because she didn't earn enough to pay for child care once her welfare benefits were cut off. She has four children—ages ten, eight, four, and one and a half. The two youngest are in subsidized child care now, and she is pleased with the quality of it. . . . Katrina needs child care so that she can work full-time.

L'Kesha [low-wage–full-time group] said that finding reliable and affordable child care . . . has been a problem. . . . Her boyfriend suggested a woman who lived in the same apartment building [who could] watch her youngest daughter. That worked for a couple of months. But a few weeks ago the child care provider never came home and was not there to watch L'Kesha's daughter when she had to go to work. This was a big problem for L'Kesha and got her in some trouble at work. She called in to the supervisor on call to say that she could not come into work because she did not have anyone to watch her child.

Three years ago, when Katie [low-wage–full-time group] was working and got pregnant with her daughter [and second child], she decided to quit work and just stay at home to take care of her two children. She said that her big motivation for staying at home at that time was that she could not find good child care. When she had just her son, she went to a number of different child care providers so she could keep working. She said that she went to private child care centers and to people who just stayed at home and watched other people's children for a little money. She said she was never satisfied with the care her son received. She said that they wouldn't feed him enough, or play with him, or change his diapers. . . . When she had Erin, she decided that she would just stay home and take care of them both.

Last year, Lisa's [not assigned to a work pathway group; an outlier in the analysis] daughter [age five] was being taken care of by her sister-in-law. . . . Her sister-in-law was a licensed in-home child care provider. [At the time], her daughter was in full-day kindergarten, but every Friday and/or Thursday she would not have school. Lisa said, "Here I am, a working mother—I can't lay off my job trying to line up day care for her. . . . It was hard because I didn't like the fact that she was out [of school] and I had to make arrangements for her to get across town. Some days your car might work, some days it didn't. . . . I would get so mad depending on somebody else to take her over there."

As can be seen in these four cases, child care concerns were often a significant reason a woman decided not to work, or to work less. Even among the women who were employed full-time, problems with child care arrangements could place their jobs in jeopardy and be a source of profound emotional distress, particularly with regard to fashioning a workable schedule for themselves and their children.

The reasons for women's difficulties in finding child care arrangements that supported their employment are quite varied. Katrina described her challenges with finding affordable child care arrangements, particularly when her access to state child care subsidies was unreliable. L'Kesha, who could only afford child care services offered by a neighbor who watched children in her apartment, ultimately found this sort of arrangement to be unreliable. Katie had serious concerns about the quality of infant care available to her in the local child care market. She ultimately chose not to work for a while after some bad experiences with the quality of the care her son received as a baby. Finally, Lisa expressed a concern over the mismatch between her work schedule, her daughter's child care needs, and her ability to bridge the gap given her time constraints, the reliability of her car, and the distance she had to travel.

The three of these four women who were assigned pathway membership were either assigned to the rapid cycler group (Katrina) or the low-wage–full-time group (L'Kesha and Katie). Did the women in the New Hope Child and Family Study who had lower levels of employment or more instability of employment tend to report that child care problems had caused them to either quit a job or fail to start a new job? Child care might have been a larger problem for women in the low-wage–full-time, rapid cycler, and full-time–wage-growth work pathway groups, since women in these groups typically worked full-time (more than thirty hours a week) *and* experienced the highest job turnover in the first two years of the study. Moreover, as we saw in Katie's case, a number of women might have chosen not to work at all owing to their concerns over child care. Therefore, many women in the no-work and low-wage–part-time work pathway groups might also have been more likely to report failing to start a job owing to child care problems.

Figure 10.1 shows the percentage of women who reported either quitting a job or failing to start a new job owing to child care problems, for each of the five work pathway groups plus the no-work group. As we expected, the women in the rapid cycler group were most likely to report that child care was a barrier to work. Just over 40 percent of the rapid cyclers reported quitting a job, and just over 33 percent reported failing to start a job, owing to child care problems (compared to about 25 percent for the entire sample). The next most likely groups to report these difficulties were the women in the low-wage–part-time and no-work groups, where about 33 percent reported problems. Just under 25 percent of the women in the full-time–wage-growth and low-wage–full-time groups reported employment problems relating to child care. As we expected, the women in the stable employment group were the least likely to report either quitting or failing to start a job owing to child care problems (10 percent and 12 percent, respectively).

Some of these percentage-point differences appear large in this sort of direct comparison. But there may be other associated characteristics that members of these different groups held in common that partially determine these apparent work pathway group differences. To check for this possibility, we tested the likelihood of a woman saying that she did quit a job or failed to start a job owing to child care problems using binary logit regression analysis. In our model, we controlled for a variety of baseline characteristics, such as age, ethnicity, household size and composition, the presence of very young children, welfare history, income, full-time employment history, and access to a car. We also controlled for whether or not the woman was enrolled in the New Hope experiment. We then added the employment groups and the unemployed group to the model, comparing each group to the rapid cyclers (who reported the most employment problems relating to child care).

Figure 10.1 Women Who Reported Quitting or Not Starting a Job Owing to Child Care Problems at Two Years, by Work Pathway Group

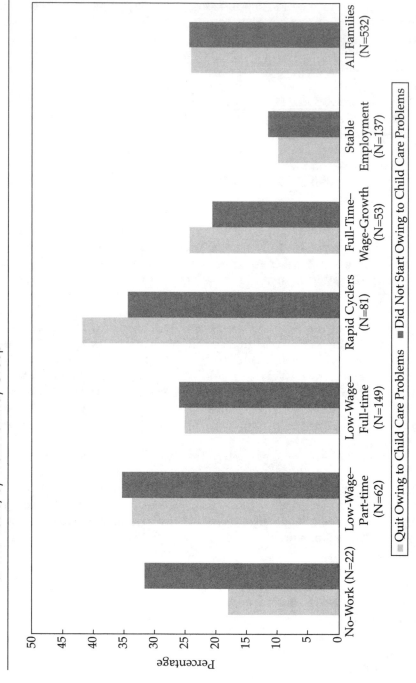

Source: Authors' compilation.

When we compared the likelihood of the women in the rapid cycler group reporting that they had quit a job owing to child care problems to the likelihoods for the women in the other clusters, we found patterns similar to, if not even stronger than, those in figure 10.1. Women in the full-time–wage-growth and low-wage–full-time groups were less than half as likely to report quitting a job owing to child care problems compared to the rapid cycler group.[1] Women in the stable employment work pathway group were less than one-fifth as likely to report quitting a job for this reason.[2] However, women in the low-wage–part-time group were not statistically different from women in the rapid cycler group with regard to having quit a job because of child care problems.[3]

The differences in the likelihood of reporting that child care problems had prevented one from *starting* a new job, however, were not as strong. This may be because exits from work because of child care problems are simply easier to remember than entries into work that did not happen for this reason. Only women in the stable employment group were significantly less likely (about one-fourth as likely) to have not started a job owing to child care problems, compared to the rapid cycler group.[4]

These results tell us that child care was sometimes a significant barrier to employment for many of the women in our study, particularly for the women in the no-work, low-wage–part-time, and rapid cycler groups. Child care problems were not perceived as posing much of a barrier to work among women in the stable employment group, although not because they used less child care than the women in the other groups. When we examined whether the women in our sample reported having at least one child in a nonmaternal child care arrangement during the two years prior to the two-year survey, we found similarly high rates of child care use across all of the employment groups. The low-wage–part-time group reported the lowest rate of child care use, at 87 percent; the stable employment and low-wage–full-time groups reported rates of child care use between 91 percent and 92 percent; and the rapid cycler and full-time–wage-growth groups reported the highest rates, 96 percent. These percentage-point differences were not statistically significant; nearly everyone needed child care in this study. However, problems with child care created problems of instability or low engagement in wage work for only some women. Those in the rapid cycler group were the most strongly influenced by the child care problems they encountered.

Since the need for child care was high in all of the work pathway groups, but the reports of child care as a barrier to employment varied significantly between the groups, the question arises: what was it about arranging and maintaining child care that could have led to such sharp differences between the women in these groups? To better understand this question we turn to the ethnographic data. These data convey a great deal of information on the New Hope mothers' concerns about securing safe and reliable care and the impact those concerns had on their child care arrangements. However, we cannot make confident estimates directly from the ethnographic data regarding the distribution of these concerns in the larger survey sample. Instead, our approach analyzes the pattern from the survey data and then from the ethnographic data, before we synthesize the results at the end of this chapter.

CHILD CARE AND THE DAILY ROUTINE

In two earlier papers (Lowe and Weisner 2004; Lowe et al. 2005), we and our colleagues argued that the problems faced by low-income families in arranging child care are often shaped by the cultural and ecological factors present in the family environment.[5] Child care arrangements must fit into the wider set of regular activities that make up the family's everyday routine, which typically includes paid work, food preparation, child care, cleaning, schooling, church, and community activities. The routines associated with child care are shaped by cultural factors—shared beliefs, values, and associated practices about child care and parenting—as well as by ecological factors such as social, legal-institutional, and material resources (Weisner 2002). Child care arrangements are more likely to be safe, stable, and reliable when they fit into the family's particular cultural and ecological circumstances.

In the analysis that follows, we identify five features of the family cultural ecology that shape the family's construction of its daily routines and examine how child care decisions are made in the context of managing that daily routine. First, child care arrangements must fit the configuration of financial and material *resources* that is characteristic of a family at a given period in time. Second, child care arrangements are dependent on the available mix of *social supports* to the family. Third, child care arrangements have to "make sense"—they must be personally and culturally *meaningful*, given family members' goals and values as participants in a local community. Fourth, parents must find some level of *interpersonal agreement* with the other members of the family about child care arrangements. Agreement is struck through the negotiations and renegotiations of their own internal conflicting goals, needs, and desires, as well as the disagreements and power struggles that inevitably emerge among family members, including the children. Finally, parents must struggle to *balance* their child care arrangements with the wider pattern of activities that they and their children follow throughout the day. These activities can compete in time and location, but those that fit together better—that is, are more balanced—are more likely to be sustained over time. Activities that often conflict in terms of time and location are harder to maintain over time. The variations in these cultural and ecological features—resources, social supports, meaning, interpersonal agreement, and balance among competing activities—can account for the problems and concerns of the women in our study with regard to their child care arrangements.

In the analysis that follows, we present ethnographic material that shows the impact of each of these five domains of the family cultural ecology on the child care arrangements of the families in our sample.

Managing Public and Family Economic Resources

Like Katrina and Lisa, whose stories opened this chapter, the women in this study often discussed their child care concerns in terms of the income and other material resources available to them and their families. Seventeen of the thirty-eight ethnographic study families (45 percent) discussed how family resources afforded certain child care options while constraining others. These parents talked about resource *configurations*, or patterns of resources within the family ecology—the pattern of available personal and public income sources and transportation, for example—not simply about the amounts of particular resources available for child care.

For example, one summer during the study, Samantha, a member of the low-wage–part-time cluster, had placed all four of her children in a day care center while she worked full-time at a local dry cleaner. She liked the day care center. It was close to work and provided transportation to and from school for her two school-age kids, and she had a close friend who also had a baby there with whom she could trade off stopping in to check on the babies once in a while. This arrangement was expensive. Even with support from the Wisconsin Shares child care subsidies for low-income families, she often had to work fifty or more hours a week to pay her child care copay and make other ends meet. A few months into the fall, Samantha quit her job at the dry cleaner after her employer cut back her hours from full-time to less than fifteen hours a week. No longer able to afford the day care center, Samantha kept her children with her at home or took them to her mother's house when she had to go out or go to work at her new part-time job in a video store.

A year later, Samantha decided to send her school-age children to the YMCA summer day camp. Although the program was expensive (it cost about $60 for each child), she felt that she could afford the program if she could obtain subsidies from Wisconsin Shares. Samantha would also have to provide her children's lunches every day. To prepare for this extra expense, Samantha used her food stamps to buy a week's worth of lunch food for the children for the first week of the camp. Thus, she was able to have her children attend the summer camp she preferred. However, even with her careful planning for using these resources, Samantha was faced with an unexpected crisis. After she bought the extra food for lunches, her children, who were not accustomed to having extra food in the house, ate all of it in one evening. Samantha, in the end, had to find additional resources to make sure the children were fed at the summer program that week.

As Samantha's case exemplifies, state child care subsidies are invaluable supports that help many families secure their child care needs. But some women's experiences with these subsidy programs were not positive, and given state and federal funding constraints, they were not always reliable financial supports for the families who needed them. For example, many families in our study who used Wisconsin Shares and began to earn slightly more than the program-mandated income thresholds—at the time of this study this threshold was 200 percent of the federal poverty level, or $28,300 for a family of three in 2000 (Wisconsin Department of Workforce Development 2001)—would lose these supports. Since subsidies were often the only way they could afford paid child care, families were forced to scramble and find alternative arrangements when they lost the program supports.

This was the case for Michol, a member of the stable employment cluster. Many parents like Michol and their employers were unaware of when they might cross these program limits and thresholds; parents often found out that they had crossed them when their benefits were stopped. In Michol's case, she had to suddenly readjust her child care use when her income rose above the state threshold and she lost the child care subsidy.

When families experience these sudden shifts in one component of their resource configuration, they must make accommodations by "refitting" their child care routines into the new resource configuration. In Michol's case, she asked her sister, a licensed child care provider, to take care of her daughter for free until after the end of the school year. In the summer, Michol enrolled her daughter Elissa in a public school summer camp that was cheaper than the after-school care she used during the school year.

Transaction costs were also important. For example, in order to use and maintain access to Wisconsin Shares, families had to complete paperwork, meet with agency personnel to find out about child care availability, and travel back and forth between home, work, and the state offices to turn in proof of employment or levels of income each month or even each pay period. Often these procedures had to be repeated as family economic and child care needs shifted. For example, when Evelia, a member of the low-wage–full-time cluster, decided to place her youngest daughter in a day care center, she first called the local agency in charge of dispensing Wisconsin Shares for her area to find out what she needed to have in order to receive the subsidized care. She was informed that she simply needed to come into the office and fill out a form. When Evelia arrived at the office, however, she discovered that she needed a number of additional pieces of information regarding her employment, income, and so on, before she could sign up for the program. Evelia ended up spending an entire day—losing that day's wages—running around to accomplish these tasks so that she could enroll her daughter in the subsidy program.

Also, as Michol's case shows, many families lose their benefits when they earn too much. Given the unstable employment and income experiences of many of the families in this study, however, those who lose eligibility for these subsidies when their income crosses the cutoff threshold only have to sign up for them again when they start earning less at a later date. Instability in one facet of their lives thus multiplied and spilled over into other areas as a result of the frequency of mandated benefit recertification.

Social Supports

As we have seen in the examples already cited, many families relied on friends and family to help meet their child care needs. In the earlier studies, we found that 61 percent of the families (twenty-three out of thirty-eight) relied on family and friends for child care at least some of the time (Lowe and Weisner 2004). Moreover, family and friends served as particularly important resources when these mothers needed to make short-term accommodations in managing their child care needs.

Although social supports were essential aids in securing child care for many of the ethnographic sample families, the mothers often described them as fragile resources that had to be carefully managed (or as helpful but costly; see chapter 11). This was true even in families with strong ties to family members and friends. Many mothers in our sample feared that their children might burden their family and friends if they asked them to care for the children too often. For example, Shaquita, a member of the full-time–wage-growth cluster, would occasionally rely on her aunts or cousins as backup child care support when she needed it. Maintaining these supports, she believed, depended on her not using them too often. She feared that if she used her relatives as a care resource too often, they might feel as though she were taking advantage, and then she might lose their support altogether. She described her sister's case as an example of how this could happen. Her sister frequently left her kids with relatives and friends for a day or two and would occasionally not return when she said she would. Shaquita was personally annoyed by her sister's behavior. As she put it: "I don't really put my kids on people, so if ever I really do need a babysitter, my auntie or my cousin don't never mind watching my kids, because I never really bring them over. My auntie and my cousin don't like watching my sister's kids, 'cause she'll tell you she'll be back on Thursday but actually it'll be Friday evening when she comes to get them."

Some ethnographic study families distributed their child care needs across many people, both as a means of enhancing their overall social supports and also so that they would not overburden any particular source of support with their child care needs. This distributed social support strategy was particularly useful in making short-term accommodations to sudden shifts in family financial resources. For example, Tiffany, a member of the rapid cycler group, often tried to rely on center-based care as a child care support for her children when she was working. However, she frequently needed others to fill in when the day care center was not available so that she could keep her job as a technician. Tiffany felt that she had "lots of backups." She distributed her secondary child care needs among her grandparents, her mother and aunt, and a brother, all of whom lived within a block of her house. Her children's father also lived a few blocks away. Demonstrating her confidence in this kith and kin–based resource set, Tiffany once exclaimed, "If something comes up with day care or something and someone has to go over, I have lots of calls I can make."

Meaning: Making Sense of Child Care

Parental child care routines and subsidy use had to "make sense" in ways other than fitting into the pattern of resources. They had to fit into the parents' goals and values concerning appropriate child care options. Thirty-four of the thirty-eight women in the ethnographic sample (89 percent) talked about these values.

These mothers reported constant conflict between the values of work and self-sufficiency and the rearing of morally "good" and successful children. Many of them struggled to be both good breadwinners and good caregivers. Also, these mothers believed that certain child care options were better for children than others. In other words, while some options for child care might have been available given family resources, they just were not "right" in the mother's view. For example, while child care centers might provide academic and social enrichment, these places were held in deep suspicion as far as the moral development of children was concerned, especially if caregivers were people whom the mother did not know very well. Some mothers felt that close family members and trusted friends would best foster their children's moral development. The values that were most motivating for parents often shaped their child care arrangements. Most of these mothers described their child care concerns and routines with reference to these kinds of morally charged values.

Caregiving Versus Breadwinning   Broadly shared American values favor the family environment as the optimal setting for the provision of love, guidance, and nurturing to children (Ellwood 1988; Hertz and Ferguson 1996; Strauss 1992). Moreover, parents are generally expected to be the best sources of nurturing for children. The women in our study wanted to be good parents and struggled to be viewed as such by other adults in their families and communities. They felt that they met these goals when they were able to provide direct, personal, and nurturing care to their children, and they often contrasted themselves with "bad" parents—those who provided inadequate care because they pursued their own self-interest. "Caring" and "hiring others to watch your child" were not interchangeable for many of our mothers; they did not have the same moral significance as forms of care. Although parental care and nonparental care coexisted in practice, they did not easily coexist in the ideal beliefs about good care held by many of the mothers in our study. For many of them who held these beliefs very strongly, child care was often a major obstacle to stable employment.

For example, Faye, a member of the rapid cycler group, did not trust anyone but very close kin and friends to take care of her toddler. Faye would often describe her difficulty in sustaining regular employment in relation to her concern for the care of her kids. If she worked more, she was concerned that her older son might get into trouble, or that her younger son would not be cared for well. She even worried that the amount of time and attention she gave to her toddler might be harming her older son in some way. She often discussed placing her toddler in a day care center but was worried that the care provider would fail to give him enough time and attention. She once said that if she ever did get child care for her son, she would want someone who would be very active with him, someone who would play with him and read to him. She did not want someone who would have him "sit somewhere and watch videos all day long." Generally, she felt she could trust close family and friends to do these things with her son, but not people she did not know.

These mothers had a sense of themselves as caregivers *and* breadwinners.[6] Coresident couples often relied on dual incomes to keep their families above poverty, making it difficult to split breadwinning and caregiving between two adults. To keep the caregiving within the family, parents had to work opposite shifts to ensure that one parent was always home to care for the children (Oliker 1995; Presser 1988). But over 80 percent of the ethnographic sample households were headed by a single mother, and most did not have another adult to share these competing responsibilities. Some of the single mothers cared for their children themselves and chose not to work, relying on both kith and kin and formal support resources to sustain themselves.[7] Others found nonparental child care and went to work in an effort to meet their breadwinning goals, while extending the direct responsibility for caregiving to trusted others.

For example, Lynette, a member of the rapid cycler group, did not use child care subsidies because she did not entrust her children to the care of people whom she did not know well. Lynette preferred staying home to provide her son Alvin with warm and attentive care for as long as she could during his toddler years. But at some point during Alvin's second year she could no longer pursue caregiving exclusively. Lynette felt that she had to go back to work. The reality of her household financial situation pressured her to seek work earlier than she had wished. She was torn between breadwinning and caregiving. Lynette left Alvin in the care of Tilly, a neighbor whom she had known for almost twenty years and trusted to give good care to her son.

Qualities of Care Environments   The women in our study also described their competing values surrounding the qualities of various care environments. For example, 61 percent of the ethnographic sample mothers (twenty-three out of thirty-eight) described care by trusted family and friends as safe and nurturing, in contrast to outside environments, which they described as potentially dangerous. Paid home-based care outside of the mother's home and child care centers was clearly held in suspicion.[8] For example, Lynette felt that the care in day care centers was "stranger care"; her use of the term "stranger" implied some element of risk for her son. Mothers feared that their children were at risk in these settings as a result of the poor caregiving they expected of them. Family and friends offered the only really safe and nurturing environments, in the opinion of many parents. But if they had to choose between paid home-based care in a provider's home and center-based care, most of them believed that center-based care offered the safer option, since care in this setting was at least public and open to the scrutiny of others.

Although their suspicion of care settings outside of trusted family and friends was occasionally based on little more than hearsay, some mothers, like Katie, based their convictions on prior experience with paid care settings outside of the circle of trusted family and friends. Lisa, a member of the stable employment group, tried day care centers twice when her kids were young; both experiences were bad. In one center, she would always find her son Conley in wet diapers when she came to pick him up. When her son Preston was in a day care center, she would often find him sitting in a sandbox without any playmates and with no caregivers looking after him. Her boys always came home dirty and unkempt. After those early experiences, Lisa was more comfortable having a friend or relative watch her children.

Positive Qualities of Center-Based Care   Most of the women did believe that care outside of the home had positive qualities and could benefit their children, and 53 percent of the ethnographic sample (twenty out of thirty-eight) discussed some of those positive qualities. Center-based care helped parents when members of their family and friend network were unavailable. Centers with reliable operating hours in a standard work week (for example, Monday to Friday, 6:00 A.M. to 6:00 P.M.) helped many parents sustain regular work. Parents also believed that center-based care offered educational and social opportunities for their children that might be missing in the home. Research shows that center-based care does appear to provide more educational opportunities than other forms of care, such as nonrelative family day care, in both lower-income and higher-income families (NICHD Early Child Care Research Network 2006). Finally, the values these mothers associated with formal care centers often changed with experience. Mothers who viewed formal care with a great deal of mistrust occasionally changed their views when, out of necessity, they placed their children in formal care. Some of them then discovered that the benefits to their children from participation in a high-quality formal care environment outweighed the perceived risks. However, as pointed out in chapter 5, center care hours often did not fit the second and third shifts worked by many of the New Hope mothers.

Mothers in the New Hope ethnographic study wanted safe and nurturing child care settings for their children. That is, they looked for centers that provided safe and hygienic environments; where providers would pay personalized attention to and interact with their children; where their child's peers were well behaved; where there was adequate discipline and supervision; and where providers expressed warmth and love to their children. Parents also believed that centers could provide educational enrichment through peer interaction, exposure to activities that promoted literacy and basic arithmetic skills, training in the proper interaction styles with adults, and age-appropriate socialization experiences, such as toilet training during the toddler years. Finally, some parents expressed a preference for child care centers that would help them better pursue their other parenting goals, aside from child-rearing. For example, two mothers said they were happy with center-based care because it allowed them to work. Another was pleased with a child care center that provided transportation for her children to and from her house each day.

These experiences show great variation in the perceived quality of the local child care market for the families in our study. The child care options available to them were highly variable in perceived quality. Some care options offered care that was both good for the child, developmentally speaking, and a good fit with parental preferences for quality of care. Other care options were understood by the women in our study to pose unacceptable risks to the well-being of their children. Such variability in terms of perceived quality is probably behind the uncertainty surrounding child care that permeates the field notes. Had care been nearly universally bad or nearly all good in these mothers' view, we would expect less ambiguity in how they discussed placing their children in child care. They would have wanted what was best for their children in either case—to avoid child care if it was deemed unacceptably risky, or to find a way to secure child care if it was deemed beneficial without reservation.

Interpersonal Agreement: Negotiations Within the Family and Care Circle

Most of the women in our study held deeply ambivalent feelings about their child care options and also described interpersonal disagreements about them among the members of their household. Given the often conflicting goals and values described in the previous section, it is no wonder that parents were in conflict about their child care decisions. (For a description of how goals and values—including goals about work and family time—often are in conflict more generally, see chapter 7.)

Moreover, sometimes the needs and preferences of other family members—including those of children—in their own daily routines conflicted with the mother's child care decisions, leading her to choose different child care options at different times in an effort to accommodate these competing interests. Sixteen of the thirty-eight families (42 percent) described various interpersonal conflicts that had an impact on their child care decisions.

In several cases, the children themselves instigated interpersonal disagreements over child care arrangements. For example, while Inez, a member of the stable employment cluster, was working two jobs to make ends meet, she left her oldest son, Jorge, in a day care center while she worked one job and with her fiancé while she worked the other. However, shortly after she began to work the second job, Jorge began having behavior problems at day care. His teachers complained frequently that Jorge refused to listen and was acting bossy with the other children. Inez believed that Jorge was unhappy about the amount of time he was spending away from his mother. She tried to talk to Jorge about his problems and to explain to him that she was away from him so often in order to provide him with nicer things. However, these explanations failed. After spending more and more time in parent-teacher conferences, Inez quit her second job to stay home with Jorge in the evenings. Shortly after she quit her job, Jorge's behavior started to improve.

Child care routines in the families also had to accommodate conflicts between adults, particularly when family and friends proved to be unreliable sources of child care support. Katrina, a member of the rapid cycler cluster, relied on her unemployed partner, Javier, to look after her children while she worked. Katrina preferred Javier as a child care option because his care saved the family money. However, she believed his support was unlikely to last. She felt that the children were "driving him crazy" and that she eventually would have to put them back in day care. Her suspicions were confirmed by Javier's behavior: he would leave the house as soon as Katrina returned from work. Katrina and Javier's relationship had often been stormy, and Katrina was unlikely to be able to convince Javier to remain in the caregiver role if he chose not to do so.[9]

Achieving Balance in the Daily Routine

Nearly all the families in our sample implicitly expressed concerns about balance, stability, and predictability in the daily routine, as these cases show. Seven of the thirty-eight families (18 percent) explicitly expressed their concerns regarding stability and predictability in their own and their children's routines.

These mothers reported wanting child care that was flexible in hours, locations, and availability. They did not want child care that was unstable and unpredictably tied to work hours or income. They also tried to arrange reliable and predictable care to ensure added stability in their children's lives. Their attempts to create predictability in their child care routine, however, were often unsuccessful. These mothers frequently made this point when discussing paid in-home child care by nonrelatives. These child care settings often proved to be unreliable, and the mothers found them to be too much of a hassle to use in the long term.

Recall Lisa's complaint that opens this chapter. She was concerned about the mismatch between her daughter's kindergarten schedule (three days a week) and her own work schedule. Her sister-in-law was glad to take care of her daughter on the two days her daughter did not have school, but this arrangement required that Lisa get across town to drop off her daughter and pick her up, a task made difficult by its distance and the unreliability of her car. Because of the imbalance between her work routines and child care arrangements, Lisa had to struggle to make a workable routine, and she worried openly that the complexity of her child care arrangements might threaten her employment.

One strategy that the women in our sample employed to help find balance between family child care routines and work routines was to work in a place that provided child care for their children. For example, Marina worked at a local day care center where she also enrolled her children when we first met her in April 1998. She had mixed feelings about having her kids at the same day care in which she worked, since the situation of having other care workers looking after her kids while she was in the same building occasionally created some tension between Marina and the other workers. But the arrangement allowed a more stable routine: she could work full-time and be near her children during the day. She even rejected another job for more money "doing cosmetics" because the day care center was not open as late as that job would have required. Marina did not want to have to juggle multiple child care arrangements in order to accept the better-paying job opportunity. So she sacrificed better earnings to maintain some balance in her family routine.

Marina believed that providing structure and some sense of stability in the family routine would be good for her children. A field-worker once complimented Marina on how well behaved her older boys were. Marina believed that their good behavior was the result of her difficult struggle to provide "structure" and "stability." "You got to reinforce structure," she said. "Well, I think that—even though I haven't been so good at this—I would say stability [is needed for well-behaved children]." To Marina, "stability" meant providing a good home and having the same group of people as a support network for her children. She believed that her children needed "a circle of people who will always be there for them."

But arranging stability and structure in her children's daily routines was not easy. Marina often found the struggle for predictability and constancy in her children's care routines frustrating and difficult. On some occasions she just wanted to give up. She reported sometimes simply wanting to say: " 'I quit! Forget it!' I want to write a note and leave. But for some reason I have a little bitty thing inside of me that says, 'You have to push it—who's gonna raise your kids?' "

HOW MUCH INSTABILITY IN CHILD CARE IS THERE?

We examined how often our families experienced unwanted and unpredicted changes or instability in their child care arrangements over the three-year ethnography (Lowe et al. 2005). Instability is quite common. Typically, between 20 and 50 percent of these families experienced instability in child care during any of the five school-year and summertime periods that were observed in the study. About one-third of all families had to make a change in their child care arrangements within any single period.

Instability in child care arrangements was related to all five of the features we argue are important for sustaining the daily routine (resources, social supports, meaning, interpersonal agreement, and balance in the daily routine). Most common among these was the mismatch between work schedules and child care needs (balance). Loss of social supports was the second most common theme in the ethnographic reports, and changes in resource availability was third. Moreover, we found that it was not necessarily each of these features operating independently that created problems in securing stable child care arrangements; often it was the dynamic relationship between all five features that mattered most.

CONCLUSION

Our first aim in this chapter was to establish how child care use and difficulties in finding child care related to New Hope mothers' work pathways. Women in the rapid cycler group were more likely to report quitting a job owing to child care problems than women in nearly all of the other employment groups. On the other hand, women in the stable employment group were the least likely to report that child care had caused them employment problems, even though they used child care at the same high level as women in the other work pathway groups.[10] The former finding underscores the importance of child care to the ability of these women to sustain employment over time.

Our second aim was to examine the New Hope mothers' concerns about the fit of child care with their work and family routines. The ethnographic material captured the dynamic management of the daily routines into which child care has to fit. In the ecological and cultural contexts of family lives, resources, social support, values and beliefs, interpersonal agreement, and the balance among the multiple activities that make up the family routine all influenced decisions about child care arrangements. These decisions were locally rational: they made sense in the moment, given the ecological and cultural context in which the family found itself at a particular period of time.

It is difficult to say from the data available to us which of these five domains contributed most to the kind of instability in child care arrangements that might put a woman's employment at risk. We do know that instability in child care was most often associated with imbalance in the family routine, much as it was for Lisa, who was among those cases with which we opened this chapter. In that account, she expressed her frustration with having to take time off work to make sure her daughter's child care needs were covered, fearing that too much such effort might put her employment at risk. Of course, social supports and resource issues are also important, and these too were often unpredictable for many of the families in our study. When social supports fail to come through or financial resources suddenly stop, a mother often must scramble to find alternative, less costly arrangements for her children. These adjustments might lead her to place

her children in a setting that is less optimal than she would prefer, adding
to her anxieties about the well-being of her children during those times
when she cannot be there to care for them herself. If these concerns become
overwhelming, she may decide to stop working for a while and stay home
with her kids until some better child care option opens up.

There can be cascading effects associated with changes in various features of the family cultural ecology. As one resource or support changes, others also shift, and the combined impact can place core family activities at risk (the mother's employment, for example). Child care stability is better viewed, not as a discrete indicator, but as an indicator of other things working well in the family context. The quality and coherence of the everyday family routines in which children participate, including but certainly not limited to child care arrangements, may be the best overall measure of the salutary elements that promote children's development as well as parents' work stability. Since shifts in child care can have negative impacts on women's employment and on children's development, the possibility that there might be this much child care instability in a population of children already at risk for developmental problems should merit concern among researchers and policymakers (De Schipper et al. 2004).

Of course, stability and instability are not the only sources of potential benefit or harm to children in their child care experiences. Many women in this study worried about the quality of the experiences their children might have in child care. Extensive assessments of the quality of the child care setting in which the children in our study were placed were not conducted as part of this study. So we cannot examine empirically the consequences of child care quality issues for children's positive developmental pathways. There are already some studies of the New Hope sample and other working-poor samples that examine the relationship of particular types of child care arrangements (for instance, formal child care centers versus care by family and friends or in-home babysitters) to children's developmental markers (Crosby, Gennetian, and Huston 2005; Crosby et al. 2006; Gennetian et al. 2006; Loeb et al. 2004). These generally find very modest, but statistically significant, positive impacts of formal child care centers on the development of children's academic skills and very modest negative impacts of formal child care on children's social-emotional characteristics (such as being either socially withdrawn or socially aggressive).

There have been other recent studies from different samples that have been able to demonstrate that these mothers' concerns about the effects of the quality of child care settings on their children's development are well founded. For example, the National Institute of Child Health and Human Development (NICHD) Early Child Care Research Network (2006) finds that the quality of adult-child interactions and the overall ambience of the child care setting were modestly associated with better verbal, cognitive, and social skills, and lower levels of conflict with teachers, at four years of age. However, the quality of the mother-child relationship and the resources provided in the home environment showed larger associations with these outcomes. Women are correct to worry about the quality of the child care environments that their children experience, but the qualities of their children's lives at home when in the care of their parents are probably more important.

As we can see, child care was a fundamental concern for the women in our study, and it had a major effect on their work pathways. But, as illustrated by the four stories that opened this chapter, the reasons child care had an impact on employment varied. Sometimes resource issues were significant: like Katrina, mothers had to struggle to put together a workable resource package to ensure that their child care needs were met. At other times, social supports mattered most, as demonstrated in L'Kesha's situation. And as Lisa's story shows, values-driven concerns over the well-being of one's children in child care settings could also matter. Negative experiences with child care quality even led some women to choose to not work for a time, particularly during their children's infancy and the early toddler years when they felt that their children were most at risk and when being a good parent meant, to some mothers, being at home. Interpersonal agreement and keeping the many activities that go into a family's routine balanced also played a role. Finally, as in Lisa's circumstances, sometimes several of these issues (resources, school schedules, work) combined to produce child care problems.

In chapter 13, we review policies and programs that might help parents with the resource, flexibility, and balance issues in their daily lives.

Chapter Eleven | The Informal Social Support, Well-Being, and Employment Pathways of Low-Income Mothers

Eboni C. Howard

WE BEGAN PART 3 with a look at child care, perhaps the most prominent work support in the daily lives of low-wage working mothers. In this chapter, we turn to the broader topic of informal social support. What is the quality of the social support sources in the family lives of mothers embarking on the uncertainties of work in low-wage labor markets? Employment can induce stress and conflict as mothers attempt to balance work demands, home life, and parental responsibilities. Because social supports can buffer the negative repercussions of low-wage employment, the role of social support is an issue central to comprehending the well-being and employment trajectories of low-income families. Among mothers attempting to secure stable employment, the availability of quality social supports may also be critical (Cohen et al. 1990; Katz and Piotrkowski 1983; Wilson, Ellwood, and Brooks-Gunn 1995). Mothers in the New Hope study readily discussed the role of social supports in their everyday lives. They told us who they relied on in times of need, the kinds of help they received, and how they felt about their supports when supports were present or absent.

It is usually assumed that low-income women, like the women in this study, regularly and heavily rely on their sources of social support, primarily their family and friends (Benin and Keith 1995; Billingsley 1992; Manns 1997; Stack 1974; Uehara 1990). Yet the experiences of the mothers discussed in this chapter suggest that consistent and high-quality supports were much less available than might be assumed, and that sometimes supports were not available or helpful at all. Indeed, even when supports were available, they sometimes had emotional or financial costs that at least partly offset their benefits for mothers' employment pathways.

In this chapter, we explore the relationships between the informal social supports and employment pathways of low-income mothers and their families, paying particular attention to the quality of help from informal sources and the trade-offs involved in receiving it. The chapter begins with a detailed account of the social support circumstances of one mother, Samantha; additional stories from other mothers are scattered throughout the chapter. We then present a brief review of the social support literature before going on to present data from the New Hope study about mothers' sources and the types and quality of the social support they received. We also examine associations between the mothers' employment patterns and the quality of their social support sources as the mothers themselves perceived them.

Overall, the evidence presented in this chapter suggests that social supports, despite the positive images often evoked by the phrase, can cause emotional and financial grief to low-income mothers who rely on them and thus influence their employment trajectories. We also see that the availability of social supports is related to the employment pathways detailed in chapter 2. Specifically, mothers in the low-wage–part-time group reported the lowest levels of social support availability. Informal work supports were lacking for mothers whose job trajectories were characterized by sporadic and part-time employment. This information, together with the findings from chapters 2 and 10 that the sporadic and part-time employment groups also reported high levels of other barriers to work, suggests the need for a program and policy focus on the low-wage workers who experience these longitudinal patterns of employment.

SAMANTHA'S SOCIAL SUPPORTS

Samantha, a twenty-five-year-old, African-American single mother, had four children—two boys ages three and four, and two girls, ages ten and twelve. Samantha was unemployed when she applied to the New Hope program; she hoped to curtail her need for welfare services but was assigned to the control group. Samantha had not been able to hold a full-time job for a long time. Her employment trajectory was typical of the low-wage–part-time cluster. During the ethnography, she worked at a dry cleaner, a fast-food restaurant, and a video store. The longest period that she held a job was six months at the dry cleaner, earning $6.50 an hour. Samantha seldom worked over thirty hours a week in any of these positions.

Samantha felt that not having the help to manage her house and children made it difficult for her to work consistent full-time hours. She had never been married, and her children's fathers were absent from their lives. Samantha did not have a boyfriend and lived alone with her four children. Her only source of support was her mother, who provided child care so that Samantha could work. Her mother also helped Samantha pay bills, especially during periods when Samantha was not working or working very little. However, Samantha's mother had financial concerns of her own; she also had a low-wage, part-time job at a fast-food restaurant. So, when she helped with Samantha's bills, she usually had to go without paying a bill or two herself. Samantha explained that her family members, like her two brothers and mother, could not offer her much help because they too were struggling to make ends meet. They might be able to give her a little help if she was in a real emergency, but most likely she would be out of luck.

Samantha's work conditions and minimal informal support had a negative impact on her work opportunities. She explained that as a single parent with little assistance, it was hard to work full-time when she also had doctor visits, sick children, school meetings, social services appointments, and other mandatory demands on her daily schedule. At the same time, having few work hours made it hard for her to earn a consistent amount of money. Under great financial strain, Samantha felt that she constantly struggled to support her family, pay her bills, and cope financially. She believed that formal supports, such as those she received through welfare and social services, never "let you ahead in the game and get you on your feet," but formal supports were what Samantha regularly ended up receiving because of the limited help she had from family and friends. Samantha said, "I don't know what to do [about money]. I feel stuck in the middle of it all, going back to welfare, in the middle of working and welfare, and I don't want it. . . . I just feel stuck struggling. . . . You know, I can't win for losing. No matter how hard I try, all I do is get farther and farther behind."

Samantha admitted that her feelings of helplessness and isolation contributed to her high levels of stress, which negatively affected her behavior with her children. She described several instances in which she didn't have the time or the patience to take care of her household chores or her children after she got home from work. The root cause of Samantha's stress was managing her family's financial and emotional needs alone. Frustrated at the lack of help in her life, she exclaimed, "Ohhhhh!!! It's hard to keep up. This is a big old house. I have too many kids, and it's just me. It's just me. No help, no fathers, no mother. . . . Yep, it's just everything [that stresses me]." Samantha said she would feel better about her life situation if she could get more help to care for her family.

THE ROLE OF SOCIAL SUPPORT

Having sources of informal social support is thought to improve self-esteem and self-mastery, provide the ability to cope with difficult circumstances, and add a sense of belonging through interpersonal relationships (Thoits 1995). Social support sources contribute to people's general well-being and satisfaction with life, while playing a protective or buffering function when people experience difficult times (Cohen and Wills 1985; Gottlieb 1994). Thus, social supports can play a crucial role in how mothers move toward and adjust to their employment situations (Jackson et al. 2000; McAdoo 1989; Pearlin and McCall 1990). Social support networks can assist in the maintenance of low-wage jobs by offering mothers instrumental assistance or material support (such as child care, transportation, sharing household expenses; Henly, Danziger, and Offer 2005). For example, Evelia relied heavily on her mother to provide regular child care for her four children. She provided her mother with a little money for the child care, but far less than she would have paid for a formal arrangement. Evelia also felt less concerned about the well-being of her children while she was at work when they were cared for by her mother.

Social support networks can also provide informational assistance in finding a job, as happened with Shaquita, a single African-American mother of two children; her coworkers told her about other job opportunities and about a technical job training program. In addition to instrumental and informational assistance, social supports can offer emotional assistance that may help mothers adjust to the extra demands, stress, and insecurity of working outside the home by providing feelings of reassurance, connectedness, and belonging (Felton and Shinn 1992; Henly 2002; House, Umberson, and Landis 1988).

Social supports have been examined as they relate to stress, physical health, mental well-being, aging, employment, single-motherhood, parenting, and the experience of racial-ethnic minority groups. Yet it still remains unclear how social supports function and have meaning in the lives of low-income mothers. One reason for this lack of clarity is the fact that definitions of "social support" vary across studies. Moreover, it is unclear which types, forms, and combinations of supports matter. There is some evidence that the quality of social support sources (for example, perceived satisfaction, concordance with needs, timing, obligatory ties, reciprocity) rather than the quantity determines the kind of influence social supports have on an individual (Fernandez, Mutran, and Reitzes 1998; Lindblad-Goldberg and Dukes 1985; Vega et al. 1991).

But how do social supports, in particular the quality of support, relate to employment patterns among low-income mothers? One study suggests that the perceived quality of social support may have more to do with coping with the daily economic hardships of low-income work than with actually securing employment or quality jobs, because low-income social networks have little information, influence, or financial resources that can facilitate upward job mobility (Henly et al. 2005). In the social support field, however, there is little research on the issue. The processes through which positive and negative aspects of support affect the work experiences, lifestyles, routines, and behaviors of low-income mothers and their families experiencing different employment trajectories is not well understood (Green and Rodgers 2001; Wijnberg and Weinger 1998). In this chapter, we explore the relationships between the informal social supports and employment pathways of low-income mothers and their families, paying particular attention to the quality and trade-offs involved with receiving help from informal sources.

SOURCES AND TYPES OF SOCIAL SUPPORT

Data from the survey indicated that informal sources of support from family members (such as older children, grandparents, siblings, aunts, uncles, or cousins) were the most common sources of support in the mothers' daily lives—and more common than formal sources of support such as those from agencies or the government. This was also true among the ethnographic sample. Interestingly, children were cited most frequently by mothers, followed closely by other relatives and friends.[1] In the social support literature, children have often been overlooked as key contributors of support to families. Research on family management and household labor more typically examines the role of children in working families (Crouter et al. 2001; Trzcinski 2002; Zukow-Goldring 1995). It has been suggested that sibling caregiving and household labor is an economic necessity in low-income working families if they are to avoid the costs of child care and the loss of scarce income (Belle 1999; Dodson and Dickert 2004; East, Weisner, and Reyes, 2006).

Current husbands, boyfriends, or male partners were a distant fourth source of support, and neighbors were mentioned much less frequently.[2] In most cases, the current male partners were not the biological fathers of these women's children. While over 75 percent of the sample said that they could rely on their children, family members, or friends for support, and 66 percent could rely on their current male partner, only 37 percent (178 mothers) stated that they could rely on their former spouse or male partner for support. The proportions of mothers who reported support from these sources were similar in the ethnographic sample.[3] Children's biological fathers were not a leading source of support. The prevalence of support from children's fathers, again, was similar in the ethnographic data. Most mothers in the ethnographic sample received support from more than one source, most frequently from family and current male partners. Support from other types of informal sources (for example, friends, neighbors, coworkers) were mentioned less frequently in the ethnography.[4]

The survey did not measure the type of informal support mothers received, but the ethnographic data indicated that the most prevalent type of support was instrumental or material—such as money, child care assistance, household help, transportation, food, or housing. Seventy-five percent of the ethnographic sample (thirty mothers) described receiving monetary assistance, most often from the current male partner, followed by family. The next most prevalent types of support were child care assistance (twenty-five mothers, or 63 percent), material goods (such as clothes and food), and transportation aid (mentioned by seventeen, or 43 percent). These types of material supports were received most often from family members. Informational and, most strikingly, emotional forms of support were described less often by mothers in the ethnographic sample. When emotional forms of support were mentioned (by twelve women, or 30 percent of the sample), the sources tended to be family members, friends, and work colleagues. Friends were rarely described as providing instrumental types of support; if they did, it was usually on an emergency basis.

The sources and types of informal support common in the ethnographic sample are illustrated by the situation of Ana, who relied heavily on her family and friends for child care assistance. Ana was a Mexican immigrant and single mother of four children whose employment was characterized by the low-wage part-time group. When Ana worked, her sister-in-law, who lived with her, typically watched her youngest child (age four) while the other children were in school. After school, Ana's father-in-law, who also lived with her, picked the children up from school and watched them until she got home from work around 8:00 P.M. Although this arrangement endured for a while, Ana did not trust her family and found them to be highly unreliable. Her father-in-law was a heavy drinker, and Ana's eleven-year-old son was often left unsupervised caring for his younger siblings. Her older children were often another significant source of support, particularly for child care. Ana could sometimes turn to her best friend on Saturday for child care assistance when her in-laws failed to show or were otherwise not able to watch her children.

THE COSTS OF SOCIAL SUPPORT

Ana's situation illustrates that even when kin or friends provide support, they may not be trustworthy or dependable. Several studies have recognized the potential costs of informal social support; however, systematic research that explores the costs as well as the benefits of receiving informal social support is limited (Lincoln 2000; McDonald and Armstrong 2001; Rook 1992; Susser 1982). When studying the effects of social support on mothers' employment patterns, especially among populations with limited resources, it is essential that the benefits of social ties be evaluated in relation to their drawbacks to the recipient. Family members and male partners may provide some emotional or instrumental support, but they may also represent additional emotional, financial, or security burdens to the mother and her children (Belle 1982; Brodsky 1999; Parish, Hoa, and Hogan 1991; Teitler, Reichman, and Nepomnyaschy 2004). For instance, support that the mother experiences as control or pressure or that includes messages that she is incompetent may have emotional costs for her. It is possible that mutually beneficial and positive social support may need to flow in both directions within the social support systems of low-income women in order to have positive impacts on their emotional, financial, and employment situations (Henly 2002).[5]

Descriptive information from the five-year survey supports the notion that mothers saw both the benefits and the costs of their social support sources. Using a measure of social support designed to capture both positive and negative aspects of informal support, we found that mothers said it was only "sometimes true" that they had positive support from adults close to them in their lives.[6] Only 26 percent (125) of the mothers surveyed indicated that their adult sources of support were consistently positive.[7] The ethnographic data parallel the survey findings, providing an enhanced understanding of how positive support is defined in the lives of these women.

The quality of social support was coded into three categories in the ethnographic data, "helpful," "not helpful," and "helpful, but has costs."[8] For the quality dimension of "helpful," mothers expressed that they felt "lucky" or "fortunate" to have the support sources and types present in their life. Almost half the sample (nineteen women, or 48 percent) held this attitude about their family sources of support, and a small proportion (seven women, or 18 percent) felt this way about their male partner or spouse as a source of support. Mothers who found their social support sources helpful demonstrated that they were less worried as a result of the help they received and felt that there were few constraints or problems with receiving the support. For example, L'Kesha, a mother of three children and in the low-wage, full-time group, described the support from her live-in boyfriend, Kevin, as very helpful and a major source of financial and emotional support. Kevin was not the biological father of her children, yet he shared half the costs of the household and cared for L'Kesha's children. He helped with household tasks such as laundry, cleaning, cooking, getting the children ready for school, and even going to parent-teacher conferences. He also shared the responsibility with L'Kesha of staying home from work with a sick child. L'Kesha said Kevin made her feel secure and that having that type of reliable support when she was stressed and worn out by work always made her feel better emotionally.

Some mothers, like Samantha, described their possible support sources as "not helpful" or totally absent. In these instances, the women believed that social support systems involved only costs, with no benefits. They did not believe that the relationship was worth the difficulties associated with it. Some mothers also felt alone, with no helpful resources available to them at all. Twenty percent (eight) of the mothers in the ethnography viewed the available support from family sources as not helpful at all or entirely absent from their lives; 13 percent (five) viewed the support available from male partners this way. Such a perspective is conveyed by Maria, a single Latina mother of five children, in the field notes:

> Maria, who has consistently worked in child care, said that she felt that her family brings her many problems. Maria said that she is very engaged with her family, yet she grows tired of all of her family's problems and getting absorbed into them. Although members of Maria's family live with her, she said that she does not get much support from her family, such as help with child care. Maria does not trust many people with her children, including her brother's wife and children. She also feels that her family relies on her more often for support than she relies on them.

Caroline also felt that she did not receive any support from her husband. She was a white woman who was married with five children, ages ten to seventeen, and lived with her husband. Caroline's employment was characteristic of low-wage, full-time work: she worked as a waitress during the ethnography. Unfortunately, Caroline perceived her husband, Tim, as a source of strain rather than support. Tim drank heavily, was involved with drugs, and cycled in and out of jail during the study.

Most mothers in the ethnographic sample described the support in their life as "helpful, but has costs"; there were trade-offs or problems associated with receiving the support. Over half of the ethnographic sample (twenty-two women, or 55 percent) felt that support from family sources was helpful but had costs. Similarly, 63 percent of the mothers (twenty-five) described their support from male partners as helpful but also associated with costs, trade-offs, and negative consequences, such as feeling stress or tense as a result of receiving the support. Some mothers also said that they felt trapped by the support, obligated to the provider of the support, or too dependent on the support. Many mothers also described the support as unreliable, untrustworthy, financially draining, emotionally challenging, or physically abusive. Others felt that their support relationships were unbalanced or asymmetrical; they felt that they gave more help than they received.

Shaquita exemplified this pattern of costly support from family sources. She consistently worked during the New Hope evaluation, achieving wage growth over the study period. Her mother lived with her, and Shaquita felt "lucky" to have her mother available for child care; having this option, she asserted, was a major element in her ability to maintain stable employment. However, Shaquita's mother was not working, nor was she looking for work while she helped with the children. This made Shaquita very angry because she ended up financially supporting her mother in addition to herself and her children. Shaquita explained the frustration with her kinship support system: "They always calling on and coming to me. Like I'm their guardian angel. I've got my own problems. . . . I got my own family, you know. I got my own kids." Shaquita seemed to have developed a reputation in her kinship network as the one who provided support, with relatively little reciprocity. Recent work in social exchange and social capital theory suggests that reputation within a network can be a key factor that determines whether help is offered or accepted in a particular dyad (Smith 2005).

Katrina, whose employment was characterized by rapid cycling, was a single mother of Filipino and African-American descent with four children. Sometimes Katrina felt supported by her boyfriend, Javier, primarily because he watched the kids, but his support also entailed several costs. As Katrina put it, "Whenever something would happen, he was there to pick up the pieces or to do the dirty work." However, she explained, Javier had a mean streak; he was abusive, drank excessively, did not contribute financially to the household, and had a bad influence on the children. Katrina said, "That's the thing, that the kids are gonna grow up and say that their lives were hell because of [Javier's drinking]. . . . That's going to be traumatizing to them. . . . [They will say,] 'He destroyed my childhood.' " Katrina described having her boyfriend around as being "equal to [having] three kids." She believed that she helped him more than he helped her and that he was just dragging her down.

Even though the mothers in the study felt that the informal support available in their lives was useful and a necessity for managing their daily life and work, they also often saw it as unreliable, untrustworthy, and fraught with off-putting tensions, problems, and abuses. Unfortunately, the support typically given to the low-income mothers in our study by their family members, partners, and friends was not always the positive and encouraging sort of support implied by the phrase "social support." Over half of the NHES mothers associated the support in their life with negative emotional, physical, or financial consequences. In addition, some perceived that support was not reciprocated within their informal social networks.

THE QUALITY OF SOCIAL SUPPORT AND EMPLOYMENT PATTERNS

How did the quality of social support perceived by the New Hope mothers relate to their work pathways? We examined this question in both the ethnographic and survey data. Examining the ethnographic data, we discovered that a smaller proportion of mothers in the stable employment and full-time–wage-growth groups portrayed support from family or male partners as *not* helpful (see figures 11.1 and 11.2). For instance, only 14 percent of the mothers in these two groups (two out of fourteen) said that their family supports were no help, compared to 29 percent (two out of seven) of the mothers in the low-wage–part-time group. Similarly, only 7 percent (one out of fourteen) of the mothers in the stable employment and full-time–wage-growth groups found that male support sources were not helpful, compared to 43 percent (three of seven) of the mothers in the low-wage–part-time group.

The ethnographic patterns suggest that mothers who did not have helpful supportive resources may have been in less stable working situations, with fewer work hours. Thus, we speculated that the five-year survey would reveal that mothers with low work hours or cycling work situations felt that they had received less informal support in their lives. In other words, negative, poor quality in social supports would be related to low work hours or unstable employment situations. However, we found no relationship between informal social support and employment patterns when we used the support measure in the five-year survey. Of course, the time period between the work pathways (assessed between baseline and two years) and the five-year survey may have been too long to expect an association.[9] Furthermore, the only measure available to measure social support combined positive and negative aspects of informal assistance.[10] When we used a measure of social support *availability* across close relationships (across six important sets of people—children, current spouse, former spouse, family members, neighbors, and friends—did the mother feel she had someone she could count on if she needed help?), a relationship between support and employment clusters did emerge.[11] As indicated in table 11.1, mothers in the low-wage–part-time group reported lower levels of support availability compared to mothers in all the other work dynamic groups, save the rapid cycler group.[12] These findings provide some additional evidence of a relationship between social support and employment clusters. Recall from

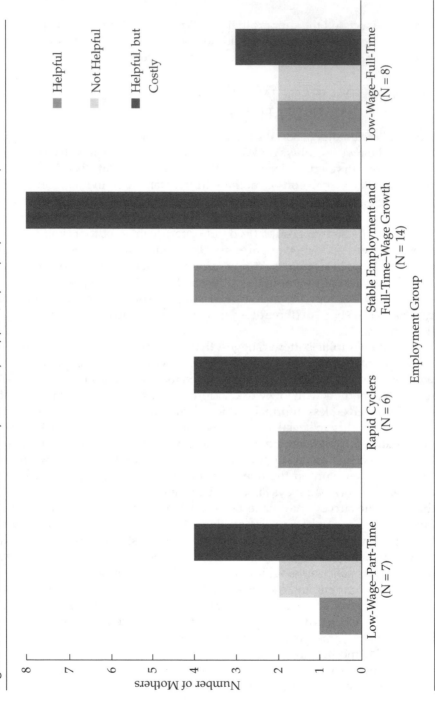

Figure 11.1 Mothers' Views of the Quality of Family Support, by Employment Group

Number of Mothers

Low-Wage–Part-Time
(N = 7)

Rapid Cyclers
(N = 6)

Stable Employment and
Full-Time–Wage Growth
(N = 14)

Low-Wage–Full-Time
(N = 8)

Employment Group

Helpful

Not Helpful

Helpful, but
Costly

Source: Authors' compilation.

Figure 11.2 Mothers' Views of the Quality of Male Partner Support, by Employment Group

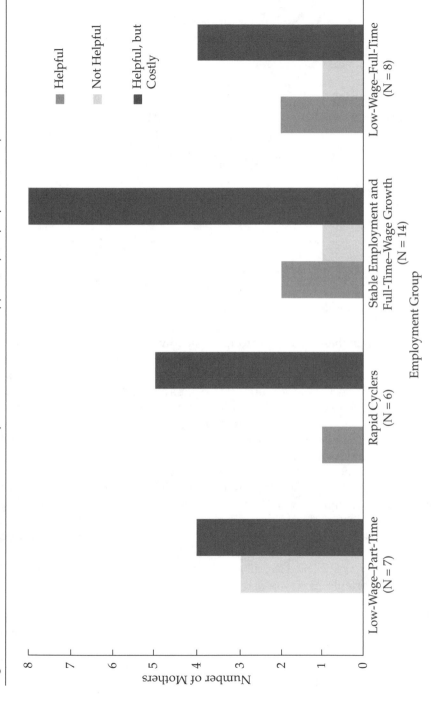

Source: Authors' compilation.

Table 11.1   OLS Regression Coefficients for Social Support
             Availability at Five Years Predicted by Work Pathway
             Cluster Membership

Employment Dynamic Cluster	Unstandardized Coefficient	Standard Error	Standardized Coefficient
No-work group	.576*	.227	1.52
Full-time–wage-growth group	.367*	.173	.147
Stable employment group	.332*	.152	.183
Low-wage–full-time group	.375*	.146	.203
Rapid cycler group	.186	.167	.079

Source: Authors' compilation.
Note: The reference group is the low-wage–part-time group.
*p < .05; **p < .01; ***p < .001

chapter 10 that these same two groups—the low-wage–part-time group and
the rapid cyclers—also reported the highest rates of child care being a barrier to work. So in addition to child care being problematic, mothers in these
two groups perceived social support to be less available than did mothers in
the other work pathway groups. Although we cannot draw causal conclusions, both child care and other, informal supports for work appear to be
lacking for mothers who have job trajectories characterized by sporadic and
part-time employment or very high job instability.

One of the most striking patterns from the ethnographic data is that most
mothers, regardless of their employment situation, perceived social support
from family members or male partners as helpful but costly and involving
trade-offs. Most of them described negative consequences of the support
they received. For example, Michol, an African-American mother of two
and a member of the stable employment group, viewed her partner as helpful but costly. She worked steadily in child care, had savings, and was financially comfortable. She was married, and her husband, Samuel (not the
biological father of her children), shared all household bills equally. However,
this financial assistance was accompanied by grave emotional and physical
costs to Michol and her children. Samuel was physically abusive. He had
broken Michol's thumbs and inflicted severe bruises all over her body.
Once, when a physical fight really escalated, Michol called the police and
Samuel was arrested. Michol explained, "He was bending me back over the

dresser, choking me, and I kind of blacked out for a little bit." She thought often about leaving him, but she also saw his good traits, like his willingness to help with the house and his habit of buying her gifts. She said, "He cooks, he cleans as much or more than I do. . . . It's not like I'm here alone. He's right here beside me, and we're both praying to the Lord." Eventually, however, she did leave him.

Elizabeth's social support situation was similar to Michol's, although her employment pattern was very different. Elizabeth was a U.S.-born, Latina, stay-at-home mother of six children ages one to eight. She lived with Victor, the father of five of her children and a Mexican immigrant whom she married during the ethnographic study. Although Elizabeth was interested in working, she did not have much work history, and her employment trajectory was characterized by almost no employment during the five-year period of study. (She was in the low-wage–part-time group.) One of the reasons she worked so little was that she could not arrange reliable child care. As Elizabeth explained, "You can't go to work here and there, missing work because you don't have anyone to look after the children." Elizabeth felt that she had no sources of support from family or friends. Throughout most of the ethnography, she described feeling secluded and alone, and she did not believe that she had anyone she could count on. In her words, "I'm isolated. I'm always around kids and don't know anything about life. . . . I don't even know the name of the vice president. It's sad, but I don't get out except with the kids." We see here that she fit the pattern of the low-wage–part-time group, which reported the lowest levels of social support availability in the five-year survey data.

Elizabeth was dependent on her husband's income; he worked full-time as a truck driver. She explained that Victor always made decisions for her, stating that "everything has to be his way." Near the end of the ethnography, she married Victor, despite his faults, because she felt obligated and for the good of her children. She explained: "When I was at the chapel and I was supposed to say, 'I do,' I just froze. I couldn't say it right away. . . . I can't see spending my entire life with him. It's kind of sad, but that's how I feel. I guess it's okay for now, until the children are older."

Several times she shared her dreams about finding a job, being away from her husband, and wanting to "just be with my children." During the ethnography, she reiterated several times her desire to separate from her husband and to have "time on her own" and establish her independence.

Similarly, Belinda was dissatisfied with her support system. Belinda transitioned to full-time work after the start of the New Hope experiment, following the pathways of low-wage employment. She also viewed the family support she received as not really helpful and the support she received from her male partner as having adverse consequences. Family support came in the form of help with child care from her sister, Stacey. Stacey was not reliable, however, and would often decide at the last minute not to watch the kids, for whatever reason. Belinda felt that such assistance just added more stress to her life. Also, Belinda claimed that Stacey expected her to help with her kids and that Belinda gave Stacey financial help as much or more than Stacey ever helped Belinda.

Belinda also received help from Rob, her live-in boyfriend and the father of her youngest child.

> Belinda said that things with Rob have been going pretty good. . . . He went and bought her the refrigerator and stove. Also, he is taking care of rent. Belinda said that they are almost caught up in past rent payments. She said that Rob is paying for all of it. . . . He usually does most of the cooking, so she can rest before going to work. Belinda said that Rob is a good man, and he does take care of her and her children. She said he takes care of all her children, even though only one is really his. "He takes care of me, he watches out for my kids, he doesn't beat me or abuse me. He pays the bills and the rent. I mean, I could have it a lot worse. . . . He is taking care of things."

Although Rob was helpful, Belinda did not feel that good about her relationship with him. She said, "Now, with Rob, I feel dependent on him, and that's not good. Being by myself would force me to do things on my own." She also felt that Rob did not respect her. Belinda said that she would like to be by herself again so that she could regain her independence and self-confidence.

Rose was a single African-American mother of two boys, four and six years old, who lived with her children, her boyfriend, and her stepfather. Rose's employment was stable, yet it was driven by a series of temporary placements with a nursing agency she worked for over four and a half years since the start of the ethnography. Her work as a temporary nursing assistant was, she felt, unpredictable and sporadic; she rarely knew whether she would be working from one day to the next. She felt that her employment as a temp was due in part to the unreliability of her support network. Rose explained that she had been given the opportunity to take more consistent and stable long-term placements but was unable to accept those placements because she had great difficulty securing reliable transportation and consistent child care. Her support system could not provide for such needs. She also got disappointed, stressed, and upset when her boyfriend continually broke his promises to help her, leaving her without child care or with the rent unpaid. Rose confessed: "Sometimes I don't go to work because I don't have nobody to come and take my kids to school for me. I have them dressed and everything, I just don't have anyone to take them to school for me, so I don't go to work." Rose was always "hustling" to get the child care and transportation assistance she needed from her family or boyfriend.

CONCLUSION

The ethnographic data indicated that the costs of social support often seemed to lead to lower work effort. Evidence from the survey data supported this contention: low availability of quality social support was associated with the part-time, sporadic work patterns characteristic of the low-wage–part-time group. The ethnographic and survey data suggested that positive social support—help that was non-obligatory, balanced, reciprocal, and non-abusive—improved the employment situations of low-income mothers. The majority of the mothers in our study, however, were integrated into support networks that were stressful and demanding. Their mothers, fathers, siblings, cousins, neighbors, and friends were also struggling to make it work—living with limited resources and handling the difficulties of impoverished circumstances. The men involved in these women's lives grappled with difficult work and financial circumstances that had negative impacts on family life. Faced with declining economic opportunities and inadequate support to address their needs, many relatives and male partners in low-income families were unable to help maintain a positive home environment and provide consistent financial support to the mothers. The qualitative analysis here and elsewhere throughout this book has suggested several reasons why other family members were struggling and were perceived by the mothers as costly sources of support; limited economic resources, physical abuse, and the use of drugs and alcohol all contributed to many women's views of support from family members and male partners as "an extra load," in the words of one mother.

The mothers' reliance on social supports that were mentally and physically costly may have had an impact on the development of their children, though we were not able to examine this directly in this dataset. As we saw from chapters 2 and 10, the ethnographic-sample members in the low-wage–part-time group, compared to the other groups, reported the highest levels of barriers to work, such as mental health problems, domestic violence, and lack of child care. In this chapter, we have found that mothers in this group also reported the lowest availability of social support. These factors can all directly influence children and may explain why children in the low-wage–part-time group (as we saw in chapter 3) had the lowest-rated achievement and highest-rated behavior problems compared to children whose mothers were in the other work pathway groups. Children whose mothers experienced costly social support may have been placed in unstable situations dominated by interpersonal conflict and financial insecurity. Extended kin often tapped into mothers' economic resources, reducing the available resources for the children. Qualitative data in this chapter indicated that too many mothers depended on informal child care that was at best inconsistent and at worst dangerous for their children. Moreover, we found that some children may have been the primary source of support for many working mothers, serving as the child care provider for themselves and their siblings.

This information, which we have accumulated across the studies in chapters 2, 10, and 11, suggests that the low-wage–part-time group experienced particularly high levels of a variety of barriers to work. Programs and policies for the working poor should focus particular attention on those working parents who experience this longitudinal pattern of employment.

As we have seen, ready access to informal support among low-income mothers was far from universal in our sample. The support received was often tenuous, unreliable, or accompanied by remarkably high costs that derailed positive work trajectories. Social support could be helpful or unhelpful, but most often it was a complex interaction of benefits and problems that had consequences for work and, potentially, the well-being of the children. In such situations, despite the general preferences of low-income parents for informal support (Edin and Lein 1997), formal support can become a viable and more consistent alternative. We turn to the role of formal work support services in chapter 12, which explores the relationship between the availability of formal services for mothers and their employment pathways.

Chapter Twelve | Do Formal Work
Support Services Work?
Experiences of the New
Hope Project and the
Wisconsin Works Program

Erin B. Godfrey and
Hirokazu Yoshikawa

WE HAVE SEEN thus far in part 3 that child care barriers and the unavailability of social support are related to difficulty finding sustained employment over time. In this chapter, we turn to the relationship of formal work support services to employment dynamics and pathways. Of course, we cannot embark on an analysis of these services without acknowledging that the New Hope Project and study, spanning the mid-1990s to the early 2000s, unfolded in the midst of historic policy change in Wisconsin and the nation. Welfare is now provided only in return for work, and only for a limited amount of time. Increasingly, the purpose of the welfare office is to provide temporary supports for work, not simply eligibility checks. Its mandate now is to increase employment through short-term job training, job search, case management, and child care subsidies. It is interesting to consider the current work supports and welfare policies from a long view. The federal cash welfare program, which began as a way to support widows so that they could care for their children (Katz 2001), is today a system whose goal is to move working-poor parents off of such public supports after providing them for only very limited periods of time. The attention to children has receded considerably, both in programs and in the public view of welfare.

Work supports to promote employment for low-income people have also changed: the emphasis has shifted from long-term human capital development strategies, such as adult education and intensive job training, to short-term job search assistance and job preparation. The intent of these relatively short-term services is to facilitate quick transitions into the workforce and decrease dependence on public aid (Sawhill and Haskins 2002). The assumption is that these shorter-term services can be successful at facilitating employment among participants. That is, making use of the available services will help participants transition to jobs with benefits and opportunities for wage growth and advancement and thus they will be able to support themselves without the aid of the state.

Wisconsin has been called a leader in attempts to reconceptualize the state welfare system. Compared to other states, Wisconsin has been relatively generous in funding its welfare-to-work programs, and it is also one of the first states to implement a cumulative lifetime limit on welfare receipt. Starting in the late 1980s, the state began implementing a number of pilot programs and demonstrations intended to reinforce the importance of family, responsibility, and work. During the period we followed New Hope participants, Wisconsin ran two major programs for families with dependent children: the Self-Sufficiency First and Pay for Performance programs from 1996 to 1997 and the Wisconsin Works (W-2) program from 1997 to 2000. (A revised version of W-2 continues to operate in the state to this day.) The Self-Sufficiency First and Pay for Performance programs were essentially the early implementation phase of W-2, and both programs were built on Wisconsin's decade of experience operating welfare reform demonstrations and pilots. Like many of the demonstration programs before it, W-2 attempted to recast the contract between the government and the people seeking aid. The receipt of cash benefits was no longer an entitlement, but contingent on work and work-related activities. All recipients were expected to participate in employment activities at some level, but those activities were intended to correspond to the recipients' level of job-readiness. Support services such as child care were available to facilitate employment (Seefeldt et al. 1999).

Despite the large number of studies that have examined how welfare reform as a whole or welfare-to-work transitions affect parents and children (Chase-Lansdale et al. 2003; Morris et al. 2001), relatively few studies have examined the particular role of work support services in both facilitating work and influencing well-being in families. A notable exception is the research conducted by Susan Clampet-Lundquist and her colleagues (2004). In "Making a Way Out of No Way: How Low-Income Single Mothers Meet Basic Family Needs While Moving from Welfare to Work," the authors analyze ethnographic data on seventy-eight mothers who made the transition from welfare to work in Philadelphia and Cleveland over four years in the mid-1990s. The authors do not analyze the relationship between work support services and job transitions, but do explore women's take-up of services and experiences with them. The authors find that formal work support services such as child care subsidies, food stamps, and health care subsidies, when they could be utilized, were instrumental in helping mothers provide for their families. The authors also find, however, that institutional barriers, such as eligibility requirements, bureaucratic red tape, caseworker misinformation and error, and extensive monitoring of ongoing eligibility, greatly limited access to and enrollment in many of these work support services. Although present in both cities, barriers to take-up differed according to the specific requirements of each state's programs.

Because of the New Hope study's experimental design, we have the unique opportunity to contrast the experiences of New Hope participants, who had access to W-2 services as well as New Hope's package of benefits, with the experiences of those who had access only to Wisconsin's work support services. As with W-2, New Hope benefits and services were aimed at facilitating employment. However, as described in chapter 1, New Hope's benefits were available only to individuals who worked an average of thirty hours per week. In addition, the program offered several employment incentives not available in W-2, including earnings supplements to bring participants' income up to 200 percent of the federal poverty limit, child care and health insurance subsidies, and case representatives who carried small caseloads and were actively involved with their clients. The mothers assigned to the New Hope group were also, of course, eligible for all W-2 work support services. In fact, since the New Hope program benefits lasted for only three years, many families in New Hope also used other state benefits over the years we followed them.

From the random-assignment evaluation of the New Hope Project, we know that not everybody given the chance to make use of New Hope services did so (Bos et al. 1999). Although New Hope offered a comprehensive package of benefits, take-up was far from universal, and participants who used some services rarely used all of them. Why might this be? Ethnographic research by Christina Gibson and Thomas Weisner (2002) provides some insight into the low rates of service use. They found that four categories of personal and family circumstances were associated with take-up of New Hope services. For two groups, take-up of benefits was limited by (1) a misunderstanding of New Hope and its benefits or (2) significant personal troubles and life instability. For the other two groups, use of services was informed by (3) cost-benefit assessments of the value of services or (4) how well the services fit into the family's daily routine. The same four categories were found to characterize take-up of W-2 and other state programs among members of the New Hope control group. In addition to personal and family characteristics, the structure of the New Hope administrative program also influenced take-up of benefits. New Hope participants who provided evidence of their employment for at least 120 hours per month were automatically sent an income supplement if they qualified. Well over 80 percent of those who did come into the New Hope offices and showed their work records received some income supplements. To receive the other benefits, however, those people either decided they wanted them, and then in fact used them, or elected not to.

This and similar research have provided essential information about the complexity and diversity underlying low-income families' decisions to use services. Once participants have done so, however, important questions remain to be answered. Benefits and services designed to foster and support work are the cornerstone of current antipoverty and welfare programs. Are the services offered to participants actually helpful in finding and keeping jobs? If so, how are they helpful? Are services only helpful for some participants, or do they facilitate employment transitions for all? Finally, how does the use of the services themselves actually affect the economic and psychological well-being of low-income families? This chapter focuses on these questions.

We use the two types of data available in the New Hope program to examine how service use was experienced by the families. In the first section, we discuss the programs and services offered to low-income people in the state of Wisconsin. We provide detail on those services and their changes. (The New Hope follow-up period spans years of extraordinary policy change in Wisconsin.) The next three sections make use of the rich ethnographic data gathered in the New Hope Project. The second section explores participants' job transitions, documenting four major patterns that capture how women in the study experienced changes in their employment over the course of the ethnography. In the third section, we capitalize on the unique opportunity we had to investigate variations in services and service providers. We contrast participants' experiences of Wisconsin's state welfare programs with experiences of the New Hope program and explore the relationship between the services available to participants and the employment transitions they made. Not only do we find striking differences in the perceived quality of the services provided, but these differences appear to influence the pattern of job transitions experienced by New Hope study participants. The fourth section focuses on individual differences in service use, finding that it was the women with the most stable life circumstances who were best able to leverage the services to improve their employment. In the fifth section, we move away from the ethnographic analysis of job transitions and use the New Hope survey data to take a broader look at the relationship between service use and more general indicators of parents' economic and psychological well-being. We show, for example, that for every additional work support service used over the first two years of the study, total yearly income over years three through five increased by an estimated $870. This impact remains, and even becomes stronger, when we exclude New Hope and other earnings supplements from the analysis. Excluding earnings supplements, we find that income over years three through five increased by $1,089 for every additional work support service used. We close the chapter with a summary of our findings and a discussion of their broader implications.

WORK SUPPORT SERVICES IN MILWAUKEE IN THE ERA OF WELFARE REFORM, 1995 TO 2000

Regardless of whether they were assigned to the control group or the experimental group, all participants in the New Hope study were eligible for a host of services offered through W-2 and other state and federal programs, such as Medicaid, food stamps, and the earned income tax credit (EITC).[1] In addition to these services, participants randomly assigned to the New Hope group were also eligible for all New Hope services, provided they worked an average of thirty hours per week each month. In months when participants did not meet the work requirement, they were denied benefits. (For a full description of the New Hope program and the services it offered, see chapter 1.) Table 12.1 provides an overview of services offered by New Hope and W-2 during the period of the New Hope study.

As mentioned, Wisconsin was an early leader in efforts to reform state welfare systems. In fact, in the two years before W-2 became Wisconsin's first Temporary Assistance for Needy Families (TANF) program, following the passage of federal welfare reform legislation, the welfare rolls in the state had already dropped by over half. In this section, we focus on Wisconsin's work support services as they operated during the bulk of the New Hope follow-up (1995 to 2000). This period spans Wisconsin's efforts to reform welfare both before and after August 1996, when President Bill Clinton signed the Personal Responsibility and Work Opportunity Reconciliation Act (PROWRA) into law.[2]

In 1994 Tommy Thompson, the Republican governor of Wisconsin, announced that Aid to Families with Dependent Children (AFDC) would end in the state. However, he did not yet have a plan for a program to replace welfare. Anger nationwide at increases in welfare rolls was peaking; Thompson had been elected governor in 1986 based on campaign promises to reduce the welfare rolls and benefits in the state. He cut benefit levels and fully implemented the federal Job Opportunity and Basic Skills (JOBS)

Table 12.1 Services Offered Through the New Hope Project and Wisconsin Works

Service	New Hope Project	Wisconsin Works and Related Federal and State Programs[a]
Job search and preparation	Provided through intensive case representation	Job search centers provided: • Computerized listings of job openings • Job search skills • Job preparation trainings • Job clubs
Job placement	Community service jobs in nonprofit organizations • Paid minimum wage • Earnings counted toward tax credits and the New Hope earnings supplements	Three tiers of job placements that differed in compensation • Trial jobs (wage employment) • Community service jobs (work in exchange for benefits totaling less than minimum wage) • W-2 transition jobs (job search and preparation or educational activities in exchange for benefits)
Earnings supplements	Monthly earnings supplements • To bring income up to the federal poverty line • Provided to participants averaging thirty hours per week of employment over the month	State and federal earned income tax credit • Available to all working participants except those in community service jobs or W-2 transition jobs
Child care	Child care subsidies • Available to participants with at least one dependent child under the age of thirteen and working thirty hours per week	Child care subsidies • Available to persons with gross incomes at or below 185 to 200 percent of the federal poverty level

	• Providers reimbursed directly by New Hope, up to a maximum of 75 percent of market rate • Participants made small copayment based on income and household size	• Providers directly reimbursed by W-2 program at 50 to 75 percent of market rate • Participants made small copayment based on income and household size
Health care	Health insurance plans through HMOs • Available to participants working thirty hours per week • Participants made small copayment based on income and family size	Joint state/federal medical assistance • Available to low-income parents (Medicaid) and their children (Badgercare) • Coverage based on sliding scale of income and assets • Participants generally not required to make copayments
Case representation	Intensive case representation • Case representatives carried small caseloads • Encouraged employment, full use of services • Provided counseling, advice, and emotional support	Case management • Case managers carried high caseloads • Focused on eligibility processing

Source: Authors' compilation.

[a]Descriptions here apply to Wisconsin Works and related federal/state programs as they operated in 2000.

program in Wisconsin by providing full state matching funds. However, the welfare rolls in Wisconsin did not start to plunge until after Jason Turner, as commissioner of the state's Department of Workforce Development (DWD), revamped the state's welfare program in 1996.

AFDC, regulated by the federal government and implemented by the states, had provided cash benefits and other services to parents and care-takers of children deprived of the support of one or both of their parents.[3] It was an entitlement program; applicants who met the eligibility criteria were guaranteed benefits, and no time limits were imposed.[4] Families who were eligible for AFDC automatically received Medicaid coverage and could qualify for a number of other state benefits, including food stamps, child care assistance, and the EITC. In Wisconsin, AFDC was managed by DWD and administered by county and Native American tribal agencies.

In March 1996, Turner and Thompson introduced two stringent varia-tions on the federal JOBS training program: the Self-Sufficiency First pro-gram and the Pay for Performance program. The JOBS program, part of the implementation of the prior wave of federal welfare reform in 1988 (the Family Support Act of 1988), had made job training, work, and education-related activities mandatory for some AFDC recipients by reducing benefits for nonparticipation (Institute for Research on Poverty 1998). But the sanc-tions were modest. These two Wisconsin programs went much further in emphasizing work over not only welfare but over education and job train-ing as well. Self-Sufficiency First was a diversion program that required that AFDC applicants complete an interview with a financial planning resource specialist before applying for benefits. They then had to participate in the state JOBS program during the thirty-day AFDC application processing period. In these thirty days, the applicant needed to devote at least sixty hours to JOBS participation, including thirty hours of direct employer con-tact. If needed, child care was provided during the applicant's hours of JOBS participation. This program was spectacularly successful in reducing wel-fare receipt among new applicants. Pay for Performance required thirty to thirty-five hours per week of work from AFDC recipients in exchange for their benefits, and the program imposed heavy sanctions on those who failed to comply.[5] It was one of the first "workfare" programs in the nation. In the first version of the program, sanctions even included reductions in food stamps. The program began in March 1996 and immediately resulted in large declines in Milwaukee's welfare rolls. In addition to these programs, begin-ning in October 1996, time limits were imposed for all active work program participants. Recipients were limited to sixty months (five years) of AFDC benefit receipt in their lifetimes. Together these reforms reduced the welfare rolls in Milwaukee by a whopping two-thirds between 1995 and 1997.

Congress passed, and President Clinton signed, the Personal Responsibility and Work Opportunity Reconciliation Act in August 1996. This law replaced AFDC with a new federal program, Temporary Assistance for Needy Families. Like AFDC, TANF was also implemented through the states. Because of its history of success in cutting its welfare rolls, Wisconsin was the first state to gain approval for its TANF plan (W-2) in late 1996. Implementation of W-2 began in the fall of 1997 and was completed in the spring of 1998, partway through the New Hope follow-up. For ease of communication, the terms "Wisconsin Works" and "W-2" are used throughout this chapter to refer to the services offered through W-2 as well as the two programs (Self-Sufficiency First and Pay for Performance) that directly preceded it (and were retained as part of W-2 after 1997).

W-2 was implemented through contracts with counties, Native American tribal regions, and public and private social service organizations.[6] In Milwaukee, W-2 was implemented through seven organizations, including the county.[7] Over the period of implementation, existing AFDC cases were converted to W-2. Interim W-2 agencies that were not permanent had a six-month period to transfer their cases to the new W-2 agencies. Before converting a case to W-2, the new agencies had the opportunity to meet with the participant, explain the program changes, and determine the employment activities in which the individual would participate. Beginning in September 1997, five-year time limits on benefit receipt were imposed on all new applicants to W-2. Time limits were also imposed on existing AFDC recipients who were not in the JOBS program as they made the transition from AFDC to W-2. Local agencies were also encouraged to begin implementing the Financial and Employment Planner (FEP) concept, a position that integrated benefit eligibility checking and work support functions.

Under W-2, receipt of cash benefits and other services was dependent on work or work-readiness activities and limited to a lifetime receipt of five years.[8] Throughout their time in the W-2 program, participants worked with a case manager (the FEP) to determine and maintain their eligibility and help find and keep employment. There were four opportunities (or tiers) for families to receive benefits under W-2. The first, and highest, tier was unsubsidized employment (employment not subsidized by the state), in which participants received job search assistance to help them find a job and then received wages from their employer. The second tier was the trial job. Some participants who had basic skills but lacked sufficient work experience to meet employer requirements were placed in a trial job. Community service jobs (CSJs) were the third tier. They were developed for individuals who lacked the basic skills and work habits needed in a regular job environment. The fourth tier was termed W-2 Transition (W-2 T). This level was reserved for individuals who, because of severe barriers, were unable to perform independent, self-sustaining work.

Determination of which tier was appropriate for each family was made through informal assessment by a FEP; in some cases, however, a more formal assessment was required. An "employability plan" was then established as a signed contract between W-2 and the participant to lay out the specific requirements for participation given the participant's tier and circumstances. Requirements were not to exceed forty hours per week of activities. Although access to services varied slightly by tier, W-2 services consisted of five main components: job search and preparation; job placements; child care; earnings supplements and health insurance; and case management. We describe each briefly here.

Job Search and Preparation Services

Job search assistance was based in the Job Center, which was billed as a focal point for employers and job-seekers. Depending on the locality, W-2 agencies were either located within Job Centers or operated independently from them and linked electronically. Job Centers, which were also open to the general public, provided an array of services, including computerized listings of job openings (JobNet), assistance with job search skills, testing and assessment, information on workforce development services, education and training programs, and links to the unemployment insurance system. The federal Workforce Investment Act of 1998 required such "one-stop centers" nationwide to co-locate federally funded work support programs; however, Job Centers were begun in Milwaukee prior to 1998. Through Job Centers, individuals could also join a job club. Job clubs met on a regular basis and provided instruction on résumé writing and interview skills, experience on personal computers loaded with adult education software to increase literacy skills, help determining suitable jobs, and training on typing and common office software. In some cases, the job club supervised participants' employment searches.

Preparation services included education and training activities in basic education, technical college courses, job skills development and vocational trainings, motivational and life skills training, and mental health services. These activities were offered through the W-2 agency, Job Centers, local schools, employers, and other community agencies. The specific hours and types of training and educational activities that qualified as participation in W-2 were laid out in each participant's employability plan. Most participants were allowed ten to twelve hours per week of educational activities, with a yearly limit of 516 hours to allow attendance in intensive short-term training and technical college classes that required more than ten to twelve hours per week of attendance.

Job Placements

Three tiers of job placements were available to participants based on their job skills, employment history, and personal circumstances. Participants who had basic job skills but lacked sufficient work experience to meet employer requirements were placed in a trial job. The employer agreed to provide the participant with on-the-job work experience and training in exchange for a wage subsidy (which did not exceed $300 a month) that would enable the participant to receive pay comparable to what a regular employee in a similarly classified position would earn (at least minimum wage). The W-2 agency contracted with the employer and paid the employer the subsidy with the expectation that if the W-2 participant performed satisfactorily, the employer would offer that participant permanent employment. Trial jobs lasted up to three months and could be extended for up to another three months. Participants were allowed to participate in more than one trial job, but a lifetime limit of twenty-four months of participation was imposed.

Community service jobs were developed for individuals who lacked basic job skills. CSJ participants received a monthly cash grant of $673 for up to forty hours per week in work, training, and education activities. (Note that at a forty-hour CSJ, this resulted in the equivalent of a less-than-minimum-wage job; in contrast, New Hope CSJs paid the minimum wage.) Failure to meet participation requirements resulted in a reduction of $5.15 for every hour of activity missed without good cause. Each CSJ placement was scheduled for a period of up to six months, with an opportunity for a three-month extension in special circumstances. CSJ placements were made with public, private nonprofit, and private for-profit employers, including municipal and other government agencies, community-based organizations, and contract organizations (private or public companies that bid for paid work). Lifetime participation in a CSJ, as with trial jobs, was limited to twenty-four months.

W-2 Transition positions were developed for individuals who, because of severe barriers, were unable to perform independent, self-sustaining work. Though termed a "position," individuals in this tier spent the majority of their participation hours in job search and preparation activities or education services. W-2 T participants received a monthly grant of $628 for up to twenty-eight hours per week of participation in work training or other employment-related activities and up to twelve hours per week in education and training. Failure to meet participation requirements resulted in a payment reduction of $5.15 for every hour of activity missed.

Child Care

Participants in all tiers of W-2 were eligible for a child care subsidy as long as their gross income was at or below 185 percent of the federal poverty level (for applicants) and 200 percent of the federal poverty level (for participants) and child care was needed in order to work or participate in a W-2 employment position. Specific eligibility for child care was determined by the FEP, and periodic documentation was required to maintain the service (particularly when transitions in jobs or hours occurred). Child care was subsidized by the W-2 program at 75 percent of the market rate for licensed child care providers and 50 percent of the market rate for provisionally certified providers. W-2 made direct payments to the child care provider. The provisional certification level (the provider had to meet minimal health and safety standards and complete a background check) was introduced to allow parents the option of using a family member or friend to provide child care. Parents at all income levels were expected to share in the cost of child care through a copayment to the child care provider. No time limits were imposed on the receipt of child care.

Earnings Supplements and Health Insurance

During the period of the New Hope study, the state of Wisconsin provided other family support services. These programs included state and federal earned income tax credits (in addition to the tax refund, advance earned income credit was given to increase the monthly income of participants in the unsubsidized-employment and trial-job tiers of W-2), the food stamp program, and HMO-based health insurance through Medicaid (adults) and Badgercare (children).

Although these programs operated separately from the W-2 program beginning in 1997, the bureaucratic separation of services was relatively recent at the time of the study, and many of the same families who participated in W-2 were also referred to these programs by W-2 caseworkers. In some but not all locales, W-2 and other supportive services were administered through the same physical location, such as the Job Center.

Case Management

W-2 case management was designed to provide the participant with access to all of the W-2 and supportive services they needed at one location. FEPs were responsible not only for determining eligibility for W-2 and related supportive services but also for developing the terms of participation through the employability plan; in addition, FEPs were integral in defining work options and providing intensive case management. For example, in the first W-2 tier (unsubsidized employment), unemployed individuals were slated to receive intensive case management services from their FEP to facilitate employment at the earliest opportunity. This included maintaining regular and frequent contact (at least once per week) with unemployed participants.

THE JOB TRANSITIONS EXPERIENCED BY PARTICIPANTS IN THE NEW HOPE ETHNOGRAPHIC STUDY

The longitudinal nature of the ethnography and its detailed collection of information about job transitions make it particularly useful for understanding the relationship between work support services and job transitions. We sought to identify the types of employment transitions that occurred for each ethnographic sample member, the types of services (from both New Hope and the state of Wisconsin) that were used, and the relationship between the two. As a first step, we determined the kinds of job transitions actually made by these low-income women, identifying four categories that characterized the changes in employment they experienced.[9,10] Note that although there is quite a bit of overlap between these job transitions and the work group pathways developed from the first two years of survey data (see chapter 2), the association is not perfect because the ethnographic period covers roughly years three to five, a period that came after the period covered by the work pathway clusters. Here we consider job transition patterns in the ethnographic data.

1. Stable Employment   Stable employment with wage growth and advancement was the job goal most often cited by New Hope mothers (see chapter 7). But only seven out of the forty women in the NHES (18 percent) experienced stable employment with wage growth and advancement for most of the three-year ethnography.[11]

2. Upward Mobility   The vast majority of the participants we followed (twenty-nine out of forty, or 73 percent) did not have stable employment and experienced a number of job transitions, both positive and negative. The mothers in what we term the upward mobility group—ten out of the forty women in the ethnography (25 percent)—experienced mostly positive job changes during the course of the ethnography. They wound their way through a series of jobs, gaining the skills, connections, and experience necessary to advance. These workers made job-to-job transitions, leaving one place of work for another offering better hours, more job security, or higher wages.

3. Supplemental Jobs   Some mothers (eleven out of forty, or 28 percent) were able to provide for themselves and their families through a combination of stable employment and supplemental employment through second or seasonal jobs or by holding down two or more part-time jobs. We consider these occasional transitions in employment to be positive because they enabled the mothers in our study to obtain additional resources when needed. However, as pointed out in chapter 5, the benefits of increased income from supplemental jobs are often accompanied by family costs such as less time to spend with children and more unstable family routines.

4. Job Instability   Finally, job instability is defined most often as a voluntary exit (quits) or an involuntary exit (firings, layoffs) from a job that results in a period of unemployment or non-employment lasting a month or longer (Gottschalk and Moffitt 1999; Jaeger and Stevens 1999; Royalty 1998). However, for low-wage workers, periods of unemployment are often interspersed with transitions from one dead-end job to another. A recent study by Harry Holzer and Douglas Wissoker (2001) finds that among previous welfare recipients, job leaving did not represent opportunities for advancement into better jobs, as it does for many people. Instead, job leaving appeared to reflect significant workplace problems, such as poor working conditions, inflexibility of hours and schedules, and harassment or discrimination. In our sample, some women appeared to be mired in cycling between unemployment and low-wage jobs with intolerable conditions. Thus, in this chapter, the term "instability" is used to refer to transitions that result in another low-wage job with few benefits or opportunity for advancement, as well as transitions that lead to periods of unemployment or non-employment. Ten out of the forty women in the NHES (25 percent) experienced this pattern of instability throughout the ethnography.

THE ASSOCIATION BETWEEN WORK SUPPORT SERVICES AND JOB TRANSITIONS

Given that both New Hope and W-2 focus on work support services as the key to fostering sustained employment, a critical question is whether services facilitated positive job transitions, such as upward mobility and supplemental jobs, and prevented negative ones, such as job instability. Among the women we followed in the ethnography, most women used at least some of the work support services offered through New Hope and W-2. Eighteen out of twenty (90 percent) of the women in the New Hope group used at least one New Hope service. Of the women in the New Hope group who used services, fifteen (83 percent) also used W-2 services at some point in the ethnography. For women assigned to the control group, fifteen out of twenty (75 percent) used at least one service offered through W-2.

To explore how work support services may have been related to job transitions, we analyzed the field notes written for each of the forty women in our sample, noting every time a job transition occurred, the type of job transition it was, and whether work support services played a role in the transition, according to the mother. We also documented what participants had to say about the experience of work support services and about their involvement (or lack of involvement) in specific services.

For sixteen out of the forty women in the NHES (40 percent; nine in the New Hope group and seven in the control group), job transitions were reported to be influenced by the use of services. However, these associations played out in some unexpected ways. First, while some types of services were related to the job transitions of the women in our sample, others were not. Second, mothers reported that the use of New Hope services generally facilitated their transitions to better-quality jobs and sustained employment with stable, higher-quality employers. This pattern did not occur with use of W-2 services.[12] Most participants used services such as W-2 cash benefits, food stamps, and Medicaid intermittently throughout the course of the ethnography, mostly as fallback measures in times of nonemployment. As soon as new employment was obtained, many of the participants went off these services until the next time they fell on tough times.

Job Search and Preparation Services

Although conceptualized as one of the major ways to foster employment and enable low-income workers to provide for their families, services related to locating employment opportunities and gaining job experience were not reported to facilitate any of the types of job transitions. Among the women eligible for New Hope services, very few even mentioned using these activities, and no women used them as a strategy to transition between jobs.

Women eligible for W-2 benefits did use W-2-sponsored Job Centers and attend job preparation seminars or basic education and job training classes. Eleven out of the thirty-three women (33 percent) who used these services took part in them at least once throughout the course of the ethnography. However, women used these services primarily because they were required to do so in order to receive benefits. What is striking is that mothers unanimously indicated that Job Centers and classes were not useful and often did not lead to any lasting, quality jobs.

Rhonda, who had been mildly disabled by a recent stroke, cycled through different kinds of benefits and used up unemployment and disability benefits before landing back at W-2's doorstep. She was put into a job placement, then started a W-2 computer and typing training class. Finally, she attempted to satisfy her work requirement by putting in applications "anywhere, just anywhere. Even if I can't do the work, I fill it out so I can say I fulfilled the requirements." When her typing didn't improve because of difficulties with her hand, she quit the computer training course and started a W-2-sponsored child care training course. She began work at a child care facility, but just a few months later she was unemployed again and considering going back to disability.

Iris, prone to depression and low self-esteem, mentioned that she attended five different types of job readiness trainings and several more when she received her GED. She seemed to think she had all the information she needed. She knew about "dress for success," she knew about showing up on time, and so on. So the field-worker asked her whether there was anything that she or anyone else could do to help her feel comfortable getting a job. Iris said that she needed to fix her weight, her hair, and her teeth, but then quickly commented that all of those things cost money, which she didn't have. She explained that if she could improve her appearance, she would be more self-confident and would not worry about potential employers judging her looks.

The lack of any perceived efficacy of the job search and preparation activities and of any relationship to actual job mobility may, of course, be due to the fact that those with less job-readiness were more likely to use these services. We explore later in this chapter how perceptions of the link between work support services and job mobility and other job transitions differed for those with different levels of job-readiness.

Community Service Job Placements

Like job search and preparation services, community service job placements were designed in Jason Turner's 1996 Pay for Performance program to push welfare recipients into the workforce by requiring them to work for their welfare benefits.[13] CSJs, the level-two job tier placement in W-2's system, were not supposed to be attractive jobs that provided advancement. On the contrary, they were designed to be unattractive alternatives that would spur recipients to find jobs in the labor market. Work in exchange for welfare did not even pay the minimum wage, given cash benefit levels. Since CSJs were work in exchange for benefits, these jobs also did not result in earned income that would have counted toward federal and state tax credits. Finally, W-2 CSJs were often tedious jobs that provided little or no opportunity for growth in skills. In contrast, New Hope CSJs were designed to pay the minimum wage (still below the pay of the majority of entry-level jobs) and to provide some opportunities for growth in job skills. New Hope CSJs were restricted to nonprofit organizations, and they did count toward both earned income tax credits and the New Hope earnings supplement. Our analysis shows that these fundamental differences in the structure and incentives created by W-2 and New Hope CSJs came through loud and clear to the mothers in the ethnographic study.

Six of the eighteen NHES women in the New Hope group who used services (33 percent) worked at a New Hope CSJ at some point during the study. In general, women who used a New Hope CSJ found their position worthwhile in terms of learning job skills. In a few cases, the placement led to a permanent position or the skills learned there were helpful in transitioning to new employment.

L'Kesha's job as a receptionist began as a CSJ placement. (Prior to this placement she had worked in another New Hope CSJ.) Thus, the CSJ placement led to a job with benefits, such as vacation, sick days, and health insurance. Over the course of the ethnography, she experienced wage growth and was promoted to office assistant. She credited New Hope for her employment trajectory, saying that the jobs she got through New Hope helped her develop job skills, especially typing and computer skills.

Janet also credited New Hope CSJs for promoting her positive job transitions. As her field-worker noted: "Janet has a clear understanding about the details of New Hope. She felt that CSJs and the wage supplement allowed people to take lower-paying jobs that taught them important skills. In the end, although the jobs paid less, they were providing workers with valuable skills."

Experiences with W-2 CSJs provide a stark contrast to those with New Hope CSJs. Twelve out of the thirty-three NHES women who used services (36 percent; three in the New Hope group and nine in the control group) held a CSJ through W-2. Although a few CSJ placements led to lasting employment, most W-2 participants saw these placements as no more than fulfillment of the mandated requirement to work in order to receive their next check. These field notes from three mothers are illustrative:

Samantha tried the W-2 program, but didn't like it. She is not receiving W-2 benefits now. She did not like W-2 because she thought the work experiences were degrading.

Nancy still has no job. She sounded a little stressed this time, unlike my last visit, when she had said that she was confident that she would find a job. Nancy was working on a CSJ job at her daughter's school, helping out in the cafeteria, but she left it after a week. She felt it was a complete waste of time—she was not learning anything, she did not get the time to look for another job, and the money from W-2 was not worth the trouble.

Christy's current work status is that she is required by W-2 to work in a day care, but she has not shown up at work for a single day and has no intention of doing it. She believes she was placed there so that the staff can keep a close look on her, and [that it] is not even a real day care, it is there to make an excuse for people like her to work.

The women saw these "workfare" jobs as simply a way to ensure receipt of their next welfare check, not as interesting, challenging, or meaningful work. In New Hope, CSJs paid the minimum wage (and counted toward the thirty-hour-a-week threshold to receive the New Hope earnings supplement); in contrast, in W-2, CSJs were truly "workfare" in that the monthly cash grant was considered the payment. At forty hours a week, or even at thirty-five, the $673 grant was the equivalent of pay below the minimum wage. Many of the W-2 job placements, in fact, represented the kinds of dead-end jobs that could promote job instability. Finally, boredom and a sense of uselessness drove many women to leave these jobs, just as they would leave other jobs they found on their own. Tellingly, the most common pattern for W-2 CSJ users was leaving without having gained any skills to promote upward mobility and ending up again in a bout of unemployment. The CSJ jobs in New Hope did not always work out, but some did, and all were offered in the context of a broader administrative program in which the interests of the New Hope staff were aligned with those of participants: to work enough to use the comprehensive set of benefits provided by New Hope. According to the accounts of the women in the control group of the ethnographic study, few of these conditions were to be found in W-2-based CSJs at the time of the New Hope study.

Earnings Supplements, Child Care, and Health Insurance

Mothers reported that New Hope services designed to maintain and support employment, such as earnings supplements, child care, and health insurance, played a larger role than job search and preparation activities and CSJs in fostering upward mobility, or positive job transitions. These services emerged as strong themes in the qualitative analysis of the ethnographic sample.

Earnings supplements were reported as relating to employment by some of the women (three of the eighteen in the New Hope group who used services, or 16 percent). Supplements motivated a couple of participants to increase their work hours and allowed another to take advantage of employer-offered fringe benefits. For example, Frida increased her work hours to thirty hours per week in order to receive supplements, and Anna Marie used the earnings supplements she received to purchase a comprehensive health care plan offered by her employer that she had not been able to afford before. When New Hope ended and she stopped receiving earnings supplements, she was motivated to increase her work hours to make up the extra income. For the majority of women who received supplements, however, there was considerable confusion over how the amount of the supplement was calculated. Mothers reported that while the supplements were helpful, they did not know how much to expect in any given month, so they could never rely on the supplement in their monthly budgeting. For two mothers, this unpredictability led them to suspect embezzlement or corruption on the part of New Hope case representatives.

Almost half of the mothers (eight) in the group who used New Hope services discussed the value of child care subsidies and health insurance. Moreover, we found that the use of these services, particularly child care, was reported to facilitate upward mobility for five of the women who used New Hope services (28 percent). These types of services are important because they address the struggles that low-income women face in balancing the time demands, energy needs, and expenses of work and family life.

> Rose said that what was really good about New Hope was their help with child care. Rose was able to arrange for child care that picked up her children from their daytime care and delivered them to the later day care so she could still work. Rose said that having that child care in the evening, so she could work [the] second shift and pick up a second job, was really helpful. She said she wouldn't have been able to do it without New Hope child care help.

For Rose, like many other New Hope mothers, New Hope child care subsidies were an extremely important service. Through the use of this service, mothers were able to take classes, take on second jobs to make ends meet, or keep up with their employment in desirable jobs. Mothers who used these services were more likely to achieve job stability and mobility than those who did not.

Child care, health care, and the earned income tax credits offered or facilitated by W-2 were used by half of the control group members in the ethnography. However, in contrast to the role these New Hope services played in facilitating positive job transitions, our ethnographic analysis found that similar services offered by W-2 were not perceived to facilitate any positive kind of job transition for the women in our sample. As we explore more fully later, mothers often felt that W-2 child care subsidies were not worth the hassle and invasion of privacy they required. The EITC was never mentioned as an impetus for starting or sustaining employment. (Research from national samples finds, however, that the EITC does encourage employment; see

Meyer 2002). Instead, it often was used by mothers in both the New Hope and control groups to purchase large-ticket items for their families, such as computers and holiday presents, or to pay off debts (for more details on the EITC and its use, see chapter 8). Jennifer Romich and Thomas Weisner (2000) analyzed the use of the EITC for the New Hope ethnographic sample and found that most participants used it as a kind of forced saving plan (rather than receiving the amount monthly, the method of receipt that one might consider more economically rational in that monthly receipt would have provided more cash over a year than a single payment, since the IRS does not pay interest on the EITC amount). They also found that the women often used the tax preparation industry to get their refunds as soon as they could. The funds were most often used to buy durable goods, keep debts at bay, make down payments on houses, buy clothes for their children or themselves, and to purchase some "extras" (see chapter 7), such as going to the mall or going out to eat, events that were rare in the lives of many families.

Case Representation and the Service Delivery System

Although the New Hope work support services mentioned here appeared to play a role in job transitions and positive employment outcomes, it was the support provided by New Hope case representatives that women reported as being most instrumental to success in their work lives. Almost half (eight of the eighteen) of the women in the New Hope group who used these services reported supportive interactions with their caseworkers, and as the following analysis shows, advice, support, and help from case representatives were linked to many kinds of positive job transitions.

For six of the eight women who reported supportive interactions, experiences with case representatives were judged helpful in leading to upward mobility, finding supplemental jobs, or facilitating stable employment opportunities. For example, some women reported that interactions with their New Hope case representative led to positive education, job training, and employment experiences, such as attending English-language and job skills classes.

Alicia has completed a lot of certificates for courses and workshops she had taken at a local technical college and through New Hope. [After] she was accepted into New Hope, . . . she says, ". . . everything changed for me." Thanks to the health insurance, Alicia was more relaxed, but most importantly, at New Hope they pushed her to go to a local community college and learn English. . . . Roque (a New Hope caseworker) called the college to get information for Alicia. He helped her a lot, frequently asking about her classes and how her life was going. Alicia went to school to get a certificate of CDA [child development associate], a program to learn to work with children. With this diploma she can start earning $9.00 per hour. The people from New Hope pushed her to take these classes. She thinks she learned English thanks to New Hope, because before New Hope she was scared about speaking English. "They built up my morale and my self-esteem."

For other women, like Inez, the support provided by New Hope case representatives helped keep them on a positive job trajectory instead of falling into a pattern of job instability.

Inez says that the only (New Hope) rep she had any significant relationship with is LaTanya. "She was a big help when I left my job at [a large chain store]. She helped me the same day I called her up. She helped me put my résumé together right away. She called a couple of places to see if they were hiring and got me interviews right away. She got me my health insurance right away. . . . She did everything possible to make sure that, you know, I got back on track. That I didn't slip between the cracks and get down on myself and just [give] up. She made sure that I stayed positive. . . . Whenever you would need someone to talk to or anything, she was there."

Case representatives served as contacts for jobs and other important services and provided emotional support and motivation to participants. In contrast to many other social service agencies these women had dealt with, participants felt that New Hope caseworkers really cared about them, and they credited their caseworkers for their economic success. Positive experiences with New Hope program reps were helpful in increasing participants' sense of worth and self-esteem and sense of hope about the future, important precursors to being able to tackle a job search, interview effectively, and hold down a job.

As opposed to the New Hope reps, who gave Wendy information about classes or jobs, the welfare people never gave her information about anything. "No kind of education or nothing . . . just whatever was going on in our household, that was it. New Hope had so much out there . . . any kind of job workshops or whatever . . . they would call and let us know." She felt like the New Hope reps were looking out for her: that they were looking for things that she could take advantage of.

New Hope participants credited the emotional and instrumental support provided by program reps not only for improving their mental well-being but for increasing their ability to find and keep solid jobs, helping them gain the skills necessary to move into better jobs, and keeping the hope of providing for their families alive. Evidence for this sentiment is also in the survey data. Evaluations of the impacts of New Hope among the survey sample at the two-year follow-up found that being assigned to the New Hope group significantly increased participants' perceptions of the amount of support they received from agencies (Bos et al. 1999). The experience of New Hope recipients was not unique. High levels of caseworker support have been found to be related to improved economic outcomes (employment and income) and psychological outcomes (depression and parenting stress) among participants in other antipoverty programs, and positive program impacts on earnings are found to be concentrated among recipients in social service offices with high levels of support (Godfrey and Yoshikawa 2005). For a few participants, positive experiences with New Hope services also seemed to translate into increased use of W-2 services when New Hope ended. Interactions with New Hope case representatives increased their knowledge of all kinds of services available to them. For example, Caroline's field-worker wrote:

> Until they came to New Hope, they did not know they could file taxes for their kind of business (and receive the earned income tax credit). For ten years, they lost $2,000 per year. That's $20,000! The New Hope caseworker told them about filing and told them they could file for the three prior years. They did and got $8,000 in six weeks. The caseworkers were therapists for her husband. We would go in there during fights, and they would help calm her husband down. "I would call there screaming, and they would call back and calm me down."

New Hope case representation was not seen as positive by all New Hope participants, a few of whom felt mistrustful of their case representatives or did not like the amount of turnover within the office.

> Tiffany appears to have mixed experiences with her NH reps. She did not like one of her reps because she felt that the rep talked down to her and acted as if she was a bit superior. "She put on airs." On the other hand, she praised another rep because she said that he had listened to her.

> Shaquita's ethnographer reported that after their first case representative left, they really didn't like their replacement rep. Apparently, the receptionist was really rude and stuck up. Additionally, they had the sense that "a lot of the

money [program administrators and staff] were using to benefit themselves and not help people."

In stark contrast to New Hope services, the services that W-2 had to offer were often not utilized because of extreme dissatisfaction with the W-2 system. Whereas case representation in New Hope emerged as the major facilitator of positive job transitions, case representation in W-2 was most often reported to be a deterrent. Our ethnographic analysis found that a large number of participants who used W-2 services were displeased with their relationship with their caseworker. Seven participants in the control group (47 percent of those who used W-2 services) and eight participants in the New Hope group (44 percent of those who used W-2 services) reported dissatisfaction. These women described cold, uncaring, and disrespectful caseworkers who misunderstood their economic and familial situations and miscalculated their benefits. In some cases, participants thought caseworkers were withholding services or deliberately slowing down paperwork out of spite or personal dislike of the participant.

Karen says she wants nothing to do with W-2. She said that it is a mess and they degrade people down there. W-2 doesn't try to help people, or support them in what they need to do to make their life better. She said that if Tommy Thompson really wanted to help people, he would give grants so people can go to school and get an education. She went down to the office when she lost her job to sign up for W-2 and found out that they wouldn't accept her because she has a good work history. They told her that she could go out and find a job without a problem and W-2 is only for those who have never worked before. She didn't understand that. She said they make it sound so easy to find a job. It is only easy if you have a college degree or know computers.

Karen went on to describe her current case manager for food stamps and health insurance as a complete idiot and a bitch. She says that her caseworker tries to deal with her like she is stupid. She said the woman is very disrespectful. She said this woman constantly messes up her food stamps. She said she signed up for food stamps way back in May when she lost her jobs and didn't get any food stamps until June. She got her food stamps for a month or two and then they stopped again. She believes that her case manager is messing with her food stamps on purpose.

Wendy doesn't feel like she was treated with much respect by the welfare workers. "Once you sit there for a while, it's like . . . there was no kind of communication, no kind of connection, nothing. No respect. They would make you feel like you lacked self-esteem. Even if you didn't, they would make you feel that way because they were snotty."

Marina thinks that W-2 is very unreliable. She walked around the room and indicated that the support she got from W-2 was not like a wall of anything solid. Instead, the support from W-2 is like a very flimsy object. "I don't depend on it . . . I can't, I don't even want to go there." She also thinks that W-2 is harsh deliberately so people won't need W-2 at all. "It's breaking down what needs to be broken. Because now, they sanction you, and they don't care if you have to pay for it. They'll just cut you off."

Many mothers also described getting hung up in bureaucratic red tape and ineptitude. Some reported investing so much time in fighting the W-2 system to get their benefits that they had no energy left over to look for a job.

Belinda is no longer getting food stamps. She said that the last stamps she got were in July. She said that she missed her appointment with her case manager. Because she forgot, they cut her off. Belinda said that she called the day after she missed her appointment (she said it was so stupid that she missed the appointment), and the people said that her case manager was on vacation. When she called back the next week, the people in the food stamps office told her that they didn't know who her case manager was, and that her old one was gone. She said that she kept calling them back, and no one would return her calls. Finally, she demanded to talk to a supervisor. She said that she talked to two different supervisors, and no one could tell her where her case was. They didn't know who her case manager was, or what her status was in the system. The people said that they would call her back, but Belinda has not heard from anyone.

Wendy, who has been on W-2 and also runs a day care facility with W-2 clients, is also critical of the fragmentary nature of the W-2 program. Her clients have to go to two different workers: one for their medical card and one for child care. "When W-2 kicked in there, it just broke it all up."

Also interesting was the overall feeling expressed by most of the participants we followed that W-2 services unduly infringed on participants' lives and that benefits were simply not worth the price they had to pay in privacy and autonomy. Trisha, for example, said, "At one point we were getting $16 a month in food stamps, and they still wanted to know everything. For that $16, I'd rather you know nothing." This sentiment was especially pervasive among participants who needed W-2 only for child care and health insurance benefits. For example:

> Rose said that she looked into W-2 child care, but it looked like too much of a hassle. She said they will have to get all in her business in order for her to get the W-2 child care, and she does not want that. Plus, she had a friend who works for W-2 who told her not to take up W-2 child care, that it is more trouble than it's worth. Her friend said that W-2 child care was bad news.

These mothers often went without these services—services that when provided through the New Hope program were effective in promoting upward mobility—because they were not worth dealing with the red tape, disrespect, and invasion of privacy that came, they felt, with participation in W-2. Contrast this opinion with that of those in the New Hope program, who did feel that participation in the program was worth the services received, even if the only service they wanted was a child care subsidy (Gibson and Weisner 2002). W-2 services were also seen as inaccessible and impractical. As often as three times a month, W-2 participants had to travel long distances to meet with caseworkers in various offices to receive their benefits.

> Katie doesn't like going to the welfare office. It is a distance from her house, she says, and they always make you wait—it doesn't matter if you have an appointment, you are going to wait at least an hour.

> When I asked her why she wasn't on food stamps, Trisha told me she would rather be out looking for a job than waiting three hours in a waiting room. She told me she couldn't do both—once she got a job, then she didn't have time to go and get food stamps, but she didn't want to spend the time right now waiting for them when she could use that time to find a job.

Meetings in W-2 offices were rarely scheduled at the convenience of the participant. Instead, participants often had to juggle work schedules and child care arrangements to meet with caseworkers at designated times. In fact, one participant lost her job and another was suspended for seven days without pay because of missing work to make a W-2 appointment.

Although negative experiences with W-2 caseworkers were much more common than they were with New Hope case representatives, a few participants reported benefiting from their relationship with their W-2 caseworker. Most positive feelings toward the W-2 system occurred among the minority of participants who were connected to one particular social service agency contracted by the state to provide W-2. This agency was often mentioned by participants, particularly those of Hispanic descent. Many participants ended up securing stable work at the agency as child care providers or caseworkers. Others spoke highly of the caseworker support provided by the agency; Karen, for example, said that "the people at [————] were really nice and . . . really helped her when she got the operation," and she loved her W-2 caseworker. Others highlighted the benefit of the information they received through the agency and the ways in which their job centers and caseworkers helped them find a good job and take basic education and job training classes. The positive experience of those participants who received W-2 benefits through this agency highlights how W-2's new service delivery system, when delivered by a capable agency, can be effective.

Informal Resources for Finding and Maintaining Employment

Slightly more than half of the women in both NHES groups felt that work support services did not play a large role in their employment transitions. These women relied on other ways to find and support employment, sometimes using those ways in tandem with New Hope and W-2 services. Women relied on personal networks of friends and families and used information from sisters, mothers, neighbors, and friends to learn about job openings and get recommended for positions. Belinda, for example, "applied for a job with the city of Milwaukee in the transportation department. It is a position similar to her (then) boyfriend's. He pushed her to apply for the job, because the pay is better than Wal-Mart." Coworkers and business connections also came in handy when women searched for new jobs, as one ethnographer noted:

> Allison's goal from the first visit—to get another job if [the car company she worked for] did not give her a raise—appears to have been realized, but she feels her initial hopes have been dashed somewhat at the new job. She found the job through a fellow worker who used to work at [her old company] and had joined [another one] last year. When he found out that Allison had left, he wanted her to join [the company he worked in]. He was the district manager and made a lot of promises to Allison, and she felt there was potential in this new place.

Other common search techniques included the local newspaper listings, as well as extensive use of temp agencies to locate jobs and transition into new positions. These data on the importance of informal support corroborate our findings from the previous chapter. There we found (using survey data) that those who reported lower social support availability were the most likely to experience the sporadic, part-time employment characteristic of the low-wage–part-time group. It also illustrates the finding from chapter 7 that women who linked their work and family goals to specific strategies and tactics they could use were more likely to meet those goals.

WHICH PARTICIPANTS BENEFIT THE MOST FROM WORK SUPPORT SERVICES?

A striking finding that emerged in our ethnographic analysis was that services were particularly helpful to those recipients who were already in a stable enough position to use them. Gibson and Weisner (2002) had found that significant personal and family barriers prevented a group of New Hope and control group participants from taking up services. Another analysis of New Hope survey data found that the benefits of the New Hope experiment for children did not extend to those from families with the highest number of barriers to employment (Yoshikawa et al. 2003). Our analysis expands on these findings by suggesting that personal and family barriers not only are a deterrent to service take-up but also hinder the effectiveness of the work support services that are used. This was true regardless of whether services were offered by New Hope or W-2.[14]

For many of the women in the New Hope ethnographic study, services such as caseworker support, earnings supplements, and child care were enough to propel them from dead-end jobs into more promising employment situations. In contrast, a large proportion of those who felt that services were not helpful (seven in the New Hope group and nine in the control group) had serious barriers to employment, such as problems with mental health, drug abuse, or domestic violence. Iris suffered from low self-esteem and depression and experienced pressure from her family not to work. Many women like Iris had problems managing their children, and little support from family members, husbands, or boyfriends. Other women like Caroline and Jackie experienced domestic abuse, and still others had serious drug abuse problems. Try as they might—and most of these women did try—these barriers consistently interfered with their ability to use services. Previous studies, such as a large study of welfare recipients in Michigan (Danziger et al. 2000), have found that these barriers hinder employment. Our data suggest that they also hinder the take-up of work support services. No matter how many suggestions their caseworkers made, how many training courses they took, or how many applications they filled out, experiences of violence, severe child behavior problems, substance use, or depression appeared to stop these women's progress dead in its tracks.

W-2 and New Hope services did not often address these serious barriers to employment. In the field notes, we found no instances of a case representative referring participants for services related to domestic violence, substance use, mental health, and so on. Of course, these are stigmatizing experiences that may have been underreported to the research team. However, chapter 9 showed that a high percentage of the ethnographic sample did reveal experiences of domestic violence to their field-worker. It seems likely that one or more of the following occurred: W-2 caseworkers and New Hope representatives did not assess all of these barriers; parents did not feel comfortable revealing the existence of these barriers in their lives; caseworkers did offer referrals, but the women did not recall or want to mention those kinds of referrals, since they did not use them; or the caseworkers did not often follow up on the information. New Hope program policy was to make referrals for such concerns (as confirmed by New Hope directors and by research on New Hope implementation; see Brock 1997), but New Hope itself was never designed to directly provide services for these kinds of personal, family, and health problems.

HOW DO WORK SUPPORT SERVICES AFFECT ECONOMIC AND PSYCHOLOGICAL WELL-BEING?

To close this chapter, we turn to the survey data to examine the association of service use with the economic and psychological well-being measures collected after New Hope benefits ended (that is, after year three of the study). We used service variables pertaining to the first two years of the New Hope Project to predict mothers' employment, income, and earnings, as well as features of their psychological well-being and parenting, in years four and five.

The New Hope Project employed an experimental design, randomly assigning participants to either the New Hope group or the control group. However, simply assigning participants to one treatment group or the other did not ensure that all participants used the services available to them; neither did it ensure that participants who took up one service took up all of them. In fact, as discussed earlier, New Hope had relatively low rates of service take-up for many benefits, and participants often took up benefits episodically, owing to the kinds of variable employment trajectories represented by the employment clusters. Thus, experimental impacts (differences between the New Hope group and the control group) on economic and psychological outcomes document the effect of being assigned to the New Hope group on those outcomes, not necessarily how the use of services affected those outcomes.

Although we can explore the associations between service use and later outcomes through techniques such as ordinary least squares regression, establishing a causal relationship between service use and families' economic and psychological characteristics is difficult.[15] Because families may differ in a variety of unmeasured characteristics in addition to their service use, the effects of using services on family outcomes may reflect these unmeasured differences. Many family characteristics, for example, could be related to both service use and well-being. To account for some of these differences our quantitative analyses capitalize on the experimental nature of the data. We combine the use of a random-assignment design with an instrumental variables (IV) estimation strategy (Angrist et al. 1996; Gennetian et al. 2005; Krueger 1999). Using a two-stage process, IV analysis uses a variable called an "instrument" to estimate the relationship between the independent variable and the outcome variables free of the biases mentioned earlier, thus strengthening the causal inference that can be made.[16] We used the variable representing assignment to New Hope versus the control group as our instrument to estimate the effect of service use on families' economic and psychological outcomes. The random-assignment variable meets the criteria for an instrumental variable.[17]

For purposes of this analysis, the independent variable, service use, was calculated as the sum of any receipt of the following variables over the two years from random assignment to the two-year follow-up: advice or help from New Hope or W-2 case representatives; a New Hope community service job or W-2 job placement; New Hope earnings supplements or the federal earned income tax credit; New Hope or W-2 child care subsidies; and New Hope or Medicaid health care subsidies. We sum all of these services together because they were designed as comprehensive policy packages, within which each service was meant to increase employment. That is, different parents may have used different combinations of services, but because they were all meant to accomplish the same purpose, we sum across them.[18] To avoid confounding the time period during which services were offered with the effects of the services, we examined all outcomes after the period covered by service use (that is, they pertained to the time between the two- and five-year follow-ups). The economic outcomes we examined included quarters employed, total yearly earnings, and total yearly income across years three to five of the study.[19] Psychological outcomes for families were examined at both the two- and five-year follow-up points, and included depressive symptoms, parenting stress, warmth, time pressure, and feelings of efficacy in achieving life goals. We also examined child outcomes at both the two- and five-year follow-up points, including mother-reported internalizing and externalizing behaviors and teacher-reported academic achievement and internalizing and externalizing behaviors. All models included covariates to adjust for background characteristics.[20]

Using this method, we conducted the two stages of the IV analysis. In the first stage, we found that New Hope did significantly predict service use (b = 1.48 (0.11), p < 0.001). In the second stage, we found that service use as instrumented by random assignment was significantly related to the amount of total yearly income garnered by the household over years three through five of the study. Service use was positively related to income (b = 870.09 (513.06), p < 0.10; β = 0.15), indicating that for every additional service used over the first two years of the study, total yearly income over years three through five increased an estimated $870. In addition, service use as instrumented by random assignment was found to be significantly related to higher perceptions of goal efficacy at the two-year follow-up (b = .09 (.04), p < .05; β = 0.21) (Snyder et al. 1996). Goal efficacy was measured as feelings of being able to achieve important life goals.[21] Finally, because of the possibility that service use might have represented primarily the effect of the New Hope earnings supplement, we reran the IV analysis using a count of services excluding the earnings supplement. In the first stage, we found that New Hope did significantly predict the count of service use excluding earnings supplements (b = 1.18 (0.10), p < 0.001). In addition, service use as instrumented by random assignment was still significantly related both to income over years three through five (b = 1088.21 (648.42), p < 0.10; β = 0.17) and to higher perceptions of goal efficacy at the two-year follow-up (b = .11 (.05), p < .05; β = 0.23). These findings show that the association of services with higher income and goal efficacy was not due solely to the provision of earnings supplements. In fact, when earnings supplements were removed from the service use index, associations between service use and income and goal efficacy were slightly larger.

CONCLUSION

In this chapter, we found evidence that the experience of service use differed across the New Hope and W-2 work support programs and that service use mattered for working mothers' earnings and for their sense of goal achievement. The qualitative analyses revealed striking differences in the perceived utility of the services offered through the New Hope program versus those offered through W-2. Services provided through the New Hope program, notably community service job placements, child care, and case representation, were perceived as linked to positive job transitions by the women we followed. They reported that their use of these services facilitated their upward mobility, supplemental jobs, and sustained employment with wage growth. They reported, on the other hand, that similar services offered through W-2 made little difference in any of these aspects of employment; moreover, they often noted that W-2 case representation and the complexity of its service delivery system were negative aspects of the state program;

these services intended by the state to facilitate work were in fact perceived as deterrents to work.[22]

The qualitative analysis also serves as an important reminder that it is the quality of services that is critical to their role in facilitating employment. Comparisons between the community service jobs provided by New Hope and those provided by W-2 revealed that this service can be effective in promoting positive job transitions only when the quality of the placement is high. Likewise, the program group's case representatives played an instrumental role in promoting job transitions and psychological well-being. Not only was case representation through W-2 perceived to lead to few positive job transitions, but it was cited often as a source of stress, depression, and low self-esteem. We should note that W-2 caseworkers' and New Hope program representatives' jobs were structured very differently: W-2 caseworkers typically had caseloads in the hundreds, whereas caseloads for New Hope program reps were no larger than fifty. Thus, the amount of personal contact with the parents was on a completely different scale in the New Hope program; this was clearly perceived as a positive by the parents who made use of New Hope benefits. Further, the interests of New Hope case representatives were more closely aligned with those of their participants. New Hope case representatives were rewarded if their clients had enough work hours to make use of the menu of New Hope benefits, as needed. Lots of client activity and service use was a sign of success for both the representative and the clients. This has often been perceived to not be the case in TANF programs (Meyers 2005).

The New Hope model of community-based work support services seems to have been perceived as more helpful than W-2 work support services for many reasons: the quality of the community service job placements; the helpfulness of program reps compared to W-2 caseworkers; the mitigation of the stigma associated with welfare offices; fewer perceptions of violations of privacy (of being "in your business"); and fewer hassles with waits and recertifications of benefits. Thus, the New Hope model of community-based work support service delivery may be an effective alternative to the W-2 Job Center model, at least as it existed in the late 1990s. The results of our analysis point to the utility of restructuring community service jobs to provide high-quality placements with opportunities for skill development and advancement. They also highlight the important role of case management in service delivery. Reorganizing the case management system to allow case managers to carry much smaller caseloads and more closely align their goals with the goals of the client could increase the effectiveness of work support services. Additional implications of these results (discussed further in the concluding chapter) include altering the delivery of child care subsidies to better fit the lives of working women and providing services after job exits to reduce extreme job instability.

Findings from the quantitative analyses indicate that service use also plays a role in the economic and psychological well-being of low-income mothers. Using an instrumental variables estimation strategy to correct for the possibility of selection bias, we found that greater use of services was associated with higher income and perceptions of goal achievement. Taken together, the qualitative and quantitative findings reinforce the important role that services can play in dynamic job transitions and more generally in economic and psychological well-being. These results also suggest that services may be helpful in placing low-income mothers on a personal and employment trajectory that ultimately allows them to provide for their families. Although service use did not appear to be directly associated with children's outcomes, it may be that the association of work support services with children's development occurs through the intervening variable of increased income.

Unfortunately, it is also clear from our qualitative analysis that not all women are able to take up or benefit from work support services equally. Indeed, we found that it was the women with the greatest initial stability in their life circumstances who were able to use services to improve their employment trajectory. Neither New Hope nor W-2 appeared to provide a sufficiently intensive level of services to help women in traumatic personal circumstances. Drug and alcohol abuse, domestic violence, depression, and poor health were major barriers that prevented some mothers from using these services and limited their effectiveness. While work support services can be effective for those able to take advantage of them, it is critical that services be designed to ameliorate the most serious barriers to employment; those barriers may not have been adequately addressed by New Hope's refer-out approach for those most at-risk. In the last chapter of this book, we consider some models that may be effective in addressing these most recalcitrant barriers to work.

Part IV | Conclusion

Chapter Thirteen | Summary and Policy Implications: Improving the World of Work for Low-Income Parents and Their Children

Hirokazu Yoshikawa,
Anna Gassman-Pines,
Thomas S. Weisner, and
Edward D. Lowe

WE BEGAN THIS book with descriptions of one neighborhood and three mothers. Our description of the North Side neighborhood, one of two in Milwaukee in the New Hope study, raised the question of how children fare in a community where work opportunities have largely disappeared. On streets with little but boarded-up storefronts, bars, dusty groceries, and only the occasional child care facility, the successful integration of work and family seemed difficult to imagine.

The stories of three mothers—Evelia, Iris, and Allison—began to provide some answers to this puzzle. Their stories suggested that successful child development in the context of extreme urban poverty is buffeted by job instability and low wages and supported by job advancement and wage growth. Over the course of the study, Evelia was mired first in a long-term post office temp job with no hope of transfer to the permanent staff. She then left that job and endured a series of short-term, low-wage jobs with little wage growth. At times she became desperate, both economically and psychologically: not knowing where the money for her next meal would come from, her sense of being a good provider for her four children was shattered. Her efforts to integrate the needs of her children, the unreliability of her partner, and the vagaries of child care provided by relatives with her own shifting work schedule were maddeningly ineffective in relieving these causes of chronic stress in her home life. Iris, in contrast, worked relatively little over the course of the study. On the one hand, her life was more stable than Evelia's. On the other, she was burdened with a number of what policy researchers might call "employment barriers," such as depression, behavior problems in one of her nephews, and a partner who did not want her to work. She became a foster parent by the end of the study period; paid to look after her two nephews at home, she finally made a steady, though very low, income. The third mother, Allison, worked in a succession of jobs in the auto industry and was able to achieve job mobility and wage growth by utilizing coworker referrals to incrementally better jobs. Of the three, it was Allison who had increases in income over the two-and-a-half-year period of the New Hope Ethnographic Study. And it was Allison who experienced continuous workplace benefits, such as health care coverage, overtime, sick days, and vacation days. Perhaps not coincidentally, Allison had fewer worries about the impact of her work life on her two "homebody" teenage sons.

There is no one work pathway among the working poor. What differences did work pathways such as Evelia's, Iris's, and Allison's make for their well-being and their children's development? We saw how different work pathways led to different prospects for children, as measured by their academic performance and social behavior. We found that variation in job experiences was associated with variation in children's development. In addition, we found that pieces of the complex, interlocking puzzle of work in low-income families—work schedules, transportation, child care, partners, work support services—made a difference for work pathways, and in turn for parents' and children's well-being.

In this chapter, we first summarize the chief findings in the book. Then we suggest several policy and program approaches that show promise in both improving the world of work and benefiting parents and children.

VARIATION IN WORK PATHWAYS OVER TIME AND ITS CONSEQUENCES FOR FAMILY AND CHILD WELL-BEING

In part I of this book, we asked how work experiences unfolded over time for our sample of low-wage working mothers in Milwaukee, and whether these work experiences affected their children's academic and social development. We examined work longitudinally over spans of years as well as hours, days, and weeks. The role of job quality, including what mothers perceived to be good or bad jobs and how job quality influenced parents' and children's well-being, was also explored. We found, in brief, that job trajectories, schedules, and quality all matter for parents' well-being and for children's academic and social behaviors.

The stories of Evelia, Iris, and Allison highlighted the variety in the work trajectories of the New Hope ethnographic sample of forty women. To examine the predictors and consequences of different patterns of work for family life and child development, we turned to the much larger survey sample. We indeed found great variety in work trajectories (see chapter 2). In an analysis that examined different combinations of hours, wages, wage change, number of jobs, and job length over two years, we found five work dynamic patterns. One pattern matched the goals of many of our parents: the full-time–wage-growth group was characterized by high wage levels, wage growth, and full-time work. Members of this group experienced average growth of $3.80 in their hourly wages over the two years, and relatively high wages on average (just over $8.00 an hour), though certainly not high in absolute terms. Another group, the stable employment group, was characterized by high stability in work (generally one job over the twenty-four months), relatively high wages, and modest wage growth of about $1.00. Each of these groups worked high numbers of hours—thirty-nine per week, on average.

The rapid cyclers held nearly five jobs, on average, over the two-year period and experienced little wage growth. This group was of concern to us because of their very high job instability. Two other groups were characterized by particularly low average wages and wage stagnation: the low-wage–part-time group reported the most sporadic and part-time work, while the low-wage–full-time group engaged in full-time work, but at similarly low wages, with an average barely above the minimum wage.

Why did mothers in our sample experience such different work pathways? To answer this question, we examined the baseline characteristics that predicted membership in the work pathway groups. The low-wage–part-time group showed lower levels of education and prior work experience than the other groups. Mothers in the full-time–wage-growth and stable employment groups, in addition to having higher levels of education and work experience, were more likely to have access to a car at baseline. This finding reflects the great importance of transportation to get to better jobs in the suburbs of Milwaukee. The New Hope program increased the probability of a mother experiencing the full-time–wage-growth or rapid cycler patterns, relative to the probability of being in the group with the lowest levels of work effort (the low-wage–part-time pattern).

When we turned to the women in these groups who were interviewed intensively in the ethnographic study, we found further differences among them in the types of jobs and job transitions they experienced. First, the groups arrayed themselves in different places in the hierarchy of low-wage work, with the low-wage–part-time group occupying some of the lowest positions on the totem pole (child care worker, home health aide, crossing guard) and holding very few clerical jobs. On the other extreme, the full-time–wage-growth and stable employment groups were most likely to have supervisory or managerial positions or to be self-employed. In between were the low-wage–full-time and rapid cycler groups. Second, the job transitions experienced by women in the different groups were strikingly different. The full-time–wage-growth group, for example, reported no experiences of being fired or suspended, and members of this group often took new jobs because of positive characteristics of the job. The rapid cyclers and the low-wage–full-time groups reported the most firings and suspensions and the fewest positive job transitions. Finally, the low-wage–part-time group appeared to experience the highest levels of barriers to work, such as mental health problems and domestic violence. This finding should be interpreted with caution, because they were derived from the fairly small ethnographic sample.

These work trajectories, then, suggested very different experiences of work and family life. Using the rich developmental and parent assessments in the survey sample, we then examined the consequences of the five work pathways. We found consistently that the pattern of very high job instability coupled with low wages and little wage growth (rapid cyclers) predicted poorer child school performance and higher levels of acting out compared to the other groups. These differences in children's development were reported by teachers who were largely unaware of the parents' work patterns and did not know that the children were in the New Hope study, much less whether their family was in the control or program group. The differences were also robust in models that controlled for earlier child outcomes.

Are these associations of work pathways with children's outcomes large enough to matter from a practical standpoint? Although the associations were not large in statistical terms, we can put them in perspective by comparing them to the size of the effects of other important contexts on children's development. The associations of .15 to .20 effect size that we found were generally comparable to the association between observed child care quality and children's preschool cognitive and social development, but smaller than the association between observed parenting quality and these outcomes.[1] In addition, mothers who were rapid cyclers showed lower levels of well-being and parenting quality compared to all of the other groups: higher levels of parenting stress, time pressure, and depressive symptoms, as well as lower levels of observed warmth. Together, these findings on parents and children represent reason to be concerned about high job instability in the low-wage workforce.

The combination of wage growth and job stability, in contrast, appeared to lead to particularly good outcomes for parents and children. This combination predicted a slew of positive family and child outcomes.[2] Parents who experienced wage growth and job stability reported higher educational expectations for their children, were more likely to report that they could achieve important goals in their lives, and reported higher levels of monitoring of their children. Teachers of these parents' children reported higher school engagement and less acting-out behavior observed in school, compared to the children of parents who experienced other work patterns.

These data help resolve one of the ongoing puzzles in the research world about the effects of low-wage work on children. Studies usually show few differences when comparing poor children whose mothers work to those whose mothers do not (Smolensky and Gootman 2003).[3] Many have speculated that this is because the effects of work on children are more complicated than simple comparisons of work to nonwork can show; the answer may be, "It depends." That is, the effects of work on development may depend on the characteristics of the work. Our results suggest that particular longitudinal patterns of work, understudied thus far, may help solve the puzzle. Very rapid job instability appears to have negative consequences for children, while the combination of job stability and wage growth may be particularly helpful.

Our evidence suggests that many of the working poor are doing well, in spite of the obstacles they face. The stable employment and full-time–wage-growth groups included many families who had higher educational levels and more work experience and who reported good experiences at work. They also were less likely to be fired, were more likely to have a car, had lower levels of reported depressive symptoms and parenting stress, reported fewer child care problems, and had somewhat more social support. These were the families in which children were doing relatively well too. Working-poor families thus showed many strengths in our data. The low-wage–part-time and rapid cycler clusters, in contrast, included many families who were struggling. They were likely to have multiple barriers to employment, and though they often benefited from income supplements, health care, and child care, many required additional assistance as well.

JOB QUALITY IN THE LOW-WAGE WORKPLACE

In addition to the New Hope mothers' experiences of hours, wages, job instability, and wage growth and stagnation, we were interested on a more basic level in what their jobs were like. What were the good and bad qualities of their jobs? What aspects of their jobs brought them stress? What brought them joy? And did job quality matter for their own well-being and their children's development? Chapter 4 probed these questions.

The aspects of job quality that were the most important to our sample included, not surprisingly, pay and benefits. Adequate pay was often cited as a problem, with those making less than $8.00 an hour more likely to say that their wages were inadequate than were those who made more. Pay raises and promotions were reported by fewer than one-third of the ethnographic sample. (Unfortunately, we do not have this information in the survey.) Second, among job benefits, health care coverage was by far the most often cited. The presence or absence of health benefits at a job was an important influence on mothers' decisions to take or leave jobs.

A majority of the mothers worked at jobs with the lowest levels of occupational complexity, as indicated by their interactions with people, things, and data at work. Not surprisingly, many of the mothers complained that their jobs were full of tedium and boredom. Relatively few of them worked in even the lowest-level supervisory positions characterized by higher levels of occupational complexity. Mothers in the full-time–wage-growth and stable employment groups were the most likely to have these jobs, and those in the low-wage–part-time group the least likely.

Relationships at the workplace made an enormous difference in mothers' overall experience of their jobs. In the supervisor-worker relationship, recognition of good work was paramount because of the relatively low degree of autonomy these mothers experienced in their jobs. Coworker support and friendship were also cited as important in the job climate. Those who experienced job mobility, such as Allison, often found new jobs through coworker referrals. However, coworker support could also turn negative. The most frequently cited irritant at work in this regard was gossip and coworkers who did not contribute their full share of work.

Flexibility at their jobs was an important issue for the New Hope mothers as well. We considered flexibility of two kinds: the ability to attend to family and other emergencies while at work, and variation in work schedules (see chapter 5). Although flexibility was valued by these mothers at their jobs, flexibility was cited almost exclusively as a prerogative of their supervisors, not as a benefit built into their jobs. When mothers had to take off days to attend, for example, a child's athletic or other school event, they had to rely on their supervisor's understanding, or the roughly 60 percent who had sick or vacation day benefits had to use one of those. Leaving the job to run an errand or tend to a child emergency was largely a matter of supervisor discretion. Those who had supervisors who were relatively lenient praised them as understanding and kind; however, many mothers reported having a supervisor who was much less willing to allow them to attend to family needs during work hours.

As for work schedules, many have observed the general shift in America's work life from a nine-to-five weekday world to a 24/7 one (Presser 2003). We found that work schedules among the working poor may have consequences for children's school performance and behavior, based on our analyses using the survey sample. In comparison to fixed daytime schedules, the combination of variable schedules (those that change from week to week) and daytime schedules was *beneficial* for children's academic and social development (see chapter 5). In contrast, the combination of variable schedules and nonstandard hours was associated with higher levels of anxious, worried, and depressed behaviors in children, as reported by teachers. These data suggested to us that flexibility during the daytime hours, when most appointments related to children occur, may have benefits for children's development. In analyses on the ethnographic sample, we found that half of the mothers indicated that they valued having flexible work hours. However, only two reported having a flextime program that gave them the option of setting their own work starting and ending hours. These data are corroborated by a national study of the workforce conducted by the Families and Work Institute, which found that flextime benefits are rare among low-wage workers; 56 percent of managers and professionals in that nationally representative sample enjoyed this benefit, while only 37 percent of workers not in those positions had access to it (Galinsky, Bond, and Hill 2004).

We found worrisomely high rates of another indicator of poor job quality: race- and sex-based discrimination (see chapter 6). Forty-three percent of the ethnographic sample reported instances of workplace discrimination. (The survey did not include questions about this topic.) Of these women, 53 percent reported sex-based discrimination, and 76 percent racial discrimination. Nearly one-quarter of the women who reported discrimination reported both kinds. The fact that questions were not asked systematically by field-workers about discrimination suggests that the prevalence we found here may be low, although the absence of any evidence from the employer or coworkers limits our understanding of these events.

Finally, in quantitative, fixed-effects analyses linking reports of job quality across a variety of dimensions to parent and child well-being, we found that job quality predicted both parents' and children's well-being (see chapter 4). Better job quality, as measured by survey measures of overall quality, job stress, and occupational complexity, predicted lower levels of acting-out and withdrawn behaviors in children, as rated by parents and teachers. These job quality indicators were also associated with parent well-being—specifically, lower depression, parenting stress, and time pressure. So job quality did appear to matter, though more for psychological well-being than for academic outcomes.

FAMILIES AND WORK

In part II, we considered how family processes might relate to and explain the effects of work pathways on children. Since the first studies of parental employment and children's development, parents' goals, values, well-being, and parenting practices have been proposed as explanatory factors that link the two (Hoffman 1961; Kohn 1969). In part II, we brought new perspectives to family and work by examining how goals for work and family brought meaning to these mothers' lives, how the economic dimensions of family and work life related to psychological ones, and how relationships and marriage related to both work and children's development in our low-income sample.

How did New Hope mothers' goals for work intersect with their goals for their own personal development and that of their children? In chapter 7, the New Hope mothers reported that they wanted "what everybody wants": a steady job that paid well, and specifically, a job that paid well enough to enable them to make progress toward the American dream of owning a car and a house and being able to take good care of their families by living in a safe neighborhood. When describing their ideal job, New Hope mothers often reported wanting these characteristics: an office job; daytime hours; benefits, with health care being the most important; job security; chances for job advancement; and flexibility to allow them to deal with the occasional child care problem, school meeting, or health crisis. The mothers were also realistic about actually achieving many of these goals, and many were not especially sanguine about their prospects. They used humor and irony in talking about their ideal goals, as well as in setting specific directions and plans. Having a goal related to education or training was likely to lead to better employment situations, particularly for younger women. And not all the women had work advancement as a strong goal in any case. Some talked about wanting to stay home with their children, particularly those who had younger children. Others wanted to work more for their church, and some older parents in our ethnographic sample were tired and wanted to find a way to retire. In this respect as well, they also often wanted what other workers want, and their hopes and work priorities varied.

Although the economic dimensions of work are obvious, they have only rarely been studied in relationship to psychological well-being and children's development. In chapter 8, we learned that increases in income, across the full five years of the New Hope study, were linked to higher school performance in children, as measured by parents, teachers, and standardized tests, through the intervening mechanisms of lower material hardship and financial worry and higher perceptions of being able to parent children effectively. These data are in agreement with other recent studies showing that higher family income is causally related to higher levels of school achievement among children in poverty (Morris, Duncan, and Rodrigues 2005). The findings also suggest that policies that increase income, contingent on work, will have benefits for poor parents' economic and psychological well-being and that these benefits will translate into improved outcomes for their children.

What kinds of psychological well-being did earnings buy? Mothers reported different kinds of satisfaction from the different kinds of household expenditures they made with their earnings. Staying on top of bills was associated with feeling only "okay." Mothers felt more satisfied when they were able to spend money on the "little extras" their children constantly asked for. Buying big-ticket, durable items, like cars or furniture, brought them long-term feelings of satisfaction, accomplishment, and, for many of these mothers, a sense of economic and psychological independence. We found a similar sense of satisfaction among women who were able to meet their goals for being a good enough breadwinner and parent and whose goals had not been thwarted either by the vagaries of low-wage work or by family and personal issues.

One of our most unexpected findings concerning the work-family interface was the power of work dynamics and the New Hope program itself in predicting marriage rates. Policymakers have been wringing their hands over the low, and declining, marriage rates among single mothers in the United States. We explored whether characteristics of work trajectories predicted marriage among the single mothers in New Hope. We found that wage growth was associated with higher rates of entry into marriage among the mothers who had never been married at the outset of the study. We speculated that this association might be due to higher relationship quality among those who experienced wage growth. Although data on relationship quality were missing from the survey, the ethnographic data in fact showed that mothers who experienced the most wage growth were also more likely to report that their relationships got better over the course of the study.

Current federal policies invest in the promotion of marriage. However, increasing wage growth or income in order to increase rates of marriage among single mothers has not been encouraged. In an analysis that is one of the first to examine long-term effects of an antipoverty experiment on marriage, we found that New Hope increased rates of marriage among single mothers (those never married at baseline). Among these mothers, New Hope group members were nine percentage points more likely to be married by the five-year point than control group members. This effect of New Hope represents nearly a doubling in the likelihood of getting married. (The control group's marriage rate was 12 percent, while the New Hope group's was 21 percent.) In mediation analyses exploring how this effect may have occurred, the most likely suspect was the increased income that the New

Hope program brought about for these mothers. These data suggest that antipoverty strategies that increase both employment and income, through earnings supplements like the one that New Hope offered, should not be neglected in efforts to promote marriage. It is worth recalling that New Hope was not a marriage promotion program and did not offer classes, refer mothers elsewhere for education, or inquire into marriage and relationship issues. The program offered a generous earnings supplement and other work supports to adults working full-time; those supports were what eventually led to the increase in marriage.

WORK SUPPORTS: CHILD CARE, SOCIAL SUPPORT, TRANSPORTATION, AND WORK SUPPORT SERVICES

Evelia's, Iris's, and Allison's stories show that managing the worlds of work and family hinges on everything from the reliability of friends in picking up your child after school to your caseworker knowing your name, to the state of your preschooler's health, to how many blocks, miles, or countries away sisters, cousins, and mothers live. We turned in part III from the influence of work pathways and family processes on children's development to the larger social contexts that can influence the work pathways themselves. The work experiences of low-income women are intertwined with a variety of contexts, including child care, informal support networks, transportation, and formal work support services. The uncertainty and instability of low-wage work were magnified by what New Hope mothers in our sample reported over and over again: the unpredictability or unreliability of these worlds that impinged on work. In part III, we found that barriers relating to child care and lack of social support predicted patterns of sporadic, part-time employment. We also found that work support services could facilitate earnings and life-goal achievement, particularly in the context of the New Hope model.

In contrast to most studies of child care, we explored the fit between child care and work-related routines for our low-wage working sample. Most New Hope mothers were single with children of different ages, requiring different care arrangements and schedules (see chapter 10). When making decisions about child care, these mothers were influenced by many factors, including the values, beliefs, and sometimes divergent preferences of others in their households. These decisions made sense given the circumstances in which the family found itself at a particular moment. The troubles occurred when the circumstances changed, as frequently happened in their child care arrangements and at work. Child care problems were associated with work pathways: The low-wage–part-time and rapid cycler groups were the most likely to report that child care problems forced them to quit a job. The low-wage–part-time group showed the lowest and most sporadic levels of employment of any of the working mothers in the sample.

The W-2 child care policy—specifically, Wisconsin Shares child care subsidies in its early stage of implementation[4]—often did not make sense to the mothers in our study. They reported having to make very frequent recertification appointments, as often as once a month, depending on changes in their work situations. Requiring recertification when job transitions occurred, such as those that reduced or increased their work hours, made little sense in the frequently shifting work worlds of low-wage mothers in Milwaukee. Mothers also often reported not knowing when they were approaching cutoffs in child care subsidy eligibility. For many, the first they heard was when the subsidy was terminated, at which point they had to scramble to rearrange their work or child care. The New Hope program offered child care subsidies that were used significantly more often than the child care programs available from W-2 or other sources among the control group, and this differential use of formal child care continued among those in the New Hope program group even after its benefits ended in 1998. Furthermore, the New Hope program families had somewhat less instability and change in their child care arrangements compared to control families, suggesting that child care programs like New Hope's can reduce the chronic changes in child care facing so many parents and children.

New Hope mothers saw the support they got from partners and informal support networks as helpful but costly (see chapter 11). Financial contributions from partners were highly valued, but for the majority of the mothers, they were also unreliable and inconsistent. Some of the mothers reported that their relationships were often stormy and troubled, and sometimes abusive, and many of them had several partners over the course of the study (see chapter 9).[5] Not surprisingly, the theme of independence from men came up frequently in the interviews with the New Hope mothers. The availability of social support was related to work trajectories. The low-wage–part-time and rapid cycler groups reported the lowest levels of support availability, and in part III a more comprehensive picture emerged of these two groups: among our work pathway groups, these two groups reported the highest levels of problems with mental health, domestic violence, child care, and social-support-related barriers. Later in this chapter, we outline some policy and program solutions for this high-risk group.

Cars enabled many residents of the two inner-city neighborhoods of Milwaukee in our study to find better jobs. As researchers at the University of Wisconsin at Milwaukee have demonstrated, job growth in the 1990s in Milwaukee was limited to the suburbs and to downtown; very few new jobs were created in the inner-city neighborhoods, such as the North Side and South Side neighborhoods included in the New Hope study (Levine 2002).

This lopsided growth in the job market made cars all-important for access to the better downtown and suburban jobs, which parents in our study craved.

One of the strongest baseline predictors (aside from prior human capital indicators like work experience and education) of being in the full-time–wage-growth or stable employment groups was having access to a car (see chapter 2). Analysis of the ethnographic data on transportation revealed, however, that having access to a car was not the same as having one that worked reliably. Of those who reported having a car, fully one-third experienced car breakdowns. When New Hope mothers did experience serious car troubles, the majority were unable to fix their cars by the end of the ethnographic study period. Lack of money for repairs was a constant barrier to reaping the benefits that having a car could have brought to their work lives. Those parents who did not have cars or access to cars commuted on the Milwaukee bus system. The majority of the mothers who talked about their bus commutes complained about unreliability, very long commutes (most often sixty to ninety minutes one way), and little bus service during second and third shifts. The cost of buying and maintaining a car through the harsh Milwaukee winters led many New Hope mothers to forgo the suburban jobs and accept the lower-paying jobs that were closer to them.

The question of how to implement work support services is important to state and local governments in this post-welfare reform era. Integrating work support services for the TANF and non-TANF populations, for example, has been vexing to state administrators. We examined work support services of two types: those offered by the New Hope program outside the welfare system, and those offered by W-2, the state's TANF program (see chapter 12). Overall, New Hope services were perceived as more helpful in securing and sustaining work. Although this may have been simply because New Hope services were offered on top of W-2 services for the experimental group members, it also appeared that the structure of some New Hope work supports made them more attractive than the parallel service under W-2.

New Hope's community service jobs, for example, were generally perceived in a more positive light than W-2's CSJs, perhaps because they were provided in nonprofit organizations and were more likely to involve clerical work than other jobs. Those mothers who experienced W-2 CSJs almost uniformly felt that they were dead-end jobs that did not prepare them for permanent positions. In addition, case management in New Hope had obvious advantages that made a real difference to parents. Caseloads of approximately fifty allowed for much more personal contact than W-2 caseworkers, with caseloads of hundreds, could ever give. And New Hope services were administered out of small storefront offices unaffiliated with the welfare system and were less stigmatizing. Finally, applying for child care benefits through New Hope required less initial paperwork than did W-2 child care subsidies. Perceptions that New Hope staff were less "in your business" went far toward explaining the more welcoming and supportive interactions that parents reported with the New Hope program reps, whose job goals were complementary: providing the benefits and helping participants to sustain work. They had an administrative support system that seldom lost files, and they knew the names of their groups of clients. As so many of our mothers put it, they showed respect.

Some New Hope supports, however, had some of the same drawbacks as W-2. For example, eligibility for New Hope child care subsidies was tied to thirty hours of work a week in a particular month. Therefore, when a New Hope program parent's hours fell below that minimum, she was ineligible for child care subsidies. This replicates the tying of child care subsidy use to transitory changes in employment, which was reported by many parents as the cause of many frustrating trips to recertify their subsidy eligibility.

PROGRAM AND POLICY SOLUTIONS FOR THE WORKING POOR

Our data suggest ways to improve the world of work to help low-wage working parents and their children. Programs and policies are needed that will accomplish the following goals:

1. *Facilitate wage growth and job stability.* We found that the combination of these two work dynamic patterns was especially beneficial to children.

2. *Reduce extreme job instability.* We found that extreme job instability (at the level of roughly five jobs in two years) was experienced by about one-sixth of the New Hope sample and that this pattern was associated with worse child school performance and behavior.

3. *Increase flexibility in work schedules,* especially during the daytime hours. The combination of standard hours and variation in start and end times from week to week appeared to be associated with positive child outcomes.

4. *Reduce the costs associated with work,* such as transportation and child care costs. New Hope mothers reported that their greatest difficulty was in maintaining and managing two work supports: transportation and child care.

Before we describe our suggested policy solutions, we caution that our data come from low-income neighborhoods in one city, Milwaukee.

Stronger policy prescriptions must await replication of our findings in other low-income samples. However, we have stated throughout this book how our findings relate to prior studies on the working poor and their children. In addition, we attempted wherever possible to use the random-assignment design of New Hope to control for selection bias and separate program impacts from other outcomes and associations, and we also used a variety of other methods to adjust for selection bias as appropriate. There could still be unobserved variables, however, that account for the associations we observed between employment characteristics, family processes, and children's development.[6] We believe that our findings do have some generalizability for families in urban poverty in the United States, given the ways in which low-income neighborhoods in Milwaukee in the late 1990s shared characteristics with neighborhood poverty in other major cities during that period.[7] We make recommendations for each of three major systems affecting low-wage working mothers: income support systems, work support service systems, and low-wage workplaces. For each area, we first propose specific guidelines for implementation of the recommendations. Then we provide information on the costs and benefits of the recommendations.

1. Income Support Policy: Expanding Work-Based Income Support for Low-Income Working Families

Parents in the New Hope study with the most positive experiences of work had access to two crucial supports: transportation and flexible child care. The forms of these supports with the greatest benefits to job quality, wage growth, and children's development—cars and center-based child care— are unfortunately also the most expensive. The benefits of these supports were out of the reach of the budgets of many families. Higher levels of work-based income support would allow parents to address these critical needs. Our recommendations in this section are focused on increasing net income for working parents. We have not done our own research on the potential costs and benefits of these policies and programs, and so we rely on others' work in this section for such economic data, when available.

Expand the Earned Income Tax Credit   One way to increase families' ability to pay for these work supports is by increasing their work-related income. The Earned Income Tax Credit is the nation's largest federally funded program that accomplishes the goal of increasing income, contingent on work effort.[8] The credit has three different structures, or tiers, pertaining to families with no children, with one child, and with two or more children. The credit phases in gradually, providing forty cents for each additional dollar earned from $1 up to an annual earned income of $10,500 for a family with two or more children (reaching a maximum of $4,204). This is known as the "phase-in" range of the EITC. The EITC benefit remains at its maximum level in the "plateau" range, which reaches up to the level of $13,750 for single-parent families and $14,750 for two-parent families. After these points, the credit is reduced by about twenty-one cents per additional dollar earned (the "phase-out" range) until the benefit disappears at the levels of $33,692 for single-parent families and $34,692 for two-parent families.

Expanding the EITC would help provide the extra financial support that parents could use for costs such as child care or transportation. It has not been expanded in the United States since 1993. In addition, critics of the EITC's current structure note that the phase-in range ends before the point that represents full-time work at a minimum-wage job. This means that, for the lowest-wage workers, the tax credit does not make additional work pay up to the point of full-time work. In addition, the phase-out range begins before the point that represents the poverty threshold for a family of three, and substantially before the poverty threshold for a family of four (Sawhill and Thomas 2001). This means that the tax credit begins to be a work disincentive before the level of income that most low-wage, full-time workers make. Because workers who pass the poverty threshold also lose access to food stamps and housing benefits, the EITC contributes to very high cumulative marginal tax rates for families in the phase-out range (Suyderhound, Loudat, and Pollock 1994). (Marginal tax rates are rates at which each additional dollar earned is taxed.)

Expansion of the EITC, however, has drawbacks. Although raising benefit levels appears to have consistent positive effects in drawing new workers into the low-wage workforce (Greenstein and Shapiro 1998), the incentives for those already working are not as clear. For example, raising the maximum while retaining the phase-in and phase-out ranges increases the work incentive in the phase-in range but also increases the work disincentive in the phase-out range. (In the plateau range, there is no work incentive one way or the other because each additional dollar in earnings results in the same maximum benefit level.) These incentives have implications for policy, in that disincentives reduce benefits to workers as well as to government in the form of earnings, taxes, and reduced welfare use. However, it is unclear whether and how such disincentives have implications for the development of children. As we have found, the relationship between work and children's development is complex and depends on the dynamics of employment as well as the quality of associated supports, such as child care.

In a recent analysis, Isabel Sawhill and Adam Thomas (2001) compared five approaches to altering the EITC that have been put forward in recent years: adding a fourth tier for families with three or more children; reducing the loss of benefits experienced by couples who marry when both work and one has children; going to a single-tier structure, thereby eliminating the distinction between families with one and two or more children, as well as the very small benefit that goes to families with no children; increasing the maximum benefit by 25 percent; and taking a make-work-pay approach by decreasing the phase-out range and increasing the maximum benefit somewhat for all three tiers.[9] In this final option, they propose increasing the maximum benefit by a fairly small amount (from $4,008 to $4,285 for single-parent families with two or more children) as well as altering the phase-out range. Specifically, they propose that EITC benefits begin to be phased out $3,000 later than under current law. These phase-out thresholds would be increased by $5,000 for two-parent families. This option addresses the shortcomings of the current EITC structure for workers in the phase-out range and is designed to provide a stronger income boost for those working full-time at the lowest wages.

Costs and Benefits of Expanding the EITC   In simulations comparing the five options for restructuring the EITC, Sawhill and Thomas (2001) found that the make-work-pay approach to expanding the EITC would bring about the largest increase in new workers and be most effective at reducing poverty rates. It was also estimated to be cost-effective, because the amount of poverty reduction was more than the amount that would be spent on the EITC expansion. However, they do not acknowledge that any expansion in the EITC, which would be funded by increased tax dollars, might have consequences for the labor supply of those paying higher taxes.

At the same time, Sawhill and Thomas do not estimate the potential benefits to children of their proposal. Would this expansion of the EITC also benefit children? Estimates from the New Hope experiment, as well as those from two other recent programs that increased employment and income for welfare recipients, indicate that these programs brought about increases in total income in the range of $1,200 to $1,500 a year.[10] These programs are roughly comparable to expansions of the EITC, in that they increased income contingent on work effort.[11] In experimental evaluations, these programs were associated with improvements in children's school performance of between .1 and .4 standard deviations. (These improvements are of the magnitude represented by increasing SAT scores by ten to forty points, though, of course, the measures of performance used were different.) They also reduced children's acting-out behaviors. In the case of the New Hope experiment, these positive child impacts benefited boys, but not girls. A recent analysis of these and other welfare and antipoverty policy demonstrations showed that the increases in income brought about by these programs appeared to be causally linked to improvements in children's school performance (Morris, Duncan, and Rodrigues 2005). This suggests that the expansion of the EITC proposed by Sawhill and Thomas (2001) would indeed improve children's development, a factor that increases its potential as a cost-effective government policy. However, the EITC is almost always used as a once-a-year lump payment. The New Hope earnings supplement, in contrast, was paid out in every month that a participant worked thirty or more hours a week. In order to approximate the benefits to children of earnings-supplement experiments like New Hope, the monthly EITC option could be encouraged.

Make the Dependent Care Tax Credit Refundable   Another federal policy that provides help specifically for child care is the Dependent Care Tax Credit (DCTC). It subsidizes child care for low- and moderate-income families, albeit at a relatively minimal level (20 to 35 percent of the amount of child care expenses claimed, depending on family structure and income). Currently, this amounts to up to $2,100 to families with two or more children under the age of thirteen (or older dependents unable to take care of themselves). The credit is not provided, however, to those who do not make enough income to pay taxes or whose taxes are less than the value of the credit itself. This means that those with the lowest levels of earned income do not receive the benefit. A simple solution to this problem, which would make a difference to low-income parents such those in New Hope, is to make the DCTC refundable.

Costs and Benefits of Making the DCTC Refundable   A recent simulation analysis showed that making the DCTC refundable is a policy that would pay for itself, through increases in earnings and reductions in poverty (Sawhill and Thomas 2001). Together, these two policy changes—expanding the EITC to increase its incentives to make work pay for low-wage workers and making the DCTC refundable—would provide an increase in support for child care and an increase in income based on work. The best current data suggest that these policy changes would be likely to improve children's development.

2. Work Support Service Systems: Building on New Hope

Although the implementation of welfare reform has been successful in getting hundreds of thousands of welfare recipients off the rolls and into more consistent employment, many have observed that the logical next step of facilitating job retention and advancement has been difficult and uncertain.

Few solid studies are available to show which kinds of job retention and advancement programs work (Blank 2002).

New Hope has several characteristics that make it an attractive model for work support services. First, as discussed in chapter 1, the program has been proven to help children's development, producing lasting improvements in boys' academic performance and social behavior. At the two-year follow-up, New Hope increased academic performance and reduced acting-out behaviors, as reported by teachers. At five years, the program children also showed higher levels of standardized reading scores and positive social behaviors, compared to their control-group counterparts (Bos et al. 1999; Huston et al. 2001, 2003). Second, in data presented in chapter 2, we found that New Hope increased the probability of work trajectories characterized by wage growth (specifically, membership in the full-time–wage-growth group) relative to those characterized by low levels of work effort (membership in the low-wage–part-time group). Thus, it is one of the very few programs shown to bring about increases in wage growth as well as improvement in children's well-being. Third, in chapter 12, we presented a stark contrast between experiences of New Hope work support services and W-2 work support services. Almost uniformly, the parents in New Hope felt that trips to W-2 centers were characterized by interminable waits, stigma, and caseworkers being "in your business." New Hope provided services in community-based storefronts unaffiliated with the welfare system. It thus avoided the problem that any work support system even partially affiliated with TANF has: colocation with the most historically stigmatized government assistance program. And finally, New Hope provided case representatives who, with caseloads averaging fifty, provided not only income support, contingent on work, but help in accessing jobs. The relatively intensive level of support provided by the case reps made a difference in motivating New Hope participants in their work lives.

Despite all of the strengths of the New Hope model, data in this book also suggest ways in which the model could be improved in wider replication. We outline several of those possible improvements here. We also caution throughout that these changes to the program should be rigorously evaluated.

Implement the New Hope Model of Work Support for Parents Not Working Full-time   In New Hope's two-year evaluation, the cost-effectiveness of the program was greater for those who were not working full-time at random assignment (Bos et al. 1999), chiefly because, for those working full-time at random assignment, the effects of New Hope on employment were weaker. Owing to the thirty-hour-a-week work requirement to qualify for the earnings supplement, many parents who were already working more than thirty hours a week could reduce their work hours and still experience an increase in income by qualifying for the earnings supplement. We suggest targeting New Hope to low-wage workers who are not working full-time. This, of course, would require assessing applicants' work hours. In the settings in which we recommend New Hope's implementation (discussed later), doing so should not be a problem. Work hours could be assessed for continued eligibility for New Hope every three months, instead of every month, as in the original program.[12] This would reduce the transaction costs of being in the program and the frequent changes in eligibility experienced by some New Hope families whose work hours repeatedly crossed the thirty-hour mark.

We also suggest retaining New Hope's income guidelines, which were set at 150 percent of the federal poverty threshold, and making New Hope a permanent program instead of one offered only for three years. Implementing New Hope without a time limit might raise the specter of welfare for some. However, recall that the earnings supplement and other supports are contingent on full-time work. And the majority of workers would eventually increase their earnings so that they would no longer be eligible. However, for those families finding it difficult to raise their earnings, the New Hope work supports and earnings supplement would ensure economic security and individualized help when their income falls below the 150 percent line.

Restructure Child Care Subsidy Recertification to Better Fit Families' Routines   As chapter 10 noted, the New Hope child care subsidy system was based on meeting the program's thirty-hour-a-week work requirement. If a New Hope participant did not work thirty hours a week in a particular month, the program did not pay the child care provider the full reimbursement for the child's care. So if a parent failed to turn in her wage stubs for a particular month, New Hope paid only 75 percent of the normal reimbursement to the provider. If the parent failed to turn them in for a second month, New Hope stopped paying the provider entirely. This system amounted to monthly recertification and often caused friction for all three parties involved: the New Hope program representative, the child care provider, and the parent (Bos et al. 1999).

Child care subsidy maintenance in the W-2 system, similarly, required a high level of interaction between parents and caseworkers. For some parents, visits to offices to recertify state-administered child care subsidies (the Wisconsin Shares program) were required as often as every month during the time of the study, depending on their employment transitions. A report of subsidy systems in twelve states by the Urban Institute found that this pattern was by no means unusual across the United States (Adams, Snyder, and Sandfort 2002a, 2002b). Although some agencies allow recertification by mail or fax, many require in-person visits. These can easily take up half a day of transportation and waiting. Recertification is required whenever employment circumstances shift in a way that could affect eligibility. For example, changes in hours or shifts, as well as job turnover, necessitate recertification. As the work pathway clusters showed, some parents experienced very frequent job turnover, and thus their eligibility status for child care subsidies changed just as frequently, necessitating multiple visits for certification and recertification. The authors of the Urban Institute report found that some agencies did structure their recertification guidelines to better fit families' busy schedules. For example, in some sites, changes in work status, hours, or shifts could simply be called in to the caseworker, with follow-up mail-in of the required documents, such as pay stubs.

Recertification in both the W-2 and New Hope approaches was not timed to fit changes in children's schedules. The primary shifts in child schedules during the year are at the beginning and end of the school year. It seems to us, and might to many parents as well, that child care should be tied to predictable changes in the rhythm of the child's school year rather than to the highly unpredictable world of low-wage work. Summer necessitates often-drastic changes in household routines in any case, and somewhat predictably, older siblings and other caretakers take over child care then, as chapter 10 showed. A shift in the timing of child care benefits would recognize that it is the child who benefits from stable and consistent child care, not only the parent-worker. The child's developmental goals should be taken into account. Recertification could be requested once or twice a year, at the end of the school year or before the beginning. This change could be helpful for infant and toddler care as well, in that many children of that age have older siblings going to school. (Adams, Snyder, and Sandfort 2002b).

Restructure Community Service Jobs and Provide Services After Job Exits to Reduce Extreme Job Instability   As we reported in chapter 2, the New Hope program increased the probability of experiencing not only the full-time–wage-growth trajectory but also the rapid cycler trajectory. This is worrisome, because the latter work pattern was associated with negative consequences for children's school performance and social behavior. Several steps could be taken to help reduce the extreme job instability that was the hallmark of the rapid cycler pattern. First, the community service jobs in New Hope, which were generally limited to six months—though in some cases they were renewable for a second six months—could be extended. CSJs were used more often by young parents who were early in their work careers or by parents who otherwise had little work experience. Getting them off to a start in the labor market with a very short-term job experience makes little sense, especially if the CSJs, like the ones at nonprofits supplied by New Hope, provide opportunities for skills development. The suggested minimum length of a CSJ could be lengthened to twelve months, for example. CSJs could also build in increases in wages, contingent on work performance. One of the most discouraging aspects of work for the New Hope parents was the lack of opportunities for raises at work. More frequent raises, based on increases in education and training, even if small in magnitude, can provide incentives for those new to the workforce to stay in jobs.[13] While making these changes, the core benefits associated with New Hope CSJs that make it different from "workfare"—benefits and eligibility for earnings supplements and tax credits from CSJ wages—should be retained.

Second, New Hope could be augmented with some proven and low-cost models that help those who have lost their jobs find another one. We found that the rapid cyclers were most likely to be suspended or fired, relative to the other work trajectories. Some of these mothers experienced multiple suspensions and firings. A program model that could be adapted for use in New Hope is the JOBS program (no relationship to the federal Job Opportunity and Basic Skills program from the 1980s) (Vinokur, Price, and Caplan 1991). In small-group sessions for workers who have lost their jobs, this program builds job search and replacement skills and provides mutual support. The program has proven cost-effective, reducing periods of unemployment, increasing earnings, and reducing depression at two-year follow-ups (Vinokur et al. 2000; Vinokur, Price, and Schul 1995). The program was tested, in two experimental evaluations, on large samples of workers applying for unemployment insurance. The program appears to have been equally effective for low-wage workers and their higher-wage counterparts. The JOBS program could be adapted to be more applicable to low-wage workers who experience job loss, whether because of being fired or for other reasons. For example, samples could be recruited from New Hope offices, based on New Hope representatives' referrals following reports of job losses.

Integrate Mental Health and Work Support Services on Site to Address the Most Serious Barriers to Work   A large segment of the working poor are exposed to risks to their mental health, violence, substance use, and legal system involvement, and these exposures threaten not only their employability but the cognitive and socioemotional development of their children (Danziger, Kalil, et al. 2000; Rutter 1979; Sameroff et al. 1998; Yoshikawa 1994). This was true of the New Hope sample as well. The low-wage–part-time group, in particular, faced high levels of barriers in the areas of mental health, domestic violence, child care, and low social support. Other work on the New Hope sample has found that among the 25 percent of families facing the greatest number of risks, the effects of the program on their children were neutral to negative. This group also experienced increases in parental stress and depression (Yoshikawa et al. 2003). Take-up and engagement with the New Hope program was low among the families who experienced serious family disorganization, drug abuse, health problems, and family violence (Gibson and Weisner 2002).

Despite the extent of these barriers to work among the New Hope parents, New Hope was a work-based support program. It did not provide services addressing mental health, substance abuse, or domestic violence, though referrals and informal help were available. But such extended services were not mentioned often by the parents who took advantage of New Hope. New Hope case reps were trained to refer out for such services, and that may be why the mothers in the ethnographic sample did not report getting help for these issues very often. Such services are also not required as part of the Workforce Investment Act of 1998 (WIA) and therefore are rarely provided at federally funded one-stop centers.

Over the past fifteen years, the field of family-focused mental health services has pioneered the integration of services addressing mental health, domestic violence, and substance use in settings such as preschools, child care centers, schools, and even family courts. These programs are characterized by several principles: the integration of prevention with treatment services; attention to both children's and parents' well-being, with services targeting each population; intensive services on-site in settings not associated with mental health (such as Head Start); and avoidance of stigmatizing labels—for instance, avoiding the use of the term "mental health" (Knitzer 2002; Raver 2002). For example, one partnership described by Jane Knitzer (2002, 13) in a recent report, the San Francisco High Quality Child Care Mental Health Consultation Program, pairs qualified mental health consultants with two hundred center- and home-based child care programs in San Francisco. The program is coordinated by several city agencies and funded by a mix of TANF, Medicaid, and city funds. A variety of activities are funded by this program, including the training of child care providers in mental health issues, case consultation with families, direct services to parents and children, and evaluation.

Although programs such as this are still too rare, they are growing in number because of recognition of the high levels of stressors affecting many low-income families. But they have not been integrated into work support centers such as the one-stop centers funded by WIA. New Hope's approach to barriers to employment could be improved through a program like this, one that provides on-site help for mental health issues and intensive case management; strengthening of collaborations with mental health, substance abuse, and domestic violence agencies; and follow-up after referrals to services. Evidence from the integration of these services into child care, preschool, and school contexts shows that no increase in stigmatization occurs; rather, families come to view these settings as more responsive to their mental health and well-being. The key principle associated with successful community-based mental health services is that of bringing mental health consultants on-site rather than simply referring parents to them (Yoshikawa and Knitzer 1997). The majority of New Hope participants had a trusting relationship with their program representative. These reps may be in a better position to engage working parents in discussions of the more difficult and personal barriers to employment if they know the providers who will address those issues and can facilitate contacts on-site. We would encourage efforts not only to field good-quality integrated programs of this sort but also to do the kind of rigorous quantitative and qualitative evaluation that New Hope data show is of such value.

Test the New Hope Model of Work Support Within and Outside the Welfare System Thus far in our discussion of work support, we have not considered where to implement the New Hope model. The New Hope Project in Milwaukee was run out of storefronts unaffiliated with the welfare system in the neighborhoods it targeted. The dominant federal model of work support after the 1996 welfare reform was put forward in the Workforce Investment Act of 1998, which established "one-stop" centers that offer the full array of federally funded employment services (job search, work experience, limited job training, and case management). In the majority of the states, these one-stop centers are linked with TANF agencies and therefore serve both TANF and non-TANF populations. Milwaukee's one-stop centers, of which there are seven, are fully integrated with TANF agencies.

A recent evaluation found that, in practice, potential users have difficulty gaining access to many work support programs at one-stop centers. A recent national review of thirty-three one-stop centers evaluated them in terms of the accessibility of seven work support services: the EITC, subsidized child care, food stamps, publicly funded health insurance, cash assistance, child support, and transportation assistance (Richer, Kubo, and Frank 2003). Job training was excluded. The review found wide variation in accessibility: some centers provided on-site applications or active referrals (making appointments) for only one out of the seven of the services, while others provided on-site applications or active referrals for all seven services. Several other worrisome trends were found. Supports that were the least likely to be consistently accessible were those that have historically been associated with welfare: cash assistance, food stamps, and health insurance. Child care subsidy applications were generally handled by outside agencies, not by one-stop center staff, so parents had to go through the paperwork process at another office to get those subsidies.

New Hope could be implemented as a model for one-stop centers, or independently from them, as was the case in Milwaukee. If New Hope were to be a model for one-stop centers, it could be combined with TANF functions. Aligning New Hope with TANF would require in most cases a major restructuring of the caseworker role. New Hope program reps had much lower caseloads of about fifty, compared to the hundreds typically allotted to a welfare caseworker. In addition, obtaining services at one-stop centers is associated with cash welfare, the most stigmatized form of government assistance in the United States (Gilens 1999). Low rates of take-up of one-stop center services by non-TANF recipients may be due to this stigma by colocation. On the other hand, housing TANF within one-stop centers would provide some benefits of convenience, in that certain forms of government assistance, such as TANF, food stamps, or Medicaid, might be more accessible in a one-stop center than in an independent storefront office unaffiliated with the government.

A restructuring of one-stop centers to provide New Hope–type benefits and alter the caseworker role might have impressive effects on the work behavior and well-being of both TANF and non-TANF working-poor families. This would require skilled management at all levels, from administration to middle management down to frontline caseworkers. The level of skill and individualized attention that New Hope caseworkers provided would be difficult to attain; however, in the best cases, some current one-stop centers might approach this level of quality in service delivery and work facilitation (Richer et al. 2003). We believe that models of New Hope–type work support services should be tested and compared—both within and outside the welfare system, because the populations of welfare recipients and the larger group of working-poor adults are quite different.

New Hope Program Costs Versus Projected Benefits   The New Hope program's costs were $5,300 per program group member per year (Huston et al. 2003, table 2.5). However, its health insurance and child care subsidy components, in states that already provide those benefits to working-poor parents, could be reduced; this would substantially lower the overall costs of the program in a replication. In the mid-1990s New Hope cost roughly $2,500 per participant more than W-2, which was phased in at the same time and was available to the New Hope families as well as the control group

(Duncan, Huston, and Weisner 2007). For the subgroup of participants not employed full-time at random assignment, every $1.00 of benefits accruing to participants costs program funders and nonparticipant taxpayers $1.41 (Bos et al. 1999). However, this estimate did not take into account any benefits to children or to parents' well-being, both of which were sustained across the two-year and five-year follow-ups. The improvements to the New Hope model that we suggest here are likely to increase work-related benefits in domains such as sustained employment and wage increases. The addition of program components to address serious barriers to employment might be accompanied by reductions in the long run in mental health costs and potentially larger improvements in children's outcomes, in addition to increases in employment. Each of these costs and benefits deserves to be tested in the same ways that New Hope program costs and benefits were tested.

3. Low-Wage Workplaces: Implementing Workplace Policies That Increase Flexibility

Implement Flextime and Time-Off Policies in Low-Wage Workplaces   One of the findings in our book is that flexibility in work schedules, particularly during the daytime hours when most family health and service appointments occur, benefits parents and children (see chapter 5). However, almost none of the parents reported having this benefit formally. Instead, flexibility at work was determined by the individual preferences of supervisors (see chapter 4): those who had an understanding supervisor reported the benefits of flexibility; those who did not have such a supervisor suffered from their inability to address child and household needs during work hours. Two sets of employer-provided benefits can address this issue: flextime and time-off policies.

As implemented most often, flextime allows employees to start and end their workday on an individual but consistent basis. More rarely, employers allow employees to vary their start and end times on a day-to-day basis (Friedman 2001). Being able to take time off during the workday for family emergencies and important appointments could be allowed as a matter of policy rather than left up to supervisor discretion. Employees report that making use of flextime benefits may have repercussions for their careers; in fact, 40 percent of workers from the recent National Study of the Changing Workforce reported that those in their firms who used such benefits did not advance as quickly (Galinsky, Bond, and Hill 2004). A recent study of working mothers corroborated this perception: mothers in a seven-year longitudinal study who made use of workforce flextime policies consistently showed slower wage growth, controlling for an array of workplace, occupational, and individual characteristics (Glass 2004). Flextime policies would need to be implemented in such a way that taking advantage of the benefit does not reduce chances for promotions and raises.

Time-off policies allow parents to respond quickly to family emergencies without worrying about being suspended or losing their job. Typical time-off policies allow a certain number of days per year of absence. Once a certain number of those days have been used ("occurrence" policies), some of these policies warn the employee that taking the maximum allowed may lead to being fired. As the New Hope mothers reported, unexcused absences were the most frequent reason for reports of being fired. Low-wage workplaces appear to be more likely than other firms to use occurrence policies to threaten their workers with being suspended or fired (Friedman 2001). About 40 percent of the New Hope survey sample had no access to sick days. Paid time off can be offered for general illness, or even with added days specifically for child illnesses. Such a policy would recognize that parental and child illness are both valid reasons for taking a day off from work.

Flexibility at the workplace can often seem a difficult goal to implement in the context of businesses that employ low-wage workers, especially small ones. A recent report by Corporate Voices for Working Families provides some promising leads, at least among large businesses. The report identified Eastman-Kodak as a model for implementing multiple forms of flexibility in the workplace for all employees, regardless of position. Employees can use one of several flexibility options, including a compressed workweek or flextime, upon completion of an application, permission from their supervisor, and a demonstration that the arrangement will not have a negative effect on the business (Corporate Voices for Working Families 2005). This example shows that, at least for larger companies that employ lower-wage workers, flexibility can be implemented in the workplace. Corporate Voices for Working Families suggests initial reviews by departments to assess levels of interest in flexible work arrangements, and it emphasizes the importance of instituting flexibility in work contracts to which both parties are accountable.

Costs and Benefits of Workplace Flexibility Policies   Are policies that increase workplace flexibility cost-effective? There are few data on the costs versus the benefits of flextime policies. To the extent that such policies maintain the number of hours worked but redistribute them during the workweek, costs could be argued to be minimal. However, to the extent that such shifts actually disrupt production, costs could be nontrivial. Furthermore, tensions arise within the workplace when some workers (those who are single, or older, or who have stable child care in place) have to cover for others who need flextime but do not have it. Any costs to employers might then be passed on to consumers in the form of higher prices. Enforcement and monitoring and disputes have benefits perhaps—but costs as well. On the other hand, our data suggest that increasing flexibility in work hours, particularly during the daytime hours when many services relevant to children's health and schooling are offered, could improve children's development.

4. Potential Cumulative Effects of Suggested Policy and Program Changes

Developmental studies suggest that simultaneously addressing multiple factors that improve children's well-being can have cumulative effects in improving their outcomes. In other words, in the long run, addressing multiple factors may provide a larger return on society's investment than addressing one or two alone.[14] Evidence from this book suggests that several factors—wage growth, extreme job instability, access to the crucial supports of transportation and child care, and work schedule flexibility—affect parents' and children's well-being. We crafted our recommendations to address each of these factors. Together, they could have cumulative positive effects on children's school achievement and social behavior.

The policies and programs suggested here—expanding the EITC, making the DCTC refundable, instituting and testing a revised version of the New Hope model, and implementing workplace flexibility policies—target three systems that affect low-income families: the tax system, community-based work support services, and workplaces. Let us return to the parents we introduced in chapter 2, Evelia, Iris, and Allison. The combination of these policies would have made a marked difference in their work lives, and in ways that we predict would have improved their well-being and that of their children.

Imagine that Evelia had had access to this package of policy and program improvements. In the middle of the ethnographic period, she was a single mother with four children working full-time at $8.00 an hour (making $16,000 a year, or 82 percent of the federal poverty line in 1999 for a family like hers). With our recommended changes in the EITC, she would have been within the plateau, or maximum benefit range, of the EITC instead of being in the phase-out range with a lower benefit. She would have thus received $4,285 instead of $3,065. This might have been enough to not only pay off her debts (which is what she did with her EITC) but also buy her children a computer (which she wanted to do but was not able to).

Because Evelia's income was not high enough to pay taxes, with the existing DCTC structure she would have received nothing. With a refundable dependent care tax credit, she would have received up to $1,296 (assuming that she claimed the maximum level of child care expenses, which was $4,800). New Hope would have provided her with an extra wage supplement of $96 per month, or $1,152 that year. Thus, Evelia would have received a total extra income boost of $3,668, an amount that, extrapolating from evaluations of earnings supplement programs, is associated with an improvement in children's school performance of about half a standard deviation.[15] The relevant social science literature shows that an improvement of this size is not only scientifically significant but societally significant.

New Hope's child care subsidy would have given her much needed help with before- and after-school child care for her six-year-old daughter, who lived too close to school to qualify for bus transportation but was too young to walk to school by herself in their dangerous neighborhood. (Evelia was assigned to the control group, so she had no access to New Hope benefits.) Workplace flexibility policies might have reduced the many episodes Evelia reported of child care schedule crises, and they might have averted one serious episode in which her son's stomach ailment went untreated for several days when her work schedule was particularly hectic.

For a parent with much lower levels of work effort, such as Iris, this package of policies and programs would have addressed her serious barriers to work, which threatened not only her work but also her own and her family's well-being, and it would have provided stronger financial and other incentives for work. With improvements to New Hope's capacity to address serious barriers to work, Iris might have received a referral to counseling to address her multiple mental health problems (depression, feelings about her appearance, relationship conflicts). The EITC improvements suggested here target those with the lowest levels of earnings by providing a stronger work incentive in the phase-in range. (Specifically, the EITC would provide more than the current $1.40 per additional earnings dollar in the phase-in range.) Because Iris's earnings placed her below the level of income that required tax payments in 1999, she would have received up to $1,440 of a refundable DCTC. This might also have served as a work incentive. Had she had access to New Hope (she was assigned to the control group), her program representative would have explained these incentives to her. One of Iris's chief reasons for not working was her concern about her nephew's behavior; workplace flexibility would have enabled her to respond to her nephew's behavior problems as needed, while continuing to work. With flextime available at work, she would have been able to leave during the workday to attend to a school or home crisis.

Finally, what if Allison had had access to this package of program and policy improvements? In the middle of the ethnographic period, Allison was a single mother with two children working full-time at $10.15 an hour. (Making $20,300 a year, Allison was at 146 percent of the federal poverty line in 1999 for a family of her size.) With our recommended changes in the EITC, she would still have been in the phase-out range but would have received $3,923 instead of $2,160.

Because her sons were over age thirteen, Allison was not eligible to receive the dependent care tax credit. So making that credit refundable would not have affected Allison. Because the amount she was earning put her above the poverty line but still allowed her to be eligible for a significant EITC, New Hope would not have provided Allison with an extra wage supplement. Thus, for a family in Allison's situation, only our suggested changes to the EITC would have made a difference. Those changes, however, would still have resulted in $1,763 of increased income, a change similar to ones that produced about a .20 standard deviation improvement in some children's school performance in earnings supplement programs. Arguably, Allison was in a position where she needed the intensive work supports provided by our package of benefits less than other participants, like Iris and Evelia. Our emphasis on the five varied work trajectories clearly shows that some successful workers like Allison are right at the threshold of need for support programs; the policies we are considering would make sure that if problems emerged in her work or family, Allison could hang in there until things got better for her.

By increasing resources in families to obtain work supports like licensed child care and transportation, facilitating wage growth, reducing extreme job instability, and making work schedules fit families' daily routines better, these policies and programs would improve the aspects of work that this book suggests may make a difference for children. Such changes would also improve the quality of family life, a worthy goal of policy in its own right.

Chapter Fourteen | Epilogue

Johannes M. Bos

THE RESEARCH PRESENTED in this book is based on data collected as part of an ambitious demonstration project in Milwaukee, Wisconsin. This project, New Hope, recruited over 1,300 volunteers to participate in a program that would give them some of the benefits associated with high-quality employment if they worked thirty hours or more a week: subsidized health insurance and child care, a wage supplement that would lift their family out of poverty, subsidized HMO health care, and a six-month community service job if they could not find work or did not already have work. The simple unifying idea behind this project was that anyone who works full-time should not be poor. The project was developed in the early 1990s and implemented as a demonstration project (with random assignment and a control group) to document the effects of such an approach. Prior research on similar wage support programs had found some evidence of lower work effort by participants, and the sponsors of the New Hope Project wanted to know whether that might happen in this case as well. It did not; instead, New Hope increased the work effort of its participants who had not been working thirty hours at baseline and, in an expansion of the study, funded by the MacArthur Foundation, was found to improve important outcomes for parents and for their children, including how well they did in school.

All of this prompted two additional rounds of in-depth research on families in the New Hope demonstration, both those who received New Hope services and those in the control group. That research, funded by the National Institute for Child Health and Development (NICHD), extended the follow-up period for this project to nine years and made possible much of the extended research into topics such as child care, job characteristics, work patterns, and so forth.[1] This book, which uses data from the first five years of follow-up, is special in that it combines extensive outcome data on hundreds of families in the New Hope demonstration with in-depth ethno-graphic fieldwork on forty-four families, who were also randomly selected in equal numbers from both the treatment and control groups.[2] This combination of quantitative and qualitative research allows the findings to be both representative of a large group of low-income families and very detailed in terms of specific relationships between key aspects of people's employment experiences and their other outcomes. This has resulted in a significant number of important insights that have been detailed throughout each chapter. One of the unique features of this book is the close integration of qualitative and quantitative findings in each chapter, using the same database for both quantitative and qualitative data. Rarely have these methods been used so seamlessly by a single research team.

Among the more important findings of this book is the apparent dichotomy in the direction of the effects of parental employment on children's outcomes. In the literature in this important policy area, most researchers and policy advocates tend to present only one side of the issue. They either find that maternal employment improves outcomes for children or find that it hurts children. The hypothesized pathways for these positive and negative effects are different. Positive effects are thought to be caused by parental role modeling, greater parental self-esteem, higher family income, or child exposure to high-quality child care. Negative effects, in contrast, might happen because parents spend less time with their children, parents are more stressed, or children are placed in poor child care situations, including self-care. As this book finds, which of these effects dominates in any particular study depends on who the parents and children are (their human capital and developmental background, respectively) and whether increased parental employment is stable and accompanied by increased family income and growth in earnings and benefits, as well as a range of other factors. In this book, researchers use a rich set of survey data on employment patterns, wage growth, job characteristics, and child and family outcomes and combine those data with ethnographic data on job duties, flexibility, coworker and supervisor relationships, discrimination, relations with partners, parental goals, social support, budgeting, and other job and family circumstances. These rich data show that some employment experiences have decidedly *positive* effects on families and children, while others have decidedly *negative* effects. The fact that these effects are found in a relatively homogeneous sample of low-income families in a single city suggests that they are not driven primarily by the individual backgrounds of the sample members and their children. This is an important finding, because it suggests that there are distinct and diverging positive and negative employment pathways among the working poor, a group typically lumped into a single category for policy purposes. Identifying these pathways early in program contexts, and in the lives of the working poor, and changing the employment trajectories that low-income workers follow could benefit families and children and improve program effectiveness.

SOME CAVEATS

There are several caveats to consider in interpreting the findings presented in this book. First, the fact that the findings are based on a relatively small sample of volunteers in a single city in the Midwest means that it is difficult to generalize to the larger population of low-income working parents in the United States. There are a number of characteristics of these families and their circumstances that make such generalization difficult. First, because these sample members volunteered for the New Hope program (even though half were assigned to the control group), they were motivated enough to apply for a program that was work-based. Many were already combining full-time work with their family life. This is not true for all low-income parents, many of whom may not consider themselves ready to join the workforce, especially if they have limited work experience or are caring for young children. Thus, the findings from the research presented here may not apply to the least work-ready parents and their families. Nonetheless, many in the program and control groups were in fact not working at baseline, or only working part-time, and their preparation for work varied.

Second, Wisconsin was a hotbed of welfare reform during the 1990s. Its Wisconsin Works (W-2) program was one of the most generous welfare reform programs in the nation in terms of the services and support it offered recipients who entered employment, while at the same time it had among the strongest work requirements. Finally, Wisconsin had a relatively generous state earned income tax credit during the period of this study. This policy helps to augment the effects of the federal EITC and increases the payoff from employment for low-income families relative to states that do not have a state EITC. The generous state EITC gave the New Hope families (in both experimental conditions) yet another incentive to work and also made it more likely that employment would help families leave poverty and improve their material well-being. Of course, all of these circumstances made it less likely, not more, that positive experimental impacts of the New Hope program would be found compared to states with less generous work support policies—and New Hope impacts *were* found.

Because of these factors, low-income parents in the New Hope Demonstration sample were more likely to be employed than their counterparts in a more representative national sample of parents in poverty would have been. This in turn may have affected how parental employment (and variation in parents' employment experiences) influenced subsequent child and family outcomes. With employment being supported and encouraged by New Hope and by state policy, employment may have been more sustainable for families in the New Hope sample, and work may have been more socially desirable than in other samples of low-income families. It is difficult to predict how this affected the findings presented in this book, but it is important to keep in mind the special context in which this research was conducted.

A third caveat concerns the representativeness of the findings based on the ethnographic research. Such research has great benefits in terms of the richness and depth of the data collected and their ability to uncover complex relationships and constructs that were not well understood previously. However, at the same time, because of the small samples involved in this research, the ethnographic findings are less generalizable than findings based on hundreds of individual families and children. Nevertheless, this book is unique in the field in how it addressed the generalizability of the ethnographic findings. The ethnographic families were randomly selected from the full survey sample. The qualitative data were carefully indexed and coded by the research team. All the data were incorporated into the analyses, not just a few selected cases. The entire team used the same full qualitative dataset in each chapter, so that each topic studied in ethnographic depth contributed to the others. And the ethnographic sample families were distributed across all the five employment pathways, which were derived from quantitative analyses of the full survey. The ethnographic data were collected, indexed, and coded without knowledge of these employment clusters. Hence, the ethnographic data were fully integrated with and nested within the relatively large survey sample using unusually objective methods.

A final caveat concerns the causal nature of the many relationships between parental employment and child outcomes presented in this research. Unlike the evaluation of the New Hope program itself, which used an experimental research design, analyses of the effects of parental employment on child outcomes are always non-experimental, since sample members were not randomly assigned to different employment experiences or job trajectories. The New Hope experiment was a broad package of supports that did not randomly assign parents to particular work trajectories. This means that there may be some uncontrolled biases that could explain the apparent effects of parental employment outcomes on subsequent child outcomes. For example, parents with a stronger motivation to work are more likely to have greater employment stability and may also be more confident in their ability to successfully combine work and family responsibilities. To the extent that subsequent child outcomes are positive, it may appear that employment stability improved those outcomes when it was really parental motivation. As described in the individual chapters, the researchers used a variety of techniques and a wide range of background variables to address these concerns. However, in the absence of random assignment of particular employment characteristics, these biases can never be completely ruled out.

However, even considering these caveats, the findings presented here greatly increase our understanding and awareness of the complexity of the relationships between parental employment and family well-being for low-income families. The richness of the New Hope data, the length of follow-up, and the combination of ethnographic and survey research methods have produced important new insights into these critical issues. It is important to build on these findings and develop new ways not only to increase the benefits of employment for low-income families but also to increase our understanding of when such employment is beneficial to families and children and when it is not.

KEY FINDINGS AND THEIR IMPLICATIONS

The research presented in this volume underscores the importance of three key elements of a good employment experience for low-income parents: stability, flexibility, and quality. The evidence suggests that the absence of these elements has negative effects on parental well-being and children's outcomes, which may have significant long-term costs. When the only job opportunities available to low-income parents are unstable (temporary) jobs with little wage growth and no flexibility, the negative effects of such an employment experience on children may outweigh the benefit of having these parents work at all. On the other hand, when low-income parents find jobs that enable them to grow, both materially and professionally, and to maintain a sustainable family life, their employment appears to benefit their children directly and significantly.

Research has not clearly identified pathways into these two alternative employment trajectories, but the background characteristics and past experiences of the low-income parents in the New Hope study accounted for some of the variation in their subsequent employment trajectories. For example, parents who had cars when they first entered the study had better employment experiences (with more wage growth in combination with full-time work) than those who did not. Similarly, parents with more education, prior work experiences, more social supports, clear goals for family or work, and an ability to link goals to tactics for finding and keeping better jobs had work trajectories that had positive consequences for themselves and their children. But in the end, both good and bad job trajectories were found among different groups of study participants. It appears that these job experiences often build on themselves, with good experiences following other good ones and bad experiences following other bad ones. A key in all of this appears to be the sustainability of employment within the family context. Although good jobs improve family well-being, there is also evidence that a positive family life contributes to success in the workplace. Breadwinner and caregiver and household pathways are interdependent.

Low-income working families often lack the resources that higher-income families use to make their work life compatible with their family obligations. This includes reliable and efficient transportation and good-quality child care (including at nonstandard hours). In addition, low-income workers have less autonomy in their jobs and less authority to make schedule changes and take time off from work to attend to family matters. Workers who were able to secure these resources and gain some flexibility in their work schedule (either formally or informally) were more successful in their careers and in their management of family life. Adequate government funding for child care assistance would make a major difference to many parents who do not have these resources, as would expanded and more flexible family leave policies. However, government funding is just one part of the solution. Major employers could make a significant difference by promoting policies and procedures that support low-income parents. In the long run, such increased flexibility reduces turnover and benefits low-income working parents and employers alike.

In terms of benefits for children, the research presented in this book uncovers effect sizes of positive work trajectories that are comparable to those associated with high-quality interventions that are targeted directly at children.[3] This suggests that the *indirect* effects of sustainable and stable parental employment on children's outcomes are nevertheless significant ways to benefit children. For programs and policies that seek to improve employment outcomes for low-income parents, this means that such initiatives have benefits that extend beyond the immediate financial and employment gains for participating individuals. These benefits are not always accounted for when decisions about such programs are made. If these positive outcomes were included in cost-benefit considerations, employment training and make-work-pay programs for low-income workers would be more likely to have positive net benefits. Future evaluations of such initiatives should incorporate measures to capture these important benefits.

At the same time, the findings presented in this book underscore the challenge facing policymakers who want to improve the life circumstances of low-income working families. Many New Hope parents experienced significant structural barriers to improving their employment situation, including inadequate or unreliable transportation from home to work, race- and gender-based discrimination at work, domestic violence, and lack of affordable child care—all topics that are carefully analyzed in this book. Traditional approaches to improving the employment situation of low-income workers tend to focus on linking them to better jobs or providing them with education or training to improve their human capital. The benefits of these approaches may be limited, however, unless existing structural barriers are addressed as well, which few of these programs are able to do. Instead, removing these barriers may require active intervention by state and local governments, which can help create the structural and social service supports that improve work opportunities for all workers. One such support is economic development policy that creates jobs in neighborhoods where low-income workers live. Local development improves access to jobs, reduces commuting time and expenses, and reduces the stigma that residents of inner-city neighborhoods often face when they apply for jobs elsewhere. Creative economic development does not simply seek to bring outside industries into low-income neighborhoods but builds on and supports existing enterprise, including neighborhood retail operations and important service industries, such as the provision of child care and health care. Attention to families with the highest levels of stress due to extreme poverty, mental health problems, or domestic violence should also be increased within work support systems. New Hope, of course, was not designed to address these structural and social service needs; the authors make sensible recommendations about expanding the New Hope model to include an emphasis on these barriers.

It is also important to underscore that parental employment is not a panacea for addressing the problems of low-income families. A key characteristic of many early welfare reform initiatives was that they often increased employment significantly without producing comparable increases in family income because they reduced welfare benefits as a family's earnings increased. As a result, many parents who left welfare for work were unable to earn enough to lift their family out of poverty or even experience a meaningful improvement in their financial well-being. Research suggests that parental employment under those conditions does not benefit family well-being and child development.

In the second half of the 1990s, the financial payoff associated with employment for low-income families increased significantly. During that time the federal earned income tax credit grew significantly, increasing the income of the average working family by several thousand dollars a year. Together with the tight labor market at that time, which increased the average hourly wage of low-income workers, this resulted in significant income gains for low-income families. Most families in the New Hope demonstration benefited from the expanded EITC, which is further supplemented in Wisconsin with a relatively generous state EITC. The ethnography found that these tax credits provided working families with an annual financial cushion that they often used to cover large onetime expenses, such as buying a reliable car, making a deposit on a better apartment, paying off debt and improving credit, or purchasing home furniture and appliances. Because the EITC is directly related to employment (as the New Hope earnings supplement was), it does not carry a stigma, as other government transfer programs do. Also, the bureaucratic hassle involved in applying for the EITC is minimal compared to other government programs, making it a very effective tool to reward work and increase the income and well-being of low-income families.

In addition to the usual policy levers of job development, education, child care, and income support, this book highlights a range of other factors that either moderate or mediate positive employment outcomes and subsequent benefits for families and children. These factors—usually not included in other studies of parental employment and its effects on children—include job quality, support from partners and spouses, the role of marriage, the importance of goals and values regarding work, and the ways in which low-income working families make ends meet. In each of these areas, the research presented here adds new nuances to the existing literature, uncovering in detail how job quality matters for parent and child well-being, how wage growth increases the likelihood of marriage, and how flexibility in work schedules during the daytime hours may benefit children. In pursuing and uncovering this myriad of linkages between work dynamics, family life, and children's prospects, the researchers decisively show that traditional views of parental work as either "good" or "bad" for children are outdated and no longer helpful. Instead, they have usefully focused our attention on the particular aspects of work over time that make the most difference for children of the working poor.

Methodological Appendix |

This appendix presents more detailed information on sampling, recruitment, data collection, and data analysis.

SAMPLING AND RECRUITMENT

Two neighborhoods in Milwaukee were chosen in which to implement the New Hope Project study: the "North Side" area, described at the beginning of chapter 1, was predominantly African American; the "South Side" was mixed, with a sizable Latino population. Both had high proportions of residents living in poverty: 40 percent on the North Side in 1989, five years prior to the beginning of random assignment; 37 percent on the South Side. These neighborhoods were chosen in order to concentrate the resources of the New Hope program in high-poverty neighborhoods and to achieve racial-ethnic diversity. The neighborhoods were defined by zip code boundaries (one zip code for each neighborhood).

A broad community-outreach approach to recruitment was adopted. Recruitment took place through presentations to churches and social service organizations in the neighborhoods; media announcements; invitations to welfare, food stamps, Medicaid, and general assistance recipients to attend meetings about New Hope; and more general street outreach. The word went out: you could come in and volunteer for the random-assignment lottery and have a fifty-fifty chance of being in the New Hope program.[1]

The New Hope staff recruited 1,362 adults, both men and women, from the North Side and South Side. Both neighborhoods had large percentages of households with incomes at 150 percent or less of the federal poverty standard and large numbers of households that received at least some AFDC (cash welfare).

THE CHILD AND FAMILY STUDY

The central research, program, and policy questions for the full sample were about work and income: would New Hope increase income and work hours, and would those working thirty or more hours a week take up the New Hope benefits and so move out of poverty? As part of the planning for New Hope—and indeed, at the strong suggestion of some of the funders—this question was addressed through a research evaluation team. The evaluation effort, with advice from an advisory board, was led by Manpower Demonstration Research Corporation (MDRC).[2] MDRC, based in New York, is a nonprofit policy institute with substantial expertise in leading policy program evaluations that use a random-assignment procedure. New Hope was carefully and effectively implemented, as the 1997 study by Thomas Brock and his colleagues (1997) showed.

However, there loomed another important question that was as yet unanswered by the research plans for evaluating the New Hope project: what were the effects of the program on children and parents? The original evaluation design did not focus on this question, and for understandable reasons: the program was a work-based antipoverty program for all adults, whether or not they had children, were married, or lived alone. The policy context in Milwaukee, Wisconsin, and among those establishing New Hope, was focused on increasing work and reducing poverty among adults—no mean feat if it could be done. The MacArthur Network, and then the National Institute of Child Health and Human Development (NICHD), funded a study of families with children who participated in the New Hope experimental evaluation, the Child and Family Study (CFS), to better understand these child and family questions.[3]

The CFS sample included all of the original applicants for the lottery for eligibility for New Hope who had one or more children between the ages of thirteen months and ten years, eleven months at the time of random assignment. This sample size was 745. In this book, we use the sample of mothers in this group (sample size 696). For those mothers who had one or two children, each of these children was included in the study. If the parent had more than two children in the target child age range, two were randomly selected (and if there were both boys and girls in the family, one boy and one girl were selected). Nearly all of the New Hope parents were mothers. Men caring for children in their households are an important group as well, of course, but there were too few of them to make reliable quantitative analyses, and only two were in the qualitative study that forms the other dataset for our work.[4] The sample of mothers is therefore the sample we use throughout our book. We will refer to the group of 696 mothers as the survey, or "larger," New Hope sample to distinguish it from the smaller, randomly selected, ethnographic sample we describe later. Note that both samples include those in both the New Hope program group and the control group.

Parent and Teacher Surveys
and Standardized Assessments

The Child and Family Study involved an ambitious combination of methods: a survey of parents, assessments of children, teacher reports on how the children were doing in school, and an ethnographic study of a random sample of these families in the program and control groups. In addition, administrative records from the state of Wisconsin were collected on income, earnings, and welfare for the full sample.

The survey sample from the CFS filled out a short questionnaire at baseline, capturing demographic information. At two and five years after baseline, detailed follow-up assessments were conducted. The New Hope program benefits were offered for three years after enrollment, so these two follow-up points represent one year before and two years after program benefits were ended. At the two-year follow-up, children were ages three to thirteen, and at the five-year follow-up they were six to sixteen. These CFS surveys included survey measures from the parents as well as assessments from teachers of school-age children in the sample. The parent survey measures included items about experiences of parental employment, goals and aspirations, economic and psychological well-being, parenting, child care, social support, relationships and marriage, and perceptions of their children's development.

Teachers of children in the CFS were mailed a questionnaire at their schools asking about the focal children in our sample. The mailing mentioned that the child was participating in a study, but it made no mention of New Hope (and so, of course, no mention of whether the child was in the treatment or control group), poverty, welfare, or other types of programs. If the children were in middle school or the early high school grades, the math and English teachers were sent the questionnaire, whenever possible.

The teacher reports included ratings of children's school performance, school engagement, and social behavior. Finally, at five years after random assignment, standardized assessments of the children's reading and math achievement were added (the Woodcock-Johnson Broad Math and Broad Reading tests). See table A.1 for more details on the constructs for which data were collected in the surveys. Seventy-five percent of the original group of parents, 72 percent of the original group of children, and 63 percent of the teachers of those children completed survey assessments at the five-year follow-up.[5]

Table A1 Survey and Standardized Assessment Constructs Used in This Volume, from the New Hope Child and Family Study

Construct	Baseline (at random assignment)	Two-Year Follow-up	Five-Year Follow-up
Baseline covariates (used in all multivariate analyses)	• Race-ethnicity (dummy variables for black and Latino) • Single-adult household • More than two children • Youngest child younger than age two • Working full-time • Receiving government aid (AFDC, general assistance, food stamps, or Medicaid) • Has a high school diploma • Has a car • On AFDC as a child • Earnings in the prior year	NA	NA

Employment	• Employed
	• Earnings in last year
		1. For employment across first two years:
		• Information on each of up to six jobs since baseline:
		  • Start date
		  • End date
		  • Wages (beginning and ending)
		  • Hours
		  • Beginning wage
		• Total earnings from jobs, per year
		• Time grid of last seven days, including hours of employment
		• Whether variable work schedule
		2. For current or most recent job:
		• Occupational complexity with people, data, and things
		• Benefits (employer-sponsored health insurance and pension plan; paid sick and vacation days)
		• Perceived opportunities for promotion and advancement
		• Learning valuable skills
		• Job security
			For current or most recent job:[a]
			• Start date, wages, hours, duties
			• Benefits (employer-sponsored health insurance and pension plan; paid sick and vacation days)
			• Perceived opportunities for promotion and advancement, learning valuable skills, job security, adequate pay, and flexibility to handle emergencies
			• Interpersonal conflict at work
			• Exhaustion after workday
			• Total earnings from jobs, per year

Income	Earned income in the past year	Total income, per year (sum of earnings, welfare, food stamps, and earnings supplements from tax credits and New Hope supplement)	Total income, per year (sum of earnings, welfare, food stamps, and earnings supplements from tax credits and New Hope supplement)

(*continued*)

Table A1 Survey and Standardized Assessment Constructs Used in This Book, from the New Hope Child and Family Study (Continued)

Construct	Baseline (at random assignment)	Two-Year Follow-up	Five-Year Follow-up
Goals and expectations for education, work, family and children, and financial and personal development	None	Goals: • Feeling good about having a paycheck • Successful role model for kids Expectations: • For high school graduation • For college attendance • For college graduation	Goals: • Feeling good about having a paycheck • Successful role model for kids Expectations: • For high school graduation • For college attendance • For college graduation
Parent psychological well-being	None	• Parenting stress • Parent depressive symptoms	• Parenting stress • Parent depressive symptoms
Parent economic well-being	Access to car	Parent material hardship	• Parent material hardship • Home and car ownership • Satisfaction with housing
Parenting practices	None	• Parent monitoring • Parent warmth (self-report and observed by interviewer) • Effective parenting	• Parent monitoring • Parent warmth (self-report and observed by interviewer) • Effective parenting
Child care as barrier to work	None	• Lack of child care as reason for quitting a job • Lack of child care as reason for failing to find a job	

Social support	None	None	Availability and reliability of social support
Child school performance and achievement	None	School: • Teacher-rated school engagement and performance • Parent-rated school engagement and performance	School: • Teacher-rated school engagement and performance • Parent-rated school engagement and performance Standardized achievement: • Woodcock-Johnson Reading and Math scores
Child social behavior	None	Teacher- and parent-rated internalizing (withdrawn) and externalizing (acting-out) behaviors	• Teacher- and parent-rated internalizing (withdrawn) and externalizing (acting-out) behaviors • Delinquent behavior (child self-report; for ages nine or older only)
Family structure	• Marital and cohabiting status • Number and ages of children	Marital and cohabiting status	Marital and cohabiting status
Service use	Current use of AFDC, general assistance, food stamps, or Medicaid	Use of work support services • Help from W-2 or New Hope case managers and representatives • Job placement or community service job • Earnings supplement • Child care subsidies • Health care subsidies	NA (New Hope benefits no longer provided in later years of follow-up)

Source: Authors' compilation.
[a] Data on each job since the two-year follow-up not collected.

Approach to Quantitative Analyses

Our core quantitative analysis identified subgroups of New Hope parents who differed in their longitudinal patterns of work (as defined by hours, average wages, job length, number of jobs, and wage growth). This analysis is described in detail in chapter 2. In each of the other chapters, we examined a particular aspect of work (job quality, job discrimination) or characteristics of the contexts of work experiences (for instance, child care, social support, parental goals, partners). Throughout the chapters, we aimed to use statistical methods that could strengthen our ability to infer causality in associations of work experiences with family and child well-being. For example, we report whether the New Hope experiment affected particular variables of interest in each chapter.[6] In some very limited cases, we use that information to identify a causal association between the variable of interest and parent or child well-being.[7] For the most part, our approach to modeling the association of work-related variables with parent or child well-being consists of using a comprehensive set of covariates, as well as residualized change or change-score methods. The choice of particular method in each chapter was determined both conceptually and by the structure of the data.[8] Each chapter provides a description of this analytic choice.

The three-year New Hope Ethnographic Study (NHES) began in the spring of 1998, during the final year of the New Hope experiment, and lasted until the summer of 2001 (Gibson and Weisner 2002; Gibson-Davis and Duncan 2005; Weisner et al. 2000). The NHES took a stratified random sample of sixty families from the full Child and Family Study, stratified for equal representation of both the experimental and control groups. This sampling strategy was chosen to take advantage of the random-assignment design of the full New Hope study. It ensures that as long as the complete NHES dataset is used for qualitative analyses, we can be reasonably certain that generalizations from the pattern of qualitative findings can be used to complement the findings from the quantitative analyses of the CFS sample. Moreover, the NHES sample families were all also in the CFS survey and child assessment sample. The random selection of NHES families from the larger CFS sample means that they were not selected because they were high users of New Hope, they were more visible and eager to participate, or they were nominated by New Hope staff as "successful" participants.

Initially, forty-six of these sixty (77 percent) were successfully recruited into the study. In all cases, the parent who had been recruited into the larger CFS was recruited into the NHES. However, two families dropped out in the first year, one each from the control and program groups. Two additional families did not begin until the spring of 1999, leaving a final sample of forty-two NHES parents and their families who were followed for the entire three-year ethnographic period. Of these, we use as our sample in this book the forty mothers in the NHES, excluding two male-headed households. In return for their participation, each parent in the NHES was given $50 for every three months of their participation in the study.[9] Thomas Weisner led the NHES fieldwork team through a series of planning meetings, training, and periodic team meetings over the three-plus years of the fieldwork itself.

Ethnographic Methods

Field-workers visited families roughly every ten weeks, most often in the family's home, but also in a variety of community settings (Weisner et al. 2002). When visiting families, field-workers used open-ended interviews to engage parents in conversations about their lives and their concerns and hopes and descriptions of their everyday routines. Although these interviews were not rigidly structured, the fieldwork team did develop a comprehensive set of topics that they used to guide these discussions and to ensure that comparable data were collected across the sample. The topic of "work life" received a lot of attention and included study participants' experiences surrounding their employers, earnings, hassles at work, work and career goals, and efforts to juggle work and family. The fieldwork team also covered topics relating to parenting and managing the household, including budgeting and debt, child monitoring, school, child care, parental goals, and parental concerns about their children. Topics also included a range of other sometimes difficult but important themes that could influence work and parenting, like partners and husbands, drugs and alcohol, family supports and conflicts (including episodes of abuse), and parents' and children's health. Finally, field-workers asked parents about their opinions on race, politics, and the welfare system.

Field-workers also participated in family activities (for example, meals, shopping, running errands, and church). All topics were covered with all parents—there were no false negatives. If certain topics did not come up spontaneously and get discussed in some depth, field-workers brought them up and encouraged discussion. Field-workers eventually wrote field notes on all the focal topics and domains of research interest and entered them into EthnoNotes, a process that kept them aware of what still needed covering. If a parent was interested in talking about a particular topic on a field visit—say, hassles at work, income problems, how the kids were doing in school—field-workers went with those topics. But then they would move the conversations on to other topics as well.

After each ethnographic visit with an NHES family, field-workers wrote up the conversations and their observations into visit summaries and more complete and descriptive field notes. These field-note entries were based on tape recordings made during each family visit and written notes made during and after the visit. Because of the frequency of the visits (a range of seven to forty-five visits per family averaged out to eighteen visits per family) and the volume of interview material, making verbatim transcriptions of each visit was not cost-effective. Generally, these data are paraphrased summaries of what the study participants told the field-worker during the visit. Field-workers were encouraged to quote participants verbatim and sometimes at great length in the field notes if their words were particularly poignant or revealing. The data were entered into a database for storing the notes and linked to all the other project data being collected in the EthnoNotes system (Lieber, Weisner, and Presley 2003). Our case studies of families, quotes from parents about what they think about their lives, and summaries of qualitative patterns in work and family life are all taken from this EthnoNotes field-note database. These qualitative and ethnographic data files also provided the details for the specific topics covered in each chapter, such as child care, social supports, working non-standard hours, or the mothers' different employment trajectories. And it was coding and indexing the full NHES sample through EthnoNotes that allowed us throughout the book to summarize the NHES data for topics such as work histories, child care choices, goals, partners, and social supports.

Core Qualitative Analysis of Employment

Our study focuses on the work experiences of these families and the varied contexts and consequences of work in their lives and in their children's lives. The NHES produced a lot of material on work; employment was a central construct guiding both the New Hope program and many aspects of its evaluation. We began this book with a core interest in how employment experiences change over time in the families of the working poor. The NHES data were ideal in capturing such changes because we visited these families fairly often and consistently asked about work at each visit. The ethnographic data and qualitative interviews aimed to capture the dynamic qualities of work: that is, the trajectories of each mother's employment experiences from the beginning to the end of the ethnographic period. The editors of this book considered the best ways to summarize and synthesize these data, and our "field notes and work data camps" emerged from their discussions. These meetings were held at UCLA, included many of the authors of the chapters in this book,[10] and continued thereafter in a "virtual camp" as our teams of authors corresponded through e-mails and phone calls and used our web-based EthnoNotes database. The focus of our collective qualitative data analyses was developing comprehensive analyses of the sample's work experiences during the period of the ethnography.

We first extracted all field-note excerpts with the keywords "job," "employment," "work," "boss," "supervisor," or "career" present anywhere in the excerpts, for all visits. The notes were then organized for each of the forty cases chronologically from the first field-note entry to the last. In most cases, the notes covered a period from the spring and summer of 1998 to the spring and summer of 2001.

Once the data were organized into separate case files, the ten-member analysis team developed a list of fifteen relevant codes for the purpose of indexing the case material. These codes were developed after extensive initial reading and winnowing down of work-related codes to a manageable set that would constitute the core analysis topics. These topics were not chosen in an ad hoc manner. Rather, they were the main themes that emerged from the team's reading of the ethnographic material relating to work and the work-family interface. The themes also engaged the literature in the field that we collectively knew about and shared among ourselves, and they reflected our own readings of what mattered to the parents that made their way into the field notes.

Eleven codes related to employment experiences: job description, wage issues, hours and schedule issues, benefits, work stressors and hassles, positive work experiences, transportation issues, reasons for remaining unemployed or in a bad job, job change, reasons for job change, and employment experiences prior to the ethnography. Two codes captured human capital–related goals and progress toward them; these goals included those related to employment, income, education, and expenditures on children. Another code was for any public assistance use and related experiences with public assistance programs (including New Hope), and a final code was included for any shifts or changes to household organization. The team decided that by limiting the initial set of codes to these fifteen, it would be easier to establish and maintain an acceptable level of inter-rater reliability. Further, these codes captured the major concerns of parents regarding work and family that were relevant to our study.

Since the task of indexing the qualitative data was to be shared by the members of the analysis team, we spent a considerable amount of time developing an acceptable level of inter-rater reliability among the team members. We began with the whole team reading a selection of field-note materials, indexing the material separately, and then discussing the rationale we each used for assigning various codes. Based on these discussions, we developed a set of instructions for each code that was well understood by each member of the team. Then, using the coding scheme with these refined instructions, we did reliability tests by having each member index the same extended excerpt of field-note text chosen for the richness of its content. We used Cohen's kappa as the measure of inter-rater agreement. Agreement was calculated across each possible pair of coders among a team of six, and the final coding process did not start until each pair achieved a minimum kappa of .70 for each of the fifteen codes. (The average kappa across each coder-pair combination was .79.)

Having established an acceptable level of inter-rater reliability, each member of the team indexed entire cases and organized the relevant information into a standardized case-summary format. This format was designed to provide a consistent and efficient summary for each case across all family visits that related to the four relevant domains in the coding scheme—employment experiences, plans and goals, household changes, and public assistance—with an additional section for miscellaneous, yet relevant, secondary information. This team data summary and analysis work ensured that those researching different topics for our book (such as nonstandard hours, work quality, child care, or goals) did so from the same reliable, core qualitative database, coded for key topics. Extensive additional qualitative analyses were then done for each chapter, tailored to that chapter's topic. The authors of each chapter used the full ethnographic sample, not just a few selected cases, so that the results (since the ethnographic sample itself was a random sample from the CFS survey sample) are comparable to the quantitative data sample and fully nested within that larger CFS sample and random-assignment design.

Finally, in several chapters, the authors wanted to get a sense of how the participants understood and expressed these understandings in their own words. Since interviews were not all transcribed verbatim, this task often proved challenging. It was often difficult to be sure whether a paraphrased expression was that of the participant or of the field-worker. To counter this concern, authors attributed an expression to the participant only when one or more verbatim quotations from the participant containing the expression could be identified in the field-note material.

Notes |

ACKNOWLEDGMENTS

1. The members of the Successful Pathways Through Middle Childhood Network included: Jacquelynne Eccles of the University of Michigan, the chair of the network; Phyllis Blumenfeld, also of Michigan; Catherine Cooper of the University of California at Santa Cruz; Greg Duncan of Northwestern University; Cynthia Garcia-Coll of Brown University; Robert Granger of MDRC/the William T. Grant Foundation; Jennifer Greene of the University of Illinois at Urbana-Champaign; Aletha Huston of the University of Texas at Austin; James Johnson of the University of North Carolina at Chapel Hill; John Modell of Brown University; Diane Scott-Jones of Boston College; Deborah Stipek of Stanford University; Barrie Thorne of the University of California at Berkeley; and Heather Weiss of the Harvard Graduate School of Education.

CHAPTER ONE

1. Marc Levine, University of Wisconsin, personal communication, September 9, 2004. The neighborhood described here is one of the two neighborhoods sampled by the New Hope demonstration, from which all the data presented in this book were obtained.
2. "Not in the labor force" means not working or looking for work, in either a civilian or armed forces employment context; Census 2000 data downloaded for zip code 53208 (one of the two New Hope neighborhoods) from factfinder. census.gov, November 14, 2004. This rate was not appreciably different for males and females: it was 33 percent for working-age men and 38 percent for working-age women.
3. This rate was only slightly higher in the state of Wisconsin (U.S. Department of Labor 2000).

357

4. The Miller plant, coincidentally, is in the middle of the North Side neighborhood; that brewery and a Harley-Davidson factory are the only large manufacturing employers in the area. Not coincidentally, the most beautiful street in the neighborhood, with a median profusely planted with flowers, cuts in between the two factories and their guarded parking lots.

5. For extensive histories of the passage of PRWORA, see DeParle (2004) and Weaver (2000).

6. The lack of adjustment in this study for preexisting differences in these groups (a problem best addressed through a randomized experimental design) makes this difference inconclusive, however, as a measure of the *impact* of W-2.

7. The federal poverty line for a family of three with two children was $13,874 in 2000 and $14,269 in 2001.

8. The majority of our New Hope sample were members of single-mother families, in part because the CFS focused on participants in New Hope (or in the control group) who had at least one child between the ages of one and twelve at the study baseline. The working-poor parents eligible for New Hope who were men in this category were too few for us to do the kinds of survey and quantitative analyses that the CFS provides, and too few for inclusion in the New Hope Ethnographic Study (NHES) random sample of 45. However, in the full New Hope sample of 1,357, there were about two hundred men for whom there were administrative and employment records, but not data from the New Hope CFS. For reviews of the (very few) studies of father employment and children's well-being, see Jarrett, Roy, and Burton (2002) and Nelson, Clampet-Lundquist, and Edin (2002). For an MDRC study of low-income fathers, see Johnson, Levine, and Doolittle (1999). For a study of the New Hope ethnographic sample fathers, see Davis and Weisner (2005).

9. However, the relative magnitude of these causal effects is uncertain (see Blank 2002).

10. For a review of the effects of low-wage maternal employment on parenting, see Chase-Lansdale and Pittman (2002).

11. Selection bias has plagued this literature since the early research on parental employment and child well-being (see Hoffman 1961). In this book, we use a variety of methods to control for selection bias in non-experimental analyses. On occasion, we also use the experiment itself to examine effects on work, family life, and child development. (There is no selection bias when comparing the full program and control groups, since they were randomly assigned.)

12. This research extended the early work of Melvin Kohn (1969), who found that fathers in jobs with opportunity for autonomy valued that same quality in their children.

13. That is, schedules that shift from week to week.

14. Rosabeth Kanter (1977) pointed out in her review of the literature that both maternal employment and paternal unemployment were considered social problems in the social sciences until the late 1960s.

15. To put the size of these positive effects in perspective, they are comparable to the effects of increasing observed child care quality by one standard deviation (NICHD Early Child Care Research Network and Duncan 2003). Effect sizes were in the range of .10 to .20 standard deviation differences between experimental- and control–group children in the earnings-supplement programs.

16. Compare with the more recent idea that "nobody who works hard should be poor in America" (see Shipler 2004, ix). Another recent popular account of low-wage jobs and lives is Ehrenreich (2001).

17. The full list of funders of the New Hope evaluation include the John D. and Catherine T. MacArthur Foundation, the Helen Bader Foundation, the William T. Grant Foundation, the National Institute of Child Health and Human Development, the Wisconsin Department of Workforce Development, the U.S. Department of Health and Human Services, and the Annie E. Casey Foundation.

18. Once families were participating in the NHES, attrition was nil, although families were lost at times, then located again.

19. The fieldwork team that visited the New Hope ethnographic sample families from 1998 to 2001 included Conerly Casey, Ellen Chmielewski, Victor Espinosa, Christina Gibson-Davis, Eboni Howard, Katherine Magnuson, Andrea Robles, Jennifer Romich, and Devarati Syam. Lucinda Bernheimer supervised their efforts and participated in data analysis.

CHAPTER TWO

1. This broad work effort is captured by Katherine Newman in her 1999 book *No Shame in My Game: The Working Poor in the Inner City* when she notes that "the nation's working poor continue to seek their salvation in the labor market. That such a commitment persists when the economic rewards are so minimal is testimony to the durability of the work ethic, to the powerful reach of mainstream American culture, which has always placed work at the center of our collective moral existence" (61).

2. Cluster analysis was initially developed as a classification method in biology but has since been used extensively in other sciences and social sciences. It uses algorithms based on distances between the values of the variables to identify subgroups whose patterns of distance are similar to each other and dissimilar from other subgroups. For an introduction to cluster analysis as a data analytic method, see Bergman and Magnusson (1997), Milligan (1996), and Rapkin and Luke (1993). It has been used to identify subgroups of states, based on a variety of policy dimensions (Meyers, Gornick, and Peck 2001); service utilization patterns in the New Hope and New Chance demonstrations (Gibson 2003; Yoshikawa, Rosman, and Hsueh 2001); and welfare dynamics in the National Longitudinal Survey of Youth (NLSY) (Yoshikawa and Seidman 2001).

3. Variables tapping the participants' perceptions of the quality of these jobs were not available for each of their one to six jobs. We therefore discuss job quality in a separate chapter. Attrition across the two years was 20 percent—that is, 80 percent of the original sample was reinterviewed at twenty-four months. Attrition analyses for this sample have shown few differences among those retained and those who were not on baseline characteristics (Bos et al. 1999; Huston et al. 2001).

4. With standard deviations, the average number of jobs was 2.47 (SD 1.37); the average job length was 11.80 months (SD 7.60); average weekly hours were 36.84 (SD 8.08); the average hourly wage was $6.53 (SD $1.48); and the average wage change was $.98 (SD $1.69).

5. These studies of welfare leavers generally do not report data on the average length of jobs or the number of jobs (Loprest 2001; National Academy of Sciences 2001).

6. We used the cluster analysis program SLEIPNER for these analyses (Bergman and El-Khouri 1998). The goal of these analyses was to obtain a solution that minimized within-cluster variance and maximized differences among clusters by assigning each individual to the nearest cluster or multidimensional centroid. As suggested by several cluster analysis methodologists (Milligan 1996; Rapkin and Luke 1993), we took a two-stage approach: first we employed hierarchical cluster analysis, using Ward's algorithm, and then we performed a k-means iterative cluster analysis, based on the centroids obtained in the hierarchical analysis. In addition, we undertook initial identification of outliers in the dataset, using the SLEIPNER program. Outliers were deleted from the analyses (using the criterion of average squared Euclidean distances from all other cases greater than .5).

7. Homogeneity of the clusters was found to be sufficient, according to Bergman and El-Khouri's (1998) criteria, with coefficients below 1.00 for each of the clusters.

8. Six of the women in the ethnographic sample were not assigned to employment clusters, so are not included in the timelines in figures 2.2 to 2.5. Two women (Jackie and Gladys) were part of the "no work" group. Three women (Marisa, Janet, and Christy) were missing data for the cluster analysis variables. Finally, one woman (Lisa) was removed from the final cluster analysis due to being an outlier on multiple cluster variables.

9. Unfortunately, a full job calendar covering the period between the twenty-four- and sixty-month interviews was not obtained from respondents. Therefore, the cluster analysis could not be extended to this time period.

10. We conducted a multinomial logit regression, with the low-wage–part-time group as the reference group; all results reported were significant at the $p < .05$ level. Aside from the five groups obtained from the cluster analysis, there was an additional group of respondents who did not report any work over the two-

year follow-up. We termed this group the "no-work" group and included it in the multinomial regression, so the no-work group was also compared to the low-wage–part-time group. No differences were found.

11. Results are reported in Yoshikawa et al. (2000). We also examined the effects of New Hope on particular two-way combinations of work dynamic variables (for instance, working with wage growth of at least $1.00 and working with wage growth of under $1.00, with the no-work group as the reference group; working with job length of at least twelve months and working with job length under twelve months, again with the no-work group as the reference group). We found no significant effects of New Hope on these two-way combination variables.

CHAPTER THREE

1. The exceptions were the mothers whose employment allowed their children to be with them. For example, Wendy, during the ethnography, began a child care business out of her home that allowed her to supervise her own children at her workplace.

2. The parent report measure of school performance consisted of a single item ("Based on your knowledge of the child's schoolwork, including report cards, how has he or she been doing in school overall?") on a five-point Likert scale from "very good" to "poor." The school performance measure collected from teachers was the ten-item Academic Subscale of the Social Skills Rating System (Gresham and Elliott 1990). For this measure, teachers rated the child's overall school performance in comparison to others in the same classroom in terms of reading and math skills, intellectual functioning, motivation, oral communication, and classroom behavior. Parents and teachers completed the same measures of behavior problems, drawn from the Problem Behavior Scale of the Social Skills Rating System (Gresham and Elliott 1990). Externalizing behaviors were represented by a seven-item scale, and internalizing behaviors by a five-item scale.

3. At each point, we also compared effects for the younger group of children (ages three to eight at the two-year follow-up and ages six to eleven at the five-year follow-up) with the older group (ages eight to thirteen at the two-year follow-up and ages eleven to sixteen at the five-year follow-up). We found few differences. However, our statistical power to detect these differences in associations by age was quite low.

4. All of the parent mediators were assessed at twenty-four months. A two-item scale of parent time pressure was used; mothers were asked how often they felt rushed and how often they had extra time. Responses were recorded on a five-point scale from "never" to "all of the time." Higher scores represented higher levels of pressure. The correlation between the two items was $r = .31$. Depressive

symptoms were measured using the widely used twenty-item CES-D (Center for Epidemiological Studies—Depression scale; Radloff 1977). Parenting stress was measured with five questions about the degree of difficulty parents experienced interacting with and caring for their children (for example, "My child seems to be much harder to care for than most").

5. Measures at baseline that we included in our regressions were: child's sex (coded as 1 = female, 0 = male), child's age (in years), whether the parent had access to a car, whether the parent received AFDC as a child, whether the parent graduated from high school or received a GED, whether the parent currently received AFDC, and whether the parent worked full-time in the prior quarter. Two dummy-coded variables representing black and Hispanic categories were created. Respondent's age was represented by two dummy-coded variables for parents younger than twenty-five and parents between twenty-five and thirty-four years old (with thirty-five or older as the default category). Household structure was represented by three variables: whether the parent lived in a one-adult household, whether three or more children resided in the household, and whether a child younger than two lived in the household. Two dummy-coded variables represented the parent's income at random assignment: whether the parent earned less than $5,000, and whether the parent earned more than $5,000 (with no income as the default category). We also included two control measures at twenty-four months that were unavailable at baseline: maternal depression (the CES–D scale) and a measure of perceived job quality, including items representing opportunities for advancement, adequacy of wage, job security, and benefits. We were not able to utilize fixed-effects models to account for selection bias (for example, to change score models; see NICHD Early Child Care Research Network and Duncan 2003) because the time period covered by our employment dynamics variables—baseline to two years—did not overlap with the time period across which we could have calculated change in children's outcomes (two to five years). However, as indicated later in the chapter, we did run models with lagged dependent variables (controlling for two-year child outcomes when predicting five-year child outcomes from cluster group membership).

6. This approach can account for selection factors that are correlated in a time-invariant way with a particular child's developmental outcome or a particular parent outcome, measured across two or more points in time. It does not account for selection factors whose relationship to the developmental outcomes changes between those points. It also does not account for selection factors that might influence both the predictor (in this case, longitudinal work patterns) and the parent or child outcome (see Blau 1999). Our method represents a residualized-change analysis; a change-score analysis was not possible owing to the lack of child development data at baseline and the lack of detailed work dynamics data between the two- and five-year follow-up points.

7. These results are drawn in part from Nikulina and Yoshikawa (2004). To reduce collinearity between the variables of wage growth, job stability, and their interaction term (the two variables multiplied together), we centered the wage growth and job stability variables and then calculated their interaction (see Cohen et al. 2003).

8. Significant indirect associations were assessed using methods described in MacKinnon et al. (2002).

CHAPTER FOUR

1. The DOT list of nine-digit codes for over twelve thousand occupations was developed with independent raters in the field. The last three digits indicate complexity, with one digit assigned to each of three complexity domains: data, people, and things.

2. U.S. Department of Labor (1991, appendix A), available at: http://www.oalj.dol.gov/LIBDOT.HTM#definitions.

3. One survey item asked whether the employer sponsored health insurance coverage. There were no additional items, however, asking whether such coverage included children, and if so, whether their children were insured.

4. Rubin (1994, 257, n. 8) comments on the differential impact of being laid off on men's and women's sense of self and cites another of her books in which she elaborates on the topic, *Just Friends: The Role of Friendship in Our Lives* (1985).

5. This effect was found at several sites of the National Evaluation of Welfare-to-Work Strategies and the Minnesota Family Investment Program (Gennetian and Miller 2000; Hamilton et al. 2001). Across recent experimental evaluations of welfare-to-work policies, for example, counter to many researchers' expectations, decreases in reports of domestic abuse appear to be more frequent than increases (Smolensky and Gootman 2003).

6. As the previous chapters indicated, detailed dynamic data on each job's hours, wages, and length were not available between the twenty-four- and sixty-month assessments.

7. Because of the lack of New Hope impacts on indicators of job quality (Huston et al. 2001), we were unable to use the experiment to leverage exogenous variation in job quality. Instead, we use a variation on fixed-effects approaches, using change scores. All of our predictors (the job quality characteristics) were measured at sixty months. (No parallel measures of job quality were available from the twenty-four-month assessment.) The change-score approach (also called difference or gain scores) involves, in our case, subtracting the initial twenty-four-month scores on each of our parent and child well-being outcomes from the sixty-month scores for the parallel measure. This creates one "change-score" variable for assessing changes in outcomes. This approach may

be preferable to using sixty-month scores alone because it can address unobserved sources of bias that are highly correlated with the sixty-month outcomes and do not change between twenty-four and sixty months. This approach is based on the assumption that unobserved variables have similar effects on both early and later outcomes and that errors in assessments at both points of time are random (see Gliner, Morgan, and Harmon 2003; NICHD Early Child Care Research Network and Duncan 2003). In addition, family and maternal baseline characteristics are used as controls. The family baseline characteristics used are single-parent household; three or more children in the household; youngest child is two years old or younger; ever worked full-time; ever received AFDC, general assistance, or Medicaid. The maternal baseline characteristics used are race-ethnicity; access to a car; in an AFDC household as a child; earnings in the past twelve months between $1 and $4,999; earnings in the past twelve months $5,000 or greater. Experimental status (assignment to New Hope or control conditions) was also included as a covariate.

8.   Overall, we tested forty-four associations between job quality variables and indicators of parent well-being and child outcomes. Of those forty-four, we would expect two findings to be significant at the .05 level by chance. We found three associations at the .05 level, and three associations at the .10 level—above those we would expect by chance.

9.   The number of benefits was computed by creating a count variable from four yes/no items about benefits in the survey. The survey asked if the job offered: a health plan paid by the employer, paid sick days, paid vacation days, and a pension plan.

10.   See note 2 for more information about the source of occupational complexity scores. Each score was standardized. A factor analysis of the twelve indicators of job quality used in the analyses described in the chapter revealed that complexity having to do with people and data was a factor separate from complexity having to do with things. Thus, a composite variable was created that represented the mean of the standardized values of complexity with people and data. The correlation coefficient of these two variables was $r = .62, p < .001$.

11.   We found that these five constructs, each measured by a single item, loaded in a factor analysis onto a single factor. They were therefore combined into a single, multi-item scale. Cronbach's alpha coefficient of reliability for the scale of five items was .67. Exclusion of any of these items would reduce the magnitude of the coefficient. The five-point response scale ranged from "not true at all of my job" to "always true of my job."

12.   Job stress was estimated as the mean of two items in the survey. On a five-point scale ranging from "not true at all of my job" (1) to "always true of my job" (5), mothers indicated the extent to which in their jobs (a) they felt drained of energy at the end of the day and (b) they often felt angry with people at work. The correlation coefficient between the items was $r = .37, p < .001$.

CHAPTER FIVE

1. The term "second shift" is used to characterize work shifts that start at about 3:00 to 4:00 P.M. and end at about 11:00 P.M. to midnight (Hedges and Sekscenski 1979).

2. The effects of New Hope on work schedules, defined in this way, had not been reported in prior evaluation reports. Teacher ratings of children's school achievement were obtained using two measures collected twenty-four months after random assignment into New Hope. The first was a twelve-item measure of classroom skills, adapted from Wright and Huston's (1995) Classroom Behavior Scale. Sample items included "remains on-task with minimal supervision," "complies with teacher requests," and "moves quickly to next activity." The coefficient alpha was .90. The second was the ten-item Academic Subscale of the Social Skills Rating System (Gresham and Elliott 1990), which rates a child's overall school performance in comparison to others in the same classroom on skills such as reading, math, intellectual functioning, motivation, oral communication, and classroom behavior. The five-point scale ranged from "bottom 10 percent" to "top 10 percent." The correlation between the two measures was .63.

   Parent ratings of children's school achievement were obtained from a single item collected at the twenty-four-month follow-up interview. Parents were asked, "Based on your knowledge of the child's schoolwork, including report cards, how has he or she been doing in school overall?" Responses were recorded on a five-point Likert scale from "poor" to "very good." The correlations of parent-reported school achievement with teacher-reported classroom skills and overall performance were .35 and .44, respectively.

   Teachers and parents rated child behavioral outcomes using two subscales from the Problem Behavior Scale of the Social Skills Rating System (Gresham and Elliott 1990) twenty-four months after random assignment. A six-item externalizing subscale tapped behaviors, such as "is aggressive toward people or objects" and "has temper tantrums." A nine-item internalizing subscale tapped behaviors such as "appears lonely" and "acts sad or depressed." All of these items were answered on a five-point scale from "never" to "all of the time." The internal consistencies for parent-reported subscales ranged from .61 to .81. The internal consistencies for teacher-reported subscales ranged from .78 to .92. Correlations among parent-reported and teacher-reported externalizing and internalizing subscales ranged from .06 to .30.

3. These work schedule definitions parallel those used by Harriet Presser (2003). To assess work schedules, parents completed a self-report time use grid for the seven days prior to the twenty-four-month interview post-random assign-

ment. Mothers were prompted with questions such as, "What times did you work at a job away from home?" This included the time it took them to travel to and from their jobs. Responses were recorded on a time grid. Mothers were also asked, "How long does it usually take you to get to the place where you work? That is, how long does it take you to travel from your front door to the front door of your work one way, including any time you may spend dropping children off along the way?" To adjust mothers' start and end times on the job, the length of their commute was added to the job start times and subtracted from the job end times that were reported on the time grid. A continuous variable of total hours worked in the prior week was created. This measure and whether mothers were not working in the prior week were used as covariates in the analyses.

To assess work on variable shifts, parents were asked, "Do you generally work the same hours every workday or different hours?" A dichotomous variable was created with the response categories "almost always work the same hours" and "usually work the same hours" combined to represent fixed shifts, and the response category "different hours on different days" representing variable shifts.

4. Rounding may prevent percentages from summing to 100.

5. No significant associations of nonstandard or variable work schedules with the employment dynamic clusters presented in chapters 2 and 3 were found.

6. To establish mean differences in school achievement and behavior problems between children whose mothers worked fixed standard, fixed nonstandard, variable standard, and variable nonstandard schedules, we conducted OLS regressions with three dummy variables representing work schedules, covariates for background, family, and human capital characteristics, and total number of work hours, as well as one dummy variable representing no work in the prior week. We also examined the interactions of variable shifts with nonstandard schedules (results not presented). These two methods produced the same pattern of associations between work schedules and child outcomes. We conducted separate analyses for each measure of school achievement and behavioral outcomes. We used the STATA software package to estimate Huber-White standard errors (White 1980) to adjust for non-independence among error terms for siblings.

7. A two-item scale of maternal time pressure was used; at the twenty-four-month follow-up interview, mothers were asked how often they felt rushed and how often they had extra time. Responses were recorded on a five-point scale from "never" to "all of the time." Higher scores represented higher levels of pressure. The correlation between the two items was $r = .31$.

A single item was used to assess the regularity of family mealtime; at the twenty-four-month follow-up interview, mothers were asked how often the family ate dinner at the same time on weekdays. Responses were recorded on a three-point scale from "different times on different weekdays" to "almost always the same."

At the twenty-four-month follow-up interview, maternal stress was assessed by a single item. Mothers were asked how much of the time during the past month they felt stressed. Responses were recorded on a four-point scale ranging from "none of the time" to "almost all of the time." Higher scores represented higher levels of stress.

To establish indirect associations of nonstandard or variable schedules with achievement and behavioral outcomes through maternal time pressure and stress and the regularity of family mealtimes, we employed current non-experimental methods for testing mediation (MacKinnon et al. 2002; Shrout and Bolger 2002). Several conditions for mediation had to be met: (1) work schedules had to be significantly associated with the potential mediator; (2) adjusting for differences in work schedules, the potential mediator had to be significantly associated with the child outcome measure; (3) the association of work schedules with the child outcome had to change substantially as a result of adding the potential mediator to the model. The overall significance of a mediated association was tested by determining whether the product of the association from a parent's work schedule to a mediator and the mediator to an outcome was significantly different from zero (MacKinnon et al. 2002).

8. We selected excerpts with the keywords "job," "employment," "work," "boss," "supervisor," "career," "hour," "shift," and "schedule."

9. In the following sections, we highlight only the benefits and costs of nonstandard or variable work schedules that were mentioned by more than 10 percent of the mothers in the NHES sample.

10. A phenomenon noted by some researchers in the post–welfare reform era (Moffitt et al. 2002).

11. The extent to which mothers felt that nonstandard work schedules eased work-family dilemmas varied with the schedules they worked. Compared to the mothers who worked nonstandard schedules for most of the ethnographic period (standardized residual = 1.4), only 21 percent of the mothers who worked standard schedules for most of the ethnography said that nonstandard work schedules eased work-family dilemmas (standardized residual = –1.2).

12. The term "first shift" refers to work shifts that start at about 7:00 a.m. to 8:00 a.m. and end at about 3:00 p.m. to 4:00 p.m. (Hedges and Sekscenski 1979).

13. Unfortunately, Presser and her colleagues were unable to delve further and determine what parents meant when they cited "better child care arrangements."

14. The term "third shift" refers to work shifts that start at about 11:00 P.M. to midnight and end at about 7:00 A.M. to 8:00 A.M. (Hedges and Sekscenski 1979).

CHAPTER SIX

1. Based on a comparison of the coefficients, standard errors, and odds ratios for perceived workplace discrimination ($b = -.915$, $SE = .246$, $EXP(b) = .40$), having less than a high school education ($b = -.685$, $SE = .196$, $EXP(b) = .504$), and having less than four job skills ($b = -.717$, $SE = .228$, $EXP(b) = -.488$).
2. The topic domain of race and ethnicity was explored by all of the field-workers, and of course work was perhaps the central topic of the ethnography. However, the specific topic of workplace-based discrimination based on race, ethnicity, or gender was not solicited at the level of a topic domain.
3. It was impossible to categorize one woman's experience of sexual discrimination because she did not provide any details about the episode.
4. The New Hope neighborhood boundaries for sampling were defined by particular zip codes in Milwaukee.
5. Of the ethnographic sample of forty available cases, six women were either not working or did not provide enough information for us to be able to identify cluster membership. Therefore, these analyses include only the thirty-four women for whom cluster membership was determined.
6. The stable employment and full-time–wage-growth groups are combined because of the small number of women in the latter group.
7. $(1, N = 34) = 5.812$, $p = .016$. Results of the chi-square analysis suggest that experiences of discrimination were related to membership in the low-wage–part-time or rapid cycler group when compared to the other three employment clusters. The number of sample members in the low-wage–part-time and rapid cycler groups who experienced discrimination was higher than expected, while the number of those who did not experience discrimination was lower than expected (standardized residuals = 1.4 and –1.3, respectively). Conversely, the number of sample members in the full-time–wage-growth, stable employment, and low-wage–full-time groups who experienced discrimination was lower than expected, while the number who did not experience discrimination was higher than expected (standardized residuals = –1.0 and 1.0, respectively).

CHAPTER SEVEN

1. These controls include baseline measures for age, high school diploma or better, race-ethnicity, single-adult household with children, household with three or more children, household with youngest child age two years or younger, participants who had ever worked full-time at baseline, household receiving government assistance, earnings, access to a car, having grown up in an AFDC household, and New Hope experimental condition.
2. When educational goals are entered into the model without controlling for the other goals, it is associated with higher hourly wages ($\beta = .11$, $p < .05$).

CHAPTER EIGHT

1. Multilevel modeling procedures (PROCMIXED in SAS) were used to estimate initial levels (quarter one) and rates of change in income across the study period for each adult in the New Hope sample. Calculations were based on twenty quarters of administrative data from the state of Wisconsin on earnings, EITC receipt, welfare (AFDC/TANF), food stamps amounts, and, for participants in the New Hope program group, New Hope income supplements for the first twelve quarters. Individual estimates were derived for total income and each income source separately. Separate estimates were calculated across all five years of the study, for years one and two only, and for years three to five only. Because we were less interested in experimental impacts, we collapsed across the New Hope treatment and control groups in these analyses. We did, however, control for the influence of the experimental treatment effect by including group assignment as a covariate in all analyses.

2. For more details on the changes in welfare policy in Milwaukee during these years, see chapter 1, DeParle (2004), and Pawasarat (2000).

3. Measures at baseline that we included in our regressions were: whether the parent had access to a car; whether the parent received AFDC as a child; whether the parent had graduated from high school or received a GED; whether the parent currently received AFDC; and whether the parent had worked full-time in the prior quarter. Two dummy-coded variables representing black and Hispanic categories were created. Household structure was represented by two variables: whether three or more children resided in the household, and whether a child younger than two lived in the household. Two dummy-coded variables represented the parent's income at random assignment: whether the parent earned less than $5,000, and whether the parent earned more than $5,000 (with no income as the default category). We also included parent's total income at quarter one as a control for initial income, and whether the family was assigned to the New Hope experimental group or the control group.

4. See note 16 for analysis details.

5. See note 17 for analysis details.

6. Our findings are consistent with those observed by Scott et al. (2004).

7. Some of our own observations confirmed that families had little *time* to engage in the "extras." For instance, we saw that a large park located in one of the North Side neighborhoods where many of the study families lived was relatively empty because residents had little time for "extra" activities such as biking and picnicking with family members.

8. We used path analysis instead of creating latent composites because of our explicit interest in replicating findings from the ethnographic data regarding the distinct relations between the indicators of economic resources, expenditure categories, and maternal psychological well-being. All path analysis

models were estimated with Amos 4.0 (Arbuckle and Wothke 1999). We used the comparative fit index (CFI) and the root mean square error of approximation (RMSEA) goodness-of-fit indices to assess overall model fit. The CFI ranges from zero to one, with zero indicating the absence of model fit and one indicating perfect model fit. RMSEA values of less than .05 are generally accepted as indicators of good model fit in the social sciences; those between .05 and .08 are indicative of an adequate model fit.

9. To more formally examine the indirect (mediated) effects, we restricted the sample to those cases (N = 328 and 222 for models predicting children's academic and social behavioral outcomes, respectively) that had complete data in order to bootstrap significance tests for the total and indirect effects.

10. We included three separate indicators of children's academic performance: scores on a standardized test of achievement, and teacher and parent reports of overall school performance. At the five-year follow-up, children were administered four subtests of the Woodcock-Johnson Tests of Achievement: the Letter-Word and Comprehension subtests, which index reading ability, and the Applied Problems and Calculations subtests, which index math ability. For the current analysis, we used a total score based on the sum of the four subtests. Teachers completed the Academic Subscale of the Social Skills Rating System (SSRS) (Gresham and Elliott 1990). On this ten-item measure, the teacher rates, on a five-point scale (1 = "lowest 10 percent of class," and 5 = "highest 10 percent of class"), the child's academic performance in comparison to others in the same classroom. Responses were summed and averaged to create a total score ($\alpha = .94$). Parents' ratings on a five-point scale ("not at all well" to "very well") of their child's current school performance across six subject matter areas (reading, oral language, written language, math, social studies, and science) were summed and averaged ($\alpha = .87$) and represented the final measure of academic achievement included in the study.

11. Assessment of children's social behavior was based on three measures. Teachers completed the Problem Behavior Scale of the SSRS (Gresham and Elliott 1990). The total score comprises two scales: *externalizing* problems and *internalizing* problems, which were included as separate indicators of social behavior in the current analysis. Externalizing problems are defined as aggression, assertiveness, and lack of behavior control (for example, "is aggressive toward people or objects" or "has temper tantrums"). Internalizing problems indicate social withdrawal and excessive fearfulness (for example, "appears lonely" or "acts sad or depressed"). Each subscale consists of six items answered on a five-point response scale (1 = "never," and 5 = "all of the time"). Internal consistencies ranged from .78 to .92. In addition, we included children's responses to fifteen items about the frequency with which they had participated in the past year in *delinquent* behavior, including fighting, stealing, vandalism, and drug use (adapted from LeBlanc and Tremblay 1988). Children

selected their response based on a scale of 1 ("never") to 5 ("five or more times") (α = .66). Because of the nature of the questions on the delinquency measure, it was only asked of children ages nine and older.

12. Baseline measures included in our path analyses included whether the parent: had access to a car, received AFDC as a child, graduated from high school or received a GED, currently received AFDC, and had worked full-time in the prior quarter. Two dummy-coded variables representing black and Hispanic categories were created. Household structure was represented by two variables: whether three or more children resided in the household, and whether a child younger than two lived in the household. We also included a dummy variable indicating whether the family was assigned to the New Hope experimental group or the control group. Child gender was accounted for by a dummy variable (0 = boy, 1 = girl). In addition to baseline covariates, we controlled for women's reports of depressive symptoms and their budgeting strategies, both of which were assessed during the five-year follow-up survey. Depressive symptoms were measured using the twenty-item CES-D (Center for Epidemiological Studies—Depression scale; Radloff 1977). The internal consistency of the items was adequate (α = .82). Women's budgetary strategies were based on their responses to several items having to do with whether or not they budgeted their expenses, had a savings and/or checking account, set aside cash for emergencies, or had a credit card. Responses were summed to create a total score. Additional covariates, such as maternal age and the presence of young children in the household, were trimmed from the final model because they were unrelated to a majority of the study variables and because of concerns regarding sample size and power.

13. At the five-year follow-up, participants were asked to indicate whether they currently owned their home (yes/no) and a car, truck, or other vehicle (yes/no). For our purposes, we summed responses across these two items.

14. The material hardship index was the sum of six questions asking whether the family had been without utilities, medical care, housing, or other necessities because of a lack of financial resources (Mayer and Jencks 1989).

15. Participants rated their satisfaction with their "overall standard of living, such as food, housing, medical care, furniture, clothing, recreation, and things like that" on a five-point scale ranging from "very unhappy" to "very happy." They also rated their satisfaction with their current housing, based on a four-point scale (1 = "very unhappy with housing," and 4 = "very happy"). Participants' financial worry was assessed through five questions about how much they worried about paying bills and about lacking money for important needs (such as food and housing). Participants responded on a five-point scale ranging from "not at all worried" to "worried a great deal." Responses to individual items were summed and averaged to create a total score (α = .90).

16.   We include a measure labeled "effective child management" as our indicator of parenting behavior. The measure is a composite of four variables: parents' control, frequency of discipline, parenting stress, and parents' confidence in their ability to prevent their children from getting into trouble. Parents' lack of control was measured on a five-item scale describing the frequency with which the child ignored or failed to obey the parent (for instance, how often the child ignored the parent's threat of punishment) (Statistics Canada 1995). The frequency of discipline was measured with six items assessing the frequency, in the past week, with which parents had punished the child by grounding, taking away privileges, spanking, or threats (Statistics Canada 1995). Parenting stress was measured with five questions about the degree of difficulty parents experienced interacting with and caring for their children (for example, "My child seems to be much harder to care for than most"). Confidence in preventing harm was assessed with a single item from the parent interview: "How confident are you that you will be able to prevent your child from getting into trouble?" For the composite variable, all scores were arranged so that more effective management was the high end of the scale. We elected to use the composite over the individual variables because it was more parsimonious and reliable than any of the individual scales composing it. The composite has also been used in previous analyses with this sample (for a complete reference, see Huston, Mistry, et al. 2002, n. 12) and has demonstrated both concurrent as well as predictive validity.

17.   The relationship between financial worry and parenting behavior was in the same direction for both models (see figures 8.2 and 8.3) but reached statistical significance for only the child academic outcomes model. The lack of statistical association observed for the model predicting children's behavioral outcomes is probably a function of the reduced sample size (222, versus 328 for the model predicting academic outcomes). The sample size was reduced by the inclusion of the measure of child reports of delinquent behaviors, which was assessed only for the older children in the sample (age nine and older).

18.   No new analyses were necessary for these results. The coefficients were estimated as part of the path analyses described earlier. The software program we used, Amos 4.0, is capable of calculating the significance of total and indirect effects in addition to those included in the model specification, but it requires complete data to do so. Listwise deletion of cases with any missing data across the set of analysis variables left us with a final sample size of 328 children for the academic outcomes model and 222 children for the model predicting social behavioral outcomes. Tests of the significance of total and indirect (mediated) effects were bootstrapped based on the bias-corrected percentile confidence interval with 1,000 resamples conducted on the cases with complete data.

19. Standardized indirect effects estimates for income slope: Woodcock-Johnson Test of Achievement: $\beta = .001$, $p < .10$; teachers' ratings of school performance: $\beta = .002$, $p < .10$; and parents' ratings of school performance: $\beta = .002$, $p < .10$.
20. Standardized indirect effects estimates for financial worry: Woodcock-Johnson Test of Achievement: $\beta = -.02$, $p < .01$; teachers' ratings of school performance: $\beta = -.037$, $p < .01$; and parents' ratings of school performance: $\beta = -.053$, $p < .01$.
21. Standardized indirect effects estimates for income slope: youth self-reports of delinquent behaviors: $\beta = -.002$, $p < .05$; teachers' ratings of internalizing problems: $\beta = -.002$, $p < .05$; and teachers' ratings of externalizing problems: $\beta = -.003$, $p < .05$.
22. See Romich and Weisner (2001) for more in-depth discussion of how New Hope families viewed and spent the EITC.

CHAPTER NINE

1. At baseline, 406 women reported that they had never been married. Of those women, only 21 reported getting married between baseline and year two. When missing data are taken into account, 263 sample members are included in the analyses.
2. Analyses were conducted, using logistic regression, to predict marriage at year five from wage growth (in dollars) and job stability (average length of job, in months). The wage-growth statistics are as follows: $b = .11$; $SE = .07$; odds ratio $= 1.12$; 95 percent $CI = 0.98–1.27$; $p < .10$.
3. The demographic characteristics, measured at baseline, were race-ethnicity (dummy variables for black and Latino); children and one adult in the home; more than two children; youngest child younger than age two; working full-time; receiving government aid; had a high school diploma; had a car; on AFDC as a child; earnings in the prior year. The job characteristics, measured over years one and two, were job quality, average hours per week, and average hourly wage. The focal child characteristics were age, gender, externalizing behavior problems (measured at year two), and internalizing behavior problems (measured at year two). Maternal mental health variables, measured at year two, were self-esteem, mastery, ability to meet goals, ability to generate different pathways to meet goals, depressive symptoms, and parenting stress.

    Although the significance of the relationship is altered after all covariates are added, the estimates are very close to the estimates in the first model ($b = .10$; $SE = .07$; odds ratio $= 1.10$; 95 percent $CI = 0.96–1.27$; $p = .17$). The change in the p-value is probably due to reductions in power after all covariates are included in the model rather then a change in the relationship between wage growth and marriage.

4. For the New Hope impact on wage growth among never-married mothers, the statistics are as follows: $b = .45$; $SE = .26$; $\beta = .10$; $p < .10$. For the New Hope impact on total income among never-married mothers, the statistics are as follows: $b = 548.27$; $SE = 270.58$; $\beta = .10$; $p < .05$. These analyses controlled for a full set of baseline covariates and a dummy variable representing work/no work (with "no work" coded as 1) over the two-year follow-up.

5. The means presented here are adjusted for baseline demographic characteristics (see note 3 for the specific baseline variables used as controls).

6. Analyses were conducted, using logistic regression, to predict marriage at year five from the New Hope program group dummy and the baseline demographic characteristics (see note 3 for the specific baseline variables used as controls). The New Hope impact statistics are as follows: $b = .71$; $SE = .32$; odds ratio $= 2.04$; 95 percent $CI = 1.09$–3.79; $p < .05$. For more details regarding this impact, see Gassman-Pines and Yoshikawa (2006).

7. For the relationship between material hardship and marriage at year five, the statistics are as follows: $b = -0.33$; $SE = 0.17$; odds ratio $= 0.72$; 95 percent $CI = 0.52$–0.99; $p < .05$.

8. The analyses examining associations between entry into marriage and children's five-year outcomes adjust for child outcomes at year two, child gender, child age, and all of the covariates used in the other analyses described in this chapter (see note 3 for a complete list).

   Another way of examining whether changes in marital status made a difference for child outcomes is to examine the New Hope program impacts on child outcomes for the children of never-married mothers. Because New Hope increased marriage among this group, if impacts on child outcomes are also found, that provides additional evidence that marriage and children's outcomes may be related. However, this method does not provide causal links between entry into marriage and child outcomes. Among all children of never-married mothers, New Hope significantly decreased sad and withdrawn behavior problems, as reported by teachers at the five-year follow-up ($b = -.20$; $SE = .10$; $\beta = -.16$; $p < .05$). This decrease was especially pronounced among the boys ($b = -.39$; $SE = .14$; $\beta = -.30$; $p < .01$). Among boys of never-married mothers, New Hope also increased five-year teacher-reported school performance ($b = .38$; $SE = .22$; $\beta = .18$; $p < .10$).

9. For the association between entry into marriage and teacher-reported internalizing behavior problems, the statistics are as follows: $b = -.003$; $SE = .002$; $\beta = -.17$; $p = .05$.

10. For the association between entry into marriage and parent-reported externalizing behavior problems, the statistics are as follows: $b = -.002$; $SE = .001$; $\beta = -.10$; $p < .10$.

11. Coding occurred in two phases. In the first phase, we noted each time a participant described a positive or negative aspect of one of her relationships. From that phase, we developed a list of all the positive and negative aspects mentioned. In

the second phase, for each relationship described by a participant, we coded the presence or absence of each aspect of relationships on the list. The aspects of relationships described in this paragraph were those mentioned spontaneously by participants and compiled in phase one. After the second phase was complete, we were able to apply overall codes of positive, negative, or mixed.

12. This rate, though high, may be a conservative estimate because reports of abuse were provided spontaneously by participants rather than in response to direct questioning by field-workers, and some of the sample members may have denied or underreported incidents of abuse as a consequence of the shame and fear that many victims of abuse feel.

The principal types of abuse described by the women in our sample were emotional abuse, physical abuse, and, in some cases, both emotional and physical abuse. Only one woman reported that she had been sexually abused by her partner.

13. The General Accounting Office (1998) reviewed and summarized estimates of the prevalence of domestic violence in the welfare population. They found that rates of lifetime prevalence, or ever experiencing domestic violence, ranged in different studies from 55 percent to 65 percent.

14. William Julius Wilson posits that lower rates of marriage among African Americans are due to a lack of "marriageable men." That is, among African-American males, rates of employment are low and rates of imprisonment are high. Thus, the potential pool of partners for African-American women is smaller than for other racial-ethnic groups. Based on this theory, if women were exposed to a different pool of partners or if the characteristics of the partners changed, they would become more likely to marry. For more details, see Wilson (1987) and Wilson and Neckerman (1986). Standard economic theory (Becker 1981) would also predict that changes in the composition and characteristics of the pool of partners would be related to changes in marriage rates.

15. Many developmental theorists—beginning with Sigmund Freud and Erik Erikson—have described the formation of intimate relationships as one of the key stages of adult development. More modern theorists posit that early adulthood is a time when individuals are trying out different relationships as they seek a life partner. For all of these theorists, as women age and engage in different relationships over time, they acquire a better sense of the type of person they want to have as a life partner. For more details, see Erikson (1950), Bee and Boyd (2002), and Schaie and Willis (2002).

16. There may be other reasons wage growth and entry into marriage are related. For example, it may be that those who experience higher wage growth perceive the quality of eligible men differently than those who experience less wage growth. Perhaps increased wage growth facilitates interactions with different men, changing women's perceptions of the types of men who are available for romantic relationships. Or it could be that wage growth is related to goal-setting. Having a stable job that included wage growth was a goal of most of

the ethnographic sample members. Achieving this goal may have made them feel successful and confident in their ability to meet goals. In turn, they might have set goals in other areas of their lives, including relationships. However, the field notes do not contain much information about the sample members' perceptions of the men who were available or their relationship goals, so we cannot explore these alternative hypotheses.

17. Results of a chi-square analysis support the notion that wage growth was related to improvements in relationship quality over time. The number of sample members in the high-wage-growth group who experienced improvements in relationship quality was higher than expected, while the number who experienced declines in quality was lower than expected (standardized residuals = .8 and −.9, respectively). For the no-wage-growth group, the opposite pattern was found: the number of sample members in this group who experienced improvements in relationship quality was lower than expected, while the number who experienced declines in quality was higher than expected (standardized residuals = −1.0 and .9, respectively).

18. The results of a chi-square analysis indicate that among those in the high-wage-growth group, the number of individuals in positive relationships was higher than expected and the number in negative relationships was lower than expected (standardized residuals = .5 and −.5, respectively). The opposite pattern was found for the no-wage-growth group: the number of individuals in positive relationships was lower than expected, while the number in negative relationships was higher than expected (standardized residuals = −1.0 and .6, respectively).

19. Results of a chi-square analysis provide support for the notion that members of the New Hope and control groups differed in the quality of their current relationships. This is especially true for negative quality: fewer New Hope group members than expected were in negative relationships, while more control group members than expected were in negative relationships (standardized residuals = −1.1 and 1.0, respectively).

CHAPTER TEN

1. For the full-time–wage-growth group: odds ratio = .41, SE = .44, p < .05. For the low-wage–full-time group: odds ratio = .41, SE = .34, p < .01.

2. Odds ratio = .18, SE = .41, p < .001.

3. Odds ratio = .59, SE = .41, not significant. For the entire model, $X^2(19) = 83.66$, p < .001, −2 log likelihood = 442.16.

4. Odds ratio = .24, SE = .42, p < .001. For the entire model, $X^2(19) = 67.37$, p < .001, −2 log likelihood = 450.42.

5. We did not find that child care beliefs differed strongly between ethnic groups in our sample, and so we have focused on the employment cluster and work influences.

6. Claudia Strauss (1992) describes the breadwinner model in depth for a sample in Providence, Rhode Island.

7. Some of these parents felt that they had to sacrifice work and family income to care for children. Several of these parents had an alternative source of income, such as SSI, working at home, caring for other children informally at their home, working fewer hours during the week, using support from Wisconsin Works, or working in some aspect of the informal economy.

8. Our findings are very similar in this regard to those reported in Holloway et al. (1997).

9. After Javier was imprisoned later that year, Katrina ended her relationship with him and placed her children back in a child care center.

10. This finding is influenced in part by the way the questions in the twenty-four-month survey were asked. The women in the stable employment group were the least likely to have changed jobs during the time preceding the two-year survey, and they were also not likely to have either quit or failed to start a job for any reason, including child care problems. So the finding is a blend of work and child care stability for this group, versus less of both for the rapid cyclers.

CHAPTER ELEVEN

1. The sample size for this analysis is 486. Survey responses from the New Hope sample at sixty months indicated that 88 percent (427) of the mothers responded that it was "sometimes true" to "always true" that they could count on their children for support, 83 percent (403) said that they could rely on their family, and 77 percent (376) of the mothers responded that they could count on friends.

2. The sample size for this analysis is 486. Sixty-six percent (322) of the sample said that it was "sometimes true" to "always true" that they could count on help from their current spouse or partner. Neighbors were a source of reliable support for only 37 percent (182) of the mothers in the survey.

3. The sample size for this ethnographic analysis was 40. One case was missing data about family support, and three cases were missing data about male support. Eighty-eight percent (35) of the mothers in the ethnographic sample described receiving support from family members. Sixty-three percent (25) described receiving support from male sources. Fifty-eight percent of the mothers in the survey sample said that they relied on their children some to most of the time for support. Only eight mothers in the ethnographic study said that their ex-partner, typically the father of their children, provided support.

4. The design of the ethnography, which focused most intensively on the family, children, men, and work in the daily routine of mothers, may have biased field-workers from consistently gathering data on the role of friends as supports. However, friends certainly were important and mentioned by many

parents, and we saw them often in the homes, helping with transportation and child care and filling other roles.

5.   In fact, recent research by Niall Bolger, Adam Zuckerman, and Ronald Kessler (2000) finds that the most helpful support is often "invisible" support, or support given in dyads that the provider but not the recipient reports as having occurred.

6.   The mean level of the influences of support by close people reported by the full survey sample was 3.1 (SD = .82). The social support scale is based on a five-point Likert scale ranging from "not true at all" (1) to "always true" (5) (alpha = .56). The scale comprises eight items like "There are adults I am close to who: support me emotionally; take more from me than they give; would help me out financially in a pinch; cause me worry and strain; show their trust and confidence in me." Negative items are reverse-coded so that a higher score represents higher, more positive support.

7.   Social support scores greater than 3.67. The sample size for this analysis is 490.

8.   The ethnographic data were coded into mutually exclusive categories, and some cases were missing data on social support resources (see note 3). The initial reliability of the codes was checked with the field-workers, who were asked to review the coding summaries of their cases and the supporting notes to determine whether the coded schema fit, based on their perspective and in-depth knowledge of the participant. Discrepancies in coding were discussed until agreement was obtained.

9.   Unfortunately, measures of social support quality were not available in the twenty-four-month CFS survey.

10.   See note 6.

11.   This social support scale is based on a five-point Likert scale ranging from "not true at all" (1) to "always true" (5). The scale comprises six items that list people (children, current spouse, former spouse, family members, neighbors, and friends) the respondent could "count on" if "I should find myself in a jam and needed help."

12.   For this analysis, an OLS multiple regression was run, with social support availability as the dependent variable. The six-item social support availability measure (see note 11) was drawn from the five-year survey. Baseline control variables included: experimental status; maternal age less than twenty-five years; maternal age between twenty-five and thirty-four years; race-ethnicity; single-parent household; three or more children in the household; youngest child age two years or younger; ever worked full-time; zero earnings in the past twelve months; received AFDC, general assistance, or Medicaid; in an AFDC household as a child; earnings in the past year between $1 and $4,999; currently employed; two or more moves in the past two years. The work pathway clusters were entered as dummy variables, with the low-wage–part-time group as the reference group.

CHAPTER TWELVE

1. Other state programs during the years of the study included job access loans, the Children's Services Network, transportation assistance, Kinship Care, SSI (supplemental security income), child support, and emergency assistance. This analysis focuses on the largest W-2 and state services in terms of funding and take-up and the services discussed most often by the study participants. We have gathered information from the Wisconsin Department of Workforce Development website: http://www.dwd.state.wi.us/; see also Seefeldt et al. (1999).

2. For a complete history of this period of welfare policy change in Wisconsin and the United States as a whole, see DeParle (2004).

3. The monthly cash benefit amount was based on family size and counted the other income the family received against the family allowance.

4. Nonfinancial eligibility requirements included: being a parent or caretaker with children who had been deprived of the support of one or both of their parents owing to death, divorce, separation, or continued absence; American citizenship or legal alien status; cooperation with child support regulations; Wisconsin residency; and provision of Social Security numbers. Financial eligibility requirements included: family income at or below 185 percent of the AFDC Assistance Standard of Need (based on family size); family assets not exceeding $1,000, excluding $1,500 vehicle equity and homestead property.

5. In the Pay for Performance program, for each missed hour of required JOBS participation, a penalty equal to the federal hourly minimum wage was imposed, first on AFDC benefits and then on food stamp benefits. Recipients who participated in JOBS for less than 25 percent of the scheduled hours received the full penalty, which reduced the AFDC grant for the next month to $0 and the food stamp benefit to the federal minimum of $10. Subsequent participation in JOBS restored benefits for future months. In the spring of 1997, two modifications to the Pay for Performance program were made to ease the transition to the full W-2 program. First, food stamps for Pay for Performance recipients who failed to participate in job training, work, and education-related activities were no longer reduced. Second, recipients received credit for each hour of participation, even if they completed less than 25 percent of the requirement. Exempted from the Pay for Performance program were: those age sixteen or younger and those age sixty or older; adult caretakers receiving supplemental security income (SSI); those required to participate in Learnfare; caretakers of a child under the age of one; those incapacitated for more than thirty days; those needed at home to care for a disabled family member; full-time Volunteers in Service to America (VISTA) volunteer; and non-legally responsible relatives (NLRRs) not included in the AFDC assistance group.

6. Counties that did not adequately reduce their caseloads were opened up to competition for administration by public and private organizations.

7. The state contracted with five private agencies to administer W-2 in Milwaukee County: region 1—YW Works; region 2—United Migrant Opportunity Services, Inc.; region 3—Opportunities Industrialization Center of Greater Milwaukee, Inc.; region 4—Employment Solutions, Inc.; region 5—Employment Solutions, Inc.; region 6—Maximus, Inc. YW Works and Maximus were for-profit corporations; the others were nonprofit.

8. Eligibility requirements were: household income at or below 115 percent of the federal poverty line; resident of the state of Wisconsin for at least sixty consecutive days before applying for W-2; could not have refused a job within the last 180 days; custodial parent with children eighteen and under; asset limitation (up to $2,500, excluding vehicles worth up to $10,000, and one home in which householders reside).

9. We employed a staged coding technique to analyze the ethnographic material. In the first stage, ethnographies were read for general themes and codes were developed. In the second stage, dichotomous codes were assigned to each case to represent the participant's employment trajectory. There was no overlap in the cases assigned to stable employment, upward mobility, or instability. For a minority of cases, a supplemental jobs code was assigned to women with stable employment and upward mobility codes.

10. Researchers have focused on three patterns of employment: job stability, job mobility, and job instability. "Job stability" is defined differently across studies, but it is most often considered employment in the same position with the same employer for one year or more. The term "job mobility" is used to describe job-to-job transitions in which the period of unemployment between jobs is less than one month. Job mobility can occur within the same employer or across different employers and can take the form of upward mobility (moving to a position of greater authority), lateral mobility (moving to a different position of the same authority), or downward mobility (moving to a position of less authority). The third kind of job change, "job instability," or exiting employment, is either a voluntary exit or "quit" or an involuntary exit due to a layoff; job instability is differentiated from job mobility by long periods of non-employment or unemployment.

   To understand how work support services were related to changes in employment among our sample of low-income mothers, some of the definitions of job changes in the existing literature need to be expanded or modified. Models of job mobility typically assume an educated workforce with the ability to choose between jobs on the basis of benefits. However, the labor market for less-educated and lower-skilled workers now consists of many low-end service or factory jobs without benefits or opportunities for advancement. In light of these concerns, we used the rich data in the ethnographic data to determine the kinds of transitions experienced by these low-income women, expanding or modifying existing definitions of job transitions where necessary.

11. An additional four women (10 percent of the available NHES) experienced stable employment throughout the ethnography; however, these four did not experience wage growth or job advancement.

12. Twelve out of twenty women in the New Hope group experienced stable employment with wage growth and advancement, upward mobility, or supplemental jobs. Eleven out of twenty women in the control group had these employment trajectories. Six of the twelve in the New Hope group (50 percent) used New Hope services in their transitions. However, of the eleven women in the control group, only two (18 percent) used W-2 services in their transitions.

13. The policy assumed that welfare recipients were not in fact already working. However, by the mid-1990s many studies, such as those by Mary Jo Bane and David Ellwood (1994) and Rebecca Blank (1994), had shown that over 50 percent of welfare recipients in national studies were in fact working. A local study conducted in Milwaukee had similar results (Pawasarat and Quinn 1995).

14. In the New Hope group, four women who had severe personal barriers to employment used services in a job transition. For three of them, the use of services resulted in job instability rather than upward mobility or stable employment. In the control group, five women who had severe personal barriers to employment used services in a job transition. For four of them, the use of services also resulted in job instability.

15. We used multiple regression to examine the relationship between service use and employment characteristics over the full five-year follow-up. This analysis was intended to extend the ethnographic analysis and examine associations between service use and the longer-term employment outcomes hypothesized to be representative of successful job transitions. In these models, service use over the first two years of the study is used to predict employment characteristics over the last three years of the study. Because New Hope services were available only to participants randomly assigned to the New Hope group, the analysis of New Hope services was conducted only on the 214 participants in the New Hope group. Both New Hope participants and control group participants were eligible for W-2 and other state services. Thus, analyses of these services included all 442 participants in both groups in examining the relationship between service use and employment outcomes, adjusting for group membership. The New Hope work support service measures included: number of weeks spent in job club or job search activities; number of months employed through a CSJ; number of quarters received earnings supplement; any use of New Hope child care subsidies; receipt of health care subsidy; any receipt of New Hope advice or support; and any receipt of New Hope help in finding a full-time job. The W-2 work support services included: number of weeks in job club or job search activities; ever in the JOBS program; number of months in a job placement; any use of W-2 child care subsidies; and any receipt of advice or support from W-2 staff. All service variables were measured over the first

two years of the study. Employment outcomes were selected to represent positive outcomes of successful job transitions. They included: number of quarters employed over the last three years of the study; wage growth over the last three years of the study; a measure of job quality at five years; and self-employment at five years. To help correct for the possibility that some of the reasons people choose to take part in services might be related to their employment outcomes, all analyses adjust for a host of individual characteristics, such as background demographic information, levels of human capital, employment characteristics over the first two years of the study, and maternal and child well-being.

16. In the first stage, an instrument (along with covariates) is used to isolate variance in the independent variable (in our case, service use) that is unrelated to the dependent variables (work outcomes). The coefficient estimates from the first-stage equation are then used to derive a predicted value for the independent variable. In the second-stage equation, the predicted independent variable replaces the actual independent variable (the same first-stage covariates are also included in the model), and the standard errors are corrected to allow statistical inferences to be made about the coefficient for the predicted independent variable.

17. The difficulty in implementing the IV estimation strategy is finding an appropriate variable to use as the instrument. The analysis must meet several assumptions (Angrist et al. 1996; Gennetian et al. 2005). First, the instrument must be truly exogenous—that is, other variables in the model should not predict it. Second, the effect of the instrument on any one participant must not be influenced by the effect of the instrument on any other participant. Third, the instrument must predict the independent variable (in our case, service use). Fourth, the only way for the instrument to affect the dependent variables (in our case, parents' economic and psychological outcomes) must be through the independent variable (service use). This criterion is often referred to as the exclusion restriction. Fifth, the coefficients for the instrument and the independent variable must be in the same direction for each outcome. The random-assignment variable meets these criteria. Since assignment was random, it is truly unrelated to all other family characteristics, and we would not expect the assignment of any one participant to be affected by the assignment of another. In addition, random assignment to the New Hope group does strongly and significantly predict service use, and the services included in the analysis effectively represent the New Hope program components, making service use the only way for assignment to New Hope to affect outcomes. Finally, for each outcome of interest, the assignment to New Hope and service use coefficients were in the same direction. For these reasons, the variable of service use is particularly well suited to an IV approach in the New Hope data. (Other characteristics of work that we have discussed in this book are not as well suited, primarily because analyses using them would violate the exclusion restriction to a much greater degree.)

18. In addition, because we have only one instrumental variable (assignment to experimental condition) available to us in the dataset, we do not have the ability to instrument multiple indicators of different types of service use.

19. These were all obtained from administrative data.

20. Covariates in multiple regression and IV estimation analyses were as follows: dummy variables for black and Hispanic; single-parent household; three or more children in the household; youngest child age two or younger; ever worked full-time; currently receiving AFDC, general assistance, food stamps, or Medicaid; had a high school diploma; had access to a car; in an AFDC household as a child; earnings in past year from $1 to $4,999; earnings in past year $5,000 or higher; focal child gender; age of child at two-year follow-up; ever participated in job search club or work experience program; and current participation in job search club or work experience program. Multiple regression analyses included additional covariates measured at the two-year follow-up: self-esteem; mastery; hope scale; depression; total quarters employed in years one and two; job quality at current job; wage change from years one to two; average job length; and parent-reported child externalizing and internalizing behavior.

21. The scale consists of six items that are averaged to create a total score ranging from 1 to 4; higher values represent higher goal efficacy. The items include: "At this time I am meeting the goals I set for myself," and, "I can think of many ways to reach my current goals."

22. Of course, our sample, whether randomly assigned to the program group or the control group, were volunteers. W-2 was asked to provide services for anyone, not just those who "volunteered" for W-2 services, so W-2 clients in general were not fully equivalent to the New Hope sample. The W-2 staff and procedures were no doubt affected by this difference. However, most New Hope sample participants had received welfare support in the past, and many did so even when they were in the New Hope program, so differences between the New Hope sample and others in W-2 were unlikely to have been very large. The New Hope sample certainly was representative of the range of variation in the general W-2 population.

CHAPTER THIRTEEN

1. That is, we found associations of between .15 and .20 as stated in effect sizes. See McCartney and Rosenthal (2000) for a discussion of effect sizes and their practical importance in developmental research. In data from the NICHD Early Child Care Research Network, the largest study of child care conducted to date in the United States, observed child care quality was associated with improvements of between .04 and .12 effect size in preschool children's cognitive development, across twenty-four months to fifty-four months, and improvements

of between .04 and .16 effect size in children's caregiver-rated social skills across this developmental period. Observed parenting quality in that study was associated with improvements in cognitive development of between .21 and .34 effect size and improvements in caregiver-rated social skills of .08 to .18 (NICHD Early Child Care Research Network and Duncan 2003; NICHD Early Child Care Research Network 2006).

2. Again, on the order of a roughly .10 to .25 standard deviation difference in these outcomes.

3. As we discussed more fully in chapter 1, the overall associations of maternal employment with low-income children's development are small, though more likely to be positive than negative.

4. This was around 1999; these implementation problems have to some extent been addressed in more recent versions of the program.

5. Fifty-eight percent of the mothers in the ethnographic sample—a figure that is in the range found in a review of studies of welfare recipients (U.S. General Accounting Office 1998)—reported some abusive event occurring on at least one occasion; although this certainly is a high number, we cannot know what a comparable group of mothers from the general population would say.

6. To summarize, we used a variety of statistical techniques to adjust for forms of selection bias. Most simply, when we were able to leverage the experimental impact of New Hope, we reported those data. In addition, we used several non-experimental techniques, including residual-change, change-score, and instrumental variable approaches. The particular approach used in a given chapter depended on the structure of the data available to answer the research questions of that chapter. For more details, see each chapter and the methodological appendix.

7. See chapters 1 and 12 for discussion of the economic and policy context of Milwaukee during this period.

8. Another approach to increasing work-related income at the bottom of the income distribution is to raise the minimum wage. However, the vast majority of New Hope parents were earning above the minimum wage. As many have noted, increasing the minimum wage is a quite inefficient way to target work-related income increases to the working poor because many of those earning the minimum wage are from higher-income families, such as high school or college students (Greenstein and Shapiro 1998; MaCurdy and MacIntyre 2004). The situation for some immigrant labor contexts differs yet again and more often can be closer to minimum wage.

9. Other proposals have been put forward. For example, Thomas MaCurdy and Frank MacIntyre (2004) propose a wage- and hours-based EITC that would address the EITC's shortcomings in making transitions from part-time to full-time work pay. However, their proposal would require federal monitoring of

hours, not just earnings, and is therefore less feasible than the five alternatives that Sawhill and Thomas (2001) review.

10. In New Hope, this increase in income occurred for those not working full-time at random assignment. For the other programs, which include the Self-Sufficiency Project (SSP), carried out in two provinces in Canada, and the Minnesota Family Investment Program (MFIP), carried out in several counties in that state, these increases in income applied to entire samples, which, unlike New Hope, were entirely made up of welfare recipients (Morris and Michalopoulos 2000; Gennetian and Miller 2000).

11. It is very difficult to evaluate the effects of an expansion of the EITC on children because such expansions occur simultaneously for the entire nation and therefore cannot be reliably disentangled from effects of other factors influencing the entire economy. This is true even of expansions in state earned income credits; comparisons across states in degree of expansion are confounded with a multitude of other policy differences between states. Experiments such as New Hope, MFIP, and SSP have the advantage of a randomized design, so that we can be confident of the causality of their effects. However, although they are somewhat similar to the EITC in providing additional income, with contingencies, they differ in other respects, so the analogy is imperfect. For example, New Hope and MFIP both provided additional services, such as child care assistance, which the EITC does not provide; New Hope and SSP rewarded specific thresholds of work hours (thirty hours a week), which the EITC does not do; MFIP and SSP targeted welfare recipients, while the EITC is available to all workers meeting eligibility guidelines, regardless of welfare receipt status. Finally, none of the three demonstration programs were implemented through the tax filing system, as the EITC is.

12. Julie Kerksick, personal communication with the authors.

13. For examples of this "career ladder" approach to work support services, see Miller et al. (2004, ch. 5); Fitzgerald and Carlson (2000).

14. This principle has been demonstrated in the field of early childhood programs for low-income families. Programs that address multiple risks, including parent risks such as harsh parenting and low educational attainment, and child risks such as problems in early cognitive development, appear to be more likely to produce cost-effective outcomes in reducing antisocial behavior and delinquency than programs that address only one issue (Yoshikawa 1995).

15. The Minnesota Family Investment Program, New Hope, and the Self-Sufficiency Project, three earnings supplement programs recently evaluated using experimental designs, produced average positive effects on school performance in the .20 effect size range, for average yearly income boosts of about $1,500 a year. Multiplying .20 by (3,668/1,500) equals .49 standard deviation (Morris and Michalopoulos 2000; Gennetian and Miller 2000; Huston et al. 2003).

CHAPTER FOURTEEN

1. The Packard Foundation, the MacArthur Foundation, and the W. T. Grant Foundation also heavily supported this research through MDRC's Next Generation Project.
2. Random selection of subjects for ethnographic research is rare. This book demonstrates many of the advantages of doing so, especially within the context of an existing random-assignment evaluation.
3. For example, effect sizes are comparable to, if not larger than, effects on child school achievement of observed child care quality (NICHD Early Child Care Research Network 2006), Early Head Start (Love et al. 2002), and reduced classroom size (the Tennessee Star experiment; see Mosteller 1995).

METHODOLOGICAL APPENDIX

1. For more details about sampling, recruitment, and implementation in the New Hope Project, see Brock et al. (1997). New Hope was also the product of its founders' visions and the political context of its time; see Duncan, Huston, and Weisner (2007).
2. Judith Gueron, Fred Doolittle, Robert Granger, Hans Bos, and Thomas Brock, among others, led this MDRC team.
3. The principal investigators (PIs) were Robert Granger, Thomas Weisner, Aletha Huston, and Greg Duncan. Bob Granger, then senior vice president of MDRC, along with Fred Doolittle, were the PIs for the evaluation of New Hope's work and income impacts at MDRC, and Bob Granger was a member of the MacArthur Research Network on Successful Pathways Through Middle Childhood. It was Bob Granger who brought the MDRC/New Hope connection to the MacArthur Network and saw the potential for doing further research on the child and family impacts of New Hope. Duncan, Huston, and Weisner were also Network members, and it was through these Network members, and with the advice of the full Network, that the design and methods for the CFS were worked out.
4. We restrict both our quantitative and qualitative samples to mothers in the CFS sample because we do not feel confident making conclusions about fathers in New Hope, given the very small percentage of them in both samples. (For instance, the New Hope Ethnographic Study included only two fathers and a number of coresident men who were not the fathers of the children in the household.) Evidence on the fathers, partners, and men in family life is summarized in Davis and Weisner (2005).
5. Research on attrition patterns showed few differences between those followed up and not followed up at twenty-four and at sixty months on the baseline demographic characteristics that had been collected at entry into the study,

and it also showed no differences in these characteristics by experimental condition (Bos et al. 1999; Huston et al. 2001).

6. For the most part, however, we do not review already released experimental effects of the New Hope program at the two- and five-year follow-ups. For those, we refer the reader to Bos et al. (1999); Huston et al. (2003); and Duncan, Huston, and Weisner (2007).

7. We are limited in our ability to leverage the experiment in this way (using instrumental variables estimation) by the exclusion restriction requirement of this statistical procedure. That is, if there are other plausible pathways through which New Hope could have affected parent or child well-being other than through changes in the particular variable being considered, this statistical approach is not warranted. In our service use chapter (chapter 12), we use this approach because we can argue that the bulk of New Hope's effects on children occurred through the services and benefits that it offered. However, in other cases such as social support, job quality, or marriage (each of which is the focus of a chapter), we cannot argue that New Hope's effects on parents and children occurred only through that construct. See Angrist, Imbens, and Rubin (1996); Gennetian et al. (2005).

8. For a summary of residualized change and change-score approaches to modeling causal associations, see NICHD Early Child Care Research Network and Duncan (2003).

9. Attrition once families were participating in the NHES was nil, although families were lost at times, then located again.

10. They included the three editors, as well as Faye Carter, Noemí Enchautegui-de-Jesús, Anna Gassman-Pines, Erin Godfrey, Eboni Howard (one of the original NHES field-workers), JoAnn Hsueh, Rashmita Mistry, and Amanda Roy. In addition, several other original NHES field-workers met informally with the book team.

References

Acs, Gregory, and Pamela Loprest. 2001. *Synthesis of Welfare Leaver Studies.* Washington: U.S. Department of Health and Human Services, Office of the Assistant Secretary for Planning and Evaluation.

Adams, Gina, Kathleen Snyder, and Jody R. Sandfort. 2002a. *Getting and Retaining Child Care Assistance: How Policy and Practice Influence Parents' Experiences.* Washington, D.C.: Urban Institute.

———. 2002b. *Navigating the Child Care Subsidy System: Policies and Practices That Affect Access and Retention.* Washington, D.C.: Urban Institute.

America's Second Harvest. 2001. "Hunger in America." Available at: www.secondharvest.org/learn_about_hunger/Hunger_Study_2001.

Angrist, Joshua D., Guido W. Imbens, and Donald B. Rubin. 1996. "Identification of Causal Effects Using Instrumental Variables." *Journal of the American Statistical Association* 91(434): 444–72.

Arbuckle, James L., and Werner Wothke. 1999. *Amos Users' Guide, Version 4.0.* Chicago: SmallWaters Corporation.

Bane, Mary J., and David T. Ellwood. 1994. *Welfare Realities: From Rhetoric to Reform.* Cambridge, Mass.: Harvard University Press.

Bartel, Ann P. 1995. "Training, Wage Growth, and Job Performance: Evidence from a Company Database." *Journal of Labor Economics* 13(3): 401–25.

Becker, Gary S. 1981. *A Treatise on the Family.* Cambridge, Mass.: Harvard University Press.

Bee, Helen L., and Denise Boyd. 2002. *Lifespan Development.* 3rd ed. Boston, Mass.: Pearson Allyn & Bacon.

Belle, Deborah. 1982. *Lives in Stress: Women and Depression.* Beverly Hills, Calif.: Sage Publications.

———. 1999. *The After-School Lives of Children: Alone and with Others While Parents Work.* Mahwah, N.J.: Erlbaum Associates.

Benin, Mary, and Verna M. Keith. 1995. "The Social Support of Employed African-American and Anglo Mothers." *Journal of Family Issues* 16(3): 275–97.

Bergman, Lars R., and Bassam M. El-Khouri. 1998. *SLEIPNER: A Statistical Package for Pattern-Oriented Analyses (Version 2)*. Stockholm: Stockholm University, Department of Psychology.

Bergman, Lars R., and David Magnusson. 1997. "A Person-Oriented Approach to Research on Developmental Psychopathology." *Development and Psychopathology* 9(2): 291–320.

Bergman, Mindy E., and Fritz Drasgow. 2003. "Race as a Moderator in a Model of Sexual Harassment: An Empirical Test." *Journal of Occupational Health Psychology* 8(2): 131–45.

Bernheimer, Lucinda P., Thomas S. Weisner, and Edward D. Lowe. 2003. "Impacts of Children with Troubles on Working-Poor Families: Mixed-Methods and Experimental Evidence." *Mental Retardation* 41(6): 403–19.

Besharov, Douglas J., and Nazanin Samari. 2001. "Child Care After Welfare Reform." In *The New World of Welfare*, edited by Rebecca Blank and Ronald Haskins. Washington, D.C.: Brookings Institution.

Billingsley, Andrew. 1992. *Climbing Jacob's Ladder: The Enduring Legacy of African-American Families*. New York: Touchstone.

Blank, Rebecca M. 1989. "Analyzing the Length of Welfare Spells." *Journal of Public Economics* 39(3): 245–73.

———. 1994. "Short-term Recidivism Among Public Assistance Recipients." *American Economic Review* 84(2): 49–53.

———. 1997. *It takes a Nation: A New Agenda for Fighting Poverty*. Princeton, N.J.: Princeton University Press.

———. 2002. "Evaluating Welfare Reform in the United States." *Journal of Economic Literature* 40(4): 1105–66.

Blau, David. 1999. "The Effect of Income on Child Development." *Review of Economics and Statistics* 81(2): 261–76.

Blau, Francine D., Lawrence M. Kahn, and Jane Waldfogel. 2000. "Understanding Young Women's Marriage Decisions: The Role of Labor and Market Conditions." *Industrial and Labor Relations Review* 53(4): 624–47.

Bloom, Howard S., Larry L. Orr, Stephen H. Bell, George Cave, Fred Doolittle, Winston Lin, and Johannes M. Bos. 1997. "The Benefits and Costs of JTPA Title II-A Programs: Key Findings from the National Job Training Partnership Act Study." *Journal of Human Resources* 32(3): 549–76.

Bolger, Niall, Adam Zuckerman, and Ronald C. Kessler. 2000. *Journal of Personality and Social Psychology* 79(6): 953–61.

Bond, James T. 2003. *Information for Employers About Low-Wage Employees from Low-Income Families*. New York: Families and Work Institute.

Bos, Johannes, Aletha C. Huston, Robert Granger, Greg J. Duncan, Thomas Brock, and Vonnie C. McLoyd. 1999. *New Hope for People with Low Incomes: Two-Year Results of a Program to Reduce Poverty and Reform Welfare*. New York: Manpower Demonstration Research Corporation.

Bradley, Robert H., and Robert F. Corwyn. 2004. " 'Family Process': investments that matter for child well-being." In Ariel Kalil and Thomas DeLeire (eds). Family investments in children's potential: Resources and parenting behaviors that promote success. Monographs in parenting: 1–32. Mahwah, N.J.: Lawrence Erlbaum Associates.

Brauner, Sarah, and Pamela J. Loprest. 1999. "Where Are They Now? What States' Studies of People who Left Welfare Tell Us." Assessing the New Federalism, Series A-32. Washington D.C.: Urban Institute.

Brock, Thomas, Fred Doolittle, Veronica Fellerath, Michael Wiseman, David H. Greenberg, and Robinson G. Hollister Jr. 1997. Creating New Hope: Implementation of a Program to Reduce Poverty and Reform Welfare. New York: MDRC.

Brodsky, Anne E. 1999. "Making It: The Components and Process of Resilience Among Urban, African-American, Single Mothers." American Journal of Orthopsychiatry 69(2): 148–60.

Brooks-Gunn, Jeanne, Wen-Jui Han, and Jane Waldfogel. 2002. "Maternal Employment and Child Cognitive Outcomes in the First Three Years of Life." Child Development 73(4): 1052–72.

Brooks-Gunn, Jeanne, Pamela K. Klebanov, and Fong-ruey Liaw. 1995. "The Learning, Physical, and Emotional Environment of the Home in the Context of Poverty: The Infant Health and Development Program." Child & Youth Services Review 17(1–2): 251–76.

Card, David, Charles Michalopoulos, and Phillip K. Robins. 2001. "The Limits of Wage Growth: Measuring the Growth Rate of Wages for Recent Welfare Leavers." Working paper 8444. Cambridge, Mass.: National Bureau of Economic Research.

Carlson, Marcia J., and Frank F. Furstenberg. Forthcoming. "The Prevalence and Correlates of Multipartnered Fertility Among Urban U.S. Parents." Journal of Marriage and Family.

Chase-Lansdale, P. Lindsay, Robert A. Moffitt, Brenda J. Lohman, Andrew J. Cherlin, Rebekah L. Coley, Laura D. Pittman, Jennifer Roff, and Elisabeth Votruba-Drzal. 2003. "Mothers' Transitions from Welfare to Work and the Well-being of Preschoolers and Adolescents." Science 299(5612): 1548–52.

Chase-Lansdale, P. Lindsay, and Laura Pittman. 2002. "Welfare Reform and Parenting: Reasonable Expectations." The Future of Children 12(1): 167–83.

Chaudry, Ajay. 2004. Putting Children First: How Low-Wage Working Mothers Manage Child Care. New York: Russell Sage Foundation.

Cherlin, Andrew J., Frank F. Furstenberg, P. Lindsay Chase-Lansdale, Kathleen E. Kiernan, Philip K. Robins, Donna R. Morrison, and Julien O. Tietler. 1991. "Longitudinal Studies of Effects of Divorce on Children in Great Britain and the United States." Science 252(June): 1386–89.

Clampet-Lundquist, Susan, Andrew S. London, Kathryn Edin, Ellen K. Scott, and Vicki Hunter. 2004. "Making a Way Out of No Way: How Low-Income Single

Mothers Meet Basic Family Needs While Moving from Welfare to Work." In *Work-Family Challenges for Low-Income Workers and Their Children*, edited by Ann C. Crouter and Alan Booth. Mahwah, N.J.: Erlbaum Associates.

Clark, Andrew E. 2005. "What Makes a Good Job? Evidence from OECD Countries." In *Job Quality and Employer Behavior*, edited by Stephen Brazen, Claudio Lucifora, and Weimer Salverda. Houndsmills, Basingstoke, Hampshire, Eng.: Palgrave Macmillan.

Cohen, Jacob, Patricia Cohen, Stephen West, and Leona Aiken. 2003. *Applied Multiple Regression/Correlation Analysis for the Behavioral Sciences*. 3rd ed. Mahwah, N.J.: Erlbaum Associates.

Cohen, Patricia, James Johnson, Stephen A. Lewis, and Judith S. Brook. 1990. "Single-Parenthood and Employment: Double Jeopardy?" In *Stress Between Work and Family*, edited by John Eckenrode and Susan Gore. New York: Plenum Press.

Cohen, Sheldon, and Thomas A. Wills. 1985. "Stress, Social Support, and the Buffering Hypothesis." *Psychological Bulletin* 98(2): 310–57.

Collins, Ann M., Jean Layzer, Lee Kreader, Alan Werner, and Fred B. Glantz. 2000. *National Study of Child Care for Low-Income Families: State and Community Subsidy Interim Report*. Cambridge, Mass., and New York: Abt Associates and Columbia University, National Center for Children in Poverty.

Conger, Rand D., and Glen H. Elder. 1994. *Families in Troubled Times: Adapting to Change in Rural America*. New York: Aldine De Gruyter.

Conger, Rand D., Xiaojia Ge, Glen H. Elder, Frederick O. Lorenz, and Ronald L. Simons. 1994. "Economic Stress, Coercive Family Process, and Developmental Problems of Adolescents." *Child Development* 65(2): 541–61.

Conger, Rand D., Martha A. Rueter, and Glen H. Elder, Jr. 1999. "Couple Resilience to Economic Pressure." *Journal of Personality and Social Psychology* 76(1): 54–71.

Connolly, Helen, and Peter Gottschalk. 2001. "Returns to Tenure and Experience Revisited: Do Less-Educated Workers Gain Less from Work Experience?" Working paper. Boston: Boston College, Department of Economics.

Corbie-Smith, Giselle, Erica Frank, Herbert W. Nickens, and Lisa Elon. 1999. "Prevalences and Correlates of Ethnic Harassment in the U.S. Women Physicians' Health Study." *Academic Medicine* 74(6): 695–701.

Corporate Voices for Working Families. 2005. *Low-Wage Best Practices Report*. Washington, D.C.: Author.

Cox, Martha J., Blair Paley, Margaret Burchinal, and C. Chris Payne. 1999. "Marital Perceptions and Interactions Across the Transition to Parenthood." *Journal of Marriage and the Family* 61(3): 611–25.

Crosby, Danielle A., Chantelle Dowsett, Lisa Gennetian, and Aletha C. Huston. 2006. "The Effects of Center-Based Care on the Problem Behavior of Low-Income Children with Working Mothers." Unpublished paper.

Crosby, Danielle A., Lisa A. Gennetian, and Aletha C. Huston. 2005. "Child Care Assistance Policies Can Affect the Use of Center-Based Care for Children in Low-Income Families." *Applied Developmental Science* 9(1): 86–106.

Crouter, Ann C., and Alan Booth, eds. 2004. *Work-Family Challenges for Low-Income Parents and Their Children*. Mahwah, N.J.: Erlbaum Associates.

Crouter, Ann C., and Matthew Bumpus. 2001. "Linking Parents' Work Stress to Children's and Adolescents' Psychological Adjustment." *Current Directions in Psychological Science* 10(5): 156–59.

Crouter, Ann C., Matthew F. Bumpus, Mary C. Maguire, and Susan M. McHale. 1999. "Linking Parents' Work Pressure and Adolescent Well-being." *Developmental Psychology* 35(6): 1453–61.

Crouter, Ann C., Melissa R. Head, Matthew F. Bumpus, and Susan M. McHale. 2001. "Household Chores: Under What Conditions Do Mothers Lean on Daughters?" *New Directions for Child and Adolescent Development* 94(Winter): 23–41.

D'Andrade, Roy G., and Claudia Strauss. 1992. *Human Motives and Cultural Models*. New York: Cambridge University Press.

Danziger, Sandra, Mary Corcoran, Sheldon Danziger, and Colleen M. Heflin. 2000. "Work, Income, and Material Hardship After Welfare Reform." *The Journal of Consumer Affairs* 34(1): 6–30.

Danziger, Sandra K., Mary Corcoran, Sheldon Danziger, Colleen Heflin, Ariel Kalil, and Judith Levine. 2000. "Barriers to the Employment of Welfare Recipients." In *Prosperity for All? The Economic Boom and African Americans*, edited by Robert Cherry and William M. Rodgers III. New York: Russell Sage Foundation.

Danziger, Sandra K., Ariel Kalil, and Nathaniel J. Anderson. 2000. "Human Capital, Physical Health, and Mental Health Characteristics of Welfare Recipients." *Journal of Social Issues* 56(4, Winter): 635–54.

Danziger, Sheldon, Colleen M. Heflin, Mary E. Corcoran, Elizabeth Oltmans, and Hui-Chen Wang. 2002. "Does It Pay to Move from Welfare to Work?" *Journal of Policy Analysis and Management* 21(4): 671–92.

Daniziger, Sheldon, and Hui-Chen Wang. 2004. "Does It Pay to Move from Welfare to Work? A Reply to Robert Moffitt and Katie Winder." April. Available at: http://www.fordschool.umich.edu/research/poverty/pdf/danziger-wang-reply.pdf.

Davis, Helen, and Thomas S. Weisner. 2005. "Fathers and Father Support in Low-Income Families." Paper presented to the meeting of the Society for Cross-Cultural Research. Santa Fe, N.M. (February).

Deitch, Elizabeth A., Adam Barsky, Rebecca M. Butz, Suzanne Chan, Arthur P. Brief, and Jill C. Bradley. 2003. "Subtle yet Significant: The Impact of Everyday Racial Discrimination in the Workplace." *Human Relations* 56(11): 1299–1324.

DeParle, Jason. 2004. *American Dream: Three Women, Ten Kids, and a Nation's Drive to End Welfare*. New York: Viking.

Department of Energy. 2004. The Effect of Income on Appliances in U.S. Households. Washington: Energy Information Administration, U.S. Department of Energy. Available at: http://www.eia.doe.gov/emeu/recs/appliances/appliances.html.

Desai, Sonalde, P. Lindsay Chase-Lansdale, and Robert T. Michael. 1989. "Mother or Market? Effects of Maternal Employment on the Intellectual Ability of Four-Year-Old Children." *Demography* 26(4): 545–61.

De Schipper, J. Clasien, Marinus van Ijzendoorn, and Louis W. C. Tevecchio. 2004. "Stability in Center Day Care: Relations with Children's Well-being and Problem Behavior in Day Care." *Social Development* 13(4): 531–50.

Dion, M. Robin., and Barbara Devaney. 2003. "Strengthening Relationships and Supporting Healthy Marriage Among Unwed Parents." Building Strong Families Brief, No. 1. Princeton, N.J.: Mathematica Policy Research, Inc.

Dodson, Lisa, and Jillian Dickert. 2004. "Girls' Family Labor in Low-Income Households: A Decade of Qualitative Research." *Journal of Marriage and Family* 66(2): 318–32.

Downey, Geraldine, and James C. Coyne. 1990. "Children of Depressed Parents: An Integrative Review." *Psychological Bulletin* 108: 50–76.

Duncan, Greg J., and Jeanne Brooks-Gunn. 2000. "Family Poverty, Welfare Reform, and Child Development." *Child Development* 71(1): 188–96.

Duncan, Greg J., Aletha C. Huston, and Thomas S. Weisner. 2007. *Higher Ground: New Hope for the Working Poor and Their Children.* New York: Russell Sage Foundation.

Durkheim, Emile. 1893/1960. *The Division of Labor in Society.* Reprint, Glencoe, Ill.: Free Press.

Dworsky, Amy, Mark Courtney, and Irving Piliavin. 2003. *What Happens to Families Under W-2 in Milwaukee County, Wisconsin?* Chicago: University of Chicago, Chapin Hall Center for Children.

East, Patricia L., Thomas S. Weisner, and Barbara T. Reyes. 2006. "Youths' Caretaking of Their Adolescent Sisters' Children: Its Costs and Benefits for Youths' Development." *Applied Developmental Science* 10(2): 86–95.

Edin, Kathryn, and Maria Kefalas. 2005. *Promises I Can Keep: Why Poor Women Put Motherhood Before Marriage.* Berkeley, Calif.: University of California Press.

Edin, Kathryn, and Laura Lein. 1997. *Making Ends Meet: How Single Mothers Survive Welfare and Low-Wage Work.* New York: Russell Sage Foundation.

Ehrenreich, Barbara. 2001. *Nickel and Dimed: On (Not) Getting by in America.* New York: Henry Holt.

Elder, Glen H., Jr. 1974/1999. *Children of the Great Depression: Social Change in Life Experience.* 25th Anniversary Edition. Boulder, Colo.: Westview Press (originally published by University of Chicago Press).

Ellwood, David T. 1988. *Poor Support: Poverty in the American Family.* New York: Basic Books.

Ellwood, David T., and Christopher Jencks. 2004. "The Spread of Single-Parent Families in the United States Since 1960." Working paper No. RWP04-008. Boston, Mass.: John F. Kennedy School of Government, Harvard University.

Erikson, Erik H. 1950. *Childhood and Society*. New York: Norton.

———. 1968. *Identity: Youth and Crisis*. New York: Norton.

Fain, Terri C., and Douglas L. Anderton. 1987. "Sexual Harassment: Organizational Context and Diffuse States." *Sex Roles* 17(5–6): 291–311.

Farley, Lin. 1978. *Sexual Shakedown: The Sexual Harassment of Women on the Job*. New York: Warner.

Fein, David J., Nancy R. Burstein, Greta G. Fein, and Laura D. Lindberg. 2003. *The Determinants of Marriage and Cohabitation Among Disadvantaged Americans: Research Findings and Needs*. Cambridge, Mass.: Abt Associates Inc.

Felton, Barbara J., and Marybeth Shinn. 1992. "Social Integration and Social Support: Moving 'Social Support' Beyond the Individual Level." *Journal of Community Psychology* 20(2): 103–15.

Fernandez, Maria E., Elizabeth J. Mutran, and Donald C. Reitzes. 1998. "Moderating the Effects of Stress on Depressive Symptoms." *Research on Aging* 20(2): 163–82.

Fields, Jason, and Lynne M. Casper. 2001. "America's Families and Living Arrangements." *Current Population Reports*, series P20, no. 537. Washington: U.S. Government Printing Office for U.S. Bureau of the Census.

Fitzgerald, Joan, and Virginia Carlson. 2000. "Ladders to a Better Life." *The American Prospect* 11(15): 54–61.

Fitzgerald, Louise F., Fritz Drasgow, Charles L. Hulin, Michele J. Gelfand, and Vicki J. Magley. 1997. "Antecedents and Consequences of Sexual Harassment in Organizations: A Test of an Integrated Model." *Journal of Applied Psychology* 82: 578–89.

Fitzgerald, Louise F., Michele J. Gelfand, and Fritz Drasgow. 1995. "Measuring Sexual Harassment: Theoretical and Psychometric Advances." *Basic and Applied Social Psychology* 17(4): 425–27.

Fitzgerald, Louise F., and Sandra L. Shulman. 1993. "Sexual Harassment: A Research Analysis and Agenda for the 1990s." *Journal of Vocational Behavior* 42(1): 5–27.

Fitzgerald, Louise F., Sandra L. Shulman, Nancy Bailey, Margaret Richards, Janice Swecker, Yael Gold, Mimi Ormerod, and Lauren Weitzman. 1988. "The Incidence and Dimensions of Sexual Harassment in Academia and the Workplace." *Journal of Vocational Behavior* 32: 152–75.

Forman, Tyrone A. 2003. "The Social Psychological Costs of Racial Segmentation in the Workplace: A Study of African-Americans' Well-being." *Journal of Health and Social Behavior* 44(3): 332–52.

Forman, Tyrone A., David R. Williams, and James S. Jackson. 1997. "Race, Place, and Discrimination." *Perspectives on Social Problems* 9: 231–61.

Freire, Paolo. 1971. *Pedagogy of the Oppressed*. New York: Seabury Press.

Friedlander, Daniel, and Gary Burtless. 1995. *Five Years After: The Long-Term Effects of Welfare-to-Work Programs*. New York: Russell Sage Foundation.

Friedman, Dana E. 2001. "Employer Supports for Parents with Young Children." *The Future of Children* 11: 63–77.

Fuller, Bruce, Sharon L. Kagan, Gretchen L. Caspary, and Christiane A. Gauthier. 2002. "Welfare Reform and Child Care Options for Low-Income Families." *The Future of Children* 12(1): 97–119.

Galinsky, Ellen, James T. Bond, and E. Jeffrey Hill. 2004. *A Status Report on Workplace Flexibility: Who Has It? Who Wants It? What Difference Does It Make?* New York: Families and Work Institute.

Ganzach, Yoav. 1998. "Intelligence and Job Satisfaction." *Academy of Management Journal* 41(5): 526–39.

Garey, Anita I. 1999. *Weaving Work and Motherhood.* Philadelphia: Temple University Press.

Gassman-Pines, Anna, and Hirokazu Yoshikawa. 2006. "Five-Year Impacts of an Anti-Poverty Program on Marriage Among Never-Married Mothers." *Journal of Policy Analysis and Management* 26(1): 11–30.

Gennetian, Lisa, Danielle Crosby, Chantelle Dowsett, and Aletha C. Huston. 2006. "Center-Based Care and the Achievement of Low-Income Children: Evidence Using Data from Experimental Employment-Based Programs." Working paper. New York: Manpower Demonstration Research Corporation.

Gennetian, Lisa A., Greg J. Duncan, Virginia W. Knox, Wanda G. Vargas, Elizabeth Clark-Kauffman, and Andrew S. London. 2002. *How Welfare and Work Policies Affect Adolescents: A Synthesis of Research.* New York: Manpower Demonstration Research Corporation.

Gennetian, Lisa A., and Cynthia Miller. 2000. *Reforming Welfare and Rewarding Work: The Final Report on the Minnesota Family Investment Program,* vol. 2, *Effects on Children.* New York: Manpower Demonstration Research Corporation.

Gennetian, Lisa A., Pamela A. Morris, Johannes M. Bos, and Howard Bloom. 2005. "Constructing Instrumental Variables from Experimental Data to Explore How Treatments Produce Effects." In *Learning More from Social Experiments,* edited by Howard Bloom. New York: Russell Sage Foundation.

Gibson, Christina. 2003. "Privileging the Participant: The Importance of Subgroup Analysis in Social Welfare Evaluations." *American Journal of Evaluation* 24(4): 443–69.

Gibson, Christina M., and Kathryn Edin. 2004. "The Effect of Multiple Partner Fertility on Father Involvement." Paper presented at the Association for Public Policy Analysis and Management Annual Meeting. Atlanta (October 28–30).

Gibson, Christina, and Thomas S. Weisner. 2002. " 'Rational' and Ecocultural Circumstances of Program Take-up Among Low-Income Working Parents." *Human Organization* 61(1): 154–66.

Gibson-Davis, Christina M., and Greg J. Duncan. 2005. "Qualitative/Quantitative Synergies in a Random-Assignment Program Evaluation." In *Discovering Successful Pathways in Children's Development: Mixed Methods in the Study of*

Childhood and Family Life, edited by Thomas S. Weisner. Chicago: University of Chicago Press.

Gibson-Davis, Christina M., Kathryn Edin, and Sara McLanahan. 2005. "High Hopes but Even Higher Expectations: The Retreat from Marriage Among Lower-Income Couples." *Journal of Marriage and the Family* 67(5): 1301–12.

Gilens, Martin. 1999. *Why Americans Hate Welfare: Race, Media, and the Politics of Antipoverty Policy.* Chicago: University of Chicago Press.

Glass, Jennifer. 2004. "Blessing or Curse? Work-Family Policies and Mothers' Wage Growth over Time." *Work and Occupations* 31(3): 367–94.

Gliner, Jeffrey A., George A. Morgan, and Robert J. Harmon. 2003. "Pretest-Post-test Comparison Group Designs: Analysis and Interpretation." *American Academy of Child and Adolescent Psychiatry* 42(4): 500–503.

Godfrey, Erin B., and Hirokazu Yoshikawa. 2005. "Opening the Black Box: The Role of Office-Level Characteristics in Welfare." Unpublished paper. New York: New York University.

Gottlieb, Benjamin H. 1994. "Social Support." In *Perspectives on Close Relationships,* edited by Ann L. Weber and John H. Harvey. Needham Heights, Mass.: Allyn & Bacon.

Gottschalk, Peter, and Robert Moffitt. 1999. "Changes in Job Instability and Insecurity Using Monthly Survey Data." *Journal of Labor Economics* 17(4): 91–126.

Green, Beth L., and Ann Rodgers. 2001. "Determinants of Social Support Among Low-Income Mothers: A Longitudinal Analysis." *American Journal of Community Psychology* 29(3): 419–41.

Greenberger, Ellen, Robin O'Neil, and Stacy K. Nagel. 1994. "Linking Workplace and Homeplace: Relations Between the Nature of Adults' Work and Their Parenting Behaviors." *Developmental Psychology* 30(6): 990–1002.

Greenstein, Robert, and Isaac Shapiro. 1998. "New Research Findings on the Effects of the Earned Income Tax Credit." Washington, D.C.: Center for Budget and Policy Priorities.

Gresham, Frank M., and Stephen N. Elliott. 1990. *Social Skills Rating System Manual.* Circle Pines, Minn.: American Guidance Service.

Gruber, James E. 1998. "The Impact of Male Work Environments and Organizational Policies on Women's Experiences of Sexual Harassment." *Gender and Society* 12(3): 301–20.

Guo, Guang, and Kathleen M. Harris. 2000. "The Mechanisms Mediating the Effects of Poverty on Children's Intellectual Development." *Demography* 37(4): 431–47.

Gurda, John. 1999. *The Making of Milwaukee.* Milwaukee, Wisc.: Milwaukee County Historical Society.

Gutman, Leslie M., and Jacquelynne S. Eccles. 1999. "Financial Strain, Parenting Behaviors, and Adolescents' Achievement: Testing Model Equivalence Between African American and European American Single- and Two-parent Families." *Child Development* 70(6): 1464–1476.

Hamilton, Gayle, Stephen Freedman, Lisa Gennetian, Charles Michalopoulos, Johanna Walter, Diana Adams-Ciardullo, Anna Gassman-Pines, Sharon McGroder, Martha Zaslow, Sujeet Ahluwahlia, and Jennifer Brooks. 2001. *National Evaluation of Welfare-to-Work Strategies: Five-Year Impacts on Adults and Children in Eleven Programs*. Washington: U.S. Department of Health and Human Services, Administration for Children and Families, Office of the Assistant Secretary for Planning and Evaluation.

Han, Wen-Jui. 2005. "Maternal Nonstandard Work Schedules and Child Cognitive Outcomes." *Child Development* 76(1): 137–54.

Han, Wen-Jui, Jane Waldfogel, and Jeanne Brooks-Gunn. 2001. "The Effects of Early Maternal Employment on Later Cognitive and Behavioral Outcomes." *Journal of Marriage and the Family* 63(2): 336–54.

Heclo, H. Hugh. 1997. "Values Underpinning Poverty Programs for Children." *The Future of Children* 7(2): 141–48.

Hedges, Janice N., and Edward S. Sekscenski. 1979. "Workers on Late Shifts in a Changing Economy." *Monthly Labor Review* 102(2): 14–22.

Henly, Julia R. 2002. "Informal Support Networks and the Maintenance of Low-Wage Jobs." In *Laboring Below the Line: The New Ethnography of Poverty, Low-Wage Work, and Survival in the Global Economy*, edited by Frank Munger. New York: Russell Sage Foundation.

Henly, Julia R., Sandra K. Danziger, and Shira Offer. 2005. "The Contribution of Social Support to the Material Well-being of Low-Income Families." *Journal of Marriage and Family* 67(1): 122–40.

Hershey, Alan M., Barbara Devaney, M. Robin Dion, and Sheena McConnell. 2004. *Building Strong families: Guidelines for Developing Programs*. Princeton, N.J.: Mathematica Policy Research, Inc.

Hertz, Rosanna, and Faith I. T. Ferguson. 1996. "Child Care Choice and Constraints in the United States: Social Class, Race, and the Influence of Family Views." *Journal of Comparative Family Studies* 27(2): 249–80.

Hetherington, E. Mavis, and Margaret Stanley-Hagan. 1999. "The Adjustment of Children With Divorced Parents: A Risk and Resiliency Perspective." *Journal of Child Psychology and Psychiatry* 40(1): 129–40.

Heymann, S. Jody. 2000. *The Widening Gap: Why America's Working Families Are in Jeopardy and What Can Be Done About It*. New York: Basic Books.

Heymann, S. Jody, and Alison Earle. 1999. "The Impact of Welfare Reform on Parents' Ability to Care for Their Children's Health." *American Journal of Public Health* 89(4): 502–5.

Heymann, S. Jody, Alison Earle, and Brian Egleston. 1996. "Parental Availability for the Care of Sick Children." *Pediatrics* 98(2): 226–30.

Hicks-Clarke, Deborah, and Paul Iles. 2000. "Climate for Diversity and Its Effects on Career and Organizational Attitudes and Perceptions." *Personnel Review* 29: 324–45.

Hoffman, Lois W. 1961. "Effects of Maternal Employment on the Child." *Child Development* 32(2): 187–97.

Hoffman, Lois, and Lisa Youngblade, with Rebekah L. Coley, Allison S. Fuligni, and Donna D. Kovacs. 1999. *Mothers at Work: Effects on Children's Well-being.* New York: Cambridge University Press.

Holloway, Susan D., Bruce Fuller, Marylee Rambaud, and Costanza Eggers-Pierola. 1997. *Through My Own Eyes: Single Mothers and the Cultures of Poverty.* Cambridge, Mass.: Harvard University Press.

Holzer, Harry J., and Robert J. LaLonde. 1999. "Job Change and Job Stability Among Less-Skilled Young Workers." Discussion paper 1191–99. Madison, Wisc.: Institute for Research on Poverty.

Holzer, Harry J., and Douglas Wissoker. 2001. *How Can We Encourage Job Retention and Advancement for Welfare Recipients?* Washington, D.C.: Urban Institute.

House, James S., Debra Umberson, and Karl R. Landis. 1988. "Structures and Processes of Social Support." *Annual Review of Sociology* 14: 293–318.

Houseman, Susan N. 1995. "Job Growth and the Quality of Jobs in the U.S. Economy." *Labor* 9 (special issue): S93–124.

Hsueh, JoAnn, and Hirokazu Yoshikawa. Forthcoming. "Nonstandard Schedules and Variable Shifts Among Low-Income Families: Associations with Parental Psychological Well-being, Family Functioning, and Child Well-being." *Developmental Psychology.*

Hughes, Diane. 2003. "Correlates of African-American and Latino Parents' Messages to Children About Ethnicity and Race: A Comparative Study of Racial Socialization." *American Journal of Community Psychology* 31(1–2): 15–33.

Hughes, Diane, Ellen Galinsky, and Anne Morris. 1992. "The Effects of Job Characteristics on Marital Quality: Specifying Linking Mechanisms." *Journal of Marriage and the Family* 54(1): 31–42.

Huston, Aletha, Greg J. Duncan, Robert Granger, Johannes Bos, Vonnie C. McLoyd, Rashmita Mistry, Danielle Crosby, Christina Gibson, Katherine Magnuson, Jennifer Romich, and Ana Ventura. 2001. "Work-Based Antipoverty Programs for Parents Can Enhance the School Performance and Social Behavior of Children." *Child Development* 72(1): 318–36.

Huston, Aletha C., Cynthia Miller, Lashawn Richburg-Hayes, Greg J. Duncan, Carolyn A. Eldred, Thomas S. Weisner, Edward Lowe, Vonnie C. McLoyd, Danielle A. Crosby, Marika N. Ripke, and Cindy Redcross. 2003. New Hope for families and children: Five-year results of a program to reduce poverty and reform welfare. New York: MDRC.

Huston, Aletha C., Rashmita S. Mistry, Johannes M. Bos, Mi-Shuk Shim, Sylvia Havadtoy, Chantelle Dowsett, and Jessica Cummings. 2002. "Changes in Employment, Welfare Receipt, and Income as Predictors of Family and Child Care Contexts and Youth Risk and Resilient Behavior." Final Report Submitted to Assistant Secretary for Planning and Evaluation, U.S. Department of Health and

Human Services. December. Washington: U.S. Department of Health and Human Services.

Institute for Research on Poverty. 1998. *Evaluating Comprehensive State Welfare Reforms.* Madison: University of Wisconsin, Institute for Research on Poverty.

Institute for the Study of Homelessness and Poverty. 2001. "Just the Facts: Housing and poverty in Los Angeles." July. Available at: http://www.weingart.org/institute/.

Jackson, Aurora P., Jeanne Brooks-Gunn, Chien-Chung Huang, and Marc Glassman. 2000. "Single Mothers in Low-Wage Jobs: Financial Strain, Parenting, and Preschoolers' Outcomes." *Child Development* 71(5): 1409–23.

Jaeger, David A., and Ann H. Stevens. 1999. "Is Job Stability in the United States Falling? Trends in the Current Population Survey and Panel Study of Income Dynamics." *Journal of Labor Economics* 17(4): 1–28.

Jarrett, Robin L., Kevin M. Roy, and Linda M. Burton. 2002. "Fathers in the 'Hood': Insights from Qualitative Research on Low-Income African-American Men." In *Handbook of Father Involvement,* edited by Catherine S. Tamis-LeMonda and Natasha Cabrera. Mahwah, N.J.: Erlbaum Associates.

Johnson, Earl S., Ann Levine, and Fred C. Doolittle. 1999. *Fathers' Fair Share: Helping Poor Men Manage Child Support and Fatherhood.* New York: Russell Sage Foundation.

Johnson, Rucker, and Mary Corcoran. 2002. "Welfare Recipients' Road to Economic Self-sufficiency: Job Quality and Job Transition Patterns, Post-PRWORA." Working paper. Ann Arbor: University of Michigan, Ford School of Public Policy, Center for Poverty Research.

Kalil, Ariel, Heidi Schweingruber, and Kristin Seefeldt. 2001. "Correlates of Employment Among Welfare Recipients: Do Psychological Characteristics and Attitudes Matter?" *American Journal of Community Psychology* 29(5): 701–23.

Kalil, Ariel, and Kathleen Ziol-Guest. 2005. "Single Mothers' Employment Dynamics and Adolescent Well-being." *Child Development* 76(1): 196–211.

Kanter, Rosabeth M. 1977. *Work and Family in the United States: A Critical Review and Agenda for Research and Policy.* New York: Russell Sage Foundation.

Karney, Benjamin R., Cynthia R. Garvan, and Michael S. Thomas. 2003. "Family Formation in Florida: 2003 Baseline Survey of Attitudes, Beliefs, and Demographics Relating to Marriage and Family Formation." Unpublished paper. University of Florida, Department of Psychology, December.

Katz, Michael B. 2001. *The Price of Citizenship: Redefining the American Welfare State.* New York: Metropolitan Books.

Katz, Mitchell H., and Chaya S. Piotrkowski. 1983. "Correlates of Family Role Strain Among Employed Black Women." *Family Relations* 32(3): 331–39.

Kessler, Ronald C., Kristin D. Mickelson, and David R. Williams. 1999. "The Prevalence, Distribution, and Mental Health Correlates of Perceived Discrimination in the United States." *Journal of Health and Social Behavior* 40(3): 208–30.

Knitzer, Jane. 2002. "Promoting the Emotional Well-being of Children and Families," policy brief 1, "Building Services and Systems to Support the Healthy

Emotional Development of Young Children." New York: Columbia University, National Center for Children in Poverty.

Kohn, Melvin. 1969. *Class and Conformity: A Study in Values.* Chicago: University of Chicago Press.

Kreader, J. Lee, Jessica B. Piecyk, and A. Collins. 2000. *Scant Increases After Welfare Reform: Regulated Child Care Supply in Illinois and Maryland, 1996–1998.* New York: National Center for Children in Poverty.

Krein, Sheila F., and Andrea H. Beller. 1988. "Educational Attainment of Children from Single Parent Families: Differences by Exposure, Gender and Race." *Demography* 25(2): 221–34.

Krieger, Nancy. 2003. "Does Racism Harm Health? Did Child Abuse Exist Before 1962?—On Explicit Questions, Critical Science, and Current Controversies: An Ecosocial Perspective." *American Journal of Public Health* 93(2): 194–99.

Krieger, Nancy, Stephen Sidney, and Eugenie Coakley. 1998. "Racial Discrimination and Skin Color in CARDIA: Implications for Public Health Research." *American Journal of Public Health* 88(9): 1308–13.

Krueger, Alan B. 1999. "Experimental Estimates of Education Production Functions." *Quarterly Journal of Economics* 114(2): 497–532.

Ku, Leighton, and Timothy Waidmann. 2003. *How Race-Ethnicity, Immigration Status, and Language Affect Health Care Coverage Among the Low-Income Population.* Washington, D.C.: Urban Institute.

Kusserow, Adrie. 2004. *American Individualisms: Child Rearing and Social Class in Three Neighborhoods.* New York: Palgrave Press.

Lareau, Annette. 2003. *Unequal Childhoods: Class, Race, and Family Life.* Berkeley: University of California Press.

Larson, Reed W., and David M. Almeida. 1999. "Emotional Transition in the Daily Lives of Families: A New Paradigm for Studying Family Process." *Journal of Marriage and the Family* 61(1): 5–20.

LeBlanc, Marc, and Richard E. Tremblay. 1988. "A Study of Factors Associated with the Stability of Hidden Delinquency." *International Journal of Adolescence and Youth* 1(3): 269–91.

Lengermann, Paul A. 1999. "How Long Do the Benefits of Training Last? Evidence of Long-Term Effects Across Current and Previous Employers." *Research in Labor Economics* 18(3): 439–61.

Lerner, Jacqueline V. 1994. *Working Women and Their Families.* Thousand Oaks, Calif.: Sage Publications.

Levine, Marc. 2002. *The Economic State of Milwaukee's Inner City: 1970–2000.* Milwaukee: University of Wisconsin, Center for Economic Development.

Levine, Marc, and J. F. Zipp. 1993. "A City at Risk: The Changing Social and Economic Context of Public Schooling in Milwaukee." In *Seeds of Crisis: Public Schooling in Milwaukee Since 1920,* edited by John L. Rury and Frank A. Cassell. Madison: University of Wisconsin Press.

Lieber, Eli, Thomas S. Weisner, and Matthew Presley. 2003. "EthnoNotes: An Internet-Based Field-Note Management Tool." *Field Methods* 15(4): 405–25.

Lincoln, Karen D. 2000. "Social Support, Negative Social Interactions, and Psychological Well-being." *Social Service Review* 74(2): 231–52.

Lindblad-Goldberg, Marion, and Joyce L. Dukes. 1985. "Social Support in Black, Low-Income, Single-Parent Families." *American Journal of Orthopsychiatry* 55(1): 42–58.

Loeb, Susanna, Bruce Fuller, Sharon L. Kagan, and Bidemi A. Carroll. 2004. "Child Care in Poor Communities: Early Learning Effects of Type, Quality, and Stability." *Child Development* 75(1): 47–65.

London, Andrew S., Ellen K. Scott, Kathryn Edin, and Vicki Hunter. 2004. "Welfare Reform, Work-Family Trade-offs, and Child Well-being." *Family Relations* 53(2): 148–58.

Loprest, Pamela. 2001. "How Are Families That Left Welfare Doing? A Comparison of Early and Recent Welfare Leavers." New Federalism: National Survey of America's Families, working paper B-36. Washington, D.C.: Urban Institute, Assessing the New Federalism Project (April 1).

Love, John M., Ellen E. Kisker, Christine M. Ross, Peter Z. Schochet, Jeanne Brooks-Gunn, Diane Paulsell, Kimberly Boller, Jill Constantine, Cheri Vogel, Allison S. Fuligni, and Christy Brady-Smith. 2002. *Making a Difference in the Lives of Infants and Toddlers and Their Families: The Impacts of Early Head Start.* Washington: U.S. Department of Health and Human Services, Administration on Children, Youth, and Families.

Lowe, Edward D., and Thomas S. Weisner. 2004. "'You Have to Push It—Who's Gonna Raise Your Kids?': Situating Child Care and Child Care Subsidy Use in the Daily Routines of Lower-Income Families." *Children and Youth Services Review* 26(2): 143–71.

Lowe, Edward D., Thomas S. Weisner, Sonya Geis, and Aletha C. Huston. 2005. "Child Care Instability and the Effort to Sustain a Working Daily Routine: Evidence from the New Hope Ethnographic Study of Low-Income Families." In *Hills of Gold: Rethinking Diversity and Contexts as Resources for Children's Developmental Pathways*, edited by Catherine R. Cooper, Cynthia Garcia-Coll, Todd Bartko, Helen M. Davis, and Celine M. Chatman. Mahwah, N.J.: Erlbaum Associates.

Lynch, Lisa. 1992. "Private-Sector Training and the Earnings of Young Workers." *American Economic Review* 82(1): 299–312.

MacKinnon, Catherine A. 1979. *Sexual Harassment of the Working Woman: A Case of Sex Discrimination.* New Haven, Conn.: Yale University Press.

MacKinnon, David P., Chondra M. Lockwood, Jeanne Hoffman, Stephen West, and Virgil Sheets. 2002. "A Comparison of Methods to Test Mediation and Other Intervening Variable Effects." *Psychological Methods* 7(1): 83–104.

MaCurdy, Thomas, and Frank MacIntyre. 2004. "Helping Working-Poor Families: Advantages Of Wage-Based Tax Credits over the EITC and Minimum Wages." Washington, D.C.: Employment Policies Institute.

Manns, Wilhelmina. 1997. "Supportive Roles of Significant Others in African American Families." In *Black Families*, edited by Harriett Pipes McAdoo. Thousand Oaks, Calif.: Sage Publications.

Mayer, Susan E., and Christopher Jencks. 1989. "Poverty and the Distribution of Material Hardship." *Journal of Human Resources* 24(1): 88–113.

McAdoo, Harriet P. 1989. "Strategies Used by Black Single Mothers Against Stress." In *Slipping Through the Cracks: The Status of Black Women*, edited by Margaret Simms and Julieanne Malveaux. New Brunswick, N.J.: Transaction Publishers.

McCartney, Kathleen, and Robert Rosenthal. 2000. "Effect Size, Practical Importance, and Social Policy for Children." *Child Development* 71(1): 173–80.

McDonald, Katrina B., and Elizabeth M. Armstrong. 2001. "Deromanticizing Black Intergenerational Support: The Questionable Expectations of Welfare Reform." *Journal of Marriage and the Family* 63(1): 213–23.

McLanahan, Sara S., and Gary Sandefur. 1994. *Growing Up with a Single Parent: What Hurts? What Helps?* Cambridge, Mass.: Harvard University Press.

McLoyd, Vonnie. 1990. "The Impact of Economic Hardship on Black Families and Children: Psychological Distress, Parenting, and Socioemotional Development." *Child Development* 61(2): 311–46.

McLoyd, Vonnie C., Toby Jayaratne, Rosario Ceballo, and Julio Borquez. 1994. "Unemployment and Work Interruption Among African-American Single Mothers: Effects on Parenting and Adolescent Socioemotional Functioning." *Child Development* 65(2): 562–84.

Menaghan, Elizabeth G., and Toby L. Parcel. 1990. "Parent Employment and Family Life: Research in the 1980s." *Journal of Marriage and the Family* 52(4): 1079–1098.

———. 1991. "Determining Children's Home Environments: The Impact of Maternal Characteristics and Current Occupational and Family Conditions." *Journal of Marriage and the Family* 53(2): 417–31.

Meyer, Bruce D. 2002. "Labor Supply at the Extensive and Intensive Margins: The EITC, Welfare, and Hours Worked." American Economic Review 92(2): 373–79.

Meyers, Marcia K. 2005. "The Decline in Welfare Caseloads: An Organizational Perspective." Paper presented to the National Poverty Center conference "Mixed-Methods Research on Economic Conditions, Public Policy, and Family and Child Well-being." University of Michigan, Ann Arbor (June 26–28).

Meyers, Marcia, Janet Gornick, and Laura Peck. 2001. "Public Policies That Support Families with Young Children: Variation Across the U.S. States." *Journal of Policy Analysis and Management* 20(3): 457–83.

Mezy, Jennifer, Rachel Schumacher, Mark H. Greenberg, Joan Lombardi, and John Hutchins. 2002. *Child Care for Low-Income Families Since 1996: Implications for Federal and State Policy*. Washington, D.C.: Center for Law and Social Policy.

Miller, Jennifer, Frieda Molina, Lisa Grossman, and Susan Golonka. 2004. *Building Bridges to Self-sufficiency: Improving Services for Low-Income Working Families.* New York: Manpower Demonstration Research Corporation.

Milligan, Glenn W. 1996. "Clustering Validation: Results and Implications for Applied Analyses." In *Clustering and Classification,* edited by Phipps Arabie, Lawrence J. Hubert, and Geert DeSoete. River Edge, N.J.: World Scientific.

Mistry, Rashmita S., Elizabeth A. Vandewater, Aletha C. Huston, and Vonnie C. McLoyd. 2002. "Economic Well-being and Children's Social Adjustment: The Role of Family Process in an Ethnically Diverse Low-Income Sample." *Child Development* 73(3): 935–51.

Moffitt, Robert, Andrew Cherlin, Linda Burton, Mark King, and Jennifer Roff. 2002. "The Characteristics of Families Remaining on Welfare." Working paper. Welfare, Children, and Families: A Three-City Study. Baltimore: Johns Hopkins University.

Moffitt, Robert, and Katie Winder. 2004. "Does It Pay to Move from Welfare to Work? A Comment on Danziger, Heflin, Corcoran, Oltmans, and Wang. Welfare, Children, and Families: A Three City Study." August. Available at: http://www.jhu.edu/~welfare/danziger_wang_08_19_04.pdf.

Moore, Kristin A., and Anne K. Driscoll. 1997. "Low-Wage Maternal Employment and Outcomes for Children: A Study." *The Future of Children* 7(1): 122–27.

Morris, Pamela A., Greg J. Duncan, and Christopher Rodrigues. 2005. "Does Money Really Matter? Estimating Impacts of Family Income on Children's Achievement with Data from a Random-Assignment Experiment." Unpublished paper.

Morris, Pamela, Aletha C. Huston, Greg J. Duncan, Danielle Crosby, and Johannes Bos. 2001. *How Welfare and Employment Policies Affect Children: A Synthesis of Research.* New York: Manpower Demonstration Research Corporation.

Morris, Pamela A., and Charles Michalopoulos. 2000. "The Self-Sufficiency Project at Thirty-six Months: Effects on Children of a Program That Increased Parental Employment and Income." New York: Manpower Demonstration Research Corporation.

Mosteller, Frederick. 1995. "The Tennessee Study of Class Size in the Early Grades." *The Future of Children* 5(2): 113–27.

National Academy of Sciences. 2001. *Studies of Welfare Populations: Data Collection and Research Issues.* Washington, D.C.: National Academy Press.

Nelson, Timothy J., Susan Clampet-Lundquist, and Kathryn Edin. 2002. "Sustaining Fragile Fatherhood: Father Involvement Among Low-Income, Noncustodial African-American Fathers in Philadelphia." In *Handbook of Father Involvement,* edited by Catherine S. Tamis-LeMonda and Natasha Cabrera. Mahwah, N.J.: Erlbaum Associates.

Newman, Katherine A. 1999. *No Shame in My Game: The Working Poor in the Inner City.* New York: Alfred A. Knopf and Russell Sage Foundation.

NICHD Early Child Care Research Network. 2006. "Child Care Effect Sizes for the NICHD Study of Early Child Care." *American Psychologist* 61(2): 99–116.

NICHD Early Child Care Research Network and Greg J. Duncan. 2003. "Modeling the Impacts of Child Care Quality on Children's Preschool Cognitive Development." *Child Development* 74(5): 1454–75.

Nikulina, Valentina, and Hirokazu Yoshikawa. 2004. "Wage Growth, Job Stability, and Children's Academic Achievement." Working paper. New York: St. John's University.

Nock, Steven L. 1995. "A Comparison of Marriages and Cohabiting Relationships." *Journal of Family Issues* 16(1): 53–76.

Oliker, Stacy J. 1995. "The Proximate Contexts of Workfare and Work: A Framework for Studying Poor Women's Economic Choices." *Sociological Quarterly* 36(2): 251–72.

Oppenheimer, Valerie K. 1997. "Women's Employment and the Gain to Marriage: The Specialization and Trading Model." *Annual Review of Sociology* 23: 431–53.

Orum, Anthony. 1995. *City-Building in America.* Boulder, Colo.: Westview Press.

Parcel, Toby L., and Elizabeth G. Menaghan. 1990. "Maternal Working Conditions and Children's Verbal Facility: Studying the Intergenerational Transmission of Inequality from Mothers to Young Children." *Social Psychology Quarterly* 53(2): 132–47.

———. 1994a. "Early Parental Work, Family Social Capital, and Early Childhood Outcomes." *American Journal of Sociology* 99(4): 972–1009.

———. 1994b. *Parents' Jobs and Children's Lives.* New York: Aldine de Gruyter.

———. 1997. "Effects of Low-Wage Employment on Family Well-being." *The Future of Children* 7(1): 116–21.

Parish, William L., Lingxin Hao, and Dennis P. Hogan. 1991. "Family Support Networks, Welfare, and Work Among Young Mothers." *Journal of Marriage and the Family* 53(1): 203–15.

Parsons, Talcott. 1949. "The Social Structure of the Family." In *The Family: Its Function and Destiny,* edited by Ruth N. Anshen. New York: Harper & Brothers.

Pawasarat, John. 1997. "The Employer Perspective: Jobs Held by Milwaukee County AFDC Single-Parent Population." Milwaukee: University of Wisconsin, Milwaukee Employment and Training Institute.

———. 2000. "Analysis of Food Stamp and Medical Assistance Caseload Reductions in Milwaukee County: 1995–1999." Milwaukee: University of Wisconsin, Employment and Training Institute. Available at: http://www.uwm.edu/Dept/ETI/barriers/fsmasum.html.

Pawasarat, John, and Lois M. Quinn. 1995. *Demographics of Milwaukee County Populations Expected to Work Under Proposed Welfare Initiatives.* Milwaukee: University of Wisconsin, Employment and Training Institute.

Pearlin, Leonard I., and Mary E. McCall. 1990. "Occupational Stress and Marital Support: A Description of Microprocesses." In *Stress Between Work and Family,* edited by John Eckenrode and Susan Gore. New York: Plenum Press.

Perry-Jenkins, Maureen, and Sally Gillman. 2000. "Parental Job Experiences and Children's Well-being: The Case of Two-Parent and Single-Mother Working-Class Families." *Journal of Family and Economic Issues* 21(2): 123–47.

Perry-Jenkins, Maureen, Rena L. Repetti, and Ann C. Crouter. 2000. "Work and Family in the 1990s." *Journal of Marriage and the Family* 56(1): 165–80.

Presser, Harriet B. 1988. "Shiftwork and Child Care Among Young Dual-Earner American Parents." *Journal of Marriage and the Family* 50(1): 133–48.

———. 1995. "Job, Family, Gender: Determinants of Nonstandard Work Schedules Among Employed Americans in 1991." *Demography* 32(4): 577–98.

———. 2000. "Nonstandard Work Schedules and Marital Instability." *Journal of Marriage and the Family* 62(1): 93–110.

———. 2003. *Working in a 24/7 Economy: Challenges for American Families*. New York: Russell Sage Foundation.

Presser, Harriet B., and Amy G. Cox. 1997. "The Work Schedules of Low-Educated American Women and Welfare Reform." *Monthly Labor Review* 120(4): 25–34.

Puryear, Gwendolyn, and Martha Mednick. 1974. "Black Militancy, Affective Attachment, and Fear of Success in Black College Women." *Journal of Consulting and Clinical Psychology* 42(3): 263–66.

Radloff, Lenore S. 1977. "The CES-D Scale: A Self-report Depression Scale for Research in the General Population." *Applied Psychological Measurement* 1(3): 385–401.

Ramos, Maria A., and Hirokazu Yoshikawa. 2005. "Parental Goals, Children's Educational Expectations, and Antipoverty Policy." Paper presented to the Society for Community Research and Action biennial conference. Urbana-Champaign, Ill. (June 9–12).

Rapkin, Bruce D., and Douglas A. Luke. 1993. "Cluster Analysis in Community Research: Epistemology and Practice." *American Journal of Community Psychology* 21(2): 247–77.

Raver, C. Cybele. 2002. "Emotions Matter." *Social Policy Reports of the Society for Research in Child Development* 16(3): 1–16.

———. 2003. "Does Work Pay Psychologically as Well as Economically? The Role of Employment in Predicting Depressive Symptoms and Parenting Among Low-Income Families." *Child Development* 74(6): 1720–36.

Repetti, Rena L., and Jennifer Wood. 1997. "Effects of Daily Stress at Work on Mothers' Interactions with Preschoolers." *Journal of Family Psychology* 11(1): 90–108.

Reskin, Barbara F., Debra B. McBrier, and Julie A. Kmec. 1999. "The Determinants and Consequences of Workplace Sex and Race Composition." *Annual Review of Sociology* 25: 335–61.

Richer, Elise, Hitomi Kubo, and Abby Frank. 2003. "All in One Stop? The Accessibility of Work Support Programs at One-Stop Centers." Washington, D.C.: Center for Law and Social Policy.

Riemer, David R. 1988. *The Prisoners of Welfare: Liberating America's Poor from Unemployment and Low Wages*. New York: Praeger.

Ripke, Marika N., Aletha C. Huston, and Rashmita S. Mistry. 2005. "Parents' Job Characteristics and Children's Occupational Aspirations and Expectations in Low-Income Families." Unpublished paper. Austin: University of Texas.

Romich, Jennifer L., and Thomas S. Weisner. 2000. "How Families View and Use the EITC: Advance Payment Versus Lump Sum Delivery." *National Tax Journal* 53(4): 1245–65.

———. 2001. "How Families View and Use the Lump-Sum Payments from the Earned Income Tax Credit." In *For Better or for Worse: Welfare Reform and the Well-Being of Children and Families,* edited by G. J. Duncan and P. L. Chase-Lansdale. New York: Russell Sage Foundation.

Rook, Karen S. 1992. "Detrimental Aspects of Social Relationships: Taking Stock of an Emerging Literature." In *The Meaning and Measurement of Social Support: The Series in Clinical and Community Psychology,* edited by Hans O. F. Veiel and Urs Baumann. New York: Hemisphere.

Royalty, Anne. 1998. "Job-to-Job and Job-to-Non-employment Turnover by Gender and Education Level." *Journal of Labor Economics* 16(2): 392–443.

Rubin, Lillian B. 1985. *Just Friends: The Role of Friendships in Our Lives.* New York: Harper & Row.

———. 1994. *Families on the Fault Line.* New York: HarperPerennial.

Rury, John L., and Frank A. Cassell, eds. 1993. *Seeds of Crisis: Public Schooling in Milwaukee Since 1920.* Madison: University of Wisconsin Press.

Rutter, Michael. 1979. "Protective Factors in Children's Responses to Stress and Disadvantage." In *Primary Prevention in Psychopathology,* vol. 8, *Social Competence in Children,* edited by Mark W. Kent and Jon E. Rolf. Hanover, N.H.: University Press of New England.

Rynes, Sara, and Benson Rosen. 1995. "A Field Survey of Factors Affecting the Adoption and Perceived Success of Diversity Training Programs." *Personnel Psychology* 48(2): 247–70.

Sameroff, Arnold J., W. Todd Bartko, Alfred Baldwin, Claire Baldwin, and Ronald Seifer. 1998. "Family and Social Influences on the Development of Child Competence." In *Families, Risk, and Competence,* edited by Michael Lewis and Candace Feiring. Mahwah, N.J.: Erlbaum Associates.

Sameroff, Arnold J., Ronald Seifer, Alfred Baldwin, and Claire Baldwin. 1993. "Stability of Intelligence from Preschool to Adolescence: The Influence of Social and Family Risk Factors." *Child Development* 64(1): 80–97.

Sawhill, Isabel, and Ron Haskins. 2002. "Welfare Reform and the Work Support System." Policy brief 17. Washington, D.C.: Brookings Institution.

Sawhill, Isabel, and Adam Thomas. 2001. *A Hand Up for the Bottom Third: Toward a New Agenda for Low-Income Working Families.* Washington, D.C.: Brookings Institution.

Schaie, K. Warner, and Sherry L. Willis. 2002. *Adult Development and Aging.* 5th ed. Upper Saddle River, N.J.: Prentice-Hall.

Schneider, Kimberly T., Robert T. Hitlan, and Phanakiran Radhakrishnan. 2000. "An Examination of the Nature and Correlates of Ethnic Harassment Experiences in Multiple Contexts." *Journal of Applied Psychology* 85(1): 3–12.

Schneider, Kimberly T., Suzanne Swan, and Louise F. Fitzgerald. 1997. "Job-Related and Psychological Effects of Sexual Harassment in the Workplace: Empirical Evidence from Two Organizations." *Journal of Applied Psychology* 82: 401–14.

Schultze, Steve, and Thomas Held. 2002. "Welfare Rolls Plunge in State." *Milwaukee Journal Sentinel*, June 5.

Scott, Ellen K., Kathryn Edin, Andrew S. London, and Rebecca J. Kissane. 2004. "Unstable Work, Unstable Income: Implications for Family Well-Being in the Era of Time-Limited Welfare." *Journal of Poverty* 8(1): 61–88.

Scott, Ellen K., Kathryn Edin, Andrew London, and Joan Mazelis. 2001. "'My Children Come First': Welfare-Reliant Women's Post-TANF Views of Work-Family Trade-offs and Marriage." In *For Better and for Worse: Welfare Reform and the Well-being of Children and Families*, edited by Greg J. Duncan and P. Lindsay Chase-Lansdale. New York: Russell Sage Foundation.

Scott, Ellen K., Andrew S. London, and Nancy A. Myers. 2002. "Dangerous Dependencies: Welfare Reform and Domestic Violence." *Gender and Society* 16(6): 878–97.

Seefeldt, Kristin S., Laura K. Kaye, Christopher Botsky, Pamela A. Holcomb, Kimura Flores, Clara Herbig, and Karen C. Tumlin. 1999. *Income Support and Social Services for Low-Income People in Wisconsin: Highlights from State Reports*. Washington, D.C.: Urban Institute.

Seefeldt, Kristin S., and Pamela J. Smock. 2004. "Marriage on the Public Policy Agenda: What Do Policy Makers Need to Know From Research?" National Poverty Center Working Paper Series No. 04-2. Ann Arbor, Mich.: Gerald R. Ford School of Public Policy, University of Michigan.

Shipler, David. 2004. *The Working Poor: Invisible in America*. New York: Vintage Books.

Shonkoff, Jack, and Deborah A. Phillips, eds. 2000. *From Neurons to Neighborhoods: The Science of Early Childhood Development*. Washington, D.C.: National Academy Press.

Shrout, Patrick E., and Niall Bolger. 2002. "Mediation in Experimental and Non-experimental Studies: New Procedures and Recommendations." *Psychological Methods* 7(4): 422–45.

Siegel, Alberta E., Lois M. Stolz, Ethel A. Hitchcock, and Jean Adamson. 1959. "Dependence and Independence in the Children of Working Mothers." *Child Development* 30(3): 533–47.

Siegel, Gary L., and L. Anthony Loman. 1991. *Child Care and AFDC Recipients in Illinois: Digest of Findings and Conclusions*. St. Louis: Institute of Applied Research.

Smith, Sandra S. 2005. " 'Don't Put My Name on It': Social Capital Activation and Job-Finding Assistance Among the Black Urban Poor." *American Journal of Sociology* 111(1): 1–57.

Smock, Pamela J., and Wendy D. Manning. 1997. "Cohabiting Partners' Economic Circumstances and Marriage." *Demography* 34(3): 331–41.

Smolensky, Eugene, and Jennifer Gootman, eds. 2003. *Working Families and Growing Kids: Caring for Children and Adolescents*. Washington, D.C.: National Academy Press.

Snyder, C. Rick, Susie C. Sympson, Florence C. Ybasco, Tyrone F. Borders, Michael A. Babyak, and Raymond L. Higgins. 1996. "Development and Validation of the State Hope Scale." *Journal of Personality and Social Psychology* 70(2): 321–35.

Stack, Carol. 1974. *All Our Kin: Strategies for Survival in a Black Community*. New York: Harper & Row.

Statistics Canada. 1995. "Self-Sufficiency Project: Self Complete Questionnaire, Parents." Montreal, Quebec, Canada: Statistics Canada.

Strauss, Claudia. 1992. "What Makes Tony Run? Schemas as Motives Reconsidered." In *Human Motives and Cultural Models*, edited by Roy G. D'Andrade and Claudia Strauss. New York: Cambridge University Press.

———. 2002. "Not-So-Rugged Individualists: U.S. Americans' Conflicting Ideas About Poverty." In *Work, Welfare, and Politics: Confronting Poverty in the Wake of Welfare Reform*, edited by Frances Fox Piven, Joan Acker, Margaret Hallock, and Sandra Morgan. Eugene: University of Oregon Press.

Susser, Ida. 1982. *Norman Street: Poverty and Politics in an Urban Neighborhood*. New York: Oxford University Press.

Suyderhound, Jack P., Thomas A. Loudat, and Richard L. Pollock. 1994. "Cumulative Tax Rates on the Working Poor: Evidence of a Continuing Poverty Wall." *Journal of Economic Issues* 28(1): 155–71.

Sweeney, Meghan. 2002. "Two Decades of Family Change: The Shifting Economic Foundations of Marriage." *American Sociological Review* 67(1): 132–47.

Tangri, Sandra S., Martha R. Burt, and Leonor B. Johnson. 1982. "Sexual Harassment at Work: Three Explanatory Models." *Journal of Social Issues* 38(4): 33–54.

Teitler, Julian O., Nancy E. Reichman, and Lenna Nepomnyaschy. 2004. "Sources of Support, Child Care, and Hardship Among Unwed Mothers, 1999–2001." *Social Service Review* 78(1): 125–48.

Thoits, Peggy A. 1995. "Stress, Coping, and Social Support Processes: Where Are We? What Next?" *Journal of Health and Social Behavior* 35(5): 53–79.

Topel, Robert, and Michael Ward. 1992. "Job Mobility and the Careers of Young Men." *Quarterly Journal of Economics* 107(2): 439–79.

Trzcinski, Eileen. 2002. "Middle School Children's Perceptions on Welfare and Poverty: An Exploratory, Qualitative Study." *Journal of Family and Economic Issues* 23(4): 339–59.

Uehara, Edwina. 1990. "Dual Exchange Theory, Social Networks, and Informal Social Support." *American Journal of Sociology* 96(3): 521–57.

University of Wisconsin. Center for Economic Development. 2001. *Cracks in the Glass Ceiling? Diversity and Management in Metro Milwaukee's Private Industry in the 1990s*. Milwaukee: University of Wisconsin (August).

———. 2003. "Stealth Depression": Joblessness in the City of Milwaukee Since 1990. Milwaukee: University of Wisconsin.

U.S. Census Bureau. 2004. "Highlights from the Census 2000 Demographic Profiles." Available at: http://factfinder.census.gov/home/saff/main.html (last updated October 10, 2004).

U.S. Department of Energy. 2004. "The Effect of Income on Appliances in U.S. Households." Washington: Energy Information Administration, U.S. Department of Energy. Available at: http://www.eia.doe.gov/emeu/recs/appliances/appliances.html.

U.S. Department of Health and Human Services. 2001. "ACF Data and Statistics: U.S. Welfare Caseloads Information." Washington: U.S. Department of Health and Human Services. Available at: http://www.acf.dhhs.gov/news/stats/3697.html.

U.S. Department of Health and Human Services. The Administration for Children and Families. 2002. Strengthening Healthy Marriages: A Compendium of Approaches. Washington: U.S. Department of Health and Human Services.

U.S. Department of Labor. 1991. Dictionary of Occupational Titles. 4th ed. Available at: http://www.oalj.dol.gov/libdot.htm.

U.S. Department of Labor. Bureau of Labor Statistics. 2000. Monthly Labor Review. Washington: Bureau of Labor Statistics (September), 40.

U.S. Equal Employment Opportunity Commission. 2004. "Discrimination by Type: Facts and Guidance." Available at: http://www.eeoc.gov/index.html (last updated August 19, 2004).

U.S. General Accounting Office. 1998. Domestic Violence: Prevalence and Implications for Employment Among Welfare Recipients, GAO/HEHS-99-12. Washington: U.S. Government Printing Office.

Valentine, Charles, ed. 1968. Culture and Poverty: Critique and Counter-Proposals. Chicago: University of Chicago Press.

Vandell, Deborah A., and Barbara Wolfe. 2000. Child Care Quality: Does It Matter and Should It Be Improved? Madison: University of Wisconsin, Institute for Research on Poverty.

Vega, William A., Bohdan Kolody, Ramon Valle, and Judy Weir. 1991. "Social Networks, Social Support, and Their Relationship to Depression Among Immigrant Mexican Women." Human Organization 50(2): 154–62.

Vinokur, Amiram D., Richard H. Price, and Robert D. Caplan. 1991. "From Field Experiments to Program Implementation: Assessing the Potential Outcomes of an Experimental Intervention Program for Unemployed Persons." American Journal of Community Psychology 19(4): 543–62.

———. 1996. "Hard Times and Hurtful Partners: How Financial Strain Affects Depression and Relationship Satisfaction of Unemployed Persons and Their Spouses." Journal of Personality and Social Psychology 71(1): 166–79.

Vinokur, Amiram, Richard H. Price, and Yaacov Schul. 1995. "Impact of the JOBS Intervention on Unemployed Workers Varying in Risk for Depression." *American Journal of Community Psychology* 23(1): 39–47.

Vinokur, Amiram, Yaacov Schul, J. Vuori, and Richard H. Price. 2000. "Two Years After a Job Loss: Long-Term Impact of the JOBS Program on Reemployment and Mental Health." *Journal of Occupational Health Psychology* 5(1): 32–47.

Waite, Linda J., and Maggie Gallagher. 2000. *The Case for Marriage: Why Married People are Happier, Healthier, and Better off Financially.* New York: Doubleday.

Waldfogel, Jane. 2001. "Family and Medical Leave: Evidence from the 2000 Surveys." *Monthly Labor Review* 124(9): 17–23.

Waldfogel, Jane, Wen-Jui Han, and Jeanne Brooks-Gunn. 2002. "The Effects of Early Maternal Employment on Child Cognitive Development." *Demography* 39(2): 369–92.

Waller, Maureen R. 2001. "High Hopes: Unmarried Parents' Expectations About Marriage at the Time of Their Child's Birth." *Children and Youth Services Review* 23(6–7): 457–84.

Ward, Janie V. 1996. "Raising Resisters: The Role of Truth Telling in the Psychological Development of African-American Girls." In *Urban Girls: Resisting Stereotypes, Creating Identities,* edited by Bonnie J. Leadbeater and Niobe Way. New York: New York University Press.

Weaver, R. Kent. 2000. *Ending Welfare as We Know It.* Washington, D.C.: Brookings Institution.

Weisner, Thomas S. 2001. "The American Dependency Conflict: Continuities and Discontinuities in Behavior and Values of Countercultural Parents and Their Children." *Ethos* 29(3): 271–95.

———. 2002. "Ecocultural Understanding of Children's Developmental Pathways." *Human Development* 45(4): 275–81.

Weisner, Thomas S., Lucinda P. Bernheimer, Eli Lieber, Christina Gibson, Eboni Howard, Katherine A. Magnuson, Jennifer Romich, Devarati Syam, Victor Espinosa, and Ellen Chmielewski. 2000. "Understanding Better the Lives of Poor Families: Ethnographic and Survey Studies of the New Hope Experiment." *Poverty Research News* 4(1): 10–12.

Weisner, Thomas S., Christina Gibson, Edward D. Lowe, and Jennifer Romich. 2002. "Understanding Working Poor Families in the New Hope Program." *Poverty Research News* 6(4): 3–5.

Weisner, Thomas S., Catherine Matheson, Jennifer Coots, and Lucinda P. Bernheimer. 2005. "Sustainability of Daily Routines as a Family Outcome." In *Learning in Cultural Context: Family, Peers, and School,* edited by Ashley Maynard and Mary Martini. New York: Kluwer/Plenum.

Whitbeck, Les B., Ronald L. Simons, Rand D. Conger, K. A. S. Wickrama, Kevin A. Ackley, and Glen H. Elder Jr. 1997. "The Effects of Parents' Working Conditions and Family Economic Hardship on Parenting Behaviors and Children's Self-efficacy." *Social Psychology Quarterly* 60(4): 291–303.

White, Halbert. 1980. "A Heteroskedasticity-Consistent Covariance Matrix Estimator and a Direct Test for Heteroskedasticity." *Econometrica* 48(4): 817–30.

Wijnberg, Marion H., and Susan Weinger. 1998. "When Dreams Wither and Resources Fail: The Social Support Systems of Poor Single Mothers." *Families in Society: The Journal of Contemporary Human Services* 79(2): 212–19.

Wilson, Julie B., David T. Ellwood, and Jeanne Brooks-Gunn. 1995. "Welfare-to-Work Through the Eyes of Children." In *Escape from Poverty: What Makes a Difference for Children*, edited by P. Lindsay Chase-Lansdale and Jeanne Brooks-Gunn. New York: Cambridge University Press.

Wilson, William J. 1987. *The Truly Disadvantaged: The Inner city, the Underclass, and Public Policy.* Chicago: University of Chicago Press.

———. 1999. *When Work Disappears: The World of the New Urban Poor.* New York: Alfred A. Knopf.

Wilson, William J., and Kathryn M. Neckerman. 1986. "Poverty and Family Structure: The Widening Gap Between Evidence and Public Policy Issues." In *Fighting Poverty: What Works and What Doesn't*, edited by Sheldon H. Danziger and Daniel H. Weinberg. Cambridge, Mass.: Harvard University Press.

Wisconsin Department of Workforce Development. 2001. *An Evaluation: Wisconsin Shares Child Care Subsidy Program.* Madison: Wisconsin Department of Workforce Development.

———. 2004. *Wisconsin Works Overview.* Madison: Wisconsin Department of Workforce Development. Available at: www.dwd.state.wi.us/dws/w2/wisworks. htm (downloaded November 14, 2004).

Wright, John C., and Aletha C. Huston. 1995. *Effects of Educational TV Viewing of Lower-Income Preschoolers on Academic Skills, School Readiness, and School Adjustment One to Three Years Later.* Lawrence, Kans.: Center for Research on the Influences of Television on Children.

Yeung, W. Jean, Miriam R. Linver, and Jeanne Brooks-Gunn. 2002. "How Money Matters for Young Children's Development: Parental Investment and Family Processes." *Child Development* 73(6): 1861–1879.

Yoshikawa, Hirokazu. 1994. "Prevention as Cumulative Protection: Effects of Early Family Support and Education on Chronic Delinquency and Its Risks." *Psychological Bulletin* 115(1): 28–54.

———. 1995. "Long-Term Effects of Early Childhood Programs on Social Outcomes and Delinquency." *The Future of Children* 5: 51–75.

———. 1999. "Welfare and Work Dynamics, Support Services, Mothers' Earnings, and Child Cognitive Development: Implications for Contemporary Welfare Reform." *Child Development* 70(3): 779–801.

Yoshikawa, Hirokazu, Johannes Bos, JoAnn Hsueh, and Elisa A. Rosman. 2000. "Do Employment Characteristics Shape Longitudinal Effects of Welfare and Antipoverty Policies on Children? Evidence from the New Hope Demonstration and the Minnesota Family Investment Program." Paper presented to the annual meeting of the Association for Public Policy Analysis and Management. Seattle (November).

Yoshikawa, Hirokazu, and Jane Knitzer. 1997. *Lessons from the Field: Head Start Mental Health Strategies to Meet Changing Needs.* New York: National Center for Children in Poverty.

Yoshikawa, Hirokazu, Katherine A. Magnuson, Johannes M. Bos, and JoAnn Hsueh. 2003. "Effects of Welfare and Antipoverty Policies on Adult Economic and Middle-Childhood Outcomes Differ for the 'Hardest to Employ.' " *Child Development* 74(5): 1500–21.

Yoshikawa, Hirokazu, Pamela A. Morris, Lisa A. Gennetian, Amanda L. Roy, Anna Gassman-Pines, and Erin B. Godfrey. 2006. "Effects of Antipoverty and Employment Policies on Middle-Childhood School Performance: Do They Vary by Race-Ethnicity, and If So, Why?" In *Middle Childhood: Contexts of Development,* edited by Aletha C. Huston and Marika Ripke. New York: Cambridge University Press.

Yoshikawa, Hirokazu, Elisa A. Rosman, and JoAnn Hsueh. 2001. "Variation in Teenage Mothers' Experiences of Child Care and Other Components of Welfare Reform: Selection Processes and Developmental Consequences." *Child Development* 72(1): 299–317.

Yoshikawa, Hirokazu, and Edward Seidman. 2001. "Multidimensional Profiles of Welfare and Work Dynamics: Development, Validation, and Relationship to Child Cognitive and Mental Health Outcomes." *American Journal of Community Psychology* 29(6): 907–36.

Zaslow, Martha, and Carol Emig. 1997. "When Low-Income Mothers Go to Work: Implications for Children." The *Future of Children* 7(1): 110–15.

Zukow-Goldring, Patricia. 1995. "Sibling Caregiving." In *Handbook of Parenting,* vol. 3, *Status and Social Conditions of Parenting,* edited by Marc H. Bornstein. Mahwah, N.J.: Erlbaum Associates.

Index |

Boldface numbers refer to figures and tables.

413